Bob Dylan

Performing Artist

1986 ★ 1990
& beyond

Mind Out Of Time

by Paul Williams

OMNIBUS PRESS

LONDON / NEW YORK / PARIS / SYDNEY / COPENHAGEN /
BERLIN / MADRID / TOKYO

Exclusive Distributors
Music Sales Limited,
8/9 Frith Street,
London W1D 3JB, UK.

Music Sales Corporation,
257 Park Avenue South,
New York, NY 10010, USA.

Macmillan Distribution Services,
53 Park West Drive,
Derrimut, Vic 3030,
Australia.

To the Music Trade only
Music Sales Limited,
8/9 Frith Street,
London W1D 3JB, UK.

Every effort has been made to trace the copyright holders of the photographs in this book
but one or two were unreachable. We would be grateful if the photographers concerned
would contact us.

Typeset by Galleon Typesetting, Ipswich
Printed in Great Britain by Cox & Wyman Ltd, Reading

A catalogue record for this book is available from the British Library.

Visit Omnibus Press on the web at www.omnibuspress.com

Bob Dylan

Performing Artist

1986 ★ 1990 & beyond

Mind Out Of Time

by Paul Williams

CONTENTS

This book is dedicated to the people
listed on the Roll of Honor in the back of the book
and to the memory of John Bauldie
and to the performer himself

Introduction/Chapter Zero: "Visions of Madonna"

On the 26th of July, 1999, in a club in Manhattan, Bob Dylan delivered one of his greatest performances ever of his well-loved 1966 epic "Visions of Johanna." As if to acknowledge and signal his awareness of the power and freshness of this latest reinterpretation, the singer-bandleader effectively changed the title of the song halfway through, by starting to sing the chorus as: "And these visions of Madonna are now all that remain/... have kept me up past the dawn."

Where does genius come from? This book proposes to examine where the improbable 58-year-old artist singing in front of 900 people in Tramps that night came from, in the sense of what roads he had walked down, artistically and personally, in some of the preceding thirteen years of his life and work.

In 1997 a *Newsweek* writer reported that Bob Dylan had recently told him that ten years earlier (summer '87): "'I'd kind of reached the end of the line. Whatever I'd started out to do, it wasn't *that*. I was going to pack it in.' Onstage, he couldn't do his old songs.

'You know, like how do I sing this? It just *sounds* funny.' He goes into an all-too-convincing imitation of panic: 'I – I can't remember what it means, does it mean – is it just a bunch of *words*? Maybe it's like what all these people say, just a bunch of surrealistic nonsense.'"

Dylan told the magazine that he got help (during his 1987 nervous breakdown as a performer) from Jerry Garcia of the Grateful Dead: "He'd say, 'Come on, man, you know, this is the way it goes, let's play it, it goes like this.' And I'd say, 'Man, he's right, you know? How's he getting there and I can't get there?' I had to go through a lot of red tape in my mind to get back there."

This book is called "mind out of time," and argues that this is how Bob Dylan sees himself (what he aspires to be) as a songwriter and performer. So, although the general structure of this narrative will be chronological, I feel it's appropriate to step outside of chronological sequence for the purpose of this introduction, and start the story by looking closely at one fine example of this artist's ability to stop time and thereby encompass it and conquer it, in the timeless world of ephemeral art. Onstage in a particular club on a summer night in New York City.

This ephemeral performance art becomes accidental when it loses its ephemeral status because someone, not the artist, captures the musical performance on recording equipment so it can be heard outside of that room and that night, by people other than the fortunate few who were in the theater at the show. A book like this, by its nature, is not about the intentional art of the performer, which takes place at a particular time and place. This non-accidental art is only experienced by the people who are in the audience that day; and even being one of those people doesn't empower me or anyone to write about the experience, unless we have total emotional recall, because the simple act of taking notes creates a distraction for the observer and a distance between the listener and this remarkably alive art form.

So this book cannot meaningfully be an in-depth look at concerts I attended; it must be the report of a listener who has listened attentively to live recordings whose existence and availability is largely accidental, in terms of the artist's control or intent.

Of course, I feel better qualified to write about these recordings thanks to the large number of Dylan concerts I've experienced as an audience member over the course of 41 years (see Appendix II). And certainly it is no accident that Bob Dylan sings and plays his heart out in front of a live audience almost every third night of his life (from 1989 to 2003 he has played close to one hundred shows every year). He is a brilliant, conscious artist. But most of the body of work that this book and its companion volumes examine is accidental in its recorded form, which is the only form we can discuss together. The story of the live audience experience of these works of art is the story of hundreds of thousands of individuals in a vast array of mind-states at specific moments in their personal histories, some sitting or standing where they can see and hear well, others far in the back of a large auditorium. But accidentally, you and I can approach these works of art as though they were enduring communal objects, so that when I describe the mastery of the performing artist singing this particular piece on this particular night in 1999, you have the opportunity (if you search patiently) to listen to the same recording I'm referring to.

Okay. "Visions of Johanna" (or, if you like, "Visions of Madonna"), was the fifth song Bob Dylan and his band performed on Monday July 26th, 1999, on 21st Street in Manhattan. Larry Campbell and Charlie Sexton on acoustic guitars, Tony Garnier on string bass, David Kemper on drums, and Bob Dylan on vocals and acoustic guitar. What makes this eight-minute performance so remarkable is its expressiveness, its artistry, its structure, its musicality, its freshness, its vision. You could start here (and many young appreciators of Dylan's music have started with recent concert recordings). This is not a repeat of a work of art created back in 1966. It is unmistakably a great work of art created at the time of its performance. Something new and original and thrilling. Bob Dylan once said, "He who is not busy being born is busy dying." His greatest accomplishment as an artist has been to stay true to this demanding dictum, in the face of the inevitable obstacles from within and without that all human beings and all artists must contend with. Our story in this volume begins at a particularly difficult moment in this process, August 1986 to July 1987. ("I'd kind of reached the end of the line.") "Visions of Madonna" and thousands of other performances that will be discussed herein are evidence that a committed artist can indeed use those painful years when he finds himself busy dying as opportunities and stimuli to learn new ways to "get there," back to being busy being born. This song, this performance, on this night in 1999, is certainly about being born. As an artist, a singer, a musician. And as a lover and a human being. Listen to the way he sings, "How can I explain? It's so *hard* to get on." And the way he and his band deliver every other verbal and musical phrase in this version of "Visions."

It starts with the same old magical incantation, "Ain't it just like the night to play tricks when you're tryin' to be so quiet?" But not the same, because it doesn't arise from the harmonica wail followed by snare drums that opens the familiar original album version, nor from the guitar strums that open the live 1966 versions on *Biograph* and the *Live 1966* album. Instead it arises (to the surprise and delight of the club audience, who recognize the seldom-played favorite when they hear these words) from a guitars-bass-and-drums riff newly created for this 1999 version that for the first time in a live "Visions" captures the martial (marching drums) rhythm that so inspired Bob Dylan as a vocalist when he sang these lyrics almost as a call-and-response duet with Ken Buttrey's drumming at the *Blonde on Blonde* recording sessions. "Ain't it just like the night ..." on July 26, 1999 arises from the first few bars of a band riff so rich in personality that Bob Dylan sings to it as though confident that he as bandleader/performer is an embodiment of the trick-playing night himself (i.e. he and his band are). As on *Blonde on Blonde*, the song is sung as a duet with the rhythm instruments. It's not a replay or imitation of that 1966 recorded performance, but it inhabits the same triumphant and heartfelt and deeply humorous realm of freedom. Artistic and personal freedom made possible by the rightness of these sounds in the ears of the singer who is singing to and with them.

"We sit here stranded, though we're all doin' our best to deny it." So the song, in 1966 and 1999, is a kind of confession (not denyin' it), and a declaration of interdependence. At Tramps in '99, Dylan sings, "and these visions, visions of Johanna that conquer my mind," as though he feels satisfaction, and maybe some joy, at having his mind conquered. I hear a similar celebration of liberation a few seconds earlier when he sings (clearly duetting with the "voice" of the drummer) "there's nothing really nothing to turn off!" It is, and has always been, a song about living proudly and joyously and communally in a private realm of silence in the midst of a noisy city. No surprise that the song's author should be inspired to a particularly heartfelt performance while singing in a club in Manhattan.

This night he doesn't sing the "inside the museums" verse, but it doesn't matter, because the spirit of the verse is very much present in the long instrumental passages (*lean* into that riff, boys!) that follow the third and fourth choruses (the "Madonna" choruses).

If you want to touch the heart of this 1999 "Visions," immerse yourself in the "little boy lost" verse ... and listen to this man's voice as he sings, "he likes to live dangerously" and "speaks of a farewell kiss to me." "Dangerously" and "farewell kiss" are notably wry, and inseparable from the mosaic of drum and melodic guitar punctuations that dance around and with these words, this melodic and percussive and marvelously expressive singing. No accident that this is the verse that climaxes in a passionate, "It's so *hard* to get on!" And climaxes further when Madonna suddenly replaces Johanna in Bob's visions. (Of course, Madonna was a character in the original song too, in the middle of the final verse: "And Madonna she still has not showed." In context, clearly a nickname or alias for Johanna herself.)

It's all in the riff. That's the secret of Bob Dylan's music (and, therefore, his genius, including his genius as a lyricist). The riff calls forth the great vocal performances, as though Dylan were one of those old bluesmen he so admires. And when on this Tramps '99 performance the band is directed to vamp on the riff for long non-vocal passages, the riff itself starts speaking to the song's listeners as though these were whole new verses of evocative, mind-blowing, Bob-Dylan-in-his-prime lyrics. We're used to Dylan achieving this effect with his harmonica solos. But he's also been able, on good nights, to work the same magic through the instrument of his live band, flooding listeners with extensions of feelings and situations already evoked and described by his lyrics and singing, as though his harmonica, or his string-band-plus-drummer, were filling in the rest of the story, and filling us all with feelings by doing so. The master of language can also be a master of non-verbal language. And on this July '99 "Visions of Madonna," as on the Feb. '66 *Blonde on Blonde* "Visions of Johanna," the two collaborate to produce a transcendent work of art. In both cases, the drummer deserves almost as much credit as the singer. Nevertheless, it's easy to predict that what you'll remember of "VoM" and rave to your friends and children about is the singer's phrasing on "Johanna's not here!" and "the *bones* of her face," and "... all that remain." The drum beats and tones get into your bloodstream. But in the singer's phrasing you can see and hear and feel a man being born. At age

58, with visions of Madonna pulsing through his body and brain. "Everything's been returned which was owed," indeed.

If you want to really learn something, listen to the *Blonde on Blonde* and Tramps versions of this song back to back, again and again, contemplating the thirty-three years of life experience that separate and unite the two performances ...

I. Billy Parker

August 1986 – May 1987

1.

Put yourself in Bob Dylan's shoes, dear reader. It's August 6, 1986, and you're standing on a stage at a county fair in Paso Robles, California with the five members of your backing band, Tom Petty & the Heartbreakers, and your four backup singers, the Queens of Rhythm. It's the 61st show you all have done together so far this year, and the last, because in ten days you're flying to England to start filming a movie called *Hearts of Fire*, something you agreed to last spring and which will keep you from doing any more concerts this year, since filming is scheduled to last into November.

Right now you and the Queens are singing just the chorus from "Brownsville Girl," a song from your new album (*Knocked Out Loaded*) that is going to be released this week. A film crew from ABC-TV is filming you singing "Brownsville girl, with your Brownsville curl, teeth like pearls, shining like the moon above..." for tomorrow night's *Entertainment Tonight* program. The next song on the set list is "Masters of War." The last song you did before the "Brownsville Girl" snippet was a cover of a country song expressing regret about the loss of a marriage, "You and Me, We Had It All"; which is interesting because the only album you'll record in the next year or two, *Down in the Groove*, will lead off with a cover of a rhythm & blues tune called "Let's Stick Together" ("You know we made a vow, not to leave one another never").

Your mind is on the music, and the audience, but when it wanders for a moment you see James Dean's face. In a few days you'll tell your actor/playwright friend Sam Shepard (co-author of "Brownsville Girl"): "You know where I just was? Paso Robles. You know, on that highway where James Dean got killed? I was there at the spot. On the spot. A windy kinda place. The curve where he had the accident. I mean, the place where he died is as powerful as the place he lived. It's on this kind of broad expanse of land. It's like that place made James Dean who he is. If he hadn't've died there he wouldn't've been James Dean."

So you're onstage with your band and you're thinking about an actor. That makes sense, in a way, because your next assignment after this county fair show is to be an actor. An actor playing the part of a musician, a "legendary musician who's given it all up," named Billy Parker.

A few days later you're at your big house in Malibu and your friend Sam comes over to tape this interview with you for *Esquire* magazine, which he says is going to be more like a play constructed out of a recorded conversation than an interview. He's a Pulitzer-Prize-winning playwright, so he's entitled. When the piece appears in *Esquire* it's called "True Dylan – a one-act play, as it really happened one afternoon in California." And throughout the play, Bob Dylan keeps returning to the subject of James Dean. "The only reason I wanted to go to New York is 'cause James Dean had been there." SS: "So you really liked James Dean?" BD: "Oh, yeah. Always did." SS: "How come?" BD: "Same reason you like anybody, I guess. You see somethin' of yourself in them."

So, dear reader, we open this book with one of the most difficult stretches in Bob Dylan's career for you or me or anyone else to see something of themselves in his art: eleven months during which he recorded the *Hearts of Fire* soundtrack and *Down in the Groove*, played no concerts, and wrote and recorded only the following new songs: "Had A Dream About You, Baby," "Night After Night," "Silvio," and "Ugliest Girl In The World." Kinda bleak. What happened?

I don't know, of course. But I would be derelict in my duty as a chronicler if I failed at this moment to share with you the following exchange from the *Hearts of Fire* press conference held in London on August 17, 1986:

> Journalist: "In the words of Billy Parker, it says here, you say, 'You wake up, you're a star – so you're a star, but there ain't nothing to you no more, you're empty.' Is that a sentiment that you would agree with?"
>
> Bob Dylan: "Some stars are like that, yeah."
>
> Journalist: "Are you?"
>
> Dylan: "No, I'm not like that. But I'm playing another character who is like that. [pause] I'm getting into my character right now, so um …" [other journalists and attendees all laugh]

Ten days after the press conference, three weeks after examining the spot where James Dean exited, and two days after stepping before the camera for the first time as the star of a feature film (excluding the 1965 documentary *Don't Look Back* and his own 1975 film *Renaldo & Clara*), Bob Dylan began two days of recording at London's Townhouse recording studio, with such rock music notables as Eric Clapton and Ron Wood in his band, with the intent of getting on tape the songs that legendary semi-retired rock star Billy Parker will perform in the course of *Hearts of Fire*.

Hearts of Fire is a dreadfully bad movie. None of the characters is believable; the dialogue is predictable and flat; the dramatic hook – ambitious girl rock singer (American) in a love triangle with current rock superstar (British) and very famous has-been (American) – is entirely lacking in drama, largely because none of these lovers seems to care at all about the alleged object of his or her affections and desire. The musical performances and the rise-to-fame narrative are as unexciting and unconvincing as the love scenes. It's hard to figure how such an egg could have been laid by then-hot and highly acclaimed American screenwriter Joe Eszterhas and then-hot British director Richard Marquand (whose recent films *Jagged Edge* and *Return of the Jedi* had been great critical and commercial successes). The movie was released in Britain in October 1987 and did very poorly. In the U.S. it has never been released theatrically, only on videocassette.

But *Hearts of Fire* is worth watching if you're interested in Bob Dylan. Indeed, it's the centerpiece of a trilogy of rare opportunities for the curious observer to see the "private" or "real" Bob Dylan, the one you'd meet if you worked with the man or somehow got invited to spend a few hours hanging out with him. What's he like? Shepard's *True Dylan* and Marquand's *Hearts of Fire* and Christopher Sykes's BBC-TV documentary *Getting to Dylan* together allow you and me to be flies on the wall watching Bob Dylan living his life and interacting with friends and other strangers from August to November 1986.

Iain Smith, co-producer of *Hearts of Fire*, got it exactly right (and gave us a glimpse of the director's process and intent) when he told John Bauldie of *The Telegraph*: "I think Dylan is arguably the best thing in the film. It's not because he's a great actor, it's because Richard has worked very hard to bring out, by cutting and editing Bob's material, what is in the man, which is his natural charisma and his natural charm and graciousness. And the net result, particularly with an American audience, is that they cannot believe they're seeing Dylan in this way. He's not stodgy, he's funny and quirky and strange and you watch him on the screen and you think, 'Well he's not acting' – you can see that – but, and it's a bit odd, he's very, very watchable. You just want to watch him. And it's a totally undefinable quality, but it's a real quality."

At the August 17 press conference, Dylan was asked: "Bob Dylan's written four songs for this movie. Can he tell us anything about those, please?"

Dylan: "Well, I haven't written those songs just yet." [laughter]

Journalist: "Well, they tell us that you have."

Dylan: "I'm about to …" [laughter]

"What are they going to be about?"

"They're gonna be about the movie."

"Are they going to be protest songs?"

"I hope so, yeah. [laughter] If Richard allows them to be."

So on August 27 and 28 at Townhouse Studio, Dylan recorded "Had a Dream About You, Baby," "Night after Night," "The Usual" (by John Hiatt), and "A Couple More Years" (by Shel Silverstein and Dennis Locorriere).

Of these, the first two songs, the "originals," are insipid. They sound like – and sound as though they were *intended* to sound like – meaningless filler, the artist's Muse protesting against having to write songs on demand for somebody else's script and agenda. "Night after night you wander the streets of my mind; night after night, don't know what you think you will find … and there's never any mercy in sight." This can be heard as a "poetic" description of

Dylan's experience at the *Hearts of Fire* press conference. Indeed, the tenacious reporter from the *Sunday Times* – who wanted to know "why one of the biggest poets and musicians of this century feels he has to play someone who's a retired star? Why aren't you writing poetry? Why aren't you doing the things you're really great at?" – must have been surprised if he noticed that the really great Bob Dylan songs and performances on the *Hearts of Fire* soundtrack are the two songs he didn't write himself.

"The Usual" is a superb rock vocal and band performance, indeed the only worthwhile track on the *Hearts of Fire* soundtrack album, which also includes "Night" and "Dream," along with five songs sung by co-star Fiona and two sung by co-star Rupert Everett. "A Couple More Years" is not on the album, presumably because someone decided it was too short (less than a minute and a half) for the album context.

John Hiatt told the *New Musical Express* in 1987: "It's funny. I was asked to write some stuff for the movie and I spoke to Dylan on the phone but I was gushing like some teenage girl – hands shaking, the whole bit. He must have thought I was a complete asshole. He said he wanted some stuff with a riff, so I started thinking, 'riff, riff,' and before I know it, I'm walking around and all I'm doing is writing Bob Dylan songs. There I was doing my best Bob Dylan impressions and, you know, it's not hard but it's not exactly what the guy wants. I realize that halfway through and think, 'shit, Bob Dylan can write a Bob Dylan song better than I can.' So I just gave him one of my old songs."

As it happens, he gave Dylan exactly what he wanted and needed. I surmise that Hiatt was brought in because earlier in August Dylan began to feel panicky about the likelihood of his managing to write before August 27th a credible rock and roll single that could have been a big hit for Billy Parker back in his glory years (the 1960s, of course). So Bob confided in his director, Richard, who immediately offered to hire the best available songwriter to do a rush job. And then Bob, asked for a suggestion, thought of the guy who co-wrote "Across the Borderline," a great movie song Dylan had been performing that year at almost every show since February 5th in New Zealand.

Of course it's comic and endearing that John Hiatt, who had recently released one of the very best and most praised and enduring singer-songwriter albums of the 1980s (*Bring the Family*), admits to being so unnerved by his moment of distant proximity to Bob Dylan. As Dylan said in his 1974 song "Idiot Wind": "People see me all the time and they just can't remember how to act. Their minds are filled with big ideas, images and distorted facts." This odd gravitational pull that Bob Dylan's presence or the idea of his presence has on people is a significant subtext in *Hearts of Fire*. In one of his best scenes, Bob as Billy tells Molly (in response to her feisty "If I'm good, it [success] can't be a trap"): "It is!! The better you are, the bigger the trap." A look at the paperback novelization, which is based on the shooting script rather than the finished film, confirms that this is one of the instances in which Dylan "had a line rewritten so that he could speak it," which, according to director Marquand, "happened quite a lot." *Hearts of Fire*: "The better you are, the bigger the trap." "Idiot Wind": "You'll find out when you reach the top, you're on the bottom!"

And in "The Usual" we have the pleasure of Bob-Dylan-as-Billy-Parker (and in his best Mick Jagger voice) confessing, "My confidence is dwindling/Look at the shape I'm in," and demanding hilariously, "Where's my pearls?/Where's the swine?" – which of course takes us right into the chorus: "I'm not thirsty, but I'm standing in line/I'll have the usual!!" This song, from an album Hiatt recorded in 1985, is exactly what the legendary Mr. Dylan on the other end of the phone wanted and needed: a song with a riff that could thereby be transformed by Bob Dylan and a band of good musicians under his sway into a believable hard rock anthem that sounds like it could have been enough of a hit two decades ago to ensure that Billy Parker still inspires awe wherever he goes (and that doesn't sound too much like a "Bob Dylan song"). In the shooting script the song was called "Night Fighter," presumably Dylan's clue that Billy Parker was not remembered for a "Sounds of Silence" or "Mellow Yellow," but something more in the domain of a Rolling Stones single from their glory days.

The mark of a great artist, a Picasso or (Dylan's favorite) Cezanne, is his ability to somehow get what he wants, to meet the challenge he has, consciously or intuitively, set himself for this particular painting or sculpture or song/performance. When the result is good, a great many factors enter in, but the one consistent one is the artist's commitment to his work, to expressing his (or her) internal vision. I'm not saying that the recording of John Hiatt's "The Usual" by Bob Dylan and his pick-up band included on the

Hearts of Fire soundtrack album is great art (though it is very enjoyable), I'm saying it's an example of a great artist at work. If his songwriting Muse goes on strike, he comes up with the exact song he needs some other way. (Keep in mind that his task is not to meet the fans' or critics' expectations; it's to realize a felt, intuited vision, an assignment he has wordlessly given himself, this day or month or hour.)

Though we the public may expect great sounds from a 1987 studio band composed of guitar hero Eric Clapton and Rolling Stone Ron Wood and their peers, I believe that in fact the marvelous sonic crunch of the hard rock riff on this recording (very different from the pale sketch on Hiatt's album) and the ecstatic instrumental rave-up that follows the third verse-and-chorus (comparable to high points of the Rolling Stones' 1970 classic "Can't You Hear Me Knocking") are evidence of Bob Dylan's remarkable artistry as a bandleader – his ability, in the moment of performance, to use the unwieldy gravitational pull of his presence to awaken the collective genius of a handful of musicians, in service to the music and the artist/bandleader's internal vision. If we wonder how he does this, we can contemplate the grunt he makes after singing "I'll have the usual!!" and the effect this may have subconsciously had on the musicians, who embark on their unscheduled epiphany seconds later. (Remember that the bandleader is also guiding and sparking the band via his own rhythm guitar playing.)

Bob Dylan had been a heavy drinker for close to three decades when he recorded this song. (John Bauldie: "There's a story that Joan Baez once said that if you get drunk with Bob Dylan you can be in his band. Perhaps it's a rather unkind question to ask you if alcohol helped in establishing his enthusiasm to work with you?" Richard Marquand: "Yes! He certainly has a very nice Cabernet Sauvignon there at the house. We certainly managed to get through a few bottles, that's true!") So it's intriguing that circumstances conspired to have him select as Billy Parker's theme a song structured around the jolly self-mockery and at times self-loathing of the social drinker ("I'm stepping over downed drunks at a party ..." "Gonna drink till I sink/What am I talking about?"). "I'll have the usual," of course, is a tag-line from the social culture of alcohol, making this song a sequel to the Replacements' equally poignant "Here Comes a Regular."

"A Couple More Years," Dylan's other great performance

from the *Hearts of Fire* soundtrack, is a different sort of example of an artist getting what he needs. Sometimes, as Bob Dylan has certainly often experienced as a songwriter, when you put yourself in the hands of your Muse you get a lot more than what you consciously asked for. You (if you're Bob Dylan) read over the song you've just written and are surprised at the aptness and cleverness of certain images and words you don't remember choosing consciously – you just needed a rhyme, or something.

In this case it isn't the songwriter's Muse that was appealed to – in regard to the *Hearts of Fire* songs that Muse kept telling BD, "If your task now and for the next few months is to *be* Billy Parker, who retired from the music scene ten years ago to live his own life, why would you wanna get any writing done?" – but, as with "The Usual," the performer's Muse. There's some evidence that Dylan was still trying, on the first day of the Townhouse sessions, to write a sensitive love song for Billy to have just written for Molly when she's begun her stardom and they're both back on his chicken farm. That didn't jell, but something or someone whispered in the singer's ear that the perfect song for an older man in the same line of work to sing to a much younger girl he's fallen for and wants to address as an equal is one Dylan knows already: "Remember, Bob, 'A Couple More Years' by Shel Silverstein, which you sang four times during your shows at the end of 1980?" "Yeah!" he says. " 'Well I got a couple more years on you babe, and that's all.' Yeah, that's perfect!" So he gets in touch with feelings of tenderness he's known (or felt recently) similar to what Billy might feel towards Molly at this moment, and he records a stunning, heartfelt performance of "A Couple More Years" … and only as he sings it, or listens to the playback, does he realize that the key line in the song seems to have been written specifically for Billy and Molly and this movie! "You're heading somewhere, but I've been that somewhere, and found it's nowhere at all." Wow. How does the performer Muse *do* that?? Bob Dylan, one of the biggest poets of the century or not, thinks to himself that no matter how hard he tried, he couldn't possibly have written a more perfect lyric and tune for this moment in this script. Awesome.

I've already said, in the introduction to this volume, that the riff is the secret of Bob Dylan's music and often the inspiration for his finest vocal performances. "A Couple More Years" is a better example of this than "The Usual." The riff in "The Usual" does give shape and excitement to the recording, and in that sense gives Dylan something to jab his vocals into. But in the unique acoustic guitar figure Dylan plays and sings to in "A Couple More Years" we can recognize the singer's inspiration, the immediate source of the powerful feelings stirred up in him and the extraordinary expressiveness of his singing throughout this brief tune. He's singing to and with that riff ("a musical figure repeated persistently throughout a composition") as if his fingers were Molly and his voice Billy.

It's an astonishing performance (and, unfortunately, not yet available on any "official" Bob Dylan album). Almost every word of the vocal (for example, "fly" in "I've had more chances to fly and more places to fall") seems to be a multilayered essay describing aspects of the speaker's life and expressing and clarifying his perception of reality. The word "all" is sung five times, and carries different messages and emotions every time. The subtlety of the phrasing is impressive. I wonder if singing (and gesturing with) the same little word in thirty deeply felt performances of "You and Me, We Had It All" on tour earlier in the year helped prepare the singer for this *tour de force*?

"Night After Night" and "Had A Dream About You, Baby" are, perhaps, true to Bob Dylan's 8/86 sense of Billy Parker as a man and musician in that they're "empty." Even the fact that "Dream" has a recognizable riff doesn't seem to help. The riff makes a difference only when it inspires the singer to sing to it and with it and to express himself. But of course that can't happen every time. By way of Bob Dylan trivia, other fans besides me have noticed that the riff in "Had A Dream About You, Baby" is quite reminiscent of "Love Her with a Feeling," the "warm-up" song Dylan sang to open many of his 1978 shows (he'd found the song on an old album by blues singer Tampa Red).

But the non-emptiness of Bob Dylan as a singer-performer and even as a songwriter at the time of these Townhouse recordings is evidenced by an obscure and remarkable souvenir of these sessions that can be found on an illicit compilation called *The Genuine Bootleg Series, Take 2* ("genuine" because unlike Columbia Records' 1991 box set *Bob Dylan the Bootleg Series*, these compilations really are bootlegs, unauthorized by the artist or his record company or song publisher). This song would presumably be called "To Fall in Love with You" if it had ever been completed and released officially. It's not included in the movie in any form, and seems to have been intended for the "I wrote this song for you" slot filled by "A Couple More Years," the scene of Billy romancing Molly on his chicken farm late in the movie.

"To Fall in Love with You" is unfinished – Dylan is singing what he has called "dummy lyrics," slurred improvised words marking rhythmic and melodic spaces when a song-in-progress is close enough to have a structure and a catch-phrase, but most of the actual lyrics and the storyline that will connect them are not yet revealed to the composer – but it isn't empty. It's remarkably full of feeling. The clear message is that the speaker expects himself to fall in love with the addressee and is eager to enjoy that intoxicating experience, but at the same time that it seems enticingly imminent it also hasn't really happened yet, and so he's caught in excited anticipation and bemused uncertainty both at once. This is a rich and complex emotional moment, and "To Fall in Love with You" as a performance captures and conveys it magnificently. Not empty at all. Another idiosyncratic example of Bob Dylan's genius.

Why does it feel so authentic? Presumably because at this very moment in late August 1986, Bob Dylan really is hoping and wanting to fall in love with this movie he's agreed to make, and he's excited about the prospect and anxious and vulnerable because it hasn't quite happened to him yet. "I feel no love; I feel no shame," he sings in the last verse of the song. A year later, producer Smith told Dylan scholar Bauldie: "He came right off the tour into the beginnings of the film, just a few days away from the start of shooting – really a very heavy time for him. And I genuinely believe that he hadn't even started to think about the film. Later, once he'd become part of the team, knew us all and trusted us and began to enjoy himself, he sort of indicated that even when we started shooting he still wasn't sure that he wanted to do the film!"

What is immediately striking about this track is how much feeling the singer seems to put into what he's saying, even though the words don't quite make sense ... and, as it progresses, what a fine groove bass and drums and guitar and voice achieve – also full of feeling – even though the structure of the song seems as improvised as the lyrics. Another striking element of the performance is Dylan's pitch changes from line to line, varying the tone and intensity of his voice so deliberately you could easily imagine two different singers are duetting, trading lines, as occurs in some gospel singing. Or you could imagine two sides of Bob Dylan (born in the sign of Gemini, the Twins) are talking to each other while skillfully singing together.

The opening verse goes something like this: "Now deal go down/My day early/Like a dyin' eye/Upon the sea/And ages roll/From me from you/What pair is I?/What can I do?/Let down your mind/And the deal is done/I can believe/Fought in the dark/What I could find/Oh time is righ-lu/I feel in love/To fall in love/To fall in love [pause] with you." This is sung with great conviction. The band (led by the drummer) audibly kicks into gear after the first chorus, as though it signals them that this really is a song. The second verse begins, "Yes, day is done/My time is right/Day in the night/Deep in the night," and the music is sounding so good and so meaningful one wishes he'd been able to finish or find this song, although the rough draft is a treasure and a pleasure in itself.

In short, a very rare opportunity to watch the songwriter and the songwriter's Muse at work – like a dyin' eye, upon the sea. The powerful opening image ("Now deal go down") is straight out of the singer's subconscious and Robert Johnson's 1936 recording "Last Fair Deal Gone Down." A further glimpse of the artist's mind at work comes in the midst of the third verse, when his voices boom: "Where ages roll/Where ages fly/I hear your name/Where angel lies." Presumably "ages fly" suggested "angel lies." The next line is "What do I know?" Indeed.

"Artist at work" is also the theme (by BD's willful and clever choice) of the filmed-in-1986 BBC-TV documentary *Getting to Dylan*. This 50-minute film was shot on the set of *Hearts of Fire* in England and Canada, fall '86, and aired on BBC's *Omnibus* programme in 1987. I tend to agree with Clinton Heylin's assessment (in his biography *Behind the Shades*): "*Getting to Dylan* remains the essential filmed portrait of Dylan in the eighties, an important adjunct to *Don't Look Back*, *Eat the Document* and *Renaldo & Clara*, the three previous films to deal with the Dylan myth."

Getting to Dylan begins with footage of 22-year-old Bob Dylan singing "With God on Our Side" on a BBC programme in 1964. This segues into what appears to be Bob Dylan arriving at a British airport in 1986 with a guitar in a case on his shoulder. It turns out to be Bob Dylan acting the part of Billy Parker – cleverly, the audio track is the same young voice as the first segment, but now singing "The Times They Are A-Changin'." Soon we see director

Marquand speaking of what it's like working with Dylan: "He's a sweetheart, he's a real sweetheart" (said with affection and sincerity). And next, Bob Dylan at the *Hearts of Fire* press conference quoted earlier in this chapter.

The press conference footage is funny, and our first opportunity to be intimate with the subject of the documentary, to see what Bob Dylan is like now – 1986 press conference tactics and humor as compared with 1965 (*Don't Look Back*) tactics. And, as in the film of his wonderful 1965 San Francisco press conference, we the viewers can see (if our minds are not too full of images and distorted facts) for ourselves some of the sweetness of the private man. It's in the faces he makes, his half-shrugs and gestures, his laughter, the offbeat sincerity and dignity of his presence, his timing. He knows how to play to his audience, whether it's his director sitting next to him, or the room full of journalists and functionaries, or you and me on the other side of the camera, watching from the future. It's subtle, but it's still that Chaplin-like ability to get us to sympathize with and laugh at his predicament.

The documentary continues in a Bristol theater called Colston Hall, where a Billy Parker concert is being staged and filmed (with 1,000 paid extras in the role of "audience"). We see "Billy" tell the crowd, "I'm gonna sing this song for the millionth time. I'm so sick of it, I could puke. But I'm gonna sing it anyway ..." And he launches into "Had a Dream About You, Baby." We see a few seconds of Dylan (not Parker) signing autographs for the eager Bristol extras, then producer Smith talking about working with Dylan, and a scene in which Bob as Billy comes in drinking from a Jack Daniel's whiskey bottle. We see him tell the director, "I messed it up again." Marquand reassures him ("You almost got it, there"). The documentary shows us more footage of the film being made, and then Marquand tells how he met and spent time with Dylan back in March, "hanging around" at his Malibu house while they got to know each other. "Now I can just say, 'hi!' without worrying about it," he explains. "But when you're dealing with such an incredibly charismatic character, people do tend to advance in a very odd way, aware of the icon they're dealing with, rather than the human being."

So after some more footage of the movie being made, including a minute of Dylan improvising on electric guitar while waiting for the next concert shot, and a stunt coordinator instructing Bob on how to jump into the crowd and grab and shake a heckler, and Rupert Everett admitting that the idea of getting to know *him* (Dylan) was "really exciting" for everyone involved with the film, we get to the heart of the documentary, a 25-minute conversation with Bob Dylan in his trailer, his home during the month of shooting in Toronto.

Appropriately – since the title of the documentary is "Getting to Dylan" and since the interviewer, Christopher Sykes, starts by asking, "How do you decide when to talk to people and when not to?" – Dylan immediately takes charge of the interview and transforms it into a multilayered work of art that is as dazzling and unexpected and as stimulating and confounding in its implications as a first-rate Bob Dylan song. He does this – and we get to actually watch the idea occur to him, as though a big light bulb appears above his head in a thought balloon, as he and the interviewer and camera crew are about to enter the trailer – by getting his sketchpad and pen and then intently studying Sykes and drawing his portrait throughout the interview. So what we have is a portrait of the artist in the act of creating a portrait of his interrogator.

First of all, this gives Dylan something to do with his energy and his nervousness while he attempts to answer Sykes's questions. Like when he's singing a song on stage, he now has something to focus on, a sense of purpose. Early in the conversation, before we can see what he's doing with his hands and why he keeps looking up so keenly, he asks the interviewer, "Could you grow your beard just a little bit more, er, like … next time?" (Dylan's condition for this day's filmed interview was that it be a trial run, to see how things go before he commits himself to an actual interview. "We're just testing out here now," he says at the beginning. "Nothing's for sure; we're just casting people here.")

In the first volume of this series about Bob Dylan as a performing artist, I discuss some famous photographs of Dylan in Woodstock New York taken by Daniel Kramer in 1964. Kramer later reported, "I found him sitting at a dining booth in the kitchen reading a newspaper. He turned the pages of the newspaper, and seemed never to acknowledge my presence. This set the pace. Apparently he was not going to do anything especially for the camera. It was not that he was not cooperating. Actually he was being cooperative in his way – he allowed me to be with him, he allowed me to photograph him and to select my own pictures, as long as they derived from the situation I found him in."

In a stroke of good luck or inspired genius or manipulativeness, or all three, Dylan arrived at a set for this 25-minute screen test that is as simple and provocative and perfect and clever as the covers of his first six albums. Next to his talking head and restless body, throughout the interview, we see a page torn from a tabloid newspaper and stuck onto the wall of the trailer with the prominent headlines "Sinatra and Me – by Liz Taylor" (top) and "Pow! Rocky to the Rescue" (center of page) and a photo of Bob's friend Liz in a dress that shows two-thirds of her prominent breasts, so that often while Dylan is talking we find ourselves hypnotized by the dance of his frizzy halo of hair and Liz Taylor's decolletage. Interestingly, Dylan's costume for the moment is a white shirt with buttons open revealing his own bare chest. The insider/fan may realize that Taylor is a personal friend of Dylan's, and that Dylan is a great admirer of Sinatra's work as a singer.

The "Pow!" in the center of this bit of stage design appropriately makes us think of 1960s New York City pop art. The tabloid page resonates with the heated discussion in the interview of how people (and the press) treat and respond to famous people. The fact that the article we're staring at is, according to the headline, not only about Liz Taylor but *by* her also resonates with the performance we're watching. And no, it doesn't feel like Dylan has stuck the page up just to provide a good backdrop for this filmed interview and show off his cleverness (though, certainly, he has consciously positioned himself for this shoot) ... rather it feels as though he'd put Liz and Frank on the wall of his trailer to amuse himself and to make himself feel more at home when retreating to this bit of private space.

In that other book, I wrote: "Reading Kramer's description of working with Dylan, and looking at the photographs, I get insight into the mystery of who Dylan is. His sitting and reading the paper, not acknowledging the camera, going on about his business, is itself a performance – he knows the camera is there, perhaps even senses eyes looking at the photograph months or decades later, and he is choosing a way of being with the camera that feels right to him, that allows him to express himself accurately. It is a very conscious way of being: his presence fills the space, he has removed the camera's power to make him something he's not – not by 'being natural' but by actually expanding his performance and making the camera and cameraman work under his unspoken direction. He does the same thing with musicians on stage or in the recording studio. He doesn't tell them what to do. Rather he fills the space in such a way that whatever they do is in relation to his aesthetic presence."

Artist at work. Early in the footage, the subject of the documentary teases the producer/interviewer by telling him he may or may not show him his portrait when he's finished drawing it. "If it's good, I'll show it to you; if not, forget it!" In the end, he does hold it up so Sykes can see it (though the camera sneaks a few peeks at the work-in-progress before that). Then, in a wonderful moment, Dylan snatches up his own book *Lyrics* and holds the cover (a sketched self-portrait) in one hand next to the just-finished Sykes portrait in his other hand, and asks, "See the similarities here?" In other words, the portrayer always ends up drawing a self-portrait. Take that, Mr. Interviewer! And of course, there are striking similarities. A further nice touch on the part of producer/editor Sykes is that we the viewers never see him on camera. We hear his voice, but only see his face in Dylan's sketch. So we can't compare Dylan's drawing with his subject's "actual" appearance. We only see him as Dylan sees him, if indeed his hand has succeeded in its task. "I'm not sure I'd show this to anybody, actually," Dylan says, as he holds it up and shows it to us. Which makes me wonder how much the premise that this particular filmed interview was supposed to be a "trial run" helped free the subject from self-consciousness?

Throughout the interview, we the viewers are mesmerized by the amount of attention Dylan seems to be paying us, as his powerful eyes repeatedly look up to assess us (the camera ... actually, Sykes's face) and we feel his attempt to penetrate, to understand, to capture. A quick intent glance, then his eyes flicker down to check the results hand and pen are getting, then flicker back, staring boldly. We feel his commitment, his uncertainty, his frustrations, his excitement, the keenness and sincerity of his engagement in this creative process. It's particularly fascinating to watch his mind and mouth trying to answer questions accurately and justly at the same time that his mind and hand are doing the same thing. The juggler. "And if you hear vague traces of skippin' reels of rhyme to your tambourine in time, it's just a ragged clown behind, I wouldn't pay it any mind, it's just a shadow you're seein' that he's chasing."

The Sykes interview is, of course, a fantastic opportunity to be intimate with Bob Dylan, to see what he's really like. Not only do we watch him (in tight close-up) concentrating for more than twenty minutes on a piece of creative-work-in-progress he cares about, we also watch him (as in the press conference films) trying to answer questions, and coping with the feelings that arise in him as he does so. And we see him absently rubbing his cheeks and eyes, scratching his head, in a manner familiar to us from his television appearances. We see (particularly in his sketch-making process, but also in his animated dialogue with the interviewer) that famous nervous energy coursing through him that we've read about in descriptions of the young Bob Dylan, the leg that won't stop moving. In this case, it's more often elegant than awkward. Dylan is standing and half-standing most of the time as he sketches and answers questions on camera, and so he is constantly stretching his wiry but muscular body in a variety of ways that are expressive and attractive; yes, he's 45 years old but still lithe and vibrant, as sexy as ever in his unique Bob Dylan way, as interesting to watch as any cat. Artist at work. Nervous and curious and inventive mind pacing back and forth before your eyes.

It is of course intimate to be in the star's dressing room and living room, his private trailer on the movie set, rather like the wonderful footage of ABC-TV's Bob Brown interviewing Dylan in 1985 on a lawn overlooking the ocean at the singer's Malibu home (or the great photo in a 1995 *Newsweek* of Dylan with his dog and his canvases in his drawing studio at home). But what makes *Getting to Dylan* the "essential filmed portrait of Dylan in the eighties" is the extent to which the camera and the direction and Dylan's own devices for disarming his defenses and self-consciousness (i.e. turning the "interview" into an unpaid sitting in which Sykes is modelling for Dylan) allow us to be present with the man's feelings and perceptions and values and personality as he talks about songwriting ("I don't have any set way of writing songs"), and money, and obsessive fans, and the impact of being famous, and how he decides when to give autographs.

We see him get irritated, not because the interviewer's an idiot (he's not), but because certain topics bring up old wounds and confront him with his own sensitivity in the face of a world that makes unreasonable requests of him and criticizes him harshly for not conforming even as they claim to love him for being a non-conformist. And because we're with him from before the interview starts (and have watched him figure out how to position himself for this situation), we're able to see through his eyes and maybe even feel for a few moments how it feels to be he.

Early in the interview, Dylan says about performing: "I don't do it for love. I do it because I *can* do it and I think I'm good at it. That's all I do it for." Sykes responds: "Does that explain why the other evening at the sort of mock concert, you didn't sort of say anything to the audience? You know, people in the press, they said, 'Well, people all turned up to this thing, and why didn't Dylan just say hello?'" Dylan gets irritated: "What was I supposed to say hello for? It doesn't have nothin' to do with me. I'm there making a movie. Are you serious?"

Sykes: "Yeah, I'm serious. That's what they said." Dylan: "Well, why didn't you tell 'em?" [Implicitly: "You got a lot of nerve to say you are my friend ..."] Sykes: "No. I mean. I just read it in the paper. And that made me wonder, why didn't you say it? If it were me, I'd feel the pressure. I'd feel the pressure." Dylan: "No – no matter what you say, it's not enough, is it? You know, if I coulda gone out and said, 'Hello everybody, how ya doin' out there?' And they'd say, 'Play a song, Bob, play a song!' I'd say, 'Oh man, I don't feel like it right now.' Then that would be in the press: 'Dylan was there. He was grumpy. He's moody. He's a recluse. He came out for a few minutes and said hello to the audience and went back into his trailer ... into the seclusion of his own little kingdom.' Which is what, you know, people would say. I'm just actually quoting you almost verbatim something that has been said."

Not only will they stone you for not saying hello and stone you for saying hello and going back to your trailer, they also will of course stone you for getting irritated, even in an interview with a guy you like, which is just a trial run, and is taking place very much under controlled conditions you've wisely created yourself. In other words, no matter how careful and clever you are, you could find yourself being inducted into the Rock and Roll Hall of Fame in January 1988, and hear Bruce Springsteen say in his speech introducing you: "About three months ago, I was watching TV and a *Rolling Stone* special came on and Bob came on. And he was in a real cranky mood. It seemed like he was kind of bitching and moaning about how his fans don't know him, and nobody knows him, and that they come up to him on the street and kind of treat him like a long-lost brother or somethin'."

What Springsteen and a few million other people saw on the

Rolling Stone TV special was a two-minute excerpt from the Sykes interview, taken out of context – not maliciously, but because it was good copy, effective "entertainment." The context is a monologue following the "why didn't you say 'hello'?" exchange, on the subject of what it's like to be famous. Dylan says: "Say you're passing a little pub or inn, and you look through the window and you see all the people eating and talking and carrying on. You can see them all be very real with each other, as real as they're gonna be. Because when you walk into the room, it's over! You won't see them being real any more. Things have changed just because a person walks into a room that can be a focus point for everybody, you know? Maybe that's got something to do with it [what fame is]. I really can't say. I don't pay any attention to it!"

Sykes: "Is it a drag, then? No, you just said you don't pay any attention to it." Dylan: "No, I don't pay any attention to it! Life is short, you know? And, what do most people want from me? They want your autograph. Nobody knows me and I don't know them! You know? They walk up and they think they know me because I've written some song that, uh, happens to … uh … bother them in a certain way and they can't get rid of it, you know, in their mind. That's got nothing to do with me! They still don't know me. And I still don't know them. So they walk, you know, up as if, ah, as if we're long-lost brothers or sisters, or something! You know, that's kinda … you know. I think I could prove that in any court!"

From "Nobody knows me" to "in any court" is the excerpt that appeared (with no explanation or contexting) in the "Bob Dylan" segment of the *Rolling Stone* TV show. So put yourself in Bob Dylan's shoes again, dear reader. What is the "right" way to do a filmed interview? Take tranquilizers beforehand?

As far as context goes, a few minutes earlier Sykes told Dylan that he recently encountered a particularly scary obsessive fan who's been following Dylan around the world lately, and said: "One does think about John Lennon getting shot, and maybe you have to worry about something like that." So in context, Dylan's comments on being famous and having fans come up to you were a lot less cranky than might have been expected … And when we see him say them in *Getting to Dylan*, it's not hard to follow his train of thought, to empathize with the man caught inside the myth. "They think they know me …" False portraits everywhere. "He's moody." Even from his fellow singer-celebrity Springsteen! Even at the Hall of Fame induction! "You'll find out when you reach the top ..."

A particularly choice moment (aesthetically speaking) in the *Getting to Dylan* interview occurs after Sykes says, following an attempt to get Dylan to speculate about where his songs come from, "Plenty of people know how to do the technical stuff [of song-writing], but you know how to tell stories." Dylan [thoughtfully]: "Really?" Sykes: "Well, you like telling stories in your songs." Dylan shrugs with a very brief expressive gesture that involves moving one shoulder while pursing his lips: "Not really." Sykes [quickly]: "No?" Dylan [continuing the thought he just expressed via gesture]: "I don't know how many stories I've written." Sykes: "Just some observations?" And then comes the special moment. Dylan [still thoughtful, carefully considering the other's comments out of respect for him, but simultaneously trying to report accurately and honestly (out of respect for himself) what comes up in him now on this topic]:

> "Yeah, I wouldn't call them stories. Stories are things which have a beginning, middle, and end. My things are more like, uh ... uh ... [you can see him thinking], short, uh ... short attention span things that happens in a group of crowded people, that goes down, uh ... very quickly, so, uh, the normal eye wouldn't even notice it."

What is delightful about this is that as you watch and listen (seeing a transcript on paper is not the same), you can recognize the exact intonation and therefore state of consciousness with which Bob Dylan in 1965 wrote "my songs're written with the kettledrum in mind/a touch of any anxious color" and sang "At times I think there are no words but these to tell what's true." So we get to watch that mind at work, in close-up dialogue with a guy he trusts (for the moment), finding the words and rhythms, gestures, in which to tell what's true, with a touch of anxious color the normal eye wouldn't even notice (but we love Bob Dylan's art because he treats us with a respect that acknowledges that we're not normal eyes and ears, that suggests his trust that we might notice something that goes down very quickly).

Immediately before this brief sequence, we see his eye and hand working on his drawing. After it, is a comic moment in which Sykes nervously says, "I have to look at my list!" and scrambles trying to find the list of questions he prepared, until Dylan says, "Here's your list, I'll bet!" and pulls it out from under his drawing, where it had somehow become employed as a backup sheet between sketch and pad.

So if you want to get to Dylan, listening to his performances is the recommended path, but watching this little filmed performance will also help.

Sam Shepard's *True Dylan* interview/play recorded a few months earlier doesn't have the advantage of allowing us to see Dylan's face and body language and hear his voice and its timing and phrasing – but it has another kind of advantage, in that this really is a private exchange between friends, in the man's house, without the obtrusiveness of a camera rolling. If the subject of James Dean keeps coming up, it's not because the interviewer (Shepard) brings it up. It's because that's what's on Bob Dylan's mind at this moment, along with "I just gotta make one more phone call, all right?" We even get to hear (see on the page) parts of the phone calls: "Maria? Hi, it's me again. [pause, laughs] Yeah, I just like the sound of your voice. Listen, what's the area code for Tulsa, do you know?" Dylan has a daughter named Maria, so there's a further touch of intimacy, even if we never find out much about the party she tells him about, which he eventually decides to avoid: "Naw, I think I'm gonna pass. [pause] I dunno. Sounds like too many record producers. [pause] Yeah, I'll just hang around here, probably."

So if you wanted it, there it is, the true Dylan. The one who's being very real when you look through the window (but when you walk into the room, it's over, so look out!). For a further taste, you also have the option of watching a bad movie called *Hearts of Fire* wherein Richard Marquand, in his last film before dying suddenly of a heart attack just before the movie's release in fall '87, really did succeed in bringing out and capturing "what is in the man [Dylan, not Billy Parker], his charisma and his natural charm and graciousness."

Or, as Bob Dylan and Sam Shepard told us in "Brownsville Girl": "The only thing we knew for sure about Henry Porter was that his name wasn't Henry Porter."

2.

November 8, 1986 was the last day of filming for *Hearts of Fire*. On April 3, 1987, Bob Dylan began recording a new album. The months in between were partly filled with the sort of semipublic activities we've come to expect from once-legendary figures ("famous long ago") like Billy Parker. On 11/10/86 Dylan inducted songwriter-performer Gordon Lightfoot into the Juno Hall of Fame at the annual Canadian Academy of Recording Arts and Sciences dinner in Toronto. A month later, he dropped in on some old friends from the folk music world, Happy and Artie Traum and John Herald in Woodstock, New York; they spent the evening at Herald's cabin singing "Barbara Allen" and various Woody Guthrie songs. In January, Dylan visited the Grateful Dead in a recording studio in northern California to discuss plans for a tour together in summer 1987.

February 19, 1987, Bob Dylan and ex-Beatle George Harrison and ex-Creedence Clearwater Revival leader John Fogerty made a surprise appearance onstage at a club in Hollywood, California, playing guitar and singing backup vocals with their friends Taj Mahal and Jesse Ed Davis. On March 2nd, Dylan attended

Elizabeth Taylor's 55th birthday party at Burt Bacharach's Los Angeles home, at which, it is reported, he sang a duet with Michael Jackson and sang "Happy Birthday" with Stevie Wonder, Dionne Warwick and Gladys Knight. On March 11, 1987, along with Mikhail Baryshnikov, Rosemary Clooney, and many other performers, Dylan participated in a tribute to George Gershwin at the Brooklyn Academy of Music in New York. He sang (accompanying himself on acoustic guitar) a brief and haunting version of "Soon," a 1930 Ira and George Gershwin film song once recorded by Ella Fitzgerald.

One of the musicians invited to the April 1987 recording sessions was told that Dylan was working on *Self Portrait*, part two. And sure enough, as with *Self Portrait* (1970), every song recorded or attempted at the April sessions for what would become *Down in the Groove* (released May 1988) was a "cover," a song written and first recorded by someone else, with the exception of two songs that are lyrics from Grateful Dead lyricist Robert Hunter's notebook that Dylan liked and put music to – "Silvio" and "Ugliest Girl in the World."

In 1985, talking with Cameron Crowe for the *Biograph* box set booklet and responding to a question about what he might do in the future, Dylan said, "I guess I'd like to do a concept album like, you know, [Willie Nelson's] *Red-Headed Stranger* or something, maybe a children's album, or an album of cover songs but I don't know if the people would let me get away with that … 'A Million Miles from Nowhere,' 'I Who Have Nothing,' 'All My Tomorrows,' 'I'm in the Mood for Love,' 'More than You Know,' 'It's a Sin to Tell a Lie' …"

There are four songs on *Down in the Groove* that were written by Bob Dylan – the two collaborations with Robert Hunter, "Had a Dream About You, Baby" from the *Hearts of Fire* session in August '86, and "Death Is Not the End," an outtake from the spring '83 sessions for the *Infidels* album. The other six tracks are from the April '87 sessions; all are covers, as are three other noteworthy tracks recorded at these sessions: "Pretty Boy Floyd" (which was recorded for and released on *Folkways: A Vision Shared – a Tribute to Woody Guthrie and Leadbelly*), "Important Words" (a ballad by rockabilly singer Gene Vincent), and my current favorite performance from these sessions, "Got Love If You Want It" (a blues rocker by Slim Harpo which had also been covered by British rock groups the

Kinks and the Yardbirds and by another of Dylan's rockabilly heroes, Warren Smith).

The other songs known to have been recorded or attempted at Dylan's Los Angeles sessions in April 1987 are "Willie and the Hand Jive" and "Twist and Shout" (R&B hits from 1958 and 1962 which were both songs Dylan had participated in at the impromptu all-star club jam two months earlier), "Just When I Needed You Most" (a 1979 pop hit), "Look on Yonders Wall" and "Rollin' and Tumblin'" (blues-rock standards) and "Red Cadillac and a Black Moustache" and "Rock With Me, Baby" (rockabilly covers Dylan had sung at some of his 1986 concerts).

Down in the Groove is widely agreed to be one of Bob Dylan's weakest albums, though it has its moments – notably "Rank Strangers to Me," a plaintive bluegrass song about feeling lost in this world.

In August 1988 Dylan told Kathryn Baker of the Associated Press: "There's no rule that claims that anyone must write their own songs. And I do. I write a lot of songs. But so what, you know? You could take another song somebody else has written and you could make it yours. I'm not saying I made a definitive version of anything with this last record, but I liked the songs. Every so often you've gotta sing songs that're out there. You just have to, just to keep yourself straight."

In the same interview, he acknowledged that one factor in his recording an album of "covers" was that he hadn't been doing much songwriting himself recently: "Writing is like such an isolated thing. You're in such an isolated frame of mind. You have to get into or be in that place. In the old days, I could get to it real quick. I can't get to it like that no more. It's not that simple. I mean, just being able to shut yourself off for long periods of time, where you're so isolated no one can get to you, mentally or physically, you know? You need to be able to do that in order to come up with that kind of stuff. You're always capable of it in your youth, and especially if you're an unknown and nobody cares, like if you're an anonymous person. But once that all ends, then you have to create not only what you want to do, but you have to create the environment to do it in, which is double hard."

This of course is what Billy Parker tries to warn Molly McGuire about in *Hearts of Fire*. In the 1988 interview, Dylan went on to explain: "I don't write about things. I write from inside of something, and I sing and play the same way. It's never *about* that something, hoping to touch it. It's rather from the inside of it, reaching out."

The power of "Rank Strangers" and "Got Love" as performances is the extent to which we feel the singer's presence *inside* the characters singing these songs, reaching out to us from these particular (and evocative) life situations. "Songs are just thoughts," Bob Dylan told Bill Flanagan in 1985. "For the moment they stop time. [Mind out of time!] Songs are supposed to be heroic enough to give the illusion of stopping time. With just that thought. To hear a song is to hear someone's thought, no matter what they're describing." So the relative success of these two tracks, and the relative lack of success of most of the others recorded for or included on *Down in the Groove*, is a function of the singer/performer's presence inside that song, that thought, at the moment of performance, and the extent to which we the listeners *feel* that presence and receive, are given, the illusion that time has stopped and we are in this character's situation ourselves, we are him, we are in his moment – or not. Overwhelmingly, ecstatically. Or not quite. In this case the "not quite"s add up and sink the album as an overall listening experience.

Also in April 1987, Bob Dylan recorded some statements about Woody Guthrie for use in a forthcoming BBC radio program. These comments were also included in the liner notes for the Guthrie/Leadbelly tribute album. They are interesting for what they tell us about the speaker. Recalling his reactions when he first heard Guthrie's records (at age 18): "There are so many reasons why he was different, you could fill a book. He had a sound. Well, everybody has a sound, but he had a particular sound, more or less a Carter Family type sound. And he had something that needed to be said. And that was highly unusual to my ears. Usually you would have one or the other, you know, but he always had something to say."

It seems reasonable to guess that Bob Dylan's criteria for the songs he was choosing to sing and the recording sessions he was organizing and supervising (he was his own producer for this album) in spring '87 were that each song have something to say, and that the finished tracks and album achieve a sound that would be different from whatever the record buyers might be expecting and would be deeply true to Bob Dylan's musical and philosophical vision (his thoughts) at this moment in his life. He was reaching for something (or from inside of something). Later in the Guthrie interview/statements, Dylan said: "There was an innocence to Woody Guthrie. There was a certain type of innocence that I never regained – I know that's what I was looking for. Whether it was real or it was a dream, who's to say? But it was like a kind of lost innocence. And after him it was over."

Segue to the first track of *Down in the Groove*, "Let's Stick Together." This recording has a *sound*. As surely as the opening (title) track of *Shot of Love* (1981), of which Dylan has said, "It's my most perfect song; it defines where I am at spiritually, musically, romantically and whatever else; it shows where my sympathies lie." Other interview comments indicate that it is the sound of the performance and recording that pleases him so much in "Shot of Love," not primarily the lyrics. The lyrics and the sound and the energy and spirit of the performance work together to create a unit of expression that is very satisfying to him, possibly a magical moment of enthusiastic innocence regained. And intuitively I feel that "Let's Stick Together" leads off *Down in the Groove*, and survived the several revisions Dylan made to the sequence and contents of this album, because the punch in the vocal and in the band performance (especially the harmonica), and the feel of the mix, and the message conveyed by sound and lyrics together are in fact the closest Dylan could come or could hope to come to expressing where he was at spiritually, musically, romantically and whatever else at this moment in his artistic and personal life. This is what he had to say. Or, in any case, an arrow pointing in that direction.

"Let's Stick Together" doesn't say a lot to me, but I've always enjoyed it as a lead-off track, the energy and earnestness of the performance (particularly the intro and first verse, and the harmonica-led jam between verses three and four). Listening to Wilbert Harrison's original 1959 version (the follow-up to his big hit "Kansas City") is a revelation, because it's actually a rather dull, predictable rock and roll shuffle, with an unconvincing vocal. This tells us how much of an original statement this 1987 Bob Dylan performance-and-arrangement is. In autumn 1986 Christopher Sykes asked Dylan, "What makes a good song?" BD replied: "Melody. Rhythm. That stuff, I guess. But mostly it's sentiment – whether you can identify with what the sentiment of the song is, what the song says, as a song. That's what makes a good song. Someone would say, '*This* is a good song,' and someone else would say, '*That*'s a

good song.' Whether it's true for anybody makes it a good … anything." So though I don't identify with the sentiment and therefore
don't connect with "Let's Stick Together," as an appreciator of Bob
Dylan I am quite impressed by how clearly he conveys his own
identification with the sentiment he hears in this song, what it once
said to him and what it very passionately says for him and through
him right now.

Every moment of the vocal and band performance is vibrant,
but the standout epiphanic moments within these three minutes are
Dylan's delivery of the lines "the marriage vow you know it's very
sacred" and "consider the child, cannot be happy without his Mom
and his Pappy" … and the way these moments are framed within
the band performance, the arrangement. Dylan is mysteriously and
charmingly full of conviction here. His depth of feeling is certainly
related to the end of his own marriage (in 1977) while his children
were still young, but I find myself believing (and some little-known
biographical facts support this) that he is in fact singing the song to
himself and particularly to a lover of his who has borne him a child
and whom he wishes to "stick" with him (even though whatever
marriage they have is not a conventional one nor, probably, an
exclusive one). The song, and much of the album, is for Bob Dylan
about marriage as a question, as an ideal, as a mysterious force. The
album, as we shall see, is also about beauty as a question, and love
and sex likewise. Sung and played from the inside.

An album mostly of cover songs draws our attention to Bob
Dylan's relationship with songs. Oddly enough, the man who told
Nat Hentoff (during their *Playboy* interview in 1966), "message songs
are a drag, only college newspaper editors and single girls under
fourteen could possibly have time for them" (he went on to say he
was going to "rent Town Hall and put about thirty Western Union
boys on the bill") … this man seems to hear and receive and
remember songs as messages. By way of example, there's another
moment in the Christopher Sykes interview outtakes (not seen in
Getting to Dylan) when, in a discussion of politics, Dylan says:

"Afghanistan rebels are okay … But in El Salvador the rebels
are the bad guys … If you listen to that stuff you go crazy. It's that
Dave Mason song – 'There ain't no good guy, there ain't no
bad guy, there's only you and me and we just disagree.' True, or
what?"

Another example occurs in the *True Dylan* conversation with

Sam Shepard. As part of his response to Shepard's question "Have you ever felt like a couple?", Dylan says:

"Yeah. Sure. A couple. Sure. I've felt like that. Absolutely. Look – listen to this: [sings and plays] 'You must learn to leave the table when love is no longer being served. Just show them all that you are able. Just get up and leave without saying a word.'"

SS: "Who wrote that?" BD: "You got me. Roy Orbison or somebody, I dunno." SS: "Roy Orbison?" BD: "Naw. I dunno. Good lyric." A year earlier, in a similarly deep moment in his conversation with Cameron Crowe, Dylan's memory for who actually wrote the song in question was clearer:

"I think of a hero as someone who understands the degree of responsibility that comes with his freedom ... You gotta be able to feel your dream before anyone else is aware of it. 'Your parents don't like me, they say I'm too poor.' ... Gotta learn to bite the bullet like Tom Mix, take the blows, like the song says. Or like Charles Aznavour, 'You must learn to leave the table when love is no longer being served.' But that's a hard thing to do ..."

The point is that for Bob Dylan, songs, other people's songs, are containers for messages ("what the sentiment of the song is"). He keeps the ones that speak to him. And he repeats them, in conversation and on stage and sometimes in the recording studio, as a way of expressing himself, who he is and what he thinks and feels, at this moment. "Look – listen to this!" (sings and plays ...)

Suddenly I remember that when I was backstage talking with Dylan in December 1980, he made comments that indicated that he saw something particularly clever or humorous in an aspect of the song sequence at his new shows (shows where he'd been pressured by the press and radio and by the concert promoter into adding more "early" songs to his set lists, which had in the past year been made up entirely of new songs about Jesus and the singer's faith) ... and that he was amused and disappointed that the commentators (i.e. the San Francisco newspaper columnists and disc jockeys) hadn't noticed or made mention of it. What he was referring to was specifically his going from "I Believe in You" as number two song each night to "Like a Rolling Stone" as number three. I tried not to reveal that I wasn't sure I saw the joke myself ... Twenty years later, attempting to put myself in Bob Dylan's shoes, I feel certain that what pleased him was this juxtaposition:

> I … walk out on my own
> A thousand miles from home
> But I don't feel alone
> 'Cause I believe in You.
>
> How does it feel
> To be on your own
> With no direction home
> Like a complete unknown
> Like a rolling stone?

So what this tells us is that sometimes Dylan as a performing artist hears even his own songs as message-containers or sentiment-containers – and when he's high on a conscious juxtaposition of messages that seems particularly clever and provocative or even profound, to him, he hopes and wishes (or expects) that someone out there is listening, identifying not just with the sentiment of the songs but with the sentiment, the thought, of the juxtaposition. How does it feel? Wonderful, when you make a *bon mot* or play a hot solo and the whole world (or the people in the front row) notices and responds with appreciation, evidence of identification. And frustrating, when no one seems to notice or respond at all. You could even find yourself wanting to exhort your audience like a life partner: "You know we made a vow, not to leave one another never." (I'm not saying "Let's Stick Together" is consciously addressed to the performer's audience, except for maybe one particular woman who might even have been in the recording studio during this session. I'm just noting that when Dylan is truly *inside* of what he's singing and playing, the resulting performance tends to become so real that an I/thou message may be heard and felt as applicable to disciple/ divinity and artist/audience relationships as well as man/woman, husband/wife, parent/child, friend/friend …)

The second track on *Down in the Groove*, "When Did You Leave Heaven?" is a not-quite, a should-have-been. It's a rare case of Dylan recording a "standard," a song that could have been enjoyed by his parents before he was born. "Heaven" was written by Walter Bullock and Robert Whitney for a film called *Sing, Baby, Sing* and was a number one hit for Guy Lombardo in 1936. It's not difficult to imagine Bob Dylan singing this song and making us feel and identify with his infatuation with the angelic woman he's singing to, giving us chills with the strong message that romantic and sexual love are a link to another world, a doorway to a higher reality ("How's everything in Heaven? I'd like to know. Have they missed you? Can you get back in?"). But this performance, while pleasant (Dylan is accompanied by Madelyn Quebec on keyboards and harmony vocal, and session engineer Stephen Shelton on drums), falls short of the sort of spine-tingling presence Dylan is capable of on a good day, so the best we can say is we can feel the affection he has for the song, though in this case we can't feel the persona singing and the power of his affection for the addressee. The closing words of the song, "When did you leave Heaven, angel mine?" suggest that it could be a song about marriage, since "mine" is not an appropriate appellation in courtship. Certainly, it seems possible that Bob Dylan had occasion to sing this song privately to Sara Dylan ("sweet virgin angel, sweet love of my life") before 1977.

It's not easy to identify (or identify with) the sentiment of the third track of *Groove*, "Sally Sue Brown," because in this case the singer's lack of conviction (or his determination to give the uptempo tracks at these sessions a "loose," rock and roll feel) results in pivotal phrases of the song's lyrics being almost indecipherable. If you search the Internet in the year 2000, you'll find seven websites where Dylan fans in Denmark, France, California and all over the globe have posted the lyrics of almost any song Bob Dylan has ever sung. All of these sites (which probably tend to borrow from each other) display the following lyrics in their "Sally Sue Brown" transcriptions:

> "Don't you see by those big bright eyes
> Prefer to treat her nasty and low down lies"

and

> "I'm goin' south and doin' them things again
> Bake in a hot tub, down the line
> I'd rather see you ruin this a-heart of mine."

Whereas what Dylan is actually singing (and I had to listen *very* carefully to hear this, and I still would have been baffled were it not that Elvis Costello also sang this song – on an Arthur Alexander tribute album; "SSB" was Alexander's first single, in 1960 – and *his* fans also like to put lyrics on their websites for every song he's ever covered) is:

"Don't be deceived by those big bright eyes ["brown" in
   Alexander's original]
They're full of cheating, misery, low-down lying"

and

"I know Sal's been doin' them things again,
Breaking hearts up and down the line
Like she broke this heart of mine ..."

So it's a song about a tough-to-resist, sexy heartbreaker who
has the power (common to psychopathic personalities) to make past
victims beg for more punishment every time she crosses their paths,
in spite of their determination not to ever let this happen again.

The fourth track on *Down in the Groove*, "Death Is Not the End,"
is a challenge to my intent to discuss Dylan's art in chronological
sequence. The performance took place and was recorded in April
1983 (when Dylan also recorded a cover song very similar in theme
to "When Did You Leave Heaven?", Willie Nelson's "Angel Flying
Too Close to the Ground"). And the decision to include this particular previously unused track on the album, which we must assume
was Bob Dylan's decision, occurred in March or April 1988.

Promotional advance cassettes of *Down in the Groove* were sent to
music writers in January and February 1988, with slightly different
song selections and sequences. Apparently Dylan changed his mind
several times about which songs to put on the album. The first
advance cassette included "Got Love If You Want It" from the
4/87 sessions as the third song, "Ninety Miles an Hour (Down a
Dead End Street)" as #4, "Sally Sue Brown" as #5, and "The
Usual" from the *Hearts of Fire* soundtrack at #8. The second
advance cassette, a month later, was the same except that "The
Usual" was gone and "Important Words" from the 4/87 sessions
was in the #8 slot. Then in June the album itself was released, with
a different sequence and "Got Love" and "Important Words" and
"The Usual" all gone, and "Death Is Not the End" and "Had a
Dream About You, Baby" added. (By accident, the *Down in the
Groove* album officially released in Argentina was identical to the first
promotional cassette.)

So if we ask ourselves what message Bob Dylan had in mind
when he sang "Death Is Not the End," we're contemplating the
1983 Bob Dylan; and if we ask what he had in mind when he chose

this one (from amongst dozens of unreleased tracks available) and determined it should follow "Sally Sue Brown" and precede "Had a Dream About You, Baby," we're contemplating the spring 1988 Bob Dylan, who in turn was trying to be true to or anyway be finished with a concept and creative project that began as an expression of his spring 1987 self and intentions (what he had to say and the sound he was hearing in his head then).

I think the *sound* of "Death Is Not the End" works remarkably well on *Down in the Groove*. The melodic harmonica solo (playing a whole verse of the song's melody, accompanied by bass and drums and keyboard) that opens the track is startling and pretty and very gratifying in contrast to and in combination with everything else on the album. Indeed, whether the listener realizes this consciously or not, it is the centerpiece of an intriguing harmonica motif on this album, which opens with a powerful example of harmonica as a primary instrument in improvisatory rock and roll ensemble music-making, a theme and sound that is further explored on track six ("Ugliest Girl"). The album's penultimate track, "Shenandoah," like "Death Is Not the End," provides a surprising example of what different musical uses the harmonica can be put to while still serving as a living, vibrant extension of Bob Dylan's consciousness – where he is at spiritually, musically and romantically right now.

Going back to Dylan's insight that "whether you can identify with what the sentiment of the song is" is central to every listener's personal determination of whether or not a song is "good," it must be noted that "Death Is Not the End" is one of three songs on *Down in the Groove* whose sentiments are so discomforting to a plurality of Dylan's listeners that it seems unlikely that any of them could ever allow themselves to decide that maybe in some way this is a "good" album after all.

The other two are "Had a Dream About You, Baby" and "Ugliest Girl in the World." In the case of "Death Is Not the End," the problem is the title phrase. The song's chorus, "Just remember that death is not the end," in context is clearly meant to be reassuring, yet something about the song's structure and music (an almost confrontational extreme simplicity, similar to Dylan's 1981 song "Lenny Bruce" in its original recorded form) makes this listener and others feel they are being preached to, clumsily and inappropriately. Aversions are stirred up. This seems odd, since the title phrase is consistent with the teachings of most world religions (Islam,

Judaism and Buddhism as well as Christianity). But something about the performer's presentation in that title phrase moment makes the sentiment indigestible, in spite of the marvelous, very Bob-Dylanish harmonica passages that open and close the track, and in spite of at least one remarkable lyrical moment. Who else could have written and sung, "When the cities are on fire with the burning flesh of men/Just remember that death is not the end"? Unfortunately (and, arguably, hilariously) that daring image is immediately preceded by one of the most egregious examples of bad writing in Dylan's oeuvre, emphasized by an ascending chord sequence that suggests that the songwriter thinks this is a beautiful and noble turn of phrase: "Oh the tree of life is growing where the spirit never dies/And the bright light of salvation shines in dark and empty skies."

Track 5, "Had a Dream About You, Baby": The sound certainly fits the album. What is objectionable about the sentiment is the idea that we as listeners are expected to accept this song and performance as an expression of Bob Dylan the songwriter and Bob Dylan the lover. It doesn't work. And it makes us wonder about our sanity, and his. It might be okay or even enjoyable if there were some overt indication that it's a joke, a parody of the dumb hit rock and roll records Dylan and the rest of us have been subjected to by hundreds of "Billy Parker"'s over the years. It works in the movie when introduced by Bob Dylan saying, "I'm so sick of [this song], I could puke." On the album, since he doesn't make us feel we're laughing and grimacing along with him, it just makes us feel insulted. The only thing I like is the line "My mind's out sick and my body's breaking," which I hear him say but which isn't included in the "official" lyrics at bobdylan.com.

Track 6, "I'm in love with the ugliest girl in the world." What male or female is going to identify with *this* sentiment? Nah, the only thing to identify with is the idea that Dylan saw the lyric and decided it was a good turnaround, an opportunity to ask a question he'd always had about why is beauty such a sacred value in matters of the heart? Okay, Bob, we see where you're coming from, and it certainly makes an interesting pairing with "When Did You Leave Heaven?", which implies throughout (without ever saying so explicitly) that it's the beauty of the woman in front of you and the way that beauty makes you feel that convinces you you're looking at an angel who's hidden her halo and somehow lost her wings. But, just as you didn't quite sell us on your genuine sense of awe about the woman you're singing to in that track, on "Ugliest Girl in the World" you throw away the only chance the song had, by not making us believe you when you sing, "You know I love her, yeah I love her." You don't sound like you do. Of course you *could* be really crazy about a person who's "not much to look at," and that might be an effective subject for a performance. But this ain't it. Too bad, because you and the band do quite well with the music (much better than on "Sally Sue Brown"). But you know, even in the case of Woody Guthrie the sound wouldn't do anything for us if we didn't identify with the sentiment.

"Silvio," the seventh track on *Down in the Groove*, also appears on a 1994 album called *Bob Dylan's Greatest Hits, Volume 3*. Like many other tracks on that album, "Silvio" was never a "hit" in terms of record sales or radio airplay or fan appreciation. But perhaps partly to declare his independence from such considerations, Dylan the performer has treated it like a huge hit anyway. Christof Graf, in his book *Man on the Road*, reports "Silvio" as #4 on the list of most-played songs (572 performances) at Bob Dylan's concerts between June 1988 and July 1999, just ahead of "Maggie's Farm" (562) and "Like a Rolling Stone" (525). Dylan likes the song. He likes the response it often gets from his live audience (not because they're familiar with the song, but because the dynamics of the song's music and Dylan's enthusiasm for it as singer and bandleader tend to make it an exciting and satisfying musical experience even though it's not one of the Dylan songs the audience members were hoping to hear tonight).

Why does Dylan like it? Again, because it's fun to perform. And I think he feels liberated by the fact that it's a Dylan song without baggage; he and the band play it as though it were a big hit or a song that made him famous, and the audience can feel that and respond happily without knowing what song this is ... which allows the singer to lean into it in a way that's different from the other Dylan songs and covers he's playing. "Find out something only dead men know!" This is just the sort of lyric Dylan enjoys calling attention to (repeating it or slowing it down, doing tricks with it) during a performance – compare "No one sees my face and lives" from "I and I" or "Just like so many times before" from "Knockin' on Heaven's Door." It sounds like a Dylan line. But of course it isn't, it was written by Robert Hunter, coauthor and lyricist of most of the best-known Grateful Dead songs, including "Truckin'," "Uncle John's Band," "Dark Star," "Box of Rain," "Friend of the Devil," "Black Muddy River," "West L.A. Fadeaway" and "Alabama Getaway." The latter four are songs Dylan has covered in a number of concerts – indeed, it's possible Hunter is the lyricist other than Dylan himself whose words have been sung live by Dylan the most number of times.

What do the words mean? I don't know, but I have two unprovable theories. One is that Hunter wrote the words partly as a portrait of Bob Dylan (as Hunter intuited his friend and frequent collaborator Jerry Garcia saw him – perhaps Hunter thought this a subject Garcia might want to sing about) after seeing him on stage and hanging around backstage at the concerts Dylan and Tom Petty and the Dead performed together in summer 1986. If so, it seems Hunter didn't have a chance to mention this to Dylan before the latter chose the lyric (possibly with some prodding from Garcia) from Hunter's notebook in early '87 as one Dylan would try putting music to. The relevant lyrics to this theory are: "Stake my future on a hell of a past," and "Seen better times but who has not?" and "I'm an old boll weevil looking for a home" [*great* portrait of Billy Parker, and excellent reworking of a familiar line from American folk music, a technique Dylan would later make much use of in his 1997 song cycle *Time Out of Mind*], "If you don't like it you can leave me alone." The final verse – "Going down in the valley and sing my song, Gonna sing it loud and sing it strong, Let the echo decide if I was right or wrong" – seems deliberately reminiscent of the last verse of "A Hard Rain's A-Gonna Fall" ("I'll tell it and think it and speak it and breathe it, and reflect from the mountain so all souls can see it ... I'll know my song well before I start singin'").

But who is Silvio? Very possibly Dylan doesn't know how Hunter arrived at the word/name/title, and doesn't feel a need to know. Which would resonate with Hunter's comment on the significance of the phrase "black muddy river": "I hesitate to define it for you ... It's a deeply meaningful symbol to me, and I think just a little thought into, like, archetypal subconscious resonances gives you all you need to know about what we're talking about here. And past that you're setting it in concrete, and just as soon as that's done, that's not what it meant at all." Interestingly, the phrase "Silvio, silver and gold," was first tried out as a possible chorus in a draft of

"Black Muddy River," before becoming a song of its own. My own personal theory is that it derives from a character named Silvio Manuel in Carlos Castaneda's 1981 book *The Eagle's Gift*. "Looking at Silvio Manuel, I always experienced a deep unfamiliar feeling of fright. He seemed like a visitor from another time. He was friendly and warm during the daytime, but as soon as the twilight set in, he would become unfathomable." Silvio Manuel had crossed into another reality permanently and thereby attained a special knowledge and was a goad for Carlos to do the same, whereby he too could "find out something only dead men know" (the phrase isn't in the book but it's certainly true to what Silvio Manuel meant to Carlos and his cohorts).

Musically, "Silvio" on *Down in the Groove* is likable (with Jerry Garcia and two other members of the Grateful Dead providing "additional vocals") but a pale sketch of the powerful performance piece the song would become in concert by late '95. And what "sentiment" can we find to identify with in this song? I dunno. But the lyrics do contain an interesting counterpoint to "Let's Stick Together": "You know I love you and furthermore, when it's time to go you got an open door."

"Silvio" was the only single released from *Down in the Groove*. Perhaps one message its performer wanted to convey through it was: Bob Dylan doesn't always have to be the one who writes the words for Bob Dylan songs.

"Ninety Miles an Hour (Down a Dead End Street)," track 8 of *Down in the Groove*, written by Hal Blair and Don Robertson, was originally recorded in 1963 by country singer Hank Snow, whose 1950 hit "I'm Movin' On" had made a big impression on Bob Dylan when he was nine years old. "Ninety Miles an Hour" is about marriage in the sense that it's about infidelity ("You're not free to belong to me, and you know I could never be your own"). Presumably Dylan chose to record it at the sessions for this album because it's a striking statement about the (dangerous, even destructive) power of love and sexual attraction ("Your lips on mine are like sweet, sweet wine ... but we're heading for a wall of stone"). This fits with "Sally Sue Brown" ("See her in that very tight skirt, got what it takes just to make you hurt"), except that in this song the speaker is not victim but co-perpetrator.

What is most striking about "Ninety Miles an Hour," and perhaps another part of what the artist is saying by performing it and including it on this album, is the eccentricity of its sound (no band, again Quebec on synthesizer and harmony vocal, and soul singers Willie Green and Bobby King providing background vocals) and the grotesque quality of the verbal imagery and the weird creepiness of the way words and arrangement work together. The message of the performance is ambivalence about sex and romance and fascination with the weird spaces they can get you into. And maybe a challenge to any listener who thought they knew what to expect from a Bob Dylan record. Billy Parker refuses to wear his legend gracefully.

"Shenandoah," another change of pace, a river-bound sea shanty and familiar folk tune with an improbably rhythmic arrangement, is very pretty, and fits with the "expect the unexpected" theme that unites this album's sound. Another eccentric love song (is the object of love the Indian chief's daughter or the rollin' river?). Irreverently, I find myself wondering if it was selected partly because of the line "For seven long years I courted Sally." Dylan had indeed had an on-and-off romantic involvement with an actress named Sally for more than seven years when he recorded these songs. And playful, private messages are certainly among the many considerations that can influence songwriters and album-builders. Listeners aren't supposed to "know" this, but can be expected to incorporate private meanings and associations from their own lives into songs they like as they hear them. That's what Bob Dylan has done all his life, as a listener, and that's part of what he's telling us on this album (and why his first album of covers was titled *Self Portrait*).

Down in the Groove, like some other Dylan albums, ends with a grand statement, a summation, a reflection on where the singer has come to at this point in his life. "Rank Strangers to Me" is a country song ("bluegrass" and "gospel" would also be accurate labels) written by Albert E. Brumley and recorded by the Stanley Brothers. For me, the persona who speaks in this performance is recognizably or believably the same person who narrates "Restless Farewell" (1963) and who shows up as first-person narrator in the last verse of "Desolation Row" (1965). Unfortunately – and not inconsistent with what I'm characterizing as the "Billy Parker" interlude in Dylan's life and work – it's a particularly bleak statement ("'I ain't got no home in this world anymore' to the nth level," as I wrote in *The Telegraph* in 1988). The success of Dylan's performance here, indeed its claim to greatness, is the immediacy of the narrator's tale, the ease with which the listener finds himself experiencing and identifying with this brief visit to a hometown suddenly emptied of life, familiarity and human warmth. Hearing this track, one feels one has just awakened from a particularly vivid dream, a dark and disturbing one that is also somehow an affirmation of primary human values. The sparse instrumentation and Madelyn Quebec's subtle but evocative second vocal are a masterful setting for Dylan's *tour de force* lead vocal, as if this album of seemingly carefully planned chaos purposefully ends with a reminder of how sure-footed this musical artist can be when that's his intention.

Dante Alighieri (1265–1321) has been quoted as saying, "Who paints a figure, if he cannot be it, cannot draw it." Bob Dylan's ability to sing and play from inside of something or someone (as in this performance of "Rank Strangers") is so natural to him that this kind of projection into a fictional character who isn't and yet is himself even arises when he's trying to explain his feelings in conversation. We see this in the *Biograph* interview when he tells Crowe: "Sometimes you feel like a club fighter who gets off the bus in the middle of nowhere, punches his way through ten rounds, vomits up the pain in the back room ... Sometimes like a troubadour out of the dark ages, singing for your supper and rambling the land or singing to the girl in the window, you know, the one with the long flowing hair ..." Listen to how the man talks, the way he *becomes* these figures! No wonder he can draw them, or perform them, so convincingly sometimes.

"Got Love If You Want It," recorded April 1987 but not included on *Down in the Groove*, I find a very convincing portrait of a man (young or not so young) whose need to express himself as a sexual being (to and with "you," a particular love object) is simultaneously the source of his freedom and self-worth and the source of his confusion and self-doubt. In this case what pleases me, and the container of the "message," is almost entirely the sound, the musical performance and the mood created by the interaction between these musicians (the "groove"). It's a triumph of Dylan as bandleader rather than as vocalist, though paradoxically it is with his voice (as well as his rhythm guitar and his harmonica) that he inspires and leads the band, the ensemble of players. Something joyful happens. They all get into it. It's not just a matter of playing well. Everybody plays well on some other tracks from these sessions, but this one achieves a remarkable groove, simultaneously uplifting and harrowing. "Got love if you want it." "Quit teasin' me, baby." "If you let me love you, I wanna be your lovin' man." "Well I hear you been a-ballin' … it's all over town." In these simple statements, and by way of the presence of the singer and the players inside these statements, I hear a distillation of all of the sentiments expressed on the tracks that did make it onto *Down in the Groove*. It all seems to flow from the exquisite sound and timing of the opening guitar notes and the way they induce the other players and the singer to join in (just as the persona hopes to induce "you" to join in).

"Important Words," another unreleased outtake from these sessions, can be heard as a further inquiry into the relationship between romance and marriage, because the phrases referred to in the title are both "I love you" and "I do." Background vocals are significant in the arrangement (as is true of many of these 4/87 recordings), but ultimately neither sound nor lyrics offer this listener much to identify with.

"Pretty Boy Floyd" is the only solo acoustic recording from these sessions, and a very impressive performance. A *great* perform-ance, in fact, but not because of the singer-and-player's presence inside the title character. That's not his job in this case, because Pretty Boy isn't the song's narrator. The narrator, who only shows up in the first and next-to-last verses, is a rambling troubadour who's telling this story. And yes, Bob Dylan truly does get inside *that* character. He becomes both Woody Guthrie and himself, the self he was when he had the honor at age nineteen of being Woody Guthrie's personal jukebox, and the self he was for the next twelve months of his artistic career, when his keen intent was to express himself (and show off, excel) as a folksinger and -player.

("I went there to sing him his songs," Dylan says in the liner notes to the album this performance appears on, *A Vision Shared*. "That's all I went to do, and that's all I did [when he visited an ailing Guthrie in early 1961]. He always liked the songs, and he would ask for certain ones. I knew them all! I was like a Woody Guthrie jukebox.")

It seems unlikely that Woody got to hear Bob Dylan play guitar and harmonica as beautifully as he does in this spring 1987 perfor-mance. Maturity as an artist, and as a singer and player, does count for something.

My friend Carl Edwards, a singer and guitar player and music scholar who once recorded an album of Woody Guthrie songs, speaks enthusiastically and helpfully of this performance:

> As to Dylan's "Pretty Boy," he really claimed it as his own on that *Vision Shared* recording. The thing that struck me about his version is that he rearranged it slightly to include a quick turnaround on the D and it gave the song great momentum. Woody's version was very deliberate and, typical of Woody, uses the minimum chords and harmonic movement. Dylan plays it almost like bluegrass changes, with a nifty little ornamental riff that lays right there under the fingers for the G major chord. You could almost say it's the Lester Flatt guitar style! Simple but very effective. I liked his version so much that I learned it and used it as the basis for my own version when I was doing coffeehouses as a solo performer. Bob's recording is, for me, the definitive reading of Woody's tune. For contrast, listen to Jack Elliott's versions. Hugely different. The other thing worth noting about Dylan's performance is the clarity he brings to it, from an instrumental standpoint. The chord changes are very sharp and precise, which further adds to the sense of purpose and conviction, I think.

Thank you, Carl. The clarity of Dylan's vocal performance also adds to this recording's magic. No problem hearing these lyrics! And Dylan is very present in his phrasing, for example stretching the vowel on the fifth syllable of each of the first three verses so that a delightful and seemingly very meaningful emphasis is placed on the words "round" and "town" in the lines "If you'll gather 'round me, people ..." and "It was in the town of Shawnee ..." This also calls attention to the internal rhyme, here spanning two verses. And it is one of many subtle things the performer does with his voice and guitar to give the story a cadence, a sense of movement. The fifth syllable of the third verse is "sher" in "There a deputy sheriff approached him"; it doesn't rhyme with the other two, but when Dylan stretches it it echoes them in a way that pleases every listener and gives flavor, personality, to the narrative. This long-vowel effect is used elsewhere, notably in the word "outlaw" in the last verse and "napkin" in the seventh verse, but most wonderfully when he holds the second o in "Oklahoma" in the phrase "It was in Oklahoma City" in the eighth verse for three long seconds, as though he were yodeling.

The three harmonica solos, including a 40-second one that

ends the performance, are also delightful and memorable. And it's interesting to look at the words of Guthrie's two recorded versions of this song and see how Dylan has combined them and in some cases seems to have given much thought to small but significant matters. In the first line he asks "people" to gather 'round me instead of "children." The first time the phrase "he took to the trees and timber" occurs, he sings "hills and timber."

Lots of love and care went into this performance. Although it's from the same month of Bob Dylan's life, it would have seemed out of place amidst the deliberate disarray of *Down in the Groove*.

On April 20, 1987, Bob Dylan made a brief guest appearance at a Los Angeles concert by the then-very-popular Irish rock group U2. During the band's encore he joined lead singer Bono on "I Shall Be Released" and "Knockin' on Heaven's Door," trading verses and singing the choruses together. During "Knockin'," after singing a line addressed to Ronald Reagan, Bono said, "You know, I usually make up my own words to Bob Dylan songs. He says he doesn't mind." Dylan responded, "I do it too!"

Around this time, Bono and Dylan wrote a song together ("Words: Bono and Bob Dylan, Music: U2") called "Love Rescue Me." The words sound more like Bono than Dylan, though we can imagine the guy Springsteen saw on TV "bitching about his fans" saying, "Many strangers have I met, on the road to my regret, many lost who seek to find themselves in me. They ask me to reveal the very thoughts they would conceal. Love rescue me." The fans still waiting for Dylan to renounce his 1979 public embrace of Jesus must have been pleased if they thought (I don't) he wrote these lines from the same song: "I have cursed Thy rod and staff, they no longer comfort me."

In a newspaper interview later in the year, Bono recalled: "We were trading lines and verses off the top of our heads and Dylan comes out with this absolute classic: 'I was listening to the Neville Brothers, it was a quarter of eight. I had an appointment with destiny, but I knew she'd come late. She tricked me, she addicted me, she turned me on the head. Now I can't sleep with these secrets that leave me cold and alone in my bed.' Then he goes, 'Nah, cancel that.' Can you believe it? He thought it was too close to what people expect of Bob Dylan."

In May 1987, Dylan sang backup vocals for U2's recording of "Love Rescue Me" at Sun Studios in Memphis, where Elvis Presley first recorded. At that time, or in mid-April (when he was also in Memphis, to play harmonica on a song Ringo Starr was recording), Dylan visited Elvis's mansion, Graceland. Within the next few months he told *Us* magazine, on the occasion of the tenth anniversary of Elvis's death: "When I first heard Elvis's voice I just knew that I wasn't going to work for anybody; and nobody was going to be my boss. He is the deity supreme of rock and roll religion as it exists in today's form. Hearing him for the first time was like busting out of jail. I think for a long time that freedom to me was Elvis singing 'Blue Moon of Kentucky.' I thank God for Elvis."

II. "I'm Determined to Stand!"

May 1987 – October 1987

3.

Journalist (at a 1997 press conference in London): "Did your collaboration with the Grateful Dead change your approach to your career as a performer?"
Bob Dylan: "Absolutely. That was a turning point for me, playing with the Dead."

In the summer of 1986, Bob Dylan co-headlined five concerts with San Francisco rock band the Grateful Dead, then the most popular live music attraction in America. In the summer of 1987, Dylan and the Dead co-headlined six more concerts, again drawing very large crowds. At the 1986 shows, Dylan had been backed by Tom Petty & the Heartbreakers, his touring band that year. But at the 1987 shows, Dylan was backed by the Grateful Dead themselves – Jerry Garcia, guitar and pedal steel guitar; Bob Weir, rhythm guitar; Phil Lesh, bass; Brent Mydland, keyboards; Bill Kreutzmann, drums; Mickey Hart, drums and percussion.

It was a very short tour for Bob Dylan. In 1981 he and his band were on the road for a total of twelve weeks, and played 54 concerts in ten countries. In 1982, 1983 and 1985 he didn't tour at all. In 1984 he and his band for that year were on the road for six weeks, and played 27 concerts in twelve countries. In 1986, he and the Tom Petty band were on the road for a total of eight weeks, and they played 61 concerts in five countries. But in the summer of 1987, Dylan and the Dead played only six concerts, in the three weeks between July 4 and July 26. The first three shows were in the northeastern U.S., in the Boston, Philadelphia, and New York City areas. The other shows were on the West Coast, in Oregon, Northern California and Southern California.

There are various theories as to why the Bob Dylan segments of these concerts (he sang 13 or 14 songs at each show, backed by the Grateful Dead, who also performed a set or two of their own before he came on) are so unrewarding. Bob Dylan fans tend to blame the Dead. Grateful Dead fans tend to blame Dylan. I've tended to regard the whole project as a bold and worthy experiment that failed, maybe partly because it sometimes (1978, for example) takes Dylan more than six shows to find his voice, and his confidence as an artist and bandleader, with a new band, or at the start of a new tour.

Bob Weir has said of this pairing: "He was difficult to work with inasmuch as he wouldn't want to rehearse a song more than two times, three at the most. And so we rehearsed maybe a hundred songs two or three times ..." Mickey Hart adds: "We were trying to back up a singer on songs that no one knew. It was not our finest hour, nor his. I don't know why it was even made into a record."

Listening closely now to that album (*Dylan & the Dead*, released February 1989) and to the recordings of these July 1987 shows and the hours of recordings that have surfaced from the May '87 rehearsals, I'm inclined to believe that the most helpful (though unsettling) explanation is the one offered by Dylan himself in several interviews ten years later. "At the time of that tour I couldn't even sing [my own songs]," he said at the London press conference quoted above. "There were so many layers and so much water had gone round, that I had a hard time grasping the meaning of the songs." He told *Newsweek* that he couldn't remember [in summer 1987, on stage and in the rehearsals] what his old songs meant, as if they were nonsense or in some alien language. "I'd kind of reached the end of the line. I was going to pack it in."

That's what these recordings sound like, in sharp contrast to the Bob Dylan who over the years has had such a gift for being present with all the possible meanings and sentiments of his songs as he performs them. They (rehearsal and stage versions alike) sound like tales told by an idiot who has no idea what the words "I want you" or "there must be some way out of here" or "you're gonna serve somebody" might refer to. The examples just given are from the official *Dylan & the Dead* album, where you can also hear Dylan sing (in "Queen Jane Approximately"): "and you wish your situation be more drastic ..." Clearly, the singer's mind can remember some of the words that belong in the songs, but can't always arrange them into meaningful sentences.

Road hazard. "I'd reached the end of the line." But fortunately it turned out to be a turning point, the beginning of something (something Dylan would later call "the Never Ending Tour"). And one person was responsible for this turnaround (though in that press conference Dylan spoke as if the Dead as a whole were responsible). At Jerry Garcia's funeral in 1995, Dylan told Garcia's widow, with tears in his eyes, "He was there for me when nobody was."

> "To me he wasn't only a musician and a friend, he was more like a big brother who taught and showed me more than he'll ever know."
>
> – Bob Dylan, in a statement released through his publicist the day after Jerry Garcia died.

What did Jerry teach Bob? The 1997 *Newsweek* interview suggests he showed him a way to get back to a place of connection with his own songs. In the London press conference (also 1997) Dylan said, "Playing with the Dead taught me to look inside these songs I was singing ... I had a hard time grasping the meaning of them, although the Dead didn't. They found great meaning in them and this really made me extremely curious as to why they could and I couldn't."

"How could you not understand your own songs?" a journalist asked. "Well," Dylan replied, "on a level of musicianship and a level of concentration, a level of not so much verbally understanding literally what they're about but understanding the spirit of them. The spirit of the songs had been getting further and further away from me. Probably because I had been playing these songs with a lot of different bands, and they might not have understood them so well, you know what I mean? And it influences you. I know it influenced me until I started playing with the Dead and I realized that they understood these songs better than I did at the time."

Okay, dear reader, I have to say I doubt that anyone could listen to the Dylan/Dead rehearsals and concerts and conclude, based on what they're hearing, that this band *understands* these songs and is in touch with their meanings. (And after all, drummer Mickey Hart said, "We were trying to back up a singer on songs that no one knew.") Nor do I buy Dylan's contention that playing with bands who didn't "get" the songs was the cause of his amnesia. One has only to listen to recordings of his 1986 shows backed by Petty & the Heartbreakers (the only band he'd played with in the three years leading up to the summer '87 tour) to realize his scapegoating is unjustified. And so I conclude that the word "they" in "They found great meaning in them" and "they understood these songs better than I did at the time" refers to Dylan's experience of talking to the band's spokesperson, their articulate (and charming) mouthpiece, the venerable "Captain Trips," Jerry Garcia. The guy Dylan remembers keenly as having been there for him when nobody was, when everybody he met seemed to be a rank stranger ...

What did Jerry teach Bob? I believe (and thirteen years of evidence supports me forcefully on this) that being with Garcia and watching him and his band play their own sets for their unique and colorful followers in summer 1986 and summer 1987 taught Dylan how to reconnect with and find his way back to not only his songs but his life's work as a performer, his deep sense of the power of music and of songs and his sense of joy and purpose in singing and playing in front of, and in a kind of collaboration with, a live audience. Jerry and the Dead showed him, revealed to him as in a vision, how to get back to being a musician and a bandleader and a singer of Bob Dylan songs, a preacher deeply inside of and keen to share the meaning to him of each of these songs at the moment that he's performing it. Garcia and the Dead unlocked the door and let the light in, and Dylan ran through that door eagerly and happily, not in July 1987 but the very first chance he got to play with a band after he completed Jerry and the boys' little rehab course.

The evidence of this reawakening is not in the recordings of the July 1987 performances, but in recordings of the thirteen years of Dylan performances (as I write this) since then.

It all started, according to Garcia biographer Blair Jackson, when "Garcia attended a Dylan-Petty show at the Greek Theater [in Berkeley in early June 1986] and spent considerable time chatting with Dylan backstage. Though Garcia had played with Dylan at the Warfield Theater in 1980, it was this night at the Greek and [similar moments] on the following summer tour that cemented their close personal relationship. They were mutual admirers who shared similar roots in American folk and blues. And they had attracted more than their share of fanatics and devoted followers who placed them on uncomfortable pedestals. Garcia had more Dylan tunes in his repertoire than did any other major American singer ..." Jackson goes on to list eight Dylan songs Garcia had sung for years with the Dead and in his side project the Jerry Garcia Band.

So Garcia was an earnest Bob Dylan fan who could communicate to him his deep appreciation for the essence of Dylan's songs without scaring him away. (Garcia was almost irresistible when sharing one-on-one his sincere enthusiasms and passions and his sense of the *zeitgeist*, the spirit of our collective moment.) Dylan's appreciation of Garcia as an artist is well expressed in these words from his statement after Jerry's death: "There's a lot of spaces and advances between the Carter Family and, say, Ornette Coleman, a lot of universes, but he filled them all without being a member of any school. His playing was moody, awesome, sophisticated, hypnotic and subtle. He was much more than a superb musician with an uncanny ear and dexterity. He is the very spirit personified of whatever is Muddy River country at its core and screams up into the spheres. He really had no equal."

Dylan loves music. And he was surprised and thrilled to see and hear, in '86 and '87, that what the Grateful Dead were doing on stage and what their large and ever-growing audience was responding to was exactly the kind of music that he had been reaching for on stage for most of his life and that he had felt himself making during his favorite tours and happiest on-stage eras, 1966, 1975–76, 1981 and 1986.

He saw that they were making music in which they spoke to their audience and to each other in a spontaneous language arising out of and making reference to all the music they'd ever heard, and what they'd felt and experienced as they'd heard it and played it and lived with it and within it. Phrasing – vocal and instrumental – mattered, and shaped what each player (including the vocalist) did next, and the music built on itself in that way, as in the best jazz bands. This happened from moment to moment and from song to song, so that the transitions between songs (as in the case of "I Believe in You" and "Like a Rolling Stone" in 1980) were part of the unique communication taking place between the performers and the audience. As he saw this, Dylan knew that this was what he'd always wanted – to feel, and to feel confident that he could lean on, an interaction between himself (as singer/bandleader) and his audience that could be as alive and intelligent and subtle and rich in meaning as the interaction between him and the other musicians on stage as they played together. He wanted – and it had sometimes happened, and that was what drew him to the road, to a life of performing – to find himself in a space where the thrill of creating something meaningful, and seeing, hearing, feeling it being created all around you, could take place.

He told *Newsweek* in 1997: "Here's the thing with me and the religious thing. This is the flat-out truth: I find the religiosity and philosophy in the music. I don't find it anywhere else. Songs like 'Let Me Rest on a Peaceful Mountain' or 'I Saw the Light' – that's my religion. I don't adhere to rabbis, preachers, evangelists, all of that. I've learned more from the songs than I've learned from any of this kind of entity. The songs are my lexicon. I believe the songs." This gives us some sense of what music and songs are for Bob Dylan, as a listener as well as a writer and performer. So of course the great moments in his life have been when he could listen and create and perform all at once within this milieu, inside the lexicon. And Jerry Garcia and the Grateful Dead reminded him that it was possible to get there and helped him, in his time of great need, to find his way back. The Dead and their audience did it by example. Jerry did it by offering understanding and friendship and love, at the right moment. Many thousands of people have tried to tell Bob Dylan what his songs have meant to them, and Bob Dylan has gritted his teeth and looked around for an escape hatch, every time. But circumstances conspired to make this case different. For one thing, Dylan had actually asked this fan to tell him, if he could, what the songs mean or have meant to him. And the fan was Jerry Garcia, a man known for his ability to take you on a (psychedelic) trip upon his magic swirling ship just by talking quietly to you about the way it is, for him, and, he's sure, for you too. So he showed Bob, by singing and playing, and talking a little, what the songs mean, and Bob saw it (like a revelation) and became a Bob Dylan fan again himself.

After that, if Dylan had trouble concentrating during his performances with the Dead (and he did; the tapes make that clear), it wasn't just because the Billy Parker in him was folding his arms and growling, "I want to go back to my chicken farm!" It was also because his mind was racing, thinking about what he'd learned, and the ideas he got, watching the Dead's sets earlier that afternoon.

The first dramatic indication that Bob Dylan the performer was a changed man because of what he learned from the Dead came in the form of the set list for the second show of his autumn 1987 tour with Tom Petty & the Heartbreakers. At the first show, Tel Aviv, September 5, he sang 17 songs. At the second show, Jerusalem, Sept. 7, he sang 13 songs, *none* of which he'd performed at the previous show. This was unprecedented; in 1986, and all years before that, his set lists seldom varied by more than three songs from one night to the next. Clearly, the singer/bandleader was sending himself a message: "Behold, I make all things new!" And I'm certain he was aware, either from talking with Jerry or by wandering through the crowd with his hood up and listening to the Deadheads talking, that Grateful Dead fans are keenly aware of how long it's been since a particular song was played, and talk excitedly to each other about variations not only in the choice of songs but in the sequence in which songs are performed.

Another indication that Bob Dylan, who had once dreamed (as quoted in his high school yearbook) of "joining Little Richard," now fantasized about somehow becoming the Grateful Dead was a message in small print on the sleeve of 1988's *Down in the Groove* album: "If you are interested in receiving information about Bob Dylan concert dates, artwork, album releases, preferential seating at concerts, home videos, etc., please write to ..." Nothing came of this at the time, but it was directly modeled on the Grateful Dead's business practices which had helped them build and maintain such a dedicated fan base for their concerts.

"Okay, I think I got a line on you now," Bob Dylan said, quietly and with a little laugh, just after singing and playing "When the Night Comes Falling from the Sky" at the Rubber Bowl in Akron, Ohio on July 2, 1986. It was his second concert coheadlining with the Dead and therefore playing to huge crowds of Deadheads wearing tie-dyed T-shirts and otherwise clearly not the "regular" Bob Dylan concert audience he was used to. I was in the crowd, and I understood that the "you" he was addressing was the unfamiliar audience, and that "got a line" referred to getting a sense of who they are and how to please them and get their attention and response, as a performer. I also understood that the comment was not intended to be heard but rather was a kind of thinking aloud to himself, an indication of his presence within the creative process, his relationship with his (real or imagined) audience, like his little laughs or awkward grins when he's just sung the wrong words or misplayed a note.

I was also in the crowd (of 40,000 or more) at Autzen Stadium in Eugene, Oregon on July 19, 1987, and I don't think Dylan grinned self-consciously when he accidentally started lines with the wrong words and therefore had to improvise lyrics during "Queen Jane Approximately" and many other songs. As I believe is evident on the tapes and on the *Dylan & the Dead* album, he wasn't in that state of mind where you can feel the person you're talking to and therefore you notice when you've misspoken or when you've "gotten a line on them" (made contact, been felt and understood). The fact that Dylan ordinarily is so present with a tangible, felt audience as he sings and plays on stage or in a recording studio is what sets him apart from the majority of performers, rock and roll or "folk" or otherwise. And the fact that this experience of losing his sense of connection was so painful and memorable that he would describe it ten years later as a crisis in his life and career ("I – I can't remember what it means, does it mean – is it just a bunch of *words*?") is an indication of how much he values this gift that he has and how crushing it is for him when the mysterious cycles of the creative life confront him with the loss of it and the possibility that he won't be able to get it back. This happened to him in 1965, as I have described in chapter 13 of *Performing Artist, Volume I*: "Last spring I was going to quit singing. I was very drained. I was singing words I didn't really want to sing." In that case, the breakdown led directly to the writing of "Like a Rolling Stone" and a major new era in the life and work of Bob Dylan. In this case, the breakdown led directly to the Never Ending Tour.

During his six concerts with the Grateful Dead in summer 1987, Bob Dylan sang four songs he had never before performed live: "Queen Jane Approximately" (1965), "The Ballad of Frankie Lee and Judas Priest" (1967), "The Wicked Messenger" (1967) and

"Joey" (1975). He also surprised and pleased his fans by singing "Chimes of Freedom" (1964) in concert for the first time in 23 years and "Stuck Inside of Mobile with the Memphis Blues Again" (1966) for the first time in 11 years and "Tomorrow Is a Long Time" (1962) for the first time in nine years. "John Brown" (1962), an antiwar song that had not yet appeared on an official Bob Dylan album, was performed for the first time in 24 years.

The tapes from the rehearsals also offer "Walkin' Down the Line" (1962) and "Pledging My Time" (1966), neither of which Dylan had ever performed live, plus a variety of covers: "Stealin'" (Memphis Jug Band), "The French Girl" (Ian & Sylvia), "Don't Keep Me Waiting Too Long" (source unknown, probably a rockabilly album), "John Hardy" (the Carter Family), "Roll in My Sweet Baby's Arms" (traditional) and "The Ballad of Ira Hayes" by Peter LaFarge. (In the *Biograph* interview, Dylan said: "The guy who was best at protest-song writing was Peter LaFarge. We were pretty tight for a while. We had the same girlfriend. Actually, Peter is one of the great unsung heroes of the day. His style was just a little bit too erratic. But it wasn't his fault, he was always hurting [from rodeo and boxing and war injuries] and having to overcome it.") The inclusion of seldom-performed Dylan songs seems to have been at the band's suggestion. Garcia reported: "He said, 'What do you want me to do?' And we said, 'Well, we have a *small* list here of our favorite Dylan tunes.' And he said yes to just about all of them, so we just started working on them one by one."

Unfortunately, Dylan's uncharacteristic lack of confidence as a singer and bandleader at this moment (and his mysterious distance from the "spirit" of his own songs) makes what should have been a fascinating set of performances a disappointing and sometimes painful listening experience.

By way of example, "Tomorrow Is a Long Time" on the rehearsal tapes is so dreadful it's difficult to imagine how it could have turned out this badly, even at a rehearsal. Drugs and alcohol? Maybe, but the singer doesn't sound drunk or drugged. He just sounds like a student forced to recite in front of the class who desperately wants not to be standing here now. The words to this song are not difficult to remember, but he mumbles them and drops them and makes a consistent mess of them anyway. Sometimes he seems to improvise new lines ("I can't read the sounds that show no fear/I can't write a letter on my bed"). Nor is there ever any feeling in his singing, as there would have to be if you were teaching an unfamiliar song to a new set of musicians, so that they could get a sense of it. His guitar playing is even more listless than his singing, so that there is no possibility of the musicians getting any sense of the rhythm and form of the song, or any other aspect of its intended musical "feel."

In 1993, Bill Flanagan asked Dylan what drew him to U2 that he did not hear in other young bands. He replied: "Just more of a thread back to the music that got me inspired and into it. Something which still exists, which a group like U2 holds onto. They are actually rooted someplace and they respect that tradition. They work within a certain boundary which has a history to it, and then they can do their own thing on top of that. Unless you start someplace you're just kind of inventing something which maybe need not be invented. That's what would draw me to U2. You can tell what groups are seriously connected and [laughs] seriously disconnected. There is a tradition to the whole thing. You're either part of that or not. I don't know how anybody can do anything and not be connected someplace back there. You do have to have a commitment. Not just anybody can get up and do it. It takes a lot of time and work and belief." This is a good expression of Dylan's aesthetic. Certainly much of what made the Grateful Dead's music attractive to Dylan was its strong threads, primarily through Garcia, back to the music that first inspired him. But I bring it up now because the May 1987 rehearsal tapes (and the Dylan/Dead concerts that followed) reveal a seriously disconnected Dylan shockingly lacking in commitment. The botched lyrics on almost every song make it almost certain that he was not using his book *Lyrics* as a reference at these rehearsals, even though in the BBC documentary we saw that he carries it with him even when he's just acting in a movie.

The only live Dylan/Dead performance of "Tomorrow Is a Long Time," at the third show of the tour (Giants Stadium, East Rutherford, N.J.), is as bad as the performance on the rehearsal tape. The vocal is again listless (it starts, "If [mumble] not a crooked highway/If tonight was not a crooked trail ...") and the music shapeless, structureless, clumsy and plodding. Presumably this is what happens when singer and band are both intimidated by the other, and neither is able to provide any kind of leadership, either at rehearsals or on stage.

The rehearsal tape version of "Slow Train" is more listenable.

Apparently the band have had a chance to hear the album track before playing the song, and they do a credible job. Dylan's vocal is full of slurred and incorrect lyrics; and in any case is quite lacking in conviction, even on lines like "sometimes I feel so low-down and disgusted." Now and then he gets some bite into a word or two, but never in a way that suggests he's present with, or connected to, what he's saying.

The live version of "Slow Train" that leads off the *Dylan & the Dead* album (from the first show of the tour, Foxboro, Mass.) is a step down in terms of band performance, maybe because now it's been a month and a half since they heard the original album track. They're clearly faking it, and what they settle on is safe and uninteresting. The vocals on this track are a good example of Dylan's spaciness as a singer throughout the rehearsals and at most of the July shows. He seldom sounds like he knows, or cares about, what he's saying. He remembers the words okay for the first three verses he sings, except he drops the phrase "they don't apply no more" from the first line of the "Man's ego's inflated" verse. He compensates by adding it to the next verse he sings, which is a classic example of the word salad Dylan's mind turned his songs into in May and July '87 (amazing that he himself selected this version to be on the officially released album; in this case we know he did because the Dead have talked about how he rejected the album they first put together from the tour, and substituted his own selections from the show tapes). Here is what Dylan seems to sing as the fourth verse of "Slow Train" on this album track:

> All that foreign soil, American soil
> That don't apply no more, all from parts of Paris
> Rum-tum in the grave, in American future
> Oh God, 'cause when Amsterdam and Paris
> But there's a slow, yeah there's a slow, there's a slow train
> coming …

He sings one more verse, loosely based on the sixth and seventh verses of the original song folded together. Then the band drags out the non-drama by repeating the last words of the chorus over and over for more than a minute and a half.

There is exactly one enjoyable track on the album, and it's "Queen Jane Approximately" from Eugene, the fourth show of the tour. What makes it enjoyable is the remarkable beauty of the music the Grateful Dead are making ... and Dylan's response to their performance. It's a rare moment on this tour when he does connect, and really sings from the heart. If you can get past the liberties the singer takes (intentionally or not) with the lyrics the song had when he wrote it (and we heard it) 22 years back, you might find, as I have, that it's a startling return to form. Bob Dylan has suddenly awakened (compared to his singing of the same song at the previous show on this tour, and compared to all his other vocals on the *Dylan & the Dead* album) and is once again telling us the story of his life at this moment. His love for the song, and for the band's transcendent rendering of its melody and dynamics and subtle colors, is evident even as he invents new lyrics on the spot to compensate for his errors (i.e. in the "clowns" verse he sings "And you're tired" instead of "And you're sick" and quickly covers it by singing, "tired – trying to get out of situations") ... and to let his unconscious mind express its thought-dreams, as if he were dreaming out loud.

Some of the new phrases his unconscious delivers: "When all of the bandits you have commissioned, have beat out your destruction or your pain, and you want someone to put out your ambition ..." "Well when all your, all the bandits that you turn your other cheek to, try to steal back all your numbness, all your pain ..."

There is also an example of the sort of spontaneous rearranging, restructuring of verse dynamics, that Dylan often comes up with during inspired performances. After "clowns that you have commissioned" in the second verse he sings "have died, have died in battle" with expressive emphasis on the words he repeats. This happens again in the next verse, "When ... heave their plastic at your feet, *at your feet!* to convince you of your pain." The expressive Bob Dylan is back with a vengeance (these repeating phrases are new since the previous performance of the song, two days earlier).

And so I find myself wondering if this is an example of Bob Dylan 1987 singing a song after a consultation with Captain Trips. ("He'd say, 'Come on man, you know, this is the way it goes, let's play it, it goes like this.' And I'd say, 'Man, he's right, you know? How's he getting there and I can't get there?' I had to go through a lot of red tape in my mind to get back there.") I can imagine Garcia telling Dylan how "Queen Jane" always made him as listener identify with the speaker and hear the song as being about himself and his relationship with a particular woman, or maybe two particular women, one in his past and one in his life now as he's listening ...

And I imagine Dylan at that moment hearing with his friend's ears and heart, and reconnecting with a sense of who "all the clowns you have commissioned" could possibly be. Epiphany.

An epiphany rekindled the next day on stage in Eugene as he hears the ethereal music his band-for-the-day is playing. It really is beautiful, like a full-length concerto expanding on the lovely eight-second piano intro to the 1965 recording (first notes of side two of *Highway 61 Revisited*). And as he watches those tens of thousands of attractive strangers (mostly young people) standing before him in the sunshine and swaying to the music. So we get this excellent Freudian slip: "When your *audience* of advisers heave their plastic/At your feet to convince you of your pain ..." He's singing to himself, or to Billy Parker, and just maybe at this very moment he's wishing his situation would be more drastic, and that's why he finds himself singing that. Anyway, that improvised verse is followed by an outstanding Garcia guitar solo. So we're given the chance to eavesdrop on a heart-to-heart dialogue between these two men. All surrounded by the sort of sublime instrumental music we might have expected but never really heard earlier in the tour.

Bob Weir, of course, would point out, correctly, that by Eugene they'd already played this song three times in the past two weeks (at the first three shows) and thus were beginning to get a handle on it and could play like the tight improvisational unit they are and can be, once they've rehearsed a song enough.

Indeed, the one concert among these six that's a real pleasure to listen to from start to finish – the one I recommend if you want some kind of audio representation of the summer 1987 tour at its best or most tolerable – is Eugene. "Queen Jane" is the high point, but the band sounds good throughout the set, and the vocalist, while still iffy, is more at home with the songs and the band than at the other shows. "The Ballad of Frankie Lee and Judas Priest," "Simple Twist of Fate," and "Memphis Blues Again" are other particularly pleasing performances, though of course one wishes Dylan as vocalist and storyteller could have been even half as present on "Frankie Lee" as he was on the original 1968 recording or in his 4/87 performance of "Pretty Boy Floyd" (another outlaw story, like "Joey" – which Dylan narrates unconvincingly on the *Dylan & the Dead* album, to music that falls flat, probably for want of an inspired conductor to guide and enliven the band).

Of course, there are occasional moments of good art hidden

amidst all the bad art and failed performances of the other five Dylan/Dead concerts. For instance, "It's All Over Now, Baby Blue" from East Rutherford, N.J., offers a surprisingly fierce and focused vocal. On the other hand, stuff you'd expect to be of interest, like a rare instance of Bob Dylan singing Ian & Sylvia's "The French Girl" (on the rehearsal tapes) can turn out to be disappointments, in this case again because the singer's not present in the song and so there's no one to identify with, no story to put with the pretty music.

Another clue as to what Jerry could have taught Bob, particularly in relation to reconnecting with the meanings of one's own songs, is this quote from a Dylan interview conducted by Robert Hilburn of the *Los Angeles Times* in 1980: "It's a very fine line you have to walk to stay in touch with something once you've created it. A lot of artists say, 'I can't sing those old songs any more,' and I can understand it because you're no longer the same person who wrote those songs. However, you really are still that person someplace deep down. You don't really get that out of your system. So you can still sing them if you can get in touch with the person you were when you wrote the songs. I don't think I could sit down now and write 'It's Alright, Ma' again. I wouldn't even know where to begin, but I can still sing it, and I'm glad I've written it."

Intriguingly, in the same interview Hilburn asked, "Any of your songs that you couldn't sing today? Any song that you couldn't relate to?" And Dylan replied, "I don't think so. I could probably sing them all, even 'Queen Jane Approximately.'"

And finally, another Dylan/Hilburn conversation, in 1991, offers some further insight into what Dylan learned from the Dead and why I say the Never Ending Tour seems to have had its conception in summer 1987. On his touring bus in 1991, on the way to a show in Indiana, Dylan told Hilburn:

> "You hear sometimes about the glamor of the road ... but you get over that real fast. There are a lot of times that it's no different from going to work in the morning. Still, you're either a player or you're not a player. It didn't really occur to me until we did those shows with the Grateful Dead [in 1987]. If you just go out every three years or so, like I was doing for a while, that's when you lose touch. If you are going to be a performer, you've got to give it your all."

4.

"Obviously, you can't find in jazz the perfection of craft that is possible in contemplative music. Yet, oddly enough, this very lack of perfection can result in good jazz. For example, in classical music, a mistake is a mistake. But in jazz, a mistake can be – in fact, must be – justified by what follows it. If you were improvising a speech and started a sentence in a way you hadn't intended, you would have to carry it out so that it would make sense. It is the same in spontaneous music."

– Bill Evans (great jazz pianist, known partly for his work on Miles Davis's *Kind of Blue* album)

"He's been great to play with. Great fun as well, mostly because you can never let your mind drift. He'll give the most familiar song an odd twist – a change of rhythm or a peculiar delivery. Playing with Bob Dylan certainly gives you a good kick up the ass. One night he'll do something like he'll say – onstage – 'Right, we'll begin with "Forever Young",' and the Heartbreakers have maybe played the song once before. Then he'll say. 'And Benmont, you start it off.'"

– Benmont Tench

"Bob said to me once, 'This band is kinda like talking to one guy.' We can communicate very quickly – pick up the signals real fast. I don't think the band has ever sounded as good as it is now, which is the exciting thing. It's an interesting thing to be playing and not know who's going to take a solo. Someone'll start, and you just look for your hole. If Bob or I are starting to disintegrate, Mike'll jump in. Sometimes we all play a solo at once, which sounds really interesting!"

– Tom Petty

"Dylan knows a million songs, old delta blues songs and stuff like that. One night when we did "Clean-Cut Kid," it sounded just like Muddy Waters. He knows more chords than anyone I know."

– Benmont Tench

"Musically, Bob's certainly thrown everything at us he can, which is very good for us, because there's so few people you can really learn anything from. Maybe he'll throw out something from the Gershwins, or something with a lot of chords that rock'n'roll players normally wouldn't play. He's a very good musician. He's not to be taken lightly. You don't survive that long if you're not good."

– Tom Petty

"We've learned you don't have to worry about playing everything exactly right. Sometimes it's better to wing it and hope that the magic happens that way instead of trying to polish it into magic. And that's a good thing to know."

– Mike Campbell

"There's nothing tentative about Dylan on stage. I've seen gigs where the songs have ended in all the wrong places, where it's all fallen apart, and it's almost as if, in some perverse way, he gets energy from that chaos."

– Stan Lynch

On September 5, 1987, six weeks after the last show of his brief tour with the Grateful Dead, Bob Dylan played a concert in Tel Aviv, Israel (his first performance in that country) backed by Tom Petty & the Heartbreakers (Benmont Tench, keyboards; Howie Epstein, bass; Stan Lynch, drums; Mike Campbell, lead guitar; Tom Petty, rhythm guitar and some backing vocals) and by his backup singers the Queens of Rhythm (Carolyn Dennis, Queen Esther Marrow and Madelyn Quebec).

It was the first night of the Temples in Flames Tour, thirty shows in six weeks, all over Europe, autumn 1987. The evocative name, which appeared on tour posters, seems to have been Dylan's invention.

As I hope the quotes above suggest, this was nothing like the Dylan/Dead tour. As the concert tapes clearly demonstrate, it was the return of the real Bob Dylan, singer/bandleader/performer extraordinaire, the master of spontaneous music. True, the Grateful Dead on their own also had considerable mastery of this form; and as we've seen, Dylan gives them a lot of credit for showing him the way back to his purpose in life as a maker of music that only becomes meaningful, to its authors and its audience, in the act of performance, preferably spontaneous interactive ensemble performance. But the summer of 1987 was not the right moment, nor were Bob Dylan and the five members of the Grateful Dead the right people, at that moment and in those circumstances, for the making of great music together. Instead they were the right combination of people in the right circumstances to open a door in the mind and heart of a great artist, and inspire him to re-find himself, to reinvent himself one more extraordinary time, instead of "packing it in." So three cheers for Dylan and the Dead, even if the music they made together was mostly awful. Because they somehow bear considerable responsibility for the wonderful music Bob Dylan began making (with the Heartbreakers and the Queens of Rhythm) as soon as he hit the stage in Tel Aviv for the start of his next (and as it turns out, never-ending) tour.

I said in the previous chapter that "it sometimes takes Dylan more than six shows to find his voice, and his confidence as an artist and bandleader, with a new band, or at the start of a new tour." This is emphatically not true of the fall '87 tour, and the obvious reason is that this wasn't a new band. Dylan and TP & the Heartbreakers had played sixty-one shows together the previous year. But please note that despite the understandable fears of some fans that fall '87 would be a mere continuation in Europe of the agenda (or "style") and the sound and the standard set lists of Dylan's 1986 American tour with the Heartbreakers, this didn't turn out to be the case. In fall '87 Bob Dylan joyfully explored a new sound, new songbook (including quite a few songs introduced during his rehearsals and shows with the Dead in May and July), new "musical flavor" – yeah, triumphant return of the "old" Bob Dylan, reinventing himself successfully every time he hits the boards. [Theatrical term. "boards" = the stage of a theater. Dylan often refers to B.B. King and other hardworking (constantly touring) old bluesmen as his models when asked to explain his lifestyle of tireless touring, but he is also very much in the noble tradition of Shakespearean actors who live their lives on the road, "hitting the boards" in town after town, constantly getting up before new audiences, playing the same roles and speaking the same lines with new spirit and (often) subtly different interpretations, varying according to the performing artist's circumstances and moods and his interactions with the rest of the troupe.]

The first six shows of Bob Dylan's fall 1987 tour – Tel Aviv, Jerusalem, Basel, Modena, Turin, Dortmund – are terrific, starting strong even though Dylan reportedly arrived in Tel Aviv (by public bus from Cairo, accompanied by two of his sons) too late for soundcheck and rehearsals.

Dylan's declaration of independence, from that part of himself that might have wanted to take the easy course by following the performance map he and this band had written during their many shows in '86, was to start the Tel Aviv concert with "I ain't gonna work on Maggie's farm no more," a song not included in any of the 1986 shows. And the second song was like an announcement (to himself) of his happiness at being here with this band and this audience: "I'll Be Your Baby Tonight," another song he'd done at half of his shows with the Dead two months earlier but not at all in his previous world tour with Petty.

In effect what this unpredictable performing artist was doing was going on with his 1987 tour, not being too distracted by the fact that the band had changed. Seven of the songs he chose to sing at Tel Aviv he'd also sung at his previous show that summer, Anaheim July 26th. Altogether, eleven of the Tel Aviv songs are ones he'd performed at one or more of the Grateful Dead shows, and a twelfth, the third song in Tel Aviv, "Senor," is one he'd rehearsed with the Dead but hadn't gotten around to including on a set list until now. Only six of the seventeen songs Dylan performed at Tel Aviv were ones he and the Heartbreakers had played at the 1986 shows. These were "I and I" from the *Infidels* album (1983) and "In the Garden" from *Saved* (1980), "I'll Remember You" from *Empire Burlesque* (1985), 1968's

"All Along the Watchtower" (only played twice in '86) and two of the Tel Aviv encores, "Knockin' on Heaven's Door" (1973) and "Blowin' in the Wind" (1963).

Dylan, still in the spirit of "Maggie's Farm" ("I try my best to be just like I am, but everybody wants you to be just like them"), also didn't pay too much attention to the fact that the audience was different tonight. One carryover from the GD tour was "Dead Man, Dead Man," a 1981 song Dylan presumably started playing in July 1987 as a joking reference to the fact that 4/5ths of the audience then were Dead people. Robert Hilburn interviewed concert-goers after the Tel Aviv show and reported that: "Some of them felt the inclusion of 'In the Garden,' one of the songs associated with Dylan's born-again Christian period, sent a mixed signal about his current religious stance. 'People I know have been waiting ten years for the night Bob Dylan would perform in Israel,' said a 24-year-old engineer. 'And he doesn't do his hits, the songs that we want to hear. What if this is the only time he plays here?'" The next day Hilburn pointed out to Dylan that he hadn't played "Neighborhood Bully," his 1983 song portraying modern Israel as a misunderstood hero. Dylan responded: "'I hadn't even thought of that song. I probably should have but I didn't. It would seem to be an appropriate song. Maybe I'll play it in Germany,' he added, laughing." He did however say "Shalom!" twice after playing "Highway 61," one of the few times he spoke to the audience at all at any 1987 concert. And the final encore at Tel Aviv was a heartfelt performance of the old American spiritual, "Go Down, Moses": "When Israel was in Egypt land (let my people go), oppressed so hard that they could not stand (let my people go). Go down, Moses, way down in Egypt land, tell old Pharoah, let my people go." It's a powerful reading of a song Dylan never sang publicly before. And quite typical of Bob Dylan, though born a Jew, to identify keenly with the people of Israel as seen (and portrayed romantically) by black American songmakers … and for him to choose to honor the people of Israel, at his first concert in that nation, by singing this song. ("That's my religion. The songs are my lexicon. I believe the songs.")

"Go Down, Moses" is certainly the high point of the Tel Aviv show. Other high points include "I'll Be Your Baby Tonight," "Senor," "I and I," "Watching the River Flow," "Simple Twist of Fate," and "Stuck Inside of Mobile with the Memphis Blues Again." (These sentences are in the present tense because I wasn't at the show – I'm listening to a tape, now.)

Dylan's singing on "Senor" at this concert is so remarkably expressive that the moments when he forgets the words (this is a song he hadn't sung on stage for more than three years) and ad-libs indistinct dummy lyrics are not a problem. The song still sounds great and the sentiment of the song and of the fictional character or persona singing it comes through clearly even if we can't quite catch the words. The feelings are clear. "This place don't make sense to me no more!" Sung like a man who has recently had the experience of panicking onstage in front of 50,000 people ("I can't remember what it means, is it just a bunch of *words?*") ...

While Dylan's voice is a little pinched and unassertive on "Maggie's Farm" (partly because it's the opening song and partly because the band too are uncertain, "faking it" on a song they only played once before, in 1985), he opens his throat and delivers an earnest vocal on "I'll Be Your Baby Tonight" – so present that you feel you've never heard this particular Dylan voice before and that if you listened carefully enough you could read his mind or at least learn all about his bus ride through Egypt and how he feels to be back on stage tonight. He improvises a new verse partway through: "Shut those doors/Shut it tight/You don't have to worry about tomorrow night." This striking "slow voice" continues on "Senor," and returns, but with variations presumably reflecting how he feels after singing the three intervening uptempo songs, on a gentle and pretty "Simple Twist of Fate." On "Baby," "Senor" and "Simple Twist," Dylan's voice seems to be particularly responsive to and inspired by Benmont Tench's soulful keyboard playing (Mike Campbell's evocative guitar embellishments are also central to the spell woven in "Simple Twist").

Tench is again the linchpin and driving force of a particularly wonderful rock and roll interpretation of "Watching the River Flow." We can feel Dylan's enthusiasm at being back in the driver's seat of a great band (BD &TP & the HBs; BD & the GD didn't have it, mostly because BD never could find the driver's seat, partly due to chemistry but largely because of his own ambivalence this year, now fading – part of the joy of this splendid "River Flow" is the sound of Dylan rediscovering his confidence as singer/performer/bandleader; it's contagious, and first-rate spontaneous music results).

A ragged but likeable "Highway 61 Revisited" was the fourth song at Tel Aviv, followed by an excellent "I and I," the success of which certainly contributed to the joy of "Watching the River Flow," which in turn flows into "Simple Twist of Fate" so meaningfully you might almost think these transitions were carefully planned and rehearsed. Probably not, but they work wonderfully, as does the sequence of #9, "Simple Twist," into #10, "Stuck Inside of Mobile with the Memphis Blues Again." Bob Dylan is back in his element, having a great time reaching into his big book of songs and playing one off against another (or against two, the one that came before and the one that comes after).

Dylan and the band sound bright on "I and I," breathing new life into a song they'd performed at most of their 1986 shows. It's the same basic version, dropping the third verse ("Took an untrodden path once"), bouncing on staccato rhythm guitar notes, Queens of Rhythm doubling (or tripling) Bob's voice on the chorus, but it has a lightness and drive in the vocal as well as the band performance that suggest that a new year brings a new song ("they're waiting for spring to come, smoking down the track"). As in '86, Dylan avoids the word "faithfully," substituting "readily" in the phrase "she must have owned the world and been faithfully wed to some righteous king who wrote psalms ..." To my taste, the sloweddown gospel repetitions of "Sees my face and lives" at the end go on a little too long, but they do serve as a reminder that the songwriter-bandleader is on a personal quest, exploring the mysteries that certain words and sounds hold for him, keys to the religiosity and philosophy he finds in music. I believe that's why he includes the Queens of Rhythm in his sonic palette; and if the repetitions sometimes sound tiresome to my ears they might in fact be energizing him, setting his spirit free and thus contributing to powerful musical moments later in the show or later in the week.

"Stuck Inside of Mobile with the Memphis Blues Again" is another song the Heartbreakers have never played onstage before, and indeed a Dylan classic that until this summer he had only performed live during the second part of the Rolling Thunder Tour, spring 1976. The sureness with which TP & the HBs play the new 1987 arrangement of the song indicates that they and Bob must have managed some rehearsal time together, maybe in the States before flying to the Middle East. In any case, this Tel Aviv "Memphis Blues Again" is an example of why Bob Dylan dedicates his life to creating opportunities for spontaneous music. It is a marvelous, unique creation comparable to the great *Blonde on Blonde* and

Hard Rain performances of this exceptional song, measurably beyond the other two BD & the HBs performances of the song in fall '87, and hugely better than any of the six BD & the GD renderings of "Memphis Blues Again" on their '87 tour. Why? Because this was the first time these five musicians and Bob Dylan had attempted this song onstage (Zen mind, beginner's mind)? Because somewhere very early on band and singer accidentally find a groove that inspires and thrills them and won't let go? Like the other 1987 versions, it's several verses shorter than the original (first four verses, "ragman" to "Grandpa," then skip the next three and finish with the original last two, "Ruthie" and "the bricks" – perhaps for the sake of spontaneity, every 1987 version features a different selection of verses and often a different sequence). I'm tickled that instead of "pointed shoes," this night Shakespeare's in the alley "with his tambourine and his bell." (At the Dylan/Dead rehearsals in May, it was "his ballerina and his bell.") Shakespeare with his tambourine is a quintessentially Bob Dylan image, and I believe it made its first appearance at Hayarkon Park, Tel Aviv, 9/5/87.

Between this wonderful "MBA" (8th song) and the equally wonderful "Go Down, Moses" (#17), Dylan and his new (but comfortingly familiar) band offered: "In the Garden," "Joey," "Dead Man, Dead Man," "I'll Remember You," "Tangled Up in Blue," "All Along the Watchtower," "Knockin' on Heaven's Door" and "Blowin' in the Wind," a stimulating out-of-time and out of sequence journey across three decades of songwriting and storytelling and Bob Dylan identities. Predictably, this didn't add up to the Bob Dylan the Israeli press and public felt they'd been promised. Newspapers around the world picked up the story of Bob Dylan's "disastrous" first performance in Israel. The tapes tell a different story.

It's quite unusual for Bob Dylan to respond to public and journalistic criticism, but he is consistently unpredictable, and at his second concert in Israel, at an outdoor venue called Sultan's Pool just outside the walls of the Old City in Jerusalem, he began his show with three of the "hits" that people complained of not hearing in Tel Aviv: "The Times They Are A-Changin'" as opening song, and "Like a Rolling Stone" and "Rainy Day Women" in the #3 and #4 slots. They're unremarkable performances – although the lyrics to "Times" are more scrambled than would seem possible, and Dylan's open-throated singing on "Like a Rolling Stone" is at times quite moving – and there's none of the musical excitement of the previous show's band-singer interaction in these three numbers or the second song (a non-hit, "Man of Peace" from *Infidels*).

Sultan's Pool was a more intimate setting than Tel Aviv's Hayarkon Park (there were 9,000 people at the Jerusalem concert, versus 45,000 at the Tel Aviv show) and so, after disposing of his responsibility to sing some big hits, Bob Dylan evidently felt inspired to sing each of the next four songs on his set list as if he were singing to just one person, as though he were firmly connected not only to the meaning of the song but also to the person the song is addressed to, tonight and forever – the object, "thou": "You're the one I'm hoping for ..."/"If you're a doctor, I need a shot of love ..."/"You walk into the room ..."/"I hope that you can hear, hear me singing through these tears ..."

These four songs ("Emotionally Yours," "Shot of Love," "Ballad of a Thin Man," "You're a Big Girl Now") on this particular night (Sept. 7, 1987, full moon shining on the singer and the concertgoers and the walls of Jerusalem) stand together as a fine example of the type of provisional container that the great works of a performing artist are sometimes found in. In addition to great concerts and great single-song-performances, there are these short runs, sequences of performances that somehow arise out of and capture one inspired moment of creation – like the moment in 1965 when Dylan sang and played the final album versions of "Mr. Tambourine Man," "It's Alright, Ma" and "Gates of Eden" in a single take.

In this case there's an interesting punctuation, a brief discourse to the audience between "Emotionally Yours" and "Shot of Love," as though Dylan uncharacteristically felt called upon to explain why he chose to sing something that wasn't a recognizable hit: "Thank you! That was a little 'request' that we played tonight, 'cause we didn't play it the other night; some people wanted to hear it, I think. Here's another one some people wanted ... since we didn't play it last time, we'll play it tonight!"

Listening to this heartfelt (and musically and lyrically unique) "Emotionally Yours," I can't talk myself out of the idea that the song was indeed requested, by a lover who is at the show and whom we can see and feel as Dylan recreates before our ears Billy Parker romancing Molly McGuire ("I wrote this song for you") but totally for real this time. The gentle, deliberate electric piano notes that open the performance, arising straight out of the jocular, anthemic "everybody must get stoned" flourish that ends the previous song, are a very effective announcement that we're shifting gears here, slipping into something more intimate ... and then when we hear a couple of signature Bob Dylan harmonica inhalations, it's like he's lighting candles. "Come baby, take me, take me down to shake me," he sings in a new second verse seemingly invented at this moment, "I will be in your arms ... Show me you know me, because I – I'm so mad about your charm. I could be dreaming, still I keep believing you're the one I'm hoping for ... and I will always be emotionally yours." The musicians and backup singers sound like an extension of the singer's consciousness, so that the whole musical fabric is felt as the spontaneous creation of one heart, one mind, one earnest lover. This is most striking in the extended instrumental passage that ends the performance – it's one of those moments when Dylan seems to be conducting the band with his heart, speaking private unvoiceable feelings telepathically through their playing, painting pictures with music. Before this there's another moment of inspired lyrical improvisation. In the bridging verse Dylan sings, "When I see you I never have a prayer" instead of "it's as if I never had a thought." This requires a different rhyme, so he replaces "But it's the only one I've got" with a passionate, "But it's the only thing I can find anywhere!" And at the same time that these particular lyrics are unique to this full moon Sultan's Pool version of this song, so is the pacing, the tempo of the performance, and the feel between voice and keyboards and drums and guitars. And, not surprisingly, the magic carries over into the next three selections.

On a good night, or during a great run of four or five performances, the transitions are all perfect, all delicious. So Dylan's little speech that ends "didn't play it last time, we'll play it tonight!" and his tone of voice delivering it are such a great lead-in to the opening vamp of this Jerusalem '87 "Shot of Love" that it sounds like it was scripted, carefully planned. When you're on a roll, the music plays you. No surprise that the "Shot of Love" that resulted is not much like the version this singer and this band played 36 times in 1986 (Clinton Heylin calls it "a much punchier performance than the previous year"), and also is quite distinct from the subsequent 1987 versions. Having made a telepathic connection with his band during "Emotionally Yours" and especially in the last 30 seconds of that song, Dylan maintained this state of grace and (perhaps with the additional boost that the same lady also requested this one and he does indeed need a shot of love from her doctor kit) found himself touching and realizing aspects of the song's intrinsic musical and spiritual identity that were always there but had never revealed themselves quite so tangibly in performance before. The unique tempo of Dylan's singing and the band's playing on this version seems to be at the heart of its surprising power (there are some wonderful moments towards the end of the song when the audience starts clapping along in time to the unusual and seductive beat of the spontaneous arrangement). The accompanying and echoing vocals of the Queens of Rhythm on this "Shot of Love" are also clearly part of what is inspiring Dylan, and therefore the band, to penetrate deeper into the soul of the song. Hearing this version of "Shot," it struck me for the first time that one interpretation of the lines "What makes the wind want to blow tonight? Don't even feel like crossing the street and my car ain't acting right" might be that the speaker feels unmotivated (and so does his car) and wonders empathetically where the wind gets its energy, its will to live, from? It's a song about being depressed (and finding a way out). Somehow that never occurred to me before.

It does happen to me ocasionally that some aspect of Bob Dylan's performance of a song on stage on a particular night turns a key in me somewhere and I find myself opening to the song and its story, its "sentiment," in a new way, and feeling as though I'm hearing its meaning more clearly than I ever did the thousands of other times I'd heard it. This happened to me at a concert in Berkeley in 1986 with the closing lines of "A Hard Rain's A-Gonna Fall." And it's happened to varying degrees with every one of the four amazing performances in this Sultan's Pool "intimacy" sequence as I've listened to this concert on tape this week (walking around outside with my Walkman and headphones ... appropriate, since singer and band and audience were outside too).

With "Ballad of a Thin Man" – which is instrumentally and vocally an exceptional (and at times quite fresh and beautiful) version of this old warhorse – something in Bob Dylan's voice and in his pacing and timing of the familiar opening phrases "You walk into the room with your pencil in your hand" made me *see* the person he's speaking to. To my surprise, I was seeing the *Time* magazine reporter Dylan argues with (and belittles) in the 1965

documentary *Don't Look Back*. Of course a reporter would have a
pencil in his hand, and would look around upon arriving at the
scene of the action and start asking questions like "Who is that
man?" But obvious as that is, I had always related to the song as
such a cosmically appropriate statement of the times, our generation speaking to the rest of you confused squares, that the narrative
for me was always a dream-sequence with a square Everyman being
mocked by ominous (and uppity) freaks, and I didn't particularly
think of "Mr. Jones" as a journalist, even though I had seen that
Time guy mentioned in "Who was the real Mr. Jones?" discussions …

This 9/7/87 performance is one of those instances of Dylan
being so present inside the character he's singing as, or singing
about or singing to, that song and story take on a striking immediacy. I noticed the way he says and sings, "*Who* is that man?" –
noticed the humor in his voice – and suddenly I just saw the speaker
of these words as a reporter. It all seemed so vivid, so full of personality. Then I was further surprised to notice that the next words ("You
try so hard …") sounded sympathetic; the singer/speaker seemed
genuinely compassionate, not just smartass as I'd always heard it.

The music is wonderful, the band is at its best (not at all rehash-
ing the 1986 version, but responding to the frontman's leadership
by creating something completely new and fresh and spontaneous).
In particular, please notice Stan Lynch's drumming after the words
"Thanks for the loan" and during the "something is happening"
chorus that follows. Drummer and singer are clearly getting energy
from each other (and the other musicians and singers are responding to both of them). It's like call-and-response between Bob and
Stan. Wow. Please also notice the beauty and inventiveness of the
guitar solos and other elements in the instrumental break before the
last verse … one discovery after another, by singers and musicians
who'd thought they were pretty familiar with this song and are now
grateful that it's making itself so new tonight, and taking them along
for the ride.

So as I listened to this marvelous "Thin Man," I thought I
noticed something odd near the end. Rewind, double-check … yes,
Dylan and the Queens definitely sing "Do you, Mr. Stone?" three
times at the end of the song, instead of "Mr. Jones." And then I
remembered a note I recently saw in Clinton Heylin's chronology/
reference work, *Bob Dylan: A Life in Stolen Moments*: "Back at his hotel
after the [Jerusalem] show, Dylan is interviewed by Kurt Loder for

the 20th anniversary issue of *Rolling Stone*." So, um, no wonder I could suddenly see the "you" of the song as a journalist. The singer really was inside his song's scenario this night, reaching out from inside of something (as he said of his performance method in the previously quoted 1988 interview). Of course he knew the after-show interview was scheduled, and was playfully aware of "Mr. Stone" being in the Sultan's Pool audience, fictional character come to life and sung to (not nastily but kiddingly) in the flesh. I swear the information about Dylan being interviewed after the Jerusalem concert was not in my conscious mind when I found myself unexpectedly seeing "Mr. Jones" with new eyes because of the particular way Dylan was speaking his lines at this show, on this tape ... The method works. Especially when musicians and singers (and audience) really awaken and inspire each other. Something is happening, and we don't know what it is, except that we do know This Is It – this is what we traveling performers and players live for. "Oh my God (thank God) I'm not here all alone!!"

The fourth song in this sequence is one of the most intimate songs Bob Dylan has ever written: "You're a Big Girl Now" from 1975's *Blood on the Tracks*. This Jerusalem performance is good but not great. That's all right. The essential delicacy of the song's music and sentiment/story do come through, and that's enough to sustain the magical mood woven in the three previous songs. It's always a treat, and a moment of memorable intimacy between singer and listeners, to hear Bob Dylan sing this one. And it's interesting to think that two of Dylan's sons were in the audience, since the person being addressed in the song is certainly their mother (so certainly that Dylan has even bothered to mock this assumption publicly, in the song notes on the sleeves of the *Biograph* album: "I wish somebody would ask me first before they go ahead and print stuff like that. I mean, it couldn't be about anybody else but my wife, right?"). There's a notable lyric change or improvisation after the lines "I can change, I swear/See what you can do." It's an example of the creative stimulus of mistakes in performance that Bill Evans said can result in good jazz. The next lines of the song are "I can make it through/You can make it too," but in Jerusalem Dylan starts with "You can make it through" and carries this out by singing, "I can – I know what ought to be!"

This Sultan's Pool "You're a Big Girl Now" is the only 1987 performance of the song, indeed the only time Dylan has ever performed this song with Petty and the Heartbreakers (and the first time he'd sung it on stage since July 1, 1978). With the unpredictability and looseness that characterize his 1987 performances, Dylan follows "I know what ought to be!" with "Our conversation was short and sweet," the opening line of the song. So he ends the song by singing the first verse again, which means the song ends with its title phrase, as songs often do but as this song has done perhaps only this once. So, um, let's be thankful for the fan in the audience with the hidden tape recorder. What a rare treasure he brought us back from the Holy City!

The next five songs of the Jerusalem show are "John Brown," "License to Kill," "It's All Over Now, Baby Blue," "Gotta Serve Somebody" and "Slow Train." Regrettably, a unique and spectacularly good vocal performance of "Slow Train" is cut short by an electricity failure two-thirds of the way through the song. This ends the concert. The last words Dylan sings are, "But the enemy I see –" And then silence. Very dramatic, as if the Higher Power doesn't want him to tell the secret, or wishes to remind us that It can be unpredictable too.

"Baby Blue," instead of ending back at the beginning or in the middle, starts in the middle. After a very pretty band intro, Dylan sings, "All your seasick sailors, they are rowing/All your reindeer armies, they are going" ... and then sings the rest of the third verse of the song. Next we get the usual second verse, a nice instrumental break, and then the usual closing verse and another fine break.

The third concert of the Temples in Flames Tour took place on September 10, 1987 in St. Jakobshalle in Basel, Switzerland. This is probably the one where Dylan surprised Benmont by saying to the band onstage, "Right, we'll begin with 'Forever Young' ... which indeed they'd never played before except possibly at a rehearsal. The performances at this third show are good, though never (to my tastes) as exceptional as certain moments during the first two shows. But of course it would be a contradiction in terms to expect uniform excellence from practitioners of spontaneous music. In any case, no Dylan fans in Basel were complaining when their hero played the following sequence in the #5, #6 and #7 slots: "Queen Jane Approximately," "When I Paint My Masterpiece" and "The Ballad of Frankie Lee and Judas Priest," none of which Dylan had ever performed in Europe before ("Masterpiece" is the only one of the three that he had performed live anywhere before 1987).

What is most noteworthy about the Basel concert is that of the fourteen songs Dylan played, only the two encores were songs he'd played at one of the two previous shows. As mentioned before, *none* of the Jerusalem songs had been played in Tel Aviv. So in the first three Temples in Flames shows, Dylan and the Heartbreakers played 42 different songs. This prodigious trend, clearly inspired by observing the Grateful Dead and their fans, couldn't continue, of course. The fourth show of the fall '87 tour only introduced one song that hadn't been played at the other shows; the fifth show introduced four new selections; the sixth show was entirely songs that had been played at one or more of the first five concerts. I can't say for certain, but I believe 42 different songs in three consecutive shows is a record for Dylan up until 1987. The closest contender seems to be 29 different songs in three consecutive shows at the volatile spring 1976 Rolling Thunder shows (and 39 different songs in five consecutive shows that spring).

At the Autodromo in Modena, Italy, Sept. 12 – the fourth Temples in Flames concert – Dylan played only three songs that he'd played in Basel, and only two he'd played in Jerusalem. So the Modena set list is mostly a rerun and reshuffle of the Tel Aviv list. Eleven songs from the Tel Aviv 17 are among the 15 played at Modena. But, determined not to return to his twenty-three-year habit of usually playing almost the same set list every night of a tour, Dylan managed to work it out so only once at Modena is a song followed by the same song it led into at Tel Aviv. "All Along the Watchtower" is the pre-encore set-closer at both shows, and the encores begin with "Knockin' on Heaven's Door" both nights. Every other sequence is different. Modena begins with "Rainy Day Women" and ends with "When the Night Comes Falling from the Sky," songs not included at Tel Aviv, and both songs that were in the #4 slot at their previous Temples in Flames appearances. "It's all math, simple math, involved in mathematics," Dylan said in 1966. "There's a definite number of Colt .45s that make up Marlene Dietrich, and you can find that out if you want to." He was talking about his songwriting ("the music, the rhyming and rhythm, what I call the mathematics of a song"), but why not apply the same principle to writing a concert?

As for September '87 being a continuation of July '87 more than a resumption of the 1986 Dylan/Petty tour, here's a rough breakdown: of the 47 songs Dylan sang at these first six fall '87 shows, 28 are songs he had performed or rehearsed with the Dead earlier in the year. And the cover songs that Dylan sang at almost all of the 1986 shows, "Across the Borderline," "Lonesome Town" and "I Forgot More Than You'll Ever Know," did not turn up at all at these six shows, nor at any of the 1987 Dylan/Petty concerts. In fact, Dylan only sang two cover songs on the fall '87 tour: "Go Down, Moses" at the first and last shows and "House of the Risin' Sun" in Paris, October 7.

Between "Like a Rolling Stone," the closing song in Basel, and "Rainy Day Women," the Modena opener, Bob Dylan and the Heartbreakers traveled 250 miles through and over the Swiss Alps. But for a performing artist, the distances between gigs are less important than the distances traveled during his minutes onstage, navigating the challenging geography of the relationships between singer and audience, singer and band, and between singer and himself, and his songs. Modena is a great show, a very satisfying work of art from start to finish, and this seems to be because the spirit of the songs, which had been "getting further and further away" from Dylan, had come home to him, along with his confidence as a bandleader and music-maker, over the course of the first three Temples in Flames concerts. So he sounds like a man who knows and feels the meanings of almost every phrase he sings and in every measure of the music he and his band are playing. This can be heard in every song and every minute of this show, and it is particularly noticeable in the performances of "In the Garden," "Highway 61 Revisited," "I and I," "Joey" and "All Along the Watchtower." If Sony Records were to ask me which concert from this important transitional tour might work well as a commercial Bob Dylan album, I'd probably suggest Modena, not because it includes my favorite single-song performances from the tour (it doesn't), but because it holds together so well as a listening experience. There is a joyous, almost exuberant spirit throughout this concert that is hard to resist. A 75-minute celebration of arrival.

"In the Garden" hasn't changed structurally from past performances, but because of the way Dylan at Modena sings this song and inspires his band to play it, it sounds more than ever like the rock spiritual he must have always intended it to be. It has a universality. It makes me imagine Dylan in 1979 challenging himself as a songwriter to come up with a "Blowin' in the Wind" about Jesus, something that could speak to that many people if the moment happened to be right. So he tried the question-asking structure that worked so well in "Blowin'" as a vehicle for narrating scenes from the life of the Master. At Modena he sings it as part of a surprising drugs-sex-and-Jesus opening sequence ("Rainy Day Women"/"I Want You"/"In the Garden"), perhaps to declare his individuality to the world, and to himself, one more time.

"Highway 61" really finds a groove this time, and Dylan is so pleased he responds with the sort of dirty, energetic, comic vocal one has always wished to hear on a live version of this song. He is present in every little scene in the song's mosaic – when he says the roving gambler was "very bored," we see the man rather vividly. And I find myself noticing for the first time that when Georgia Sam asks Poor Howard "Where can I go?", he's talking to a character from a Leadbelly song. Perhaps it's not just Dylan's presence in the vocal that makes me notice this, but also the fact that I've now experienced his 1997 song cycle *Time Out of Mind*, where he makes references to specific American folk songs in almost every lyric. "Poor Howard is dead and gone (left me here to sing this song)," according to Leadbelly, which perhaps explains why he tells Sam "there's only one place I know." (Find out something only dead men know?) It's a rollicking performance in which the vocal is as rhythmic and confident as the drums and guitars and keys. This one performance defines the spirit of the whole concert, and for this reason is best heard in conjunction with everything else they played that night. Compilation albums of great moments from a tour are treasures, but to really get the experience of being there and thereby be in touch with the artist's intent and the whole canvas he was working on, you also need to listen to tapes of complete concerts. The Modena "Highway 61" informs the Modena "I and I" and the Modena "Joey" and everything else Dylan and the Heartbreakers created that night.

I wouldn't have thought the Tel Aviv "I and I" could be improved on, but that's the joy of spontaneous music – another show can bring an unexpectedly new and even more wonderful version of an already "perfect" number. Tiny changes, like a shift in the emotional state or physical condition of one musician, may alter the chemistry and overall *gestalt*, and as a result it could all fall apart or all come together in ways not previously experienced or anticipated. Every moment is a fresh set of conditions and responses, and every subsequent moment of the performance is affected, like a

stack of dominoes falling one by one, except in this case there are
many stacks falling at the same time, brushing against each other
and setting off new chain reactions in a variety of directions. And
each musician's sense of fulfillment comes from rising to the challenge and doing his best to carry on this multi-part conversation,
never losing sight of the song's essential rhythm and melody and
structure and sentiment. "I and I, in creation where one's nature
neither honors nor forgives." That's what the song's about. Uncom-
promising expression of and confrontation with one's nature. And
this time, I must say, the "Sees my face and lives" choral ending
goes on at least as long as it did in Tel Aviv and I love it, and would
welcome a further extension. Why? Stan Lynch's drumming seems
to be one fresh and very effective element. And the precise mix of
Dylan's voice with the Queens' voices also seems different and
again the change is very effective, very pleasing. And please note
how present Dylan is when he sings, "If she wakes up now, you
know she'll just want me to talk. I got nothing to say, especially
about whatever was!!" Another case where a brief scene becomes
unusually vivid, thanks to the spin the storyteller gives it with his
voice, the way he coaxes these words out of his larynx this particular
evening. It's Modena '87, and every song has a keen edge on it. "I
got nothing to say," indeed!

Even before the vocal starts, the opening notes of "Joey" at
Modena demonstrate clearly, when compared with the opening
notes of the same song on *Dylan & the Dead* (from Foxboro, Mass.,
July 4, '87), the difference between musicianship that's full of life
and purpose, and musicianship that's, um, dead ... and rudderless.
In 1991, talking about his songs in an interview with Paul Zollo for
Song Talk magazine, Dylan said of "Joey" (music by Bob Dylan,
words by Jacques Levy and Bob Dylan, 1975): "That's a tremen-
dous song. And you'd only know that singing it night after night.
You know who got me singing that song? Garcia. Yeah. He got me
singing that song again. He said, 'That's one of the best songs ever
written.' Coming from *him*, it was hard to know which way to take
that [laughs]. He got me singing that song again with them. It was
amazing how it would, right from the gate go [sic], it had a life of its
own, it just ran out of the gate and it just kept on getting better and
better and better and better and it keeps on getting better. It's in its
infant stages, as a performance thing. Of course, it's a long song.
But to me, not to blow my own horn, but to me the song is like a

Homer ballad. Much more so than 'A Hard Rain,' which is a long song too. But to me 'Joey' has a Homeric quality to it that you don't hear every day. Especially in popular music." To give the reader some perspective on when a song can be in its infant stages, as a performance thing, to Bob Dylan: he first performed "Joey" live at the first three Dylan/Dead shows, then performed it eight more times in autumn 1987 with the Heartbreakers. He performed it four times in June and July 1988. Then in 1990, the year before the above comments, "Joey" really ran out of the gate. Dylan performed it 27 times between January and November, 1990. In any case, as strong as the song starts in Modena, it does get better – band and singer and song go on inspiring each other and sustain that Homeric fire right through to a very colorful and striking evocation of the "town of Brooklyn" in the last verse and chorus. In the hands (and vocal cords) of a great performing artist, songs do indeed have a life of their own. "Joey" at Modena, and the Modena concert as a whole, stand as excellent examples of this gratifying and intriguing phenomenon.

"All Along the Watchtower," speaking of performed songs having lives of their own, is unusual in that the Tel Aviv and Modena versions are actually a continuation of a process of exploration begun when Dylan and the Heartbreakers and the Queens tried out a slowed-down version of this song at a series of shows in July 1986. This was radically different from the Jimi Hendrix arrangement of the song Dylan favored in concert throughout 1978 (and at a great many shows since 1987). In July '87, Dylan and the Dead attempted the Hendrix arrangement (extremely unsuccessfully, as demonstrated by the embarrassing version included – apparently at Dylan's request – on *Dylan & the Dead*). But reunited with the 1986 players, Dylan apparently remembered what the song had been trying to become in the last month of that tour … and the result in Modena (the last time the song was performed in 1987) is wonderful and memorable.

"Knockin' on Heaven's Door" at Modena makes another sort of leap through time. It has a musical sweetness and, I would say, an evocation of a sense of community (community of music-makers) happily reminiscent of the 1975 Rolling Thunder performances of this song, and quite different from the 1986 standard encore version and from the Dylan/Dead tour versions. It's as though this happy night of performing with old friends has reconnected Dylan with a "meaning" this song had for him in performance at one moment in his life on the road, and thus becomes, through his singing and his conducting of the musicians and singers, an expression of his love for his work (and his audience) on these special nights when everything comes together.

The Sept. 13 show – the first time on this tour that Dylan played two nights in a row – took place at the Palasport in Turin, also northern Italy. Turin is another very good tape – arguably lacking the mysterious X-factor that makes every minute of the Modena tape such a rich listening experience, and the different X-factor that makes the next concert (Dortmund, Germany, Sept. 15) so spectacular from start to finish it could even trump Modena. But let's say we want an example of Bob Dylan and his autumn '87 band and singers playing a first-rate concert that isn't transcendent … a "control" … an example of Bob Dylan singing well even when he doesn't seem to me to be keenly present inside of or passionately connected with the stories he's telling and the circumstances he's evoking in his songs. Turin will do. Because I love to write about and call attention to those special moments on the concert tapes when Bob Dylan connects with a song's "meaning" in a fresh or unusually powerful way, and when Dylan and his band inspire each other to create remarkable spontaneous music, I'm always in danger of giving a skewed picture of his opus. I skim over the "ordinary" shows, including very good and very satisfying ones like Turin '87, which opens with "Positively 4th Street," one of only three times Dylan performed this song in 1987 (versus 51 times in '86) and probably the only time he's ever opened a show with it. This is followed by "Masters of War," also performed thrice in '87, and "Lenny Bruce," only performed twice in fall '87 (24 times in '86). None of these were played on the Grateful Dead tour.

Later in the Turin tape we get two more rarities that did get single performances on the Dead tour: "The Wicked Messenger" (performed three times in '87) and "Heart of Mine" (performed four times in '87). Heylin in *A Life in Stolen Moments* calls these "particularly fine versions" and also makes note of the long harmonica solos that open "Lenny Bruce" and "License to Kill" in Turin.

These latter two performances do deserve attention, and arguably are examples of Dylan being unusually present in a song via his harmonica playing rather than his singing. In "Lenny Bruce" it's just forty seconds of harmonica, played over the piano intro (which picks out the song's melody, backed by very understated bass and drums), but it is so full of feeling, of tenderness and sympathy, that the mood of the harmonica solo lingers with the listener throughout the song, enriching the lyrics, which are delivered fairly routinely — i.e. "these are the words to this song," rather than the "I really want to tell you this story!!" of Dylan's most "present" singing ("Joey" in Modena, "In the Garden" and "Shelter from the Storm" in Dortmund, "Rank Strangers to Me" on *Down in the Groove*). ("John Brown" at Turin is an example of Dylan singing with more presence than this story-song receives at many of its 1987 performances.) In "License to Kill" at Turin, Tench "starts it off" on piano and immediately Campbell adds some tasteful lead guitar notes, and the beauty of this duet seems to inspire Dylan to jump in with a harmonica solo (again a duet with the piano) that extends for two minutes. Lynch's drumming also contributes to this very expressive "instrumental version" of "License to Kill." Again the harmonica conveys a very sweet and tender feeling of sympathy. I find myself wondering, "sympathy for what?" My question is answered when Dylan's voice interrupts the fugue to say, "Man thinks, because he rules the Earth, he can do with it as he pleases." And I realize, sympathy for the Earth, and wonder why it took me until this moment to appreciate that the song's sentiment is more environmentalist than pacifist. Again, the harmonica passage establishes the mood of the whole ensemble performance, and the result is about as fine a "License to Kill" as you could hope to find, combing through a decade and a half of concert tapes. And what makes this particular performance so special is not an unusually strong vocal, as is often the case, but the unique quality of the way the musicians (including vocalist and harmonica player) are playing together and the freshness (and success) of their approach to the song's melody and rhythm and dynamics. The harmonica returns late in the performance, during an instrumental break, and quickly gives way to a moving (and sonically very appropriate and pleasing) organ solo, which leads into the return of the vocals for the final chorus. Splendid.

Turin includes the second fall '87 performance of "Gotta Serve Somebody." In 1987 Dylan chose to improvise new lyrics (at least for the opening lines, and sometimes well beyond that) at every performance of this song. There are seventeen 1987 performances of "Gotta Serve Somebody," and no two are alike. This time, he starts by singing, "You might be a conductor, standing in the rain, might suffer from happiness, you might suffer from pain, might be too much a preacher, standing in the rows, neither tune is a harmony, to expose ... but you're gonna serve somebody." The third verse starts, "Might be the president, might be some clown ..." In addition to the fun of trying to guess what he's saying, it's a very enjoyable rockin' performance by singer and band and harmony singers – not GREAT, but not to be overlooked.

And then, if you want GREAT, there's Dortmund, 9/15/87. This concert starts with "Knockin' on Heaven's Door" (#14 at Tel Aviv, #15 in Basel) and ends with "Like a Rolling Stone" and "Forever Young." Like Modena, it's an inspired concert from start to finish, but the particular spirit that's infusing this singer and these musicians this night is not the Modena spirit. It's still joyful and at times exuberant, but it has a flavor and a character all its own, presumably shaped by the specific circumstances of this location and this day and by the ensemble's experience of the previous concert and the previous five concerts and, um, everything that's happened to each of these players, and to their leader especially, throughout their lives so far. It's all here. All those past and present life experiences and musical experiences are expressed in this unique creation, this "accidental" work of art called the Dortmund '87 Bob Dylan show, "Bob Dylan's 91,587th Dream," a dedicated artist's confident and playful declaration of existence, recorded at Westfalenhalle 1 on the 15th of September, Anno Domini 1987. "I am!!" "I am a rock and roll guitar player, singer, and bandleader, and the guy who wrote all these songs. The author of 'Knockin' on Heaven's Door' and 'Like a Rolling Stone' and 'Tangled Up in Blue' and – whether you've heard of them or not – the author of 'I'll Remember You' and 'Dead Man, Dead Man.' And proud of it. Are you ready out there? Look out, here I come!"

Bob Dylan feels good about himself and his work, this night in Dortmund. You can hear it in his voice. It's a unique, very wonderful Bob Dylan voice, special to this show. His presence this time is not a matter of being one with the protagonists of the songs or the persons being sung to. It's a matter of his enthusiasm for the act of singing, and for each of these songs that he gets to sing. In a subtle but measurable sense, this "Tangled Up in Blue" vocal is not like any other rendition. It has a unique personality – not a different arrangement or lyrics, but a subtle idiosyncrasy of delivery that gives us listeners the opportunity to be intimately present with this singer and his mood, his picture of life and reality, at this particular never-to-be-repeated moment. This, according to my theory, is what we like so much about Bob Dylan. The particular way he sings "Some are mathematicians" or "with a soulful, bounding leap" at this moment on this record, or at this moment on this concert tape. We're connoisseurs of his idiosyncrasies, his phrasing, his music, his utterances, no two alike, and of course we can't always explain what it is that seems so profound or funny or otherwise gratifying about this particular one. But we do make mental markers when we hear a good one, so we can replay the past and hear it again. You wouldn't expect, dear fellow connoisseur, to hear Bob Dylan say "Don't go mistaking Paradise for that home across the road" in 1987 in a voice that makes you think of "Lo and Behold!" or something else ("Sign on the Cross"?) from *The Basement Tapes*. Even a line as familiar as "She walked up to me so gracefully and took my crown of thorns" makes you want to go back and hear it again so you can pay more attention to the images you saw and the feelings you felt when you encountered this Dortmund reading of it. Sweet wine. Good art.

Beginnings and endings are important to the performing artist. They hold his work, contain and define it, and determine the character of the experience, both for listener and performer. On this Dortmund tape you can hear an intro to "I Want You" that gathers such momentum as piano is joined by bass and then drums and then harmonica, that its energy and personality become unstoppable and can be felt throughout the song, in the spirit of the vocal and the way singer and musicians work together. You may also notice this spirit and energy spilling over into the next performance, "Senor," which has a very different feel and tempo yet can be felt as a continuation of the same very awake vocal and musical presence. Dylan's wonderful delivery of "bogged down in a magnetic field" and of almost every phrase in "Senor" seems rooted in the sensitivity of the "Honey I want you" choruses and the breathless candor of the verse lines ("there's nothing she doesn't see ...") in the preceding number. And then "Senor" climaxes in a remarkable spaghetti western marching band ending that somehow seems responsible for the surprising musical (and vocal) freshness of the version of "Clean-Cut Kid" that follows. This could even be the night Benmont mentions when this usually routine rock number "sounded just like Muddy Waters" (it isn't; Benmont's quote is from '86). It's as though the band, and their leader/conductor, have suddenly found something in this song that wasn't there before – or was always there, waiting to be found. And in turn the reinvention of "Clean-Cut Kid" and the happy experience of performing it this way seem to contribute to the delicacy and exquisite beauty of the musical intro to the next Dortmund performance, a truly memorable "Shelter from the Storm." After a beginning like that, no wonder Dylan sings his heart out.

The very beginning of the Dortmund concert is a strummed acoustic guitar, bass notes, piano notes, oooohh-oooohhs from the Queens and then the first verse of "Knockin' on Heaven's Door" sung with so much presence and power you can feel yourself in the skin of the dying sheriff and might be surprised at the joy you and he feel as all the instruments and the singers join in on "knock, knock, knockin' on heaven's door ..." You might even find yourself thinking that the "just like so many times before" line (added to live versions for at least the past two years) must be an acknowledgment and celebration of the endless round of birth and death. Deep stuff for the start of a show, and a promise of great things to come, a promise which is certainly kept this night.

So Bob Dylan as set-list writer (probably muttering to himself, "the last shall be first ...") decided to open this show with the song that had ended every concert he performed in 1986. And then he closed the concert with "Forever Young," his opener three shows earlier. This will be a characteristic of the autumn '87 tour. Eight different songs will have the honor of being both a show-closer *and* a show-opener on this tour, even songs you wouldn't ordinarily expect to find in either position. "Joey" was the final encore in Stuttgart, Sept. 29, and then Dylan opened with "Joey" the next night in Munich. Because he recognizes the power, in his chosen art form, of beginnings and endings, he's determined to liberate himself, and his audience and his band, from any assumptions they might have about the way things are supposed to be. Or he wants to see what will happen if he tries it. He was leaning toward this when he opened and closed his 1974 shows with the same song – "Most Likely You Go Your Way (and I'll Go Mine)."

Dortmund '87 is rich in memorable endings. "Senor," "In the Garden," "Forever Young," "I'll Remember You" and "Dead Man, Dead Man" all feature unusual and impressive endings.

Listening to the tape, you can almost see Dylan waving his hands to conduct the grand finale of "Garden" (which he once described as "actually a classical piece"). After a riveting vocal performance that is equal to, though quite distinct from, the Modena version, he returns after what could have been the closing instrumental passage and sings the first line of the song very deliberately, twice, Queens echoing him the second time, and then the music the band is playing slowly rises to the crescendo it seems to have been building toward throughout the performance, while the Queens' voices swell and soar in a classical-meets-Gospel moment that is only all the more wonderful for being sandwiched between "Highway 61 Revisited" and "Tangled Up in Blue." The ending of "Forever Young," the very end of the Dortmund concert, sounds like a Rodgers and Hammerstein finale as Dylan, framed by the Queens' echoing voices, shouts the words "forever young!" five times over the band's concluding flourish. The ending of "I'll Remember You" is not structurally different from what Dylan and the Heartbreakers had been doing with the song for a while, but what is impressive is how the music in this final instruments-only verse manages to rise to the unusual heights of expressiveness and passion Dylan achieved with his singing of the other three verses of the song in this Dortmund version, so that you see pictures as you listen to the closing instrumental passage as you would if you were hearing storytelling lyrics sung with a lot of presence. Not a dramatic grand finale, but an extremely satisfying ending to a great performance nonetheless.

In that interview conducted after the Jerusalem show, the subject of compact discs came up, and Dylan said, "I don't particularly think they sound a whole lot better than a record. Personally, I don't believe in separation of sound, anyway. I like to hear it all blended together." "The Phil Spector approach," the interviewer added. "Well, the live approach," Dylan clarified. This gives us some insight into what Bob Dylan wanted to hear as a bandleader, live-music-maker, in September 1987. Another clue comes when he's talking about Levon and the Hawks (his backing musicians in 1966) and Mr. Stone asks, "What were some of the most memorable shows you guys did together?" Dylan answers, "Oh, man, I don't know. Just about every single one. Every night was like goin' for broke, like the end of the world."

Dortmund '87 is definitely like goin' for broke, particularly the

"Shelter from the Storm"/"I'll Remember You"/"Frankie Lee and Judas Priest"/"Highway 61 Revisited"/"In the Garden" segment. It isn't like the end of the world, this wasn't that kind of tour; but getting to hear Bob Dylan sing "Frankie Lee and Judas Priest" and "Shelter from the Storm" as though this might be his last chance ever and he doesn't want to waste it, is certainly a memorable experience. Indeed, if you have a bad attitude about the fall '87 shows because you saw a couple and didn't like Dylan's idiosyncratic hairpiece ("You had to feel sorry for Bob Dylan when he came onstage at Wembley with what looked like a raccoon living in his hair!" – Patrick Humphries in *Oh No! Not Another Bob Dylan Book*) and the fact that he never spoke to the audience between songs, you could probably get over that by listening to Dortmund's "Shelter" and Dortmund's "Highway 61" back to back with selections from *Live 1966* and finding that they stand up well to both the beauty of '66 acoustic set stuff and the excitement of '66 electric set performances. True, as the tour went on, you couldn't expect such transcendence every night or even every other night, but neither was it ever true, as Humphries wrote in his book, that the songs "all sounded the same" or that "Dylan's delivery was now sloppy to the point of incoherence." Don't be distracted by the raccoon and other offenses to your preconceptions, friends. Just get a copy of Dortmund '87, and listen to the sound of this singer (and harmonica player) and these musicians all blended together, and listen to this man's voice as he sings and shouts, "he soon lost all control" and "I offered up my innocence and got repaid with scorn." It's the beginning (and therefore the ending, or summation) of the Never Ending Tour, and even apart from historical significance, it's a moment of extraordinary contact between performers and listeners that can be repeated forever as long as the recordings survive and as long as we have ears to hear. And we know, from listening to *Dylan & the Dead*, that this wasn't arrived at easily. But it was well worth the struggle. Indeed, the personal struggle leading up to it may be the source of the power of the many high points of this first segment of Bob Dylan's autumn 1987 European tour with Tom Petty & the Heartbreakers.

5.

In the 1997 *Newsweek* cover story ("Dylan Lives"), after Dylan told the reporter that ten years earlier he'd "kind of reached the end of the line" and "couldn't do his old songs" onstage, he spoke of a very specific (and dramatic) turning point. According to the interviewer, David Gates:

> Then, in October 1987, playing Locarno, Switzerland, with Tom Petty's band and the female singers he now says he used to hide behind, Dylan had his breakthrough. It was an outdoor show – he remembers the fog and the wind – and as he stepped to the mike, a line came into his head. "It's almost like I heard it as a voice. It wasn't like it was even me thinking it. *I'm determined to stand, whether God will deliver me or not.* And all of a sudden everything just exploded. It exploded *every* which way. And I noticed that all the people out there – I was used to them looking at the girl singers, they were good-looking girls, you know? And like I say, I had them up there so I wouldn't feel so bad. But when that happened, nobody was looking at the girls anymore. They were looking at the main mike. After that is when I sort of knew: I've got to go out and play

these songs. That's just what I must do." He's been at it ever since.

Locarno, October 5, was the 21st show of the fall '87 tour. Of course, you can't hear everything exploding on the tape, any more than you can hear the voice in Dylan's head saying, "I'm determined to stand, whether God will deliver me or not." But the first encore certainly seems like a reference to and restatement of that crucial moment: "Trust yourself ... look not for answers where no answers can be found ... You've got to trust yourself!"

Why did everything explode? Because the man had an awakening, one that had been in process, had been coming, for a long time. Because it was the end of doubt, the end of the ambivalence the singer had been wrestling with all year. It was – in terms of Bob Dylan's relationship with the world, with his audiences, the public – the death or end of Billy Parker. The arrival of a man who finally knows, beyond any doubt or second-guessing, what his purpose is: "I've got to go out and play these songs. That's just what I must do."

"He's been at it ever since," indeed! "You're either a player or you're not a player. It didn't really occur to me until we did those shows with the Grateful Dead." Those shows were the turning point ... but the memorable moment of awakening came a few months later, on a stage set up in a market square in a small town on the shores of a lake in the Italian-speaking part of Switzerland. "It poured and poured with rain, but it was a beautiful show indeed," reported John Bauldie of the Dylan magazine *The Telegraph*.

"It wasn't like it was even me thinking it." Okay, but surely "whether God will deliver me or not" is not a line that would have come up from the subconscious of, or otherwise come into the head of, a person who hadn't ever wished or prayed for God to deliver him.

What does the line mean? Well, the beauty of these words that Bob Dylan heard in his head in Locarno is that they are as resonant and open to interpretation as any Dylan lyric. So they mean whatever the listener hears them as meaning when he or she encounters them. But if we do attempt to shovel this glimpse into the ditch of what "God will deliver me" means, it certainly makes sense for us to look into Bob Dylan's favorite collection of sacred writings, the Bible. The Lord's Prayer (Matthew 6:13) asks God to "deliver us from evil." *The Interpreter's Dictionary of the Bible* (a four-volume encyclopedia published in Nashville, Tennessee in 1962) has an entry under "Deliverer, The" which says: "The principle theme of the Bible is God's deliverance of mankind from the power of sin, death, and Satan through his action in Jesus Christ; and this mighty deliverance is foreshadowed in the history of God's people Israel by his deliverance of them from such disasters as Egyptian bondage or Babylonian exile. But the English words 'deliver' and 'deliverance' are not very frequent in our English versions of the Bible, the idea of deliverance being more usually expressed by other words, particularly 'salvation,' 'redemption,' and their cognates."

To me, the words Dylan heard sound like a response to recurrent episodes of anxiety ("he goes into an all-too-convincing imitation of panic"). What made this moment onstage a breakthrough was presumably the unconditional decision and determination to stand. In context, this seems to me to mean not only to stand on stage and perform, but to brace himself against his own anxiety, as if standing in the surf and allowing a large wave to go by. And because the first thing he noticed after everything exploded was "all the people out there" looking at him rather than at the girls "he now says he used to hide behind," I tend to think the breakthrough had to do with his perception of, and therefore relationship with, his live audiences. So it is noteworthy that one of the more powerful performances on the Locarno tape is "Seeing the Real You at Last" ("I'm still trying to get used to seeing the real you at last!").

Among the recordings of the fall '87 shows, Locarno can be considered a fairly typical example of what these shows were like. The second and third songs are "Like a Rolling Stone" and "Maggie's Farm," as was the case at nine of these 30 shows (six other shows featured the same songs in first and second position; so this brief sequence is characteristic of the tour, having been featured at half the shows, starting in Göteborg, Sweden on September 25). Dylan played fourteen songs at Locarno, also quite normal for the tour. No song was played at most of these shows ("Rolling Stone" and "Maggie's" come closest, at 23 appearances each). But Locarno does offer quite a few of the most "typical" fall '87 choices: "Dead Man, Dead Man" (played at 17 of these shows), "Rainy Day Women" (played at 16 shows, but only an opener, as it was at Locarno, at two other shows), "Shot of Love" (played at 14 shows),

"Ballad of a Thin Man" (13 fall '87 shows), "Simple Twist of Fate" (12 shows), "Seeing the Real You at Last" (12 shows), "Watching the River Flow" (11 shows), "Tomorrow Is a Long Time" (11 shows), "I'll Be Your Baby Tonight" (eight shows), and "Blowin' in the Wind" (nine shows, but only a closer, as it was at Locarno, at two other shows). To be a typical fall '87 show, Locarno also had to include a relative rarity or two, and it did: "The Ballad of Frankie Lee and Judas Priest" (played at only four fall '87 shows) and "Trust Yourself" (played three times on this tour). Also, as at almost all of these shows, Roger McGuinn of the Byrds came onstage and joined Dylan and the band on guitar for the encore songs. (McGuinn opened the Temples in Flames shows with a solo set. He would be joined partway through by Petty and the Heartbreakers, who would then play an opening set of their own. When Dylan included "Chimes of Freedom" in his segment of the show – as he did ten times, but not in Locarno – McGuinn would sing it with him.)

To be considered a fairly representative example of the autumn 1987 Dylan/Heartbreakers shows, Locarno would have to have included a show-stopping performance of Dylan singing "Tomorrow Is a Long Time" without the band, backed only by Tench on piano and Campbell on guitar – and it did, a particularly fine example of the species. This impressive moment of good theater and excellent music was a feature of the fall '87 tour starting with the Göteborg show on September 25. Dylan and Campbell and Tench performed "Tomorrow" together at the next two shows; then they replaced "Tomorrow" with a three-man "Don't Think Twice, It's All Right" for three shows. Thereafter they played one or the other in this fashion for the rest of the tour, except for seven concerts that either included both of these songs performed this way, or one of the two with an alternate companion: "The Lonesome Death of Hattie Carroll" or "To Ramona."

Although each of these Dylan/Campbell/Tench showcases is rewarding, "Tomorrow Is a Long Time" is, time and again, the most dramatic and memorable, a performance that characterizes the fall 1987 concerts for anyone who attended one of the eleven "Tomorrow" shows. On this tour, and on the summer tour with the Grateful Dead, Bob Dylan did not include a solo acoustic set or song as he had in 1986 and 1984 and 1981, and on most of his tours since he stopped playing solo acoustic concerts in 1965. These stripped-down three-man performances (no rhythm section, no backup singers) take the place of those solo acoustic interludes, as though Dylan is pleased to have found a way to make an equivalent aesthetic statement without just "giving the audience what they want" (though of course he does provide concertgoers with a similar thrill when he plays a long harmonica solo at the beginning of various fall '87 songs). Yes, Dylan does want to please audiences, but his first commitment as an artist and performer is to maintain an aesthetic space around himself in which he feels free of the pressure of anyone else's expectations. "There's but so many people an I just cant please them all," as he said in a handwritten prologue to his 1973 book *Writings and Drawings*. For me, these three-player "Tomorrow Is a Long Time" performances not only evoke the 21-year-old artist (and lover) who wrote and first sang this song in 1962, but also conjure images of Bob Dylan on his 1978 big-band tour singing "Tangled Up in Blue" accompanied only by keyboards and saxophone, trying on the stage identity of crooner, happily exploring the plasticity of his song and of his persona and chosen art form. At moments – definitely including the Locarno "Tomorrow" and the song's debut in this form at Göteborg – these 1987 "Tomorrow"'s seem more romantic and (in the best sense of the word) nostalgic and dramatic than if Dylan were singing the song alone, accompanying himself on harmonica and acoustic guitar. These 1987 performances speak of the present, including Bob Dylan's relationship with his audience and with the endless highway and crooked trail of the performing artist, at the same time that they speak of the singer's and the listeners' pasts and dreamed-of futures.

"Whether God will deliver me or not!" It is interesting to speculate about what these words meant to Bob Dylan when they came into his head. Are they an expression of doubt as to God's existence or of His love? Or are they rather a reflection of the speaker's private doubts about his own worthiness of deliverance (still drinkin', dopin' and wenching, still proud after all these years)? In either case, Bob Dylan on October 5, 1987 was determined to stand against his own anxiety/stage fright, and as a result we have the Never Ending Tour of the subsequent sixteen-plus years, a truly extraordinary body of work.*

---

* Some months after I wrote this chapter, I received a letter commenting on it from one of this book's Patrons, Jeff Taylor, of Rochester (MN) Community College, who wrote, "When I first read the line in the 1997 *Newsweek* story, I immediately thought of the

"It wasn't like it was even me thinking it." This is closely related to what Dylan has told us about how his remarkable songs have come to and through him. In 1968, in an interview with John Cohen for *Sing Out!* magazine, Dylan said:

> Then of course, there are times you just pick up an instrument – something will come, like a tune or some kind of wild line will just come into your head and you'll develop that ... Whatever it brings out in the voice, you'll write those words down. And they might not mean anything to you at all, and you just go on, and that will be what happens.

In the same interview, when asked about the germ that started him writing "I Pity the Poor Immigrant," Dylan said, "the first line." Cohen asked, "What experience might have triggered that? Like you kicked the cat, who ran away, who said 'Ouch!' which reminded you of an immigrant." Dylan answered, "To tell you the truth, I have no idea how it comes into my mind." Like it wasn't like it was even him thinking it ...

Book of Daniel. During the Babylonian exile, King Nebuchadnezzar of Babylon issued a decree requiring every person to 'fall down and worship the golden image' and those who refused would be 'cast into a burning fiery furnace' (Daniel 3:10-11). Daniel goes on to tell of the faith and defiance of Shadrach, Meshach, and Abednego (often described as Hebrew children, they were actually Hebrew or Jewish men – government officials, in fact). The king asks the three men, 'Now if you are ready ... to fall down and worship the image which I have made, well and good; but if you do not worship, you shall immediately be cast into a burning fiery furnace; and who is the god that will deliver you out of my hands?' (3:15) They respond: 'If it be so, our God whom we serve is able to deliver us from the burning fiery furnace; and he will deliver us out of your hand, O king. But if not, be it known to you, O king, that we will not serve your gods or worship the golden image which you have set up' (3:17–18). This infuriated the king, he threw them into the furnace, and they were preserved by angelic protection and a kingly change-of-mind. The Jewish men in Daniel's account refused to 'fall down' and worship. The opposite of falling down is to remain standing. Dylan, a Jewish convert to Christianity ('messianic Jew'), was 'determined to stand.' The Jewish men were determined to remain standing in the presence of the Babylonian idol even though they would be cast into the fire. They knew that God could save them from the fire, but even if he chose not to rescue them, they were determined to do the right thing. Their statement that the 'God whom we serve is able to deliver us ... and he will ... But if not ...' is very similar to Dylan's 'whether God will deliver me or not.' As you know, Dylan has been steeped in the apocalyptic portions of the Bible since his conversion in 1978. Daniel ranks right beside Revelation as a primary source of End-Times information. A Dylan thought (or Divine message) echoing the Book of Daniel, with its emphasis on defying the evils of Babylon while living in its midst, makes perfect sense." It does indeed. Thank you, Professor Taylor!

The Locarno tape is fairly typical of the Temples in Flames Tour in terms of quality as well as song selection. Indeed, it illustrates why there is not much agreement amongst tape collectors or commentators or people who attended the shows as to how good or bad this tour and the performances on these tapes were and are. Most of the Locarno performances, like the majority of the fall '87 performances, I would describe as "good but not great." That means it pretty much depends on the mood of the person listening whether Locarno's "I'll Be Your Baby Tonight," for example, is rated as disappointing, not very well played or sung (the tempo, probably set by Dylan on rhythm guitar, seems plodding, and the band performance uninspired), or as delightful, full of little pleasures (the long band/harmonica intro, Dylan's improvised lyrics – "Close the blinds, close the gate; what about tonight? It will have to wait" – and the way he says "mockingbird"). Is this another wonderful "Simple Twist of Fate" or does it feel like he's just going through the motions? Not a great "Like a Rolling Stone," certainly, but quite gratifying if you open yourself to it or if it catches you at the right moment.

The audience members' and commentators' appraisals of these shows were, as usual, influenced by what they were expecting (based on their images of Dylan from the 1960s or on their experiences of his previous European tours in the 1980s) and by their responses to his physical appearance and his presentation of himself. "He was in fine form," John Lindley wrote in late 1987 about the seven shows in England that ended the '87 tour: "Contrary to what most newspaper reviews reported – and the writers, almost without exception, seemed to equate Dylan's not speaking [to the audience between songs] with his not caring, either about his performance or about his audience – the shows were high energy. No sooner did the lights dim at the close of one song than Dylan was attacking the next." It's ironic that the performer's keen interest in the relationship between the elements of his creation (his attention to the segues between songs – another example of Dylan being influenced by watching the Grateful Dead in concert) made him appear uncommitted to many observers, because his interest in good segues, along with his struggle with stage fright, influenced him to omit the customary flattery of talking to the audience between songs. I've already quoted Patrick Humphries' comments on the tour, in which "what looked like a raccoon living in his hair" seems related to Humphries' judgment that Dylan's delivery of his songs "was now sloppy to the point of incoherence." All of us listeners and observers are of course influenced in our experiences and sincere appraisals by many such factors. Andrew Muir wrote in a letter to me in October 2000 about his recollections of Dylan's 1987 shows: "There was an attractive fragility to his yearning vocals but a frightening look about him. I was too worried about his appearance to fully like the shows. I thought I'd never see him again."

It is appropriate, in the light of Dylan's 1997 account of his epiphany in Switzerland ("I noticed that all the people out there were looking at the main mike"), that the one unequivocally great performance on the Locarno tape is a sort of collaboration between Dylan and the "people out there." Dylan's delivery of the first few lines of "Tomorrow Is a Long Time" ("If today was not an endless highway/If tonight was not a crooked trail/If tomorrow wasn't such a long time/Lonesome would mean nothing to you at all ...") is particularly moving, as though this were an invocation, a prayer, that has great meaning to him at this moment. Near the end of the first verse the audience begins clapping slowly, providing a rhythmic pulse that becomes very audible with the start of the next verse, so loud and so full of feeling that Dylan's singing and Campbell's and Tench's playing seem to rest on and lean into that pulse throughout the rest of the performance. It's a magical effect. Performers of spontaneous music usually acknowledge the part played by a live audience in the collective act of creation; but seldom is the audience's part so audible and measurable. "There's beauty in the silver, singin' river," Dylan sings, and on the recording of this performance it's as though we can hear that river, certain that just this once the singer *can* see his reflection in the waters and hear the echo of his footsteps (and maybe hear his true love's heart a-softly pounding). Magical. There is ensemble audience clapping during other fall '87 performances of this song, but never with quite the sonic and musical result heard on the Locarno recording. This, we might surmise, is why Dylan must go out and play these songs: because something new can happen every time he does.

"You might be a professor, in some rock school," Dylan seems to sing at the start of "Gotta Serve Somebody" in Munich, September 30, 1987. Of course I thought he was talking to me ("But Bob, I couldn't be, I'm a college dropout like yourself"), until I listened more carefully and decided that what he's saying is: "You might be a confessor in some rotten school …" Munich, the 17th concert of the Temples in Flames Tour, four shows before Locarno, is and was a particularly good performance, a very rewarding show. All students in my school will please listen to it a few times and then write essays on "Who Bob Dylan thought he was in autumn 1987 (on a stage in the capital of Bavaria)."

I like the sequence that opens this concert: "Joey," "Seeing the Real You at Last," "Like a Rolling Stone." If Bob Dylan thought of his set lists as messages to his audience, what inference might he want us to make from his choice of these three songs from his huge songbook, in this sequence, as the beginning of his show tonight?

1: "Joey." It's a story, the rise and fall of a gangster (told as though he were a hero to the teller). 2: "Seeing the Real You at Last." It's a love song, built around a phrase as universally applicable in love situations as "don't think twice, it's all right." Neither of these songs were hits. They're fairly obscure songs from little-known albums (*Desire, Empire Burlesque*), whereas the third selection is a signature song, Bob Dylan's biggest hit and a song that somehow seems to be about the times that he symbolizes in the eyes of many (in Munich and in Tel Aviv and London and Philadelphia): "Like a Rolling Stone." "How does it *feel?*" "I'm still trying to get used to seeing the real you at last." "Joey … Joey … King of the streets, child of clay …"

Maybe he wants to tell us (and himself) that there's more to him than just the songs he's famous for? The first two songs date from 1976 and 1985, respectively; so maybe the message is that he respects and values all his work equally, regardless of era of origin. "Joey," he told us in the *Song Talk* interview, is Homeric. That resonates nicely with this image from "Seeing the Real You at Last": "I sailed through the storm, strapped to the mast." It's Odysseus! – still trying to get used to how it feels to be on his own, like a complete unknown, with no direction home. Interesting that the fourth song in this Munich sequence seems to be about Penelope: " 'Come in', she said, 'I'll give you shelter from the storm.' "

In 1978 Dylan said of the Egyptian Umm Kulthum, "She was one of my favorite singers of all time, and I don't understand a word she sings!" This suggests that he recognizes and appreciates that the human voice is an expressive instrument that can speak powerfully to a receptive listener even when the words being sung have no more verbal or narrative meanings for him or her than the sounds made by other musical instruments … that singing is an art that exists beyond words, even though words are its primary medium. Virginia Danielson in her book *The Voice of Egypt*, about Umm Kulthum and Arabic song, writes that in Arabic culture, "a good singer is a *mutrib*, one who creates an environment of *tarab* with his or her performance. Excellent rendition generates *tarab*, literally 'enchantment,' the sense of having been deeply moved by the music."

Bob Dylan is a *mutrib*, and the first four songs of Munich '87 are a good example of his ability to generate *tarab*. Mysteriously, he achieves this with a rendition that is far from excellent by many perfectly reasonable standards. He swallows words and phrases repeatedly throughout this performance of "Joey," which would be disconcerting if one were hearing the song for the first time and attempting to understand and follow the story. What excuse is there for a storyteller to mumble like that? Only the excuse that he's singing freely and spontaneously and sincerely, and the slurred words are part of that, a peculiar by-product of his concentration on creating *tarab*. When the result is a genuinely enchanting performance, what purpose would it serve to complain about his apparent sloppiness or lack of excellence? Instead we might as well admit that it's normal for masters to break the rules and leave observers baffled at how they manage to get such great results anyway (not all the time, but often enough to make us doubt our pictures of how things ought to work).

When my students hand in their papers about the Munich tape (or CD) and who Bob Dylan thought he was at this moment in his performing life, I expect (if my students are sincere) a wide range of opinions regarding the worthiness of Dylan's intentions and achievement in this concert performance. There is much to complain about in this show (and in most of the shows from this tour) and much more to be delighted by, to fall in love with – and it's all happening at the same time. Students pointing to the flaws in Dylan's singing of "Joey" (and during the rest of the show), and students pointing to examples of Dylan's vocal artistry and charm, might well find themselves pointing to the same verses and phrases, the same musical moments. Why these contradictory assessments? I'm glad you asked. I'm not sure I can give a clear answer, but I'm certain the answer is at the heart of Bob Dylan's accomplishments as a performing artist and who this man thought he was that night in the Olymphiahalle in München.

I think he thought of himself as an artist – not in any pretentious sense, but in the sense that Bob Dylan probably thinks of a horn-player or drummer in a Mississippi juke joint blues band as an artist, a person keenly aware of the work of creative expression that he is participating in, and his responsibilities to the music and to the band as a whole (and to the audience in the sense that the music and the audience are not separable in the musician's mind). And I believe he found delight in his work, when he wrote this set list and while he and the Heartbreakers and the Queens were on stage playing and singing … and that this delight is what fuels the charm that radiates from him and from the music he and his troupe are making. He's having a great time, and as a result so are we.

Charm, in my opinion, is at the heart of Dylan's accomplishments as an artist, and I specifically include his "greatest hits," the 1965 ensemble performances of "Like a Rolling Stone" and "Maggie's Farm" and "Subterranean Homesick Blues" and solo performances of "Mr. Tambourine Man" and "It's Alright, Ma." We the public had never heard songs or music or even poems like these before, but we were struck by them immediately, by the sounds of the words and of the music and of the performances. He charmed us, enchanted us. It's his gift.

"Clarity of articulation" is one of the many virtues frequently mentioned by Arab music-lovers praising Umm Kulthum's singing. And indeed Dylan's clarity of articulation was one of the characteristics that made me praise his Modena performance of "Joey" so highly. Then how can I be so charmed by this Munich version full of slurred phrases and swallowed words? I think the answer lies in the feeling of the musical performance as a whole, which is not impeded by the singer's strange diction – in fact, it is even possible that the sound of Dylan's voice, as in the case of the 1965 ensemble performances just mentioned, is the vehicle by which his particular mood and intent, unique to this performance and this moment, are communicated to the other musicians and singers so that the end result is a collective creation with a spirit all its own … words and instruments and voices and rhythm all working together to share a mysterious and urgent truth. In Modena, Dylan told the story of Joey Gallo like a champion. In Munich, he's using this vehicle to share something different, something that clearly arises from his love of the song and his self-discovery in the process of performing it with his troupe to open this particular night's musical journey.

When I noticed Dylan's radical slurring of the line "Whatever you're gonna do" (it becomes a gentle moan) near the end of Munich's "Seeing the Real You," I realized that one of the reasons he does this is he's trying to make a certain sound with his mouth, his voice, which feels right to him at this moment. Each musical phrase created by the ensemble calls forth what each individual player does next.

On the other hand, the fact that the two most noticeably swallowed phrases early in "Joey" ("of whatever side there was" and "Joey almost hit the roof") occur at the precise same location in terms of song structure and rhythm of vocal performance – second half of the third line of an eight-line verse – strongly suggests that this swallowing or holding back is related to Dylan's intuitive sense of where he is in the metrical cadence and narrative drama of these lines. Here he doesn't seem directed by the sounds he's hearing from the ensemble but by the pulse of the song's structure and language. The logic of his bizarre delivery (which continues in this fashion throughout the concert, lots of slurred vocals and swallowed phrases – the latter sounding as though they've been half-erased from the tape) seems to me reminiscent of the vocal mannerisms of a Shakespearean actor, for whom the felt pulse of the language and of each dramatic scene may take precedence even over his beloved clarity of articulation. "The quality of mercy is not strained! It droppeth as the gentle rain from heaven, mumble mumble ..."

When my hypothetical students get their essays back, they'll find that the professor believes the key to who Dylan thought he was this night in Bavaria is found in the segues between the songs ... if you mention them, as John Lindley did, you get an A-plus. Dylan was trying to create something – an environment of *tarab*, even if he didn't know that Arabic term – and he carefully and probably gleefully rehearsed these segues with the conscious intent of creating a mood and of never losing it once he got it going.

The first of the 12 Munich segues goes like this: Dylan and the Queens sing another stirring, ennobling chorus of "Joey ... Joey ... What makes them want to come and blow you away?" ... thrilling me with the interplay of their voices and the feeling that all of this, each time they sing this chorus together, is an exploration and portrait of what performed music is and can be for Bob Dylan. We

listeners are given the opportunity to meditate on why the singer/
author has changed this chorus line to the present tense at this series
of shows, as though Joey's death were not a historical event, not
something in the past that happened only once. (Maybe he's suggesting that the question is not about the motivations of these
specific killers, but rather about human nature in general: what
makes them/us want to come and blow someone away?) In any
case, we are brought into the present moment ourselves as the last
joint vocalization of "away" is extended by guitars and keyboards
and subtle harmony voices into a wash of sound that feels like a
resolution – except for the seductive and rhythmic blues guitar
notes that are arising out of it, new life beginning ("Seeing the Real
You at Last") even as the song we were focused on is still fading
away.

It's a wonderful musical transition, imbuing us with feelings
of loss for the trance we were just in, simultaneous with feelings of
anticipation about the new one we're being pulled into – so that the
feelings combine and all we know is, he's got us and it's very engaging. "I thought the rain would cool things down, but it looks like it
don't. I'd like to get you to change your mind, but it looks like you
won't." Yeah! "From now on I'll be busy, ain't going nowhere
fast ..." Can you see why Dylan loves to perform these songs (with
these players) so much? They seem to always find new ways to speak
for him and to him about what he's feeling and doing right now.
The spell-weaver is also enchanted. "Ain't going nowhere fast."
Thirty seconds and much charming music later I like the way he
says, "I don't mind a reasonable amount of trouble, trouble always
comes to pass." Twenty seconds further he's singing, "I'm tired of
this bag of tricks," but we know and feel that that isn't true.

Since the words to "Seeing the Real You" are taken from
Bogart films [see *Performing Artist Two*, chapter 16], it's reasonable to
suppose the performer sees it as a Bogart movie (starring himself,
with Lauren Bacall as "you"). "Joey" of course is a gangster film (a
"streets of New York" story); and if we listen to the words and this
Munich performance asking ourselves what made this guy a hero to
these songwriters, I think the answer must be: his style. ("He walked
right into the clubhouse of his lifelong deadly foe ... said, 'Tell 'em
it was Crazy Joe.'" "He pushed the table over to protect his family."
At one point we're even told that "he dressed like Jimmy Cagney.")
And of course Bob Dylan, our projectionist for the evening, doesn't

miss a beat when he conducts his band and audience from "Real You" into "Like a Rolling Stone." Another great segue. Bob and girls sing a final "at last" with an inflection signifying the period at the end of a sentence; the band follows with wrap-up notes which also turn out to be start-up notes as the recognizable melody of "Like a Rolling Stone" tiptoes in, soon joined by purposeful drumbeats. The singer slurs "Onceuponatime" and suddenly it's, "y'dressed so fine, [swallow] bums a dime, in your prime, didn't you?" Melody notes and drumbeats continue the build-up and singer slurs and punctuates: "peoplecall, saybewareDoll, yrboundt'fall, y'thought-theywere all, kiddin'you!" and we're in another world, familiar and very wonderful and clearly connected to the Bogart movie we were swimming in a moment ago.

It's a new kind of "Like a Rolling Stone" – the fall '87 evolution of the song, in its exemplary Munich manifestation. I like the sound of Dylan's voice every time he re-enters from a short instrumental flourish: "You used to laugh about" and "You never turned around" and "Princess on the steeple ..." Every inflection matters, as if we can watch the painter dip his brush in just the right color and splash it on with conviction. It's the sort of performance where short phrases jump forward – "so amused," "to conceal" – either via emphasis or understatement. So it's fun to listen to again and again (as are "Joey" and "Real You" and almost everything else until the encores). And the little delights only serve to emphasize how much it's all one big musical pleasure, every musician and singer and syllable contributing to the overall Cinerama effect.

This "slow rocker" version of "Like a Rolling Stone" ends with suitably understated climactic glory, and after the closing drum flourish, the sustain of the various instruments segues into tentative yet purposeful (and familiar) rhythm guitar notes soon joined by similarly exploratory and familiar harmonica chords, little bursts of harmonica-sound dancing with the piano notes that have walked onstage simultaneously. The harmonica in-breaths and the piano and guitar notes become steadily more expressive, and then the latter provide a platform for the singer, who enters at 1:21: "'Twas in another lifetime, one of toil and blood ..." Dylan sings "Shelter from the Storm" with a lot of feeling tonight. Maybe he needs it, or he thinks that Joey does, or that Bacall or the princess on the steeple do (or he's hoping one of those two might provide it).

The fourth segue is a real surprise. Were you expecting to hear

"Dark Star" tonight? As early as Tel Aviv, there are indications on "Tangled Up in Blue" that Dylan must have said to the Heartbreakers something like, "Can you guys get more of a Grateful Dead sound on this one?" Not that he wanted them to play an arrangement he and the Dead had worked out for this song earlier in the summer, but that Dylan was yearning, after watching and enjoying the Dead's performances before his sets with them, to achieve a sound for himself something like what he heard the Dead doing with their own songs. He didn't achieve that during the Dylan/Dead sets, but the aspiration was still in him as he rehearsed and played with the Heartbreakers, and somehow "Tangled Up in Blue" became the fall '87 song on which the Heartbreakers (or just Mike Campbell at first) tried to find a way to give the boss what he was requesting. I deduce this from the unmistakable "Jerry Garcia guitar notes" that can be heard from Campbell on every fall '87 "Tangled," starting with the Tel Aviv show. I speculate that this could have started as a joke on Campbell's part – "Okay, you want the Dead sound?" So he throws in an adept Garcia imitation here and there in the song, playing high single notes in a scale or mode that produces guitar notes and noodlings that are recognizably the sound of Jerry Garcia. He does it well, and works it into the evolving fall '87 Dylan/Heartbreakers version of the song intelligently and tastefully. If someone played you one of these performances and said it was from the Dylan/Dead tour, you'd very likely believe them (though in fact there isn't any trademark Garcia guitar stuff on the Dylan/Dead performances of "Tangled").

In any case, by Munich "Tangled Up in Blue" had metamorphosed into a number with a sound quite reminiscent in significant ways of the Dead's signature performance song "Dark Star." This is particularly noticeable in the intro. The Heartbreakers don't play the identifiable "Dark Star" intro (and theme) chords, but otherwise they are quite clearly in the same unique musical territory – playing Grateful Dead music, as the Dead almost never managed to with Dylan, except for a few special moments like the aforementioned Eugene "Queen Jane."

By taking special care, as he did at Munich and many fall '87 shows, to ensure that the band would never stop playing between songs, that there would always be a flowing transition from one song to the next, a musical continuity, bandleader Bob Dylan was making an aesthetic statement – one the Grateful Dead made at every show and one which Dylan himself had made before, notably on the 1976 segment of his Rolling Thunder Revue tour (documented on the album *Hard Rain*). This statement is that songs performed live in a concert are not separate entities. For tonight, for this hour and a quarter that we're together, they all become one song – like a novel or a movie containing many characters and stories and themes and settings, all of which are connected by being part of the same sequenced experience, the time you spend reading this novel or watching this movie or listening to this concert.

By paying attention to the beginnings and endings of his songs and to the segues between them in performance, Dylan is in the tradition of many great artists who have playfully experimented with and called attention to the conceptual forms in which their work is perceived and presented. The painter Henri Matisse, for example, liked to make the "mistake" in some of his paintings of a person's head or arm being cut off by the edge of the canvas. Françoise Gilot comments on Matisse's self-portrait *Conversation*, in which the crown of his head is thus cut off: "He clearly meant to say that since his intelligence and reason were all over the canvas, in each part of it equally and in the whole totally, it could not be found in the imitative representation of the upper part of his skull within the picture." Similarly, Dylan the performer uses the edges of the forms he works within to declare his own freedom and to remind observers that aesthetic and emotional truth is not limited by the conventions of perception. In writing and performing set lists, he often wants to convey that the protagonists of his songs might all be the same person and in any given case might or might not be himself ... and that the world portrayed musically and lyrically in a song or concert might be this very place we're in right now and/or the backdrop for one interconnected never-ending story.

" 'Twas in another lifetime ..." is a good beginning for a story-song that follows another that began, "Once upon a time ..." This storytelling motif is continued in the opening lines of the fifth Munich song: "Early one morning the sun was shining, and he was laying in bed ..." Dylan the performer discovered fairly early in his relationship with "Tangled Up in Blue" that this first-person lyric could be changed on the spur of the moment to a third-person narrative and that he could switch persons and pronouns from show to show as a way of further exploring and challenging his and his audiences' relationships with the protagonists of these tales. This night in Munich in a gesture typical of this tour (typical because it is not easy for us to know whether to consider this an expression of artistic freedom or of forgetfulness), he shifts persons in mid-song, so that it goes from "he was laying in bed" and "rain fallin' on his shoes" to "I stopped in for a beer" and "I muttered something underneath my breath." This last line is amusing and revealing, because again in this song, Dylan swallows a number of words, so that in the line "he seen a lot of women" the word "women" is barely audible. No doubt Bob Dylan often does mutter something underneath his breath when accosted by a stranger who asks, "Hey, don't I know you?" After developing a technique like that you might even find yourself using it in performance. In any event, the freewheelin' Bob Dylan, while certainly leaving himself open to charges of sloppiness, sings this song with a lot of presence and panache this evening.

Listening to the Munich "Shelter from the Storm," I found myself very struck by this mind-out-of-time line: "If I could only turn back the clock to when God and her were born ..." "Wow," I muttered underneath my breath, "the two great loves of his life!!" Jesus Christ, of course, and Sara Lowndes. Sara because "Shelter from the Storm" is from *Blood on the Tracks*, a song cycle clearly arising from the songwriter's difficult break-up with the woman he'd been married to for eight years. In that context, I've always heard "Shelter" as a semi-autobiographical tribute to the remarkable woman who came into Dylan's life at a time when he really was burned out from exhaustion and blown out on the trail of youthful stardom. At a moment when "now there's a wall between us," it would be natural to wish oneself back to when she was newly born into your life and there were no walls of miscommunication at all. When Dylan wrote the song, he hadn't yet had the equivalent experience of Jesus coming into his life, so the phrase "when God and her were born" was probably just freewheelin' cleverness, a facile and well-turned phrase that might come to mean much more to him (or me) at a time when the singer was feeling a wall between himself and his other Savior.

The first four songs at Munich '87, from "Born in Red Hook, Brooklyn, in the year of who-knows-when" (the opening lines of "Joey") to "I'll give you shelter from the storm" (the final words of "Shelter," after the "when God and her were born" verse) can be heard as a hero's journey, a hero not encumbered by time and corporeality as we know them. In the next three songs, Dylan and the Heartbreakers take us on another sort of journey – a journey, as was customary on the autumn '87 tour, through a sequence of musical landscapes.

The mind- and heart-opening power of this sequence becomes evident as we experience the fifth Munich segue, in which the lovely modal music of this unique version of "Tangled Up in Blue" gently falls apart Grateful-Dead-style and, as the audience starts to cheer, is abruptly and tenderly replaced by the crisp blues-rock guitar notes and reggae rhythm section intro of Dylan and the Heart-breakers' 1987-style "I and I." This knitting-together-by-segue causes that part of our minds that responds to the pictures and stories evoked by the words of the songs to recognize the first line of "I and I," "Been so long since a strange woman slept in my bed," as a possible continuation of the story-of-my-life-as-a-series-of-man/woman-interactions theme of "Tangled Up in Blue." Clearly and delightfully we're in a whole new musical landscape, but the connectedness between the story-songs is as tangible as the contrast between musical settings and "feel"s is evident and delightful.

Dylan and the Heartbreakers and the Queens sing and play "I and I" with charming spirit and many colorful flourishes, including some fine guitar solos. Listeners may find themselves contemplating the implications of the chorus ("one says to the other" might be about the relationship between me and me, parts of myself) with new insight, as they possibly notice lyrical parallels between the preceding song and this one ("still on the road, headin' for another joint"/ "still pushing myself along the road, the darkest part") ("she opened up a book of poems and handed it to me"/ "took a stranger to teach me to look into justice's beautiful face"). But most of all, it's the contrasting and harmonious musical worlds evoked that make this sequence so magical. And then this opening gambit is trumped emphatically when an elaborate 90-second "I and I" finale (eighteen quick and bouncy repetitions of "sees my face and lives," the last line of the last chorus, followed by another 45 seconds of three slow and dramatically stretched-out SMF&Ls) ends with a closing drum flourish and, as no doubt predetermined by the bandleader, Benmont jumps in *very* quickly to start playing the melody of the next number. A few seconds later the harmonica player jumps in just as quickly to start a piano-hamonica duet that becomes a very graceful and deeply felt instrumental intro to "Forever Young." I haven't mentioned Howie Epstein much, but I believe spontaneous music as good as the ensemble segment of this two-minute intro doesn't happen without gifted and skillful and inspired playing from the bass player, who has the responsibility of connecting melody to rhythm and all of the players to each other. Wonderful music (followed by some really remarkable singing). Again, a whole new soundscape, enriched by and enriching the two that came before. In this fine setting, the blessings pronounced by the singer ("May God bless and keep you all-you" … an awkward but appealing mumble or mental error; "May your wishes all come true") can be heard as addressed to the audience or to the "she" of "Tangled Up in Blue" or to the "other" of "I and I," and do a lot to resolve and smooth off the life-story-situations depicted in those two previous songs.

A montage is "the combining of pictorial elements from different sources in a single composition." So here's an interesting tidbit of information about the montage Bob Dylan, performing artist and set-list writer, created on 9/30/87 in Munich: two of the fourteen songs he performed, "Tangled" and "Shelter," are from the same album, *Blood on the Tracks*; but the other twelve songs included in this show are taken from twelve separate Bob Dylan albums released between 1963 and 1985. Fourteen songs, thirteen albums. What a palette this artist is working from! And how skillfully, with the help of his segues and his versatile band and his love of performing, he ties all these disparate elements together into a unified whole. A concert. And, accidentally or not, a concert tape.

Dylan and the Heartbreakers' 1987 segues are often clever surprises, like the juxtapositions of words and images in his 1964–66 songs. So after this epic performance of "Forever Young" (possibly the best "FY" of the season) comes to a suitably elegant end, we hear the Chuck Berry lick from "You Can't Catch Me" (made famous by Keith Richards on the Rolling Stones' 1964 cover version) tentatively rising from a nondescript rhythm section shuffle sound, and thus we are tastefully drawn into a transition song, that all-purpose shuffle and not-quite-greatest-hit "Maggie's Farm," here serving as a chance for Dylan to take a break from all this intense creativity and just operate on cruise control for a few minutes. He enjoys it (and thus so do we), and the band shows off their ability to make particularly delicious Chuck Berry shuffle music (not like anything else they've been playing all night). It's an excellent (and seemingly very deliberate, carefully chosen) bridge between the lovely "Tangled"-"Shelter"-"Forever" sequence and the extraordinary third segment of tonight's montage: "Gotta Serve Somebody"/"Don't Think Twice, It's All Right"/"I Dreamed I Saw St. Augustine"/"Dead Man, Dead Man."

So we're back to, "You might be a confessor, in some rotten school ..." Bob Dylan is speaking in tongues. Like Umm Kulthum for him, he's one of my favorite singers of all time, even when I can't understand a word he sings. The second line of the song is something like: "Might be some churts money underneath your tool." And then, "Might go to church ... You might not go. Might be on top/talking fast [both phrases seemingly sung at the same moment], you might be talking slow, but you're gonna serve somebody ..." He and the Queens sing the standard chorus line – "It might be the Devil, it might be the Lord" – but not with any sense that this is an important part of the song's message. Bob Dylan is improvising freely, like Lester Young playing horn with a hip combo. The second verse comes out: "Might be rich, might be poor. Might be hungry, might have in store. Might be walking on the sidewalk, riding in a car, standing at your station, standing at your bar." The singer's voice is expressive, and very responsive to the music behind and around him. The third verse could be a keeper if this were a songwriting session: "Might be hot, might be cold. Might be shot, might be untold. Might be low, might be high. Might be saying hello, might be saying goodbye." And then, after an especially wonderful lead guitar solo, my favorite improvised verse, the fourth and last: "Might be regarded, livin' in France. Might be jumpin' crazy, might have a dance. Might be from century, might be unborn. Might be nahtoll, or a Christmas morn. But you'll serve somebody ..." The next two seconds manage to be both a swallowed vocal and an example of inspired scat singing, both at once. I don't think any of us, including me, can really claim to know who Bob Dylan thinks he is tonight, but there can be little question that he's performing freely and putting his heart into it. It's almost as if (during this "Gotta Serve Somebody") we're getting a chance to watch the same mind that ad-libbed "Gates of Eden" and "Desolation Row" 22 years earlier stretching its muscles, free-associating, unwinding, like in a monitored dream-session in some futuristic laboratory.

The segue from "Maggie's Farm" was very nice, and the segue from "Gotta Serve Somebody" into "Don't Think Twice" is spectacularly good. In both cases, it's like we're listening to Prokofiev's

"Peter and the Wolf," and hearing each character's theme before he or she walks onstage. Grand entrances. Shock of recognition. General happiness.

Shock of recognition partly because, as is so often the case at Dylan concerts, we can't be certain from the opening notes (or even, sometimes, the opening words) what song this is, what beloved old favorite or unexpected rarity we're about to hear. What is communicated in those first bluesy notes of "Gotta Serve Somebody" arising from the nicely executed conclusion of "Maggie" is that something portentous is coming, something worthy of this attractive and (playfully) dramatic build-up. And then the shock is not that it's "Serve Somebody" or even that the lyrics are so unfamiliar and outrageous. The shock is that some part of ourself is being spoken to, and for, so unexpectedly and so unmistakably. As if we'd been waiting all our lives for this particular character (Peter, or the Hunter, or the Wolf) to walk onstage. We recognize him. It's me! A dear part of me I'd forgotten about or lost contact with.

So the delight we feel as we hear those very pretty piano notes that arise soon after the last chord of "Serve Somebody" at Munich is not that this melody is my old favorite, "Don't Think Twice." Rather it's something like the delight we presumably all felt the first time (or one of the first times) we heard "Don't Think Twice" on the radio or on a record, and felt something evoked by those very pretty guitar notes and then the sound of the singer's voice entering. We didn't know the song or its "message" yet, but we felt the stirrings of a shock of recognition ("it's *me*; this is for me, whatever it is") that kept growing as we heard more of the performance and once we got a chance to hear it again. It's very pretty music Benmont Tench and Mike Campbell and Bob Dylan are making at the start of this song, and it awakens something in the listener quite apart from recognition that they're playing one of my favorite Dylan songs. What we recognize, with shock and pleasure, is that part of ourselves that is being awakened by this work of art; and right away, if our minds are demanding an explanation of all these powerful feelings that are rushing in, the singer tells us: "Well, it ain't no use to sit and wonder why, babe, iffen you don't know by now ..." My God, his voice sounds good! Possibly the best singing he's done all autumn.

It's February 2001 as I'm writing this. (In my class, students are asked to put their names on their papers, so we know whose views are being expressed, since no two observers see or hear the same thing in the same event or performance ... and the date of the writing, so we can locate the moment in this person's trajectory when he or she saw and heard things this way.) So I have the advantage, in my Dylan contemplations, of Clinton Heylin's just-published revised & expanded biography *Bob Dylan: Behind the Shades, Take Two.* In his preface, Heylin quotes Dylan associate Cesar Diaz (tour guitar technician from 1988 to 1993): "I think the greatest masterpiece he has ever pulled off is the fact that he can make people believe that part of him is involved in the writing of those songs. To me, each song is a play, a script, and he'll be that guy from the song for that moment, but then he'll change back to Bob. People make the mistake to think that he's the guy [who's speaking in a song's lyrics, when he performs it]. But the guy that wrote that song only existed for that moment. It took me a while to realize that. But he actually convinces you that yes, it is me who is talking to you and I'm being sincere about it ... he is able to convince you that it is him at that point when he is singing the song, when in reality he's just singing a song and just playing."

What Diaz is describing is the sort of artistry that we properly expect of that other kind of performer, a stage actor. What he calls attention to here, based on his experience of years of watching Dylan and his audiences from the side of the stage, is that most of the people who attend the shows have come to see this old trouper in a long-running drama called "The Bob Dylan Story." And, understandably, they forget that this is a play, fiction, theater – much of the excitement is that that's the real Bob Dylan up there, the one who slew all those dragons when he was a real-life hero back in the 1960s. So they don't see him as an actor, in the sense that contemporaries of Edith Piaf and Umm Kulthum and Billie Holiday naturally felt and wanted to feel that the broken hearts and frustrating love relationships they were evoking in their perform-ances were their own and as immediate and urgent to them as they were to their listeners at the moment of hearing them.

In 1963 Dylan said of "Don't Think Twice": "It's a hard song to sing. I can sing it sometimes, but I ain't that good yet. I don't carry myself yet the way that Big Joe Williams, Woody Guthrie, Leadbelly and Lightnin' Hopkins have carried themselves. I hope to be able to someday, but they're older people. I sometimes am able to do it, but it happens, when it happens, unconsciously."

Twenty-four years later, Dylan is an older person and a more experienced singer. How good is he now, how does he carry himself? (And who does he think he is? Some of you haven't handed in your papers yet.) I think anyone who listens attentively to all ten 1987 "trio format" performances of "Don't Think Twice" will probably agree that the last sentence of Dylan's quote still applies. Sometimes (but not always) he's able to carry himself with an authority and humanity quite worthy of this little script he wrote when he was 21. This is particularly true on September 30th in Munich. When he sings, "I once loved a woman, a child I'm told," he's very believable indeed. As an actor should be. It may be he even convinces himself that it's him who's talking, because when he sings the next line it comes out "I'd give her my heart" – in the present tense, instead of the colloquial past of "I give her my heart" in the original version.

If you give yourself the pleasure of listening again to the original recorded performance of this song, on Dylan's second album, while looking at the lyrics as published in his book *Lyrics*, you'll probably notice that the printed version is not the same as the "original" recorded version. You might also notice that the colloquial language of the recorded version ("We never done too much talkin' anyway"; "Iffen you don't know by now"; "It'll never do somehow") has the effect of making the song more evidently a fiction, a play, an invented character speaking to another invented entity in an imaginary (though very reality-based) situation. (So the songwriter is certainly expressing feelings he's felt in his relationship with his girlfriend Suze, but he's replaced her and their New York City setting with a woman who lives in the country and has a rooster, and himself with a ramblin' man who says things like, "we never done too much talkin' …")

So (ahem) the shock of recognition I feel when I hear the unique melody played and evoked by the opening piano notes of this Munich '87 "Don't Think Twice" and from every moment of Dylan's singing here, and when I listen to the remarkable interplay of organ and melodic guitar and rhythm guitar in the between-verse breaks, is the shock of being deeply touched by a musical creation that seems to understand me and illuminate my inner life in ways I didn't think were possible. And since I can't help being convinced that Bob Dylan is the guy talking in this performance, I also have the illusion of feeling very close to this troubadour on his way from the Billy Parker movie and the Dylan/Dead tour to the Traveling Wilburys and the "official" start of the Never Ending Tour next spring and to his rendezvous with a voice in his head in Locarno five days from now, when he sings, "I'm walking down that long, lonesome road, babe; Where I'm bound, I can't tell ..." Gooseflesh. Great music. Great performed art.

The eleventh song at Munich in 1987 is a good example of how the same moment-of-performance can be a delight to one intelligent listener (or "student") and a real disappointment to another. "I Dreamed I Saw St. Augustine" is a powerful, evocative song, and one Dylan rarely attempts in concert. So how exciting to hear its melody notes and opening words arising right after the end of "Don't Think Twice"! And how distressing that Dylan sings it so poorly and with such lack of conviction after his sublime vocal on the previous number. At moments when I'm under the spell of my excitement at hearing this song and of my keen interest in what new messages its powerful lyrics and images might unfold for the singer and for me at this moment in the performer and dreamer's spiritual life, I can find it charming and intriguing and rewarding. At other moments I'm distressed and surprised that this vocal can be or seem so flat and lifeless in contrast to the technically pleasing and wonderfully alive vocal that precedes it.

I said earlier that I believe the fact that different listeners (or, as in this case, even the same listener) may often have very different opinions regarding the quality of a particular Dylan performance is at the heart of his accomplishments as a performing artist. What I'm pointing towards is that, in my opinion, Dylan's power as a creator of performed art is the result of his ability to be true to his instincts and thus his inner self at the moment of performance, for better or worse. This allows what he creates (and this is also true of his songwriting, which can be thought of as a kind of performance) to break free of the limits his conscious mind (like all of our conscious minds) would impose if it had the opportunity.

In turn we listeners sometimes listen intuitively, and sometimes quite consciously and deliberately. For better or worse, in both cases. The power of the *mutrib* is to influence his listeners to hear a song with their hearts and instincts, not with their reasoning minds. Umm Kulthum or Billie Holiday or Bob Dylan at their best cast a spell on us. This can happen via a recording. And just as what the singer/musician expresses depends on who he (or she) is and what he's feeling at that moment, so what we hear, and the extent to which we are able to let go of our conscious judging minds in the process, depends on who we are and where we are in our own trajectories of feelings at the moment of listening. So contradictory assessments of the quality (and even the "meaning") of a particular performance are inherent in the nature of the art form, of the experience of listening and connecting or not connecting. As Bob Dylan once said, "At times I think there are no words but these to tell what's true, and there are no truths outside the Gates of Eden." At times, I also think so. "Sometime, not all the time," as Dylan also said (in "Clothes Line Saga," 1967).

There is one 1987 performance (out of the five he did) of "I Dreamed I Saw St. Augustine" that does delight me consistently – from October 11th in Birmingham, England. Inevitably, I have a theory as to what happened, for better and worse, in the case of these two performances of the song. Not surprisingly, this theory has to do with the voice Dylan says he heard in his head in Locarno, five days after Munich and six days before the 10/11 Birmingham show.

To me, the Locarno incident Dylan described to *Newsweek* in 1997 was a spiritual event, in the sense that confronting one's doubts and fears always is. And certainly a dream in which one sees a long-dead saint preaching as though he were alive now, and then feels one's own guilt or shame related to one's reactions to this vision, is also a spiritual event. A visitation. Ambiguous, like any dream, and like most spiritual events.

Interestingly, Augustine also heard voices. "So was I speaking [to the Lord] and weeping in the most bitter contrition of my heart, when, lo! I heard from a neighboring house a voice, as of boy or girl, I know not, chanting, and oft repeating, 'Take up and read; Take up and read.' Instantly my countenance altered, I began to think most intently whether children were wont in any kind of play to sing such words: nor could I remember ever to have heard the like. So checking the torrent of my tears, I arose; interpreting it to be no other than a command from God to open the book, and read the first chapter I should find." (from *The Confessions of Saint Augustine*, Book VIII, "The Struggle of Conversion")

Dylan may not have known this about Augustine when he wrote the song, as he also did not know that Augustine was not "put out to death" (he died of a fever at the age of 76, in Africa in the year 430). It certainly seems likely that as with "I Pity the Poor Immigrant," the title and first line of "I Dreamed I Saw St. Augustine" came into the author's mind unbidden, and the rest of the lyrics followed quickly. Guided by intuition, and incorporating images and bits of information (or misinformation) from the storehouse of his magpie mind. To me, the Augustine in Dylan's song is in the image of an Old Testament (Jewish, not Catholic) prophet, or possibly of John the Baptist.

My theory, for what it's worth, is that when he sang "St. Augustine" in Munich (and in East Berlin September 17 and in Milan October 4), Dylan unexpectedly, and probably unconsciously, found himself resentful that he hadn't in fact had such a dream or other message from the Higher Power, now when he particularly needed one. The result is that he sings in a voice choked (restrained) by ambivalence, and his efforts to conjure up his own fiery breath are quite unsuccessful. There are however some pleasant eccentricities in the performance which the part of me that wants to be delighted by it can seize on when that's my inclination: the wistful sound he makes with his breath after "coat of solid gold" and the striking way he phrases the guilty word "amongst." One can also find pleasure in the mental error that has him start the last verse, "I dreamed I was Augustine, alive with fiery breath ..." And of course I tend to regard the excellence of the 10/11 performance of "St. Augustine" as probably partly due to a change in the singer's personal spiritual weather report since Locarno. He had the dream or visitation he was longing for, heard the voice, and so it's no surprise he can now sing the song joyfully and with such conviction and power.

The last segue of the regular part of the Munich concert (you can't play nonstop into the encores, form requires that you act like the concert is over until the audience calls you back with their applause) is particularly gratifying. The transition itself – Campbell playing the "St. Augustine" melody very colorfully and lovingly over a rhythm section that is clearly arriving at the end of something and then a very brief jam extending that ending into the stirring introductory notes of the next song, which turns out to be "Dead Man, Dead Man" – makes a statement, one that feels very fulfilling, as though everything that's been played and sung all evening has necessarily brought us here, to this musical moment.

It's quite a moment ... band cooking happily and bandleader/

rhythm guitarist/singer dancing a fandango alongside them, celebrating the successful climax of tonight's creation, this complex and
very expressive montage of Bob Dylan thoughts and music and
visions. The last verse of "Dead Man, Dead Man" is entirely
improvised:

> "Wake up! in pajama tops,"

he sings in an enchanting whisper. I can't catch any of the words of
the next line, though I feel something from them anyway. And then:

> "The ghetto that you mumble mumble, I'll bail you out of
>   jail ...
> Every time you tell me that you're trying to survive,
> Ooh I can't stand it, I can't stand it,
> Pretending that you're alive!"

This last line might be addressed to himself, as the whole song
was when he wrote it. Bert Cartwright in his pamphlet *The Bible in
the Lyrics of Bob Dylan* reports that, "In some of his concerts Dylan
explained that he composed this song one time upon looking at
himself in the mirror." Cartwright also informs us that "Dead Man,
Dead Man" is inspired by Ephesians 5:14: "Awake thou that
sleepest, and arise from the dead, and Christ shall give thee light."
But whether Dylan is addressing himself or not, it's illustrative of
the richness of the performing artist's montaging that "pretending
that you're alive" and "dead man, dead man, when will you arise?"
tonight follow a song in which he sings, "I dreamed I saw St. Augustine, alive as you and me" and "'Arise! Arise!' he cried so loud ..."
St. Augustine is certainly a dead man, as is Joey Gallo, and if the
dead man of this song ("cobwebs in your mind, dust upon your
eyes") is Bob Dylan looking at himself in the mirror, then every song
in this montage might be about a dead man. "Every time you tell
me that you're trying to survive, ooh I can't stand it ..." Delicious
humor, if I'm not entirely off the mark about what this simultaneously accidental and very conscious artist is up to here.

One last note about the splendid segues between songs in
Dylan and the Heartbreakers' 1987 Munich concert/montage: a
friend of mine who worked for the Grateful Dead around this time
tells me that in writing their set lists and thus determining the
sequence in which songs would be performed, the Dead gave consideration to the keys in which songs were played, because the little

transitional jams they liked to play between songs would be easier and freer and sounded better when the two songs were in the same or a similar key. Dylan clearly noticed this during the summer 1987 tour, and evidently was stimulated to start thinking of his own concerts as expressive compositions in which his songs would be the movements. A new symphony each night! Let's try this sequence and see what happens ...

This led him to some bold experiments, like starting the Brussels October 8 concert with "Desolation Row." Dylan's sense of how a concert may be shaped by the selection of an opening song and closing song, how these choices could be an opportunity to make an indirect but aesthetically effective statement, even extended to the tour as a whole. This was revealed when he sang "Go Down, Moses," the last song at the first Temples in Flames show in Tel Aviv, for the second time ever at the end of the last concert of the tour, in London on October 17. Some kind of mysterious full circle. "Tell old Pharoah, let my people go." Dylan had literally been in Egypt-land the day before that first show. And now it was time to say goodbye to the Queens of Rhythm and the Heartbreakers and the Temples in Flames audiences and go back to that other world so far away from the bizarre familiarity of being on tour, knowing that your purpose in life is to do the next show in the next town. There was plenty to look back on at the end of the tour, not only Dylan's first shows in Israel but his first-ever performance in Eastern Europe (Sept. 17 in East Berlin, in front of 100,000 people). And the penultimate song of the tour, "Rainy Day Women" in London just before "Go Down, Moses" and right after "Chimes of Freedom," turned out to be a glimpse of the future, when ex-Beatle George Harrison came onstage to sing and play with Bob Dylan and Tom Petty, soon to be his bandmates in a new recording unit called the Traveling Wilburys. "They'll stone you when you're 29!" George ad-libbed, though in fact he was then 44, two years younger than the future Lucky Wilbury.

Dylan in the mid-Eighties. *(Curt Gunther/LFI)*

Dylan just before *Hearts Of Fire*, on stage with Tom Petty, Philadelphia, July 20, 1986. *(John Hume)*

On the Tom Petty tour. *(Ross Barnett/LFI)*

Wembley, 1987. *(John Hume)*

On stage with George Harrison during the
1988 Rock and Roll Hall of Fame Ceremony,
New York, Jan 20. *(Neal Preston/Corbis)*

Portland, Maine, July 3, 1988.
(John Hume)

RDS Arena, Dublin, June 3, 1989.
(John Hume)

Dylan with Roger McGuinn and David Crosby at the Roy Orbison Tribute, Los Angeles Concert, February 26, 1990 *(Neal Preston/Corbis)*

With G.E.Smith on acoustic guitar, 1990. *(Ilpo Musto/LFI)*

On stage in 1990. *(Ilpo Musto/LFI)*

Belfast, February 6, 1991.
(John Hume)

On stage at the 1994 Woodstock
Festival, August 14. *(Jon Olson/Corbis)*

Dylan with Bruce Springsteen at the Rock and Roll Hall of Fame Museum Concert,
Cleveland, September 2, 1995. *(Nick Elgar/LFI)*

Dylan on stage with Rolling Stone Ronnie Wood at the Prince's Trust Concert in London's Hyde Park, June 29, 1996. *(LFI)*

III. Bound to Ride That Open Highway

November 1987 – December 1988

6.

Bob Dylan was determined to stand, indeed. And to prove it to himself, only five weeks after the last show of his fall 1987 tour with the Heartbreakers and the Queens of Rhythm (and seven weeks after that line came into his head in Locarno), he was auditioning a new band for his next tour. The big one. The one that he would describe in a 1989 interview as "The Never Ending Tour." The one that is still ongoing as I write these words (it's June 22, 2001; he starts a seven-day stand in Norway, Sweden and Denmark in two nights, and I have tickets to see him in Arizona and southern California in August). Since he told himself in October 1987 that he was "determined to stand," this performing artist has played 1,322 shows. The tour not only has not ended, but during these fourteen years it has never paused for longer than seven months.

So among the "tapes" (recordings) in the collections and catalogues of the "serious" Dylan fans (aficionados) is one dated November 22, 1987 and labeled "Audition/Rehearsal with G. E. Smith and Others." It is not a particularly rewarding listen, although, inevitably, it has its unique and intriguing and even entertaining moments.

But in order to stay on the tack of what this book is really

117

about, I need to step out of time and chronology for a moment and advance to June 13, 1988 in Park City, Utah, and a performance of "Gates of Eden" by Bob Dylan, G. E. Smith, Kenny Aaronson and Christopher Parker that – similar to "Visions of Madonna" on July 26, 1999 and "Like a Rolling Stone" (second run-through) on June 15, 1965 – cuts to the heart of who Bob Dylan is and what his songs mean (that riddle he'd had such a hard time grasping a year before) and what he lives and performs for.

It was the fifth show of the Never Ending Tour and the third time Dylan and his '88 band played this song onstage. The first time (at the opening show of the N.E.T., in Concord, California, June 7, 1988) was in fact the first time Dylan had ever performed "Gates of Eden" onstage in an electric version (i.e. with an amplified band rather than solo acoustic). It was also the first time he'd performed the song publicly since 1978.

I'm going to go on for a while about this one performance (and for good reason), and first I'd like to share with you what the six-thousand-year-old Chinese oracle the *I Ching* just told me about Bob Dylan's 6/13/88 performance of "Gates of Eden":

> A crane calling in the shade.
> Its young answers it.
> I have a good goblet.
> I will share it with you.

This refers to the involuntary influence of a man's inner being upon persons of kindred spirit. The crane need not show itself on a high hill. It may be quite hidden when it sounds its call; yet its young will hear its note, will recognize it and give answer. Where there is a joyous mood, there a comrade will appear to share a glass of wine.

This is the echo awakened in men through spiritual attraction. Whenever a feeling is voiced with truth and frankness, whenever a deed is the clear expression of sentiment, a mysterious and far-reaching influence is exerted. . . . The root of all influence lies in one's own inner being; given true and vigorous expression in word and deed, its effect is great. The effect is but the reflection of something that emanates from one's own heart. Any deliberate intention of an effect would only destroy the possibility of producing it.

> – Richard Wilhelm/Cary Baynes translation of the *I Ching*,
> 1967 edition, page 237, "Inner Truth"

Spiritual attraction. Bob Dylan's reputation rests, in my way of looking at it, not only on his songwriting but on individual perform-ances of songs like "A Hard Rain's A-Gonna Fall" and "Desolation Row" and "Gates of Eden" and "It's Alright, Ma" and "Like a Rolling Stone," live performances in a recording studio that were released on records and that delivered the "meaning"s of these songs with such conviction and impact (such "true and vigorous expression") that multitudes of listeners then and since have recog-nized and celebrated these works as the uncanny, brilliant reflection of something that emanates from their own hearts as well as his. The genius of the man, I argue, is not so much located in his writing as in his performing – at certain remarkable and memorable moments – of those writings. I believe that neither Jerry Garcia nor anyone else could have "grasped the meaning" of Dylan's songs nor "understood the spirit of them" without having been exposed to recordings of Dylan performing them at moments when the singer/author was able to be completely present within and at one with these musical and verbal creations.

Such a moment is captured in the June 13, 1988 performance of "Gates of Eden." Believe it or not, Dylan actually seems to sing it with more authority, as much or more conviction and clarity of understanding, than he put into the original album version of the song. The lamppost that stands with folded arms at the start of verse two has never stood with such dignity before. This is a function both of Dylan's vocal and of the instrumental passage/band perform-ance that leads up to this image. Indeed, the beauty and power of this "Gates" are as much a product of the band's playing as of Dylan's singing, which is not surprising, because at moments like this the two are inseparable.

Evidence that the mysterious and far-reaching influence of a performance like this is not the result of deliberate intention can be found by listening to the two 1988 performances of "Gates of Eden" that precede this Park City version and the two that closely follow it. All are good, and were certainly rewarding experiences for the people at those shows, but all pale in comparison to what Dylan and his band happen to be doing with this song at this particular moment. So it's not so much a matter of a good arrangement worked out in rehearsals. As the *I Ching* said, it's a matter of a feeling being "voiced with truth and frankness." I was fascinated, when previously unheard takes of "Like a Rolling Stone" were released on the 1995 CD-ROM *Highway 61 Interactive*, by the fact that, to my ears, the take of "Rolling Stone" performed a few minutes after the officially released version is lacking most of the power of that great performance. Yeah, they (including the singer; in fact, singer and musicians were inseparable) got it that once; but that didn't guarantee that they could get there again. How fortunate we are, I tell myself, that the "right" take did make it onto the record and the radio and into our lives. Bob Dylan, as much as any artist of his era, has exerted a mysterious and far-reaching influence. But he has not produced this effect through deliberate intention. Maybe that's why so many of us collect and study his "accidental art" as well as his official releases.

The Park City '88 "Gates of Eden" is six minutes long – 20 seconds longer than the original album version, although three of the original nine verses are omitted. It starts like a great rock and roll single, with a series of assertive, expressive drum hits, tastefully and effectively reinforced by loud bass guitar/lead guitar grunts. "Something's coming!!" is the unmistakable message, and right away the singer justifies this build-up by singing the opening verse with a vigor and spirit appropriate to Henry V working up his troops before the Battle of Agincourt. Right away his diction and phrasing are irresistible, with the result that the cowboy angel riding four-legged forest clouds becomes quite visible. Dylan's remarkable presence in the vocal throughout the song dramatically underlines its powerful visual imagery and the skillful/playful language and theatricality of its lyrics. This is most striking in the "savage soldier" verse, when we see (and identify with) the savage soul (djer) as he sticks his head in sand like an ostrich – and because we also see the shoeless hunter, we realize he's probably "gone deaf" *because of* the soldier's complaining. The cinematic movement in this verse's lines becomes evident and very pleasing. We see that the shoeless hunter "still remains" beside the soldier despite the complaining, and the next words, "upon the beach" suddenly give us a new, more specific picture of where this action is occurring. This is immediately trumped when the phrase "upon the beach" is modified by the dependent clause "where hound dogs bay at ships with tattooed sails, heading for the Gates of Eden." It's as though I never really saw this movie until I heard this performance. Dylan's phrasing in "heading for" sounds very meaningful, and the band's rhythmic break right after "Eden" underlines this quite convincingly, and suddenly I'm amazed at how cleverly the presence of the cowboy angel astride clouds in the first verse directed our listening minds to an image of Eden as Heaven, mythical place in the sky where angels are found. And then how wonderful when the camera keeps pulling back during the "savage" verse, and we see that the soldier and hunter are walking on a beach, and then we see these ominous, thrilling ships with tattooed sails moving across the set in the distance, and with the next line we are not surprised to hear that they're "heading for the Gates of Eden." If this causes us to picture those Gates as just ahead of the ships, stage right somewhere, we get a semiconscious adrenaline rush as we experience Dylan, who often violates and challenges the listeners' sense of time, challenging our sense of space, as suddenly Heaven or Eden is felt as being on the same plane as this human world with its beach and soldier-hunter conversation. Wow ... as in Greek and Roman myths, Gods and mortals interact, coexist on the same plane, while the narrator keeps reminding us that the important distinction is not high and low but horizontal: inside or outside the Gates of Eden. Psychedelic indeed.

And what is really remarkable is that Bob Dylan the singer is so totally at one with this song this night, as though he were reliving its moment of creation, as though it were a vision that came to him irrepressibly as he wrote it, and this night onstage, thanks particularly to the stimulus of Christopher Parker's inspired drumming, he is evidently seeing and smelling and hearing that vision, reliving it, and sharing it with us. The Park City '88 "Gates of Eden" is the *sound* of "I've got to go out and play these songs – that's just what I must do!" And it is the precise opposite of "I can't remember what it means... is it just a bunch of surrealistic nonsense?" If any Bob Dylan song were to be impenetrable to its author decades later, "Gates" seems a likely candidate; but here it is, seemingly more lucid than ever before. How did he get there? It has to do with his relationship with his band ... and it's not something that happens in rehearsals. It's something that only happens for this kind of artist onstage, in front of an audience. And that, I insist, is the reason for his never-ending touring. He lives his life onstage because he lives his life primarily for moments like this, and onstage, "nowhere" or just anywhere in the world, unplanned and unexpected, with a band, is where they happen. "Sometimes I think there are no words but these to tell what's true!" See why a committed artist would have to keep touring, keep working with a band? Listen to the texture of Bob Dylan's voice as he sings "It doesn't matter inside the Gates of Eden" in Park City – you have the opportunity to encounter a truth (share a lover's dream) not available anywhere else.

At Park City, Dylan sings the first two verses of the original "Gates of Eden" followed by the "motorcycle black madonna" verse, which in turn is followed by the "savage soldier" verse. Then the song is completed with the "kingdoms of experience" verse ("what's real and what is not") and the usual final verse ("At dawn my lover comes to me …"). There is a slight lyric change in the first verse (the cowboy angel rides "with his candle burning in the sun" instead of "lit into the sun"), and an even subtler change at the end of the second verse: "No sound at all ever comes from the Gates of Eden" instead of "No sound ever comes from …"

These line changes are the same in all of the first five 1988 performances of "Gates of Eden," so they may have been pre-planned. In Berkeley, June 10th, Dylan sang the same six verses of the song, but not in the same sequence. "Savage soldier" is third, "kingdoms of experience" fourth, and "motorcycle black madonna" fifth. In Concord, he only sang five verses, dropping "savage soldier" (probably accidentally; we hear the band vamping for a while before he starts singing the last verse, suggesting he knows he forgot something and he's thinking about what to do). The next "Gates" after Park City, in East Troy, Wisconsin, June 18, features seven verses; "motorcyle" is dropped and "With a time-rusted compass blade" and "The foreign sun, it squints upon" are added, perhaps spontaneously. A week later, in Holmdel, New Jersey, "motorcycle" is back, "time-rusted compass" is retained, but "foreign sun" and "savage soldier" are dropped.

Dylan made an important and revealing statement about his aesthetic as a performing artist sometime in 1988 when he wrote a 500-word essay about Jimi Hendrix for use in a traveling exhibition celebrating Hendrix's work. In the course of this piece, he said, "my songs were not written with the idea in mind that anyone else would sing them, they were written for me to play live & that is the sort of end of it." After discussing how easy it is to "get into" and sing a Chuck Berry song or a Beatles song, he said:

> my songs are different & i don't expect others to make attempts to sing them because you have to get somewhat inside & behind them & it's hard enough for me to do it

sometimes & then obviously you have to be in the right frame of mind. but even then there would be a vague value to it because nobody breathes like me so they couldn't be expected to portray the meaning of a certain phrase in the correct way without bumping into other phrases & altering the mood, changing the understanding & just giving up so that they then become only verses strung together for no apparent reason, patter for a performer to kill time, take up space, giving a heartless rendition of what was it to begin with. jimi knew my songs were not like that. he sang them exactly the way they were intended to be sung & he played them the same way. he played them the way i would have done them if i was him. never thought too much about it at the time but now that years have gone by, i see that the message must have been his message thru & thru. not that i could ever articulate the message that well myself, but in hearing jimi cover it, i realize he mustve felt it pretty deeply inside & out & that somewhere back there his soul & my soul were on the same desert.

Bob Dylan "obviously" was in the right frame of mind while singing "Gates of Eden" in Utah 6/13/88, and because of the way he breathes during this performance I find myself with a new and satisfying (to me) idea of the meaning of a certain phrase which had puzzled me until now. The phrase as printed in Dylan's book *Lyrics* is "it shadows metal badge" but in this wonderfully articulated version I realize he's actually saying (in reference to the lamppost), *its* shadow's metal badge. Going back to the 1965 album version, I find the word has always been "its" in spite of what *Lyrics* says. This opens the door to me hearing the possibility and likelihood of an apostrophe before the final "s" in "shadows" ... and this and the particular breath of this performance allow me to recognize that the subject of the next phrase, "all in all can only fall with a crashing but meaningless blow" must be the metal badge of the lamppost's shadow. I also find myself easily hearing "holes" (in "to curbs 'neath holes where babies wail") as a clever substitution for "homes" – the sort of place from which one might occasionally hear babies wailing. Now, with the phrases not bumping into each other inappopriately, it's easy for me to hear the poet/performer as describing an old-fashioned urban lamppost with protrusions ("iron claws") attaching it to street curbs, casting shadows that may look ominous ("metal badge") to young persons in nearby homes, finally symbolizing a modern city-animus like Ginsberg's Moloch that "all in all [sooner or later] can only fall with a crashing but meaningless blow." See how helpful the right breathing (singer getting inside & behind the songs) can be?

Dylan spoke of how Hendrix played his songs as well as how he sang them, and said, "he played them the way I would have done them," acknowledging that the message of the songs depends on how the music is played, as well as on the singing. The Park City "Gates" is an example of Dylan's 1988 band at its best – very tuned in to him (and thus to his "message") and very expressive collectively.

But why are they less tuned in (and the resultant performances of the song less thrilling) three days earlier and five days later? This is where the *I Ching*'s commentary is helpful. When it speaks of "the involuntary influence of a man's inner being upon persons of kindred spirit" and "the echo awakened in men through spiritual attraction," it casts light directly upon the mystery of Bob Dylan or John Coltrane and their accompanists and the works of art they've created together, always in moments of live performance. "A crane calling in the shade. Its young answers it." Everything depends on the musicians' and vocalist/bandleader's responses to each other. The part the drummer plays before and betweeen verses is similar in each of these "Gates" performances, but its execution this day is exceptional, and the singer's response to Parker's "clear expression of sentiment" and the drummer's and guitarists' responses to the "feeling voiced with truth and frankness" in the resultant vocal all work together to create a great effect, a "true and vigorous expression in word and deed" of these persons' and this song's message. A work of art. The triumph of this 1988 tour (originally called "Interstate '88") and of the Never Ending Tour that it evolved into is the creation of a creative environment (a "joyous mood") in which moments like this can and do happen. Not every night, of course. But often enough to greatly enrich and bring fulfill-ment to these performing artists and their [present and future] listeners.

Earlier in this series of books, in a discussion of *Blood on the Tracks*, I wrote, "I need to say again that Dylan performs a song not only with his voice but also through the musicians around him; the brilliant success of these recordings is proof again that the power of his presence as a performer can transform whoever is playing with him into a perfect extension of his instincts and his unconscious will. Dylan short-circuits any intellectual approach to music ['deliberate intention of an effect'] and conducts his bands from his gut, his solar plexus, invisibly, intuitively, trusting the music to find its way into existence if they (he and the band) will just lean into it enough, press through their own limits and surrender to the sound that's trying to happen." The *I Ching* explains that this occasional transformation of one's comrades into a perfect extension of one's aesthetic instincts and non-verbalized will is an influence that has its root in one's inner being, and describes it as "the reflection of something that emanates from one's own heart." "No words but these to tell what's true. Bam! bam! bam!"

Parker and the band's glorious intro to "Gates of Eden" on June 13, 1988 is played in some exotic time signature like 12/8, and when Dylan comes in with the start of the first verse ("War and peace, the truth just twists") the band shifts into 3/4 (waltz) time. It's a fabulous transition, and Dylan's extraordinary vocal performance seems an expression of his delight at the intuitive and bizarre rightness of the sound the four of them are creating. At the end of the verse, the word "Eden" is the cue for a brief return of the exotic time signature and an expressive drum-led instrumental break, which again transitions gracefully and thrillingly into the second verse and back to waltz time. This charming dance is repeated, with variations, every time Dylan says "Eden" and every time he returns to start another verse/episode. The variations are the increasing expressiveness of G. E. Smith's lead guitar playing as the breaks between verses get longer, climaxing in a particularly wonderful instrumental break between verses five and six (after Dylan sings, "what's real and what is not doesn't matter inside the Gates of Eden"). One can't help feeling that Smith is reading Dylan's mind at this moment, painting the pictures Dylan sees by skillfully and mysteriously producing the sounds Dylan hears in the back of his mind; it's a drum/guitar duet (punctuated and held together by very sparse and tasteful bass notes from Kenny Aaronson), similar to and full of the excitement of the drum/vocals duet the entire performance seems to be. The closing instrumental break after the last verse is as satisfying and fulfilling as the opening instrumental passage was provocative and inviting. Dylan's presence in the song is extraordinary throughout every verse of this unforgettable vocal performance, but is just as palpable in the instrumental breaks, when we hear him singing wordlessly through Smith and Parker and Aaronson (and his own barely audible rhythm guitar playing).

This is it. This is the message Dylan assembled this band and embarked on this tour to deliver. And as with the "Like a Rolling Stone" sessions, I'm baffled that they could perform the song so magnificently and not come close to this level the next times they played and sang it. But that's because I forget it's not a product of deliberate intention. It's more like a moment of grace, a lot of different factors working together to create the circumstances whereby a feeling (a "message") can be collectively voiced with truth and frankness and genuine joy.

Okay, time travelers. Let's go back to November 22, 1987, New York City, the G. E. Smith & friends audition/rehearsal tape. It's interesting to hear Bob Dylan improvising new lyrics to "You're a Big Girl Now." It's interesting to hear him sing Woody Guthrie's version of the traditional song that inspired Dylan's "Isis," "Trail of the Buffalo," with an accordion and a band. It's interesting to hear him sing an unknown song called "Carrying My Cross" and another that might be called "Much Too Easy." It's interesting to hear Bruce Springsteen's 1984 hit "Dancing in the Dark" played at a Bob Dylan rehearsal. And it's interesting to hear Dylan sing "All I Really Want to Do" for the first time since his rehearsals with the Grateful Dead in spring 1987 and for the second time since 1978 and for the last time for at least the next 14 years. But –

But he's not all that present in "Big Girl," and the improvised "dummy" lyrics don't quite jell and can't quite be heard. But he doesn't sing "Dancing in the Dark" (G.E. does, way in the background, trying to teach Bob the words at the latter's request, I think). Neither are "Carrying My Cross" nor "Much Too Easy" particularly striking performances (but the former song is a bit haunting, and I'd be glad to hear him try it again someday). "Trail of the Buffalo" is experimental, as could be expected at a rehearsal, but intriguing. "Dead Man" and "I'll Be Your Baby Tonight" and "Joey," songs Dylan had sung a lot with the Heartbreakers in recent months, are attractive, likeable versions. "Heart of Mine" is quite lively and the vocal is spirited ... possibly in response to the playing of one of the musicians Smith has invited to the session, guitarist Danny Kortchmar, who knows the song well, having played on the 1981 album version. There are moments in "Folsom Prison Blues" when the texture of Dylan's voice is quite engaging. Altogether, not a great tape but a good listen, enjoyable for its unique qualities and for Dylan's evident enthusiasm for performing – which comes through on one of the takes of "Leopard-Skin Pill-Box Hat" and on "Dead Man, Dead Man" – even at this odd between-bands moment in a rehearsal hall in New York City. You can feel his readiness to get back on stage. He's not only determined to stand, but raring to go.

7.

On January 20, 1988, Bob Dylan was inducted into the Rock and Roll Hall of Fame. After the ceremony, he participated in the obligatory jam session, singing lead on "Like a Rolling Stone" and sharing lead vocals with George Harrison on "All Along the Watchtower." An audiotape survives. But a much better souvenir of the performing artist's seven months off between the last Temples in Flames show in October 1987 and the first Never Ending Tour show in June 1988 is a promotional videotape from May '88 of Dylan and Harrison and another rock and roll legend, Roy Orbison, with Tom Petty and another contemporary rock star, Jeff Lynne, performing "Handle with Care," a song they all wrote and recorded together in Bob Dylan's garage in Malibu, California, April 1988, under the name the Traveling Wilburys.

It happened like this: George Harrison had just had two hit singles (including "Got My Mind Set on You," his first #1 record in America as a solo artist since "Give Me Love" in 1973) with songs from his *Cloud Nine* album, produced by Jeff Lynne of the '60s U.K. rock group the Move and '70s hitmakers Electric Light Orchestra. The record company was asking him for an extra song to include on the German release of the second single, "When We Was Fab."

> I had to do this song [Harrison told the BBC in late 1988] because Warners needed a third song to put on a 12-inch single. I didn't have another song, I didn't have an extended version, so I just said to Jeff – I was in Los Angeles and he was also in L.A., producing a Roy Orbison album ... we were having dinner one night, and I said, "I'm just going to have to write a song tomorrow and just do it." I was just kind of think-ing of [how John Lennon wrote and recorded] "Instant Karma." And I said, "Where can we get a studio?" And he said, "Well, maybe Bob, 'cause he's got this little studio in his garage." We phoned up Bob; he said, "Sure, come on over." My guitar was at Tom Petty's house for some reason, and I had to go round and get it; Tom said, "Oh, I was wondering what I was going to do tomorrow!" And Roy Orbison said, "Give us a call tomorrow if you're going to do anything; I'd love to come along." And that was it!
>
> When we got to Dylan's house the next morning, we started to write this tune – just the tune. And then as we were doing that, I thought, "Let's just stick a bit in here for Roy; Roy can sing some of it." We got the tune and put it down, all the rhythm guitars with just a little click track, and then we needed the words. And I was walking around with a bit of paper and a pencil and I was looking around in Dylan's garage, looking at lists of his song titles, trying to think of a title. And I was saying, "Come on! Where's the words?" think-ing that all these people are great songwriters – give us some lyrics, then! And there was Bob saying, "Well, what's it about? What's it called?" And I'm trying to come up with some titles, and I look behind his garage door and there was this big card-board box that said "Handle with Care" on it. I said, "It's called 'Handle with Care'!" And he said, "Oh, that's good. I like that!" And that was it. Once we'd got the title it just went off. I thought, "Been beat up and battered around," and then the lyrics just went flying around. I mean, we could have had 29 verses to that tune. It was brilliant.
>
> I thought, it's a little bit daft having all these people sit around and then I end up singing it again, y'know ... just get them to sing it! And when they were actually doing the vocals, at one point I just said to Jeff, "Hey Jeff, this is it! The Traveling Wilburys! [Lynne: "When we were recording *Cloud*

Nine we joked about this sort of fictitious group that we might have one day, called the Trembling Wilburys – just like you do in the studio at four o'clock in the morning"] I mean, it was like magic! It just happened. You could never have planned it. If you'd have tried to phone everybody up, you would have got all these record companies and managers and it would have been impossible. But it was so spontaneous; we were doing it before we realized.

Lynne: "So this song was delivered for the C-side of a German 12-inch, but when they heard it, they said, 'Oh, you can't put it on that – it's such a waste of a good track.' And then we discussed it and George spoke to Roy and Bob and everybody, and said, 'Let's do nine more of the buggers!'"

I liked the song and the way it had turned out with all these people on it so much [Harrison told the BBC], I just carried it around in my pocket for ages, thinking, "Well, what can I do with this thing?" And the only thing I could think of was to do another nine – to make an album. And as it happened they all said yeah – they all loved the idea. It was just a question of timing, 'cause Bob had to go on the road at the end of May, and this is like early April when we did "Handle with Care." He said, "Well, I got a bit of time at the beginning of May," so we just said, "OK, we'll meet on" – I think it was the 7th of May or something. We had nine or ten days that we knew we could get Bob for, and everybody else was relatively free, so we just said, "Let's do it!" We said, "We'll write a tune a day and do it that way." And that's what happened. It was very exciting and nerve-wracking.

When the album, *Traveling Wilburys, Volume One*, was recorded in May 1988, three of the Wilburys were already members of the Rock and Roll Hall of Fame, Roy, Bob and George. Orbison: "We used to tease Tom and Jeff about when they were going to get in the Rock and Roll Hall of Fame. I was first, I think; George and Bob came in the same year. But they'll get there for sure, Jeff and Tom – so we did that with affection." Orbison also recalled, in an interview in London Nov. 29, 1988, six weeks after the album was released: "I hadn't been in a group before, and I guess Bob hadn't either, although he'd traveled with Tom. But Jeff had ELO and George had the Beatles and Tom Petty had the Heartbreakers. But even that didn't bother anything. Bob was just a prince. I still think of

him as the greatest poet of our age. I always wanted to write with
Bob, and we got the chance on the Wilburys. And we'll write again.
We both live in Malibu, and before too long I'm gonna ring him up
and go over and we'll do some work, because he's really terrific ..."
This didn't happen, because Orbison died unexpectedly at age 52
one week after this interview with Andy Bell, in which Roy provided his own account of the Wilburys' history:

> Originally the Wilburys started because George Harrison
> needed a third side for a European single. We got together
> and he said, "Let's see if we can use Bob Dylan's studio." So
> we phoned him up, and Bob Dylan answered the phone on
> the first ring, which is unusual, and he said, "Sure, come
> over." Well, George had to stop by Tom Petty's house to pick
> up his guitar, and Tom said, "Hey, I'm not doing anything.
> Can I come along?" So he came along too. Anyway, we were
> at Bob's house working on "Handle with Care," and we
> needed a couple of lines and Bob and Tom wandered in and
> just threw in the lines we needed. Then George took the
> record to his record company and they said, "This is much too
> good for a B-side. We're not sure what to do with this." And
> then we had the idea of putting together the album. We had
> all enjoyed it so much; it was so relaxed, there was no ego
> involved, and there was some sort of chemistry. So we'd go to
> Bob's house and we'd just sit outside and there'd be a barbe-
> cue and we'd all just bring guitars, and everyone would be
> throwing something in here and something in there, and then
> we'd just go to the garage, the studio, and put it down. Some
> days we'd finish just one song, sometimes two or three. We put
> down all the tracks, writing and singing and everything, in
> about ten or twelve days, then quite a lot of time in
> post-production.

Roy's recollection, while no doubt true in spirit, is inaccurate
insofar as the May sessions (roughly May 7–17) were not at Bob's
house on the Ampex tape recorder in a corner of his garage, but at
the nearby home and slightly less primitive home studio of
Dylan's friend Dave Stewart of the Eurythmics. The Wilburys (all
supposedly brothers; Orbison was Lefty Wilbury, Dylan was Lucky
Wilbury, Petty was Charlie T. Wilbury, Lynne and Harrison, who
are credited with producing the album, were Otis and Nelson
Wilbury) wrote and recorded ten songs for their first album. Dylan

sings lead on "Congratulations" and "Dirty World" and "Tweeter and the Monkey Man." About the writing of these songs, Lynne and Harrison recalled:

> Bob was the only one who had a clear-cut tune one day, when he came in and said, "What do you think of this one?" It was "Congratulations" and it was almost complete. Those are mostly Bob Dylan's lyrics, but we needed to do sort of like the bridge and a chorus or something. [Lynne]
>
> The second song [recorded] was "Dirty World." Bob's very funny – I mean, a lot of people take him seriously and yet if you know Dylan and his songs, he's such a joker, really. And Jeff just sat down and said, "OK, What are we gonna do?" And Bob said, "Let's do one like Prince! Hahaha!" And he just started banging away – "Love your sexy body! Ooooh-oooh-oooh-oooh bay-bee!" And it just turned into that tune … We decided to do this thing about "He loves your … he loves your …" and then we wrote lists. I picked up a bunch of magazines and gave everybody a magazine. Roy Orbison had *Vogue*, I had some copies of *Autosport* which I gave to Bob Dylan, and then we started reading out little things like "five-speed gearbox," wrote down a big list of things and then we reduced it to about twelve that sounded interesting. Then we just did the take, with the list on the microphone, and whoever sang first sang the first one on the list, and we sang round the group until we'd done 'em all. [Harrison]
>
> "Tweeter and the Monkey Man" was Bob Dylan and Tom Petty sitting in the kitchen. Jeff and I were there too, but they were talking about all this stuff which didn't make sense to me – Americana kind of stuff. Then we got a tape cassette and put it on and transcribed everything they were saying and wrote it down. And then Bob sort of changed it anyway. That for me was just amazing to watch, 'cause I had very little to do with writing that tune at all, except Jeff and I remembered a little bit that Bob did that he'd forgotten, which became that chorus part. It was just fantastic watching him do it, because he sang … he had one take warming himself up, and then he did it for real on take two, right through. It's just unbelievable seeing how he does it. [Harrison]

More fun to see than hear, in this case, because to my taste the song that resulted is significantly lacking in charm; and Dylan's delivery of the narrative as lead singer is void of presence or conviction (like

"Joey" on *Dylan & the Dead*) or even humor, except perhaps during the few seconds when we finally get to hear Bob Dylan sing the phrase "mansion on the hill" – made famous in a song of that title by his hero Hank Williams, a phrase and title since borrowed by Neil Young and Bruce Springsteen among others.

Much has been made (by Dylan fans and commentators) of this and other allusions to Springsteen song titles in the lyrics of "Tweeter and the Monkey Man." In the afore-quoted Roy Orbison interview, Andy Bell said, "There seems to be a bit of joshing going on in 'Tweeter and the Monkey Man.' Is there a gentle swipe at Bruce Springsteen there?" Orbison's response: "Oh no, I don't think so. Bruce is a great mate of mine." Bell: "But all the references to Springsteen songs – 'Mansion on the Hill' ..." Orbison: "Well, 'Mansion on the Hill,' of course, is Hank Williams ..." Bell: "'Thunder Road' ..." Orbison: "Well, that's Robert Mitchum ... hahaha!" This is a great moment. Lefty Wilbury, seven days before his death, reveals himself as a true Wilbury, playfully educating a Brit in "Americana kind of stuff" ... in this case the 1958 film and hit country song "Thunder Road," starring and sung by Robert Mitchum (which Springsteen was alluding to in his song title, just as he alludes to "Roy Orbison singing for the lonely" in that song's lyrics).

My favorite part of *Traveling Wilburys, Volume One* is "Handle with Care," the song that started it all. [I'm also quite fond of Derek Taylor's pseudonymous and very funny liner notes.]

To best appreciate "Handle with Care" as a pleasant footnote in Bob Dylan's canon, it helps to watch the video made to promote the song (and album) on music television. Not only do you see Bob Dylan (of "The Times They Are A-Changin'") and his guitar standing beside and singing with George Harrison of "While My Guitar Gently Weeps" and Roy Orbison of "Oh, Pretty Woman" and *their* guitars, but you have the distinct pleasure of seeing Dylan's body language harmonizing perfectly with his phrasing when he leans forward energetically (with his upper body and his voice) on the first chorus of "Everybody's got somebody to *lean* on, Put your body next to mine and *dream* on ..." This reassuring and very likeable couplet follows Orbison's standout vocal bridge "I'm so tired of being lonely/I still have some love to give/Won't you show me that you really care ..."

"Dirty World" is fun, and I suppose answers the question of

what Dylan's voice would sound like if he sang with a rock group (as opposed to being a solo performer/songwriter backed by a rock band). Dylan has written many songs over the years that are both sexier and funnier than this (i.e. "Rita May," 1975), so it's no surprise that he'd be an appreciator of Prince's work. Harrison's report above gives us an opportunity for another glimpse of what Bob Dylan is like at an intimate moment, collaborative songwriting and music-creating with friends. He really comes across as a leader. Five guys sitting around at the start of ten days of writing and recording together and one says, "What are we gonna do?" Dylan says, "Let's do one like Prince!" and starts singing and banging away at his guitar: "Love your sexy body!" So he suggests (by action and example) a collaborative technique where each thinks of a song-style and form as typified by a modern rock performer, and then spontaneously lets a song start to come forth in that vein, whatever comes into his mind. He trusts and implies that the others will come forward with ideas and suggestions, as they did when George began "Handle with Care" a month earlier. The second line Dylan comes up with – "He loves your dirty mind" – indicates his familiarity with Prince's superb 1981 song and album "Dirty Mind." Since this was the first song written and recorded at the May album-making session, we can also hear it as an example of Dylan taking charge as a bandleader, creating a new "Wilburys sound" on the spot, in collaboration with a longtime friend and collaborator, drummer Jim Keltner, who played on "Watching the River Flow" in 1971 and "Knockin' on Heaven's Door" in 1973 and toured with Dylan from 1979 to 1981.

The song that results is quite enjoyable, though not half as wonderful as "Handle with Care." Not inspired, but certainly good filler as needed. And noteworthy as another variation in lyricist Dylan's endless exploration of the shifting perspectives made possible by messing with pronouns. Each verse starts in the third person ("He loves your sense of humor …") and moves into second person and first person for the next few lines of the verse ("Oh baby, I'm on my hands and knees") … so we come to realize that the "he" being referred to must be the speaker referring to himself in the third person, a distancing that evaporates whenever "you" come on stage, perhaps because "every time he touches you, his hair stands up on end."

So "Let's do one like Prince!" leads to "Let's do one like

Bruce!" and Bob and Tom then try writing a story-song about
working-class people set in the darkness on the edge of a New Jersey
town. Of course one central figure should be a disillusioned
Vietnam Vet, and for a twist they make her a transsexual. And
while it's true the phrases "state trooper" and "Thunder Road" and
"Jersey girl" seem intended to evoke Springsteen, what are we to
make of the direct and indirect Dylan quotes and allusions in this
song's lyrics? "They could hear them tires squeal" ("Tweeter and
the Monkey Man") – "You know you can make a name for yourself,
you can hear them tires squeal" ("Sweetheart Like You," 1983).
"Sometimes I think of Tweeter, sometimes I think of Jan; sometimes I don't think about nothing but the monkey man" ("Tweeter
and the Monkey Man") – "She was thinking about her father who
she very rarely saw, thinking about Rosemary and thinking about
the law, but most of all she was thinking about the Jack of Hearts"
("Lily, Rosemary and the Jack of Hearts," 1975). "It was you to me
who taught, in Jersey anything's legal as long as you don't get
caught" in "Tweeter" is slightly reminiscent of "In Patterson [New
Jersey], that's just the way things go" from "Hurricane," 1976.

"Congratulations," the song that was "almost complete" when
Dylan brought it in to the Wilburys sessions, is again agreeable
filler ... but little more than that. Indeed, it's a remarkably spiritless
performance. Dylan sings "I'm sorrow bound" as if he were reading
from a cue card. The whole track suggests to me that Bob Dylan
knows how to deliver the message and sentiment of a song only
when he can see himself as an actor playing the part of the person
who is speaking these words ... and that perhaps this mindstate is
not easy for him to attain when singing as a member of a musical
group. He's brought in a new lyric on the universal topic of anger
and sorrow about the departure of a spouse or soulmate. But since
the idea is that it will be sung by "the Traveling Wilburys" – and
indeed it quickly gets a collective arrangement where a chorus of
W'burys sings the first word of each verse-line ("Congratulations")
and then the lead singer completes the phrase ("for breaking my
heart" "for tearing it all apart" "you finally did succeed" "for
leaving me in need") – it's not like it's about a genuine feeling felt by
the speaker. Instead, it's an expression of some kind of universal
feeling that you the listener may recognize when this ensemble sings
about it. Like "It Ain't Me Babe" sung by the Turtles. "Uh no no
no, it ain't me, babe!" – a singalong, not a dramatic, humorous,

poignant rendering of one individual's circumstances and feelings, as "It Ain't Me Babe" usually is when performed in a recording studio or onstage by Bob Dylan, singer-songwriter, bandleader.

So we can be glad that the splendid sales of *Traveling Wilburys, Volume One* (it reached number three on the U.S. album charts near the end of 1988, and, according to biographer Howard Sounes, "sold more copies than any Dylan album of the decade") didn't ulti-mately distract Bob Dylan from his chosen life as a "solo" (plus band) performing artist. And we can also be grateful that the Dead had the good taste to say no when, again according to Sounes in his 2001 book *Down the Highway, the Life of Bob Dylan*, "In February 1989 he [Dylan] called the Grateful Dead office and said he wanted to join the band. He made it clear that he was serious."

"Congratulations" is the only Traveling Wilburys song Dylan has yet performed live (at two shows in June 1989, at the beginning of the 1989 leg of the Never Ending Tour, and again at a warm-up show before the start of the early 1990 leg). In the late '88 interview Orbison was asked, "Are there any plans for a Wilburys tour?" "We did talk about it," he replied, "but there were problems with other people's commitments and we really only got about as far as talking about how we would all get off stage! I think it's something we'd all like to do but there are not really any plans for it. Perhaps we might do a single show somewhere. I'd really like that."

Apart from the three songs he sings and was a primary co-author of, Dylan's presence on *Traveling Wilburys, Volume One* is only noticeable when he takes the lead vocal on the first chorus of "Handle with Care" and on the first verse of "Margarita," which verse he probably wrote: "I was in Pittsburgh late one night/I lost my hat, got into a fight/I rolled and tumbled till I saw the light/ Went to the Big Apple, took a bite." This echoes "Lo and Behold!", a Basement Tapes song he wrote in 1967: "I come into Pittsburgh/ At six-thirty flat/I found myself a vacant seat/An' I put down my hat."

I also think I hear Dylan's presence as author of one verse of "End of the Line," the second single from the album, identifiably a George Harrison tune. Perhaps I think this because Tom Petty sings the lines with a bit of Dylan inflection in his voice: "Maybe some-where down the road a ways/You'll think of me and wonder where I am these days/Maybe somewhere down the road when somebody plays/'Purple Haze'." Since "Purple Haze" is a signature Jimi

Hendrix song, not something ever performed by Dylan or Petty or Harrison, this resonates nicely with the last words of Dylan's 1988 essay for the Hendrix exhibition: "It's not a wonder to me that he recorded my songs but rather that he recorded so few of them because they were all his." So by that logic you could think of Bob when somebody plays "Purple Haze" ("somewhere back there his soul & my soul were on the same desert").

On May 29, 1988, while in New York City rehearsing with his new band for the tour that would start on June 7th, Dylan made a guest appearance at a Levon Helm show at the Lone Star Cafe. He got on stage and played guitar and shared lead vocals with Levon on Robbie Robertson's "The Weight" and Chuck Berry's "Nadine." Presumably because he was on a stage and inspired by the hot playing of Levon's band, Dylan's brief and fragmented vocals on "Nadine" are full of the life and spirit and sense of purpose that seem missing in his "Congratulations" and "Tweeter" vocals at the Wilburys sessions earlier in the month.

When Dylan was inducted into the Rock and Roll Hall of Fame at the start of 1988, Bruce Springsteen said in the presentation, "When I was 15 and I heard 'Like a Rolling Stone,' I knew that I was listening to the toughest voice that I had ever heard … a guy that had the guts to take on the whole world and make me feel like I had to, too. The way that Elvis freed your body, Bob freed your mind." Dylan in his acceptance speech similarly acknowledged rock and roll/r&b pioneer Little Richard, who was at the ceremony: "I don't think I'd've even started out without listening to Little Richard."

8.

"When your environment changes, you change. You've got to go on, and you find new friends. Turn around one day and you're on a different stage, with a new set of characters," Bob Dylan said in 1978 (to Jonathan Cott of *Rolling Stone*). On June 7, 1988, at the Concord Pavilion in Northern California, he found himself on stage with a new band, quite different from Tom Petty & the Heartbreakers or the Grateful Dead: Christopher Parker, drums; Kenny Aaronson, electric bass; and G. E. Smith, electric lead guitar (and accompanying Dylan as second acoustic guitar on the acoustic songs – the 1988 equivalent of the solo acoustic sets included in the 1986, 1974 and 1966 shows). No backup singers this year, no keyboards and no harmonica at all. A new year, a new sound. New friends, in the sense that old songs become new friends (to the performer) when their forms change because the players and the instrumentation and the musical environment (and the performer's self-image) have changed.

I was in the audience at that first show of the year, and was thrilled when my hero opened the show by performing "Subterranean Homesick Blues," a great song he had never played on stage before. The surprises kept coming. The second song was the first-ever live performance of "Absolutely Sweet Marie" from *Blonde on Blonde*. The seventh selection was "Man of Constant Sorrow" from Dylan's first album, another song he'd never played on stage before (though there are tapes of him singing it at a party and in a friend's apartment in 1961). The acoustic set also included "Boots of Spanish Leather" – which Dylan had last sung publicly at a television taping in 1965 – and a traditional song he isn't known to have performed before, "The Lakes of Pontchartrain." Wow. We also got the first "electric" version of "Gates of Eden," and the first-ever live performance of "Driftin' Too Far from Shore," a 1984 Dylan song included on his 1986 album *Knocked Out Loaded*.

It was the singer's first North American concert since the shows with the Grateful Dead in July '87. As on the 1986 tour with the Heartbreakers, the 1988 shows had a basic format, a dramatic structure based on the alternation of electric (band) sets and acoustic sets. At Concord and at most of the shows for the rest of the year, Dylan and the band opened with "Subterranean," then played five more electrified songs, followed by the band walking off stage and Dylan and Smith performing a three-song acoustic set, followed by the return of the band and three electric songs, the last of these a rousing show-closer ("Like a Rolling Stone" at Concord and most other nights in 1988). The audience would then play its part, calling for an encore, so the fourth and last set would be the encores. At Concord Dylan played only one encore, "Maggie's Farm." For the rest of the year he played two or three or more encores, at least one of them acoustic (accompanied by Smith). A striking exception was the second show of the tour, Sacramento, June 9, at which Dylan refused the audience's request for an encore. Clinton Heylin in *A Life in Stolen Moments* suggests he was disappointed at the poor turnout ("the venue was only half-full, fewer than six thousand fans attending"). Other variations as the year went on (Dylan played 71 shows in 1988, all in the United States or Canada) were the occasional seven-song opening set or four-song second set (or, rarely, a four-song third set). Concord was thirteen songs long, about 70 minutes. At most 1988 shows, Dylan played 15, 16, or 17 songs. A notable exception: October 13 in Upper Darby, Pennsylvania, he played 21 songs – seven in the first set, four in the second, three in the third, and then seven encores.

After Concord, the next three '88 shows were also in the San

Francisco Bay Area, at Sacramento, Berkeley and Mountain View. During the rest of June, Dylan and his new stripped-down three-piece band played in Utah, Colorado, Missouri, Wisconsin, Ohio, New Jersey, and New York. In July and August they did shows in Massachusetts, Maine, Pennsylvania, Quebec, Ontario, Michigan, Illinois, Indiana, Maryland, Tennessee, Georgia, Texas, Arizona, southern California, Oregon, Washington, British Columbia, Alberta, Manitoba, Ontario again, and New York state again. The September itinerary included New York, New England, New Jersey, Pennsylvania, Virginia, the Carolinas, Tennessee, Florida, and Louisiana. The tour ended in October with two more shows in Pennsylvania and four shows at Radio City Music Hall in New York City. There was an 11-day break in August and 17 days off in late September and early October; otherwise it was a straight 19 weeks on the road. Most of the shows, until the last six weeks, were at outdoor venues.

The T-shirts and hats sold at the start of the tour referred to it as "Interstate '88." But Dylan fans have come to know it as the first leg of the Never Ending Tour, which they regard as still continuing in 2001, even though Bob Dylan said in 1993, in the liner notes to his album *World Gone Wrong*:

> by the way, dont be bewildered by the Never Ending Tour chatter. there was a Never Ending Tour but it ended in '91 with the departure of guitarist G. E. Smith. that one's long gone but there have been many others since then. The Money Never Runs Out Tour (fall of '91) Southern Sympathizer Tour (early '92) Why Do You Look at Me So Strangely Tour (European '92) The One Sad Cry of Pity Tour (Australia & West Coast American '92) Principles of Action Tour (Mexico-South American '92) Outburst of Consciousness Tour ('92) Dont Let Your Deal Go Down Tour ('93) & others too many to mention each with their own character & design. to know which was which consult the playlists.

The Never Ending Tour "chatter" began as a result of Adrian Deevoy's October 1989 interview with Dylan (published in the Dec. '89 issue of *Q* Magazine). At the start of the interview Deevoy said, "Tell me about the live thing. The last tour has gone virtually straight into this one." Dylan replied: "Oh, it's all the same tour. The Never Ending Tour ..."

Deevoy: "What's the motivation to do that?" Dylan: "Well, it works out better for me that way. You can pick and choose better when you're just out there all the time and your show is already set up. You know, you just don't have to start it up and end it. It's better just to keep it out there with breaks, you know, with extended breaks."

The interview continued with some valuable insights into the mind and method of this performing artist:

Deevoy: Does that lend itself to reassessing stuff? The songs are being constantly reinterpreted, almost. Dylan: Like which one? Like *what?* People do say that. To me it's never different. To me ... there's never any change. Deevoy: The live show is quite improvisational. Dylan: It *can* be. Some nights more than others! Heh heh. Some nights it's very structured. Some nights it just sticks right to the script and other nights it'll *skip*. Deevoy: What makes it take off? Dylan: It's hard to say. It's hard to say. It's the crowd that changes the songs.

Deevoy: You stopped playing the harmonica for a while recently ... Dylan: Uh ... yeah. When was that? Oh yeah. Sometimes I do, yeah. Those are the things that get set up and it's hard to bury them. Once there's no harmonicas on the stage, you don't play them. Then there's always some problem with harmonicas. Deevoy: Like picking up the wrong one ... Dylan: That can be very unfortunate when that happens. You've probably seen that happen a few times. Heh heh heh. Very unfortunate. You can be playing an entire harmonica solo and not be able to hear it and you'll be in the wrong key. You can usually tell by the faces in the crowd, you look and see if it's in the right key. If it's in the wrong key it's, Aauugh! (he puts his hands over his ears and grimaces.) Then you can make an adjustment to it. Heh heh heh.

Deevoy: What about your voice? Are you pleased with the way it's sounding at the moment? Dylan: Mmmmm ... Ah, that's a thing that's very hard to really pin down. You know, whether you want it that way or not. Trying to adjust the moods of the different songs can be tricky sometimes. Deevoy: Do you ever feel limited by it? Dylan: Yeah. Sure. My voice is very limiting. Vocally, it's just good enough for me. It's good for my songs. It really is good for my songs. My type of songs.

"*I'm* bound to ride that open highway ..." Bob Dylan sang/announced June 7, 1988, at the first show of his Never Ending

Tour. This was during "Man of Constant Sorrow," the opening
song of his first acoustic set in almost two years. This line is not
included in the performance of the song on Dylan's first album. Nor
is it in the Stanley Brothers' 1950 recording of "Man of Constant
Sorrow," which Dylan may have been listening to when re-
familiarizing himself with this song before the start of the tour. It's
clear he made reference to something other than his own recording
of "Man" when preparing to include it in his 1988 repertoire,
because the state he now bids farewell to and says he's from is "old
Kentucky" as on the Stanleys' recording, rather than "Colorado" as
on *Bob Dylan*.

There are two verses included in the 1988 performances
(Concord and again four nights later in Mountain View) that are
not in Dylan's 1961 recording but are new adaptations of verses in
the Stanley Brothers' version.

Bob Dylan would be the first person to tell you that songs can
have a life of their own. In 2001, as I write this, "I Am a Man of
Constant Sorrow" is reaching millions of listeners as the centerpiece
of a surprise hit album, the multiplatinum hillbilly music soundtrack
to a film called *O Brother, Where Art Thou?* about the adventures of
three prisoners who escape from a chain gang in Mississippi in
1937. Stumbling upon a guy who offers them a couple of dollars if
they'll sing something into his tape recorder, they sing "Man of
Constant Sorrow" and it immediately becomes a huge hit record,
and they're treated like celebrities when they're recognized as *the*
Soggy Bottom Boys.

The first known publication of the song was in a 1913 songbook that a blind singer from Kentucky printed to sell at his performances. He called it "Farewell Song." Sixty years later a song
scholar asked him, "What about this 'Farewell Song' – 'I Am a Man
of Constant Sorrow' – did you write it?" Richard Burnett answered,
"No, I think I got the ballad from somebody. I dunno. It may be my
song." He certainly made it his own, even if he got it from somebody. Burnett sang, "Oh, six long years I've been blind, friends. My
pleasures here on Earth are done. In this world I have to ramble, for
I have no parents to help me now." When bluegrass pioneers the
Stanley Brothers recorded the song, which they'd learned from
their father, they sang this verse as: "For six long years I've been in
trouble, no pleasure here on Earth I've found. For in this world, I'm
bound to ramble. I have no friends to help me now." Dylan at

Concord sang this as: "For six long years, I've been in trouble, no pleasure here on Earth I've found. I'm bound to ride that open highway. I have no friend to help me now." (Or, perhaps, "I have no Friend to help me now.")

The other Stanley Brothers (and Burnett) verse Dylan didn't sing in 1961 but does include in 1988 is: "You may bury me in some deep valley, where many years I may lay. Then you might learn to love another, when I am sleeping in my grave." The fact that Burnett called this "Farewell Song," calling attention to his song's musical and emotional climax in the lines "So fare you well my own true lover, I fear I never see you again" makes me notice that Dylan left these lines out of his 1961 recorded version (he reinstates them powerfully in 1988) but made up for it in 1962 when he wrote in "Don't Think Twice," "Goodbye's too good a word gal, so I'll just say fare thee well" ... and wrote another song called "Farewell" that starts, "Oh it's fare thee well my darlin' true ..."

It is a song with a life of its own. Emry Arthur's 1928 "hillbilly record" of "I Am a Man of Constant Sorrow" touched many people, and in 1936 Sarah Ogan Gunning recorded it as "A Girl of Constant Sorrow." Judy Collins named her first album (*Maid of Constant Sorrow*, 1962) after her own version of the song.

The acoustic set at Concord, even without harmonica (which was the heart and soul of Dylan's 1961 "Man of Constant Sorrow"), was and is the high point of a strong show. The second song of the set, "The Lakes of Pontchartrain," powerfully expresses Dylan's interest, at this moment in his life, in using his voice and guitar and the attention of his audience, to tell stories. Indeed, it seemed at the time and still seems now, that the 1988 shows where he sang "The Lakes of Pontchartrain" or "Trail of the Buffalo" or "Two Soldiers" or "Barbara Allen" were built around and seemed to fulfill their purpose at these dramatic moments of musical storytelling. G. E. Smith's role in this, although his playing as second guitarist in the acoustic sets was skillful and tasteful, often intelligent and always appropriate, seems to have been primarily to boost Dylan's confidence by taking away the possibility that he would make a very audible mistake in his guitar playing, a possibility that would have worried him and made it difficult for him to be as present in his singing during the "solo" sets as he needed and wanted to be. Because of this new two-guitar format, and Dylan's confidence in Smith's ability to "cover" him, Dylan was able to be more ambitious in the songs he chose to play and sing, and to set higher goals for what he hoped to achieve, musically and emotionally, during this part of the show.

Now that it has been revealed, in Howard Sounes' biography *Down the Highway*, that Dylan secretly married one of his backup singers, Carolyn Dennis, in June 1986, four months after the birth of their daughter Desiree, we can see that along with its many other attractions, this song appealed to Dylan because it gave him a chance to sing about the beauty of a black or partly black woman: "A dark girl towards me came, and I fell in love with a creole girl on the lakes of Pontchartrain." "The hair upon her shoulders in jet black ringlets fell. To try to paint her beauty, I'm sure 'twould be in vain, so handsome was my creole girl ..."

This is a theme that has made oblique appearances in various Dylan songs over the years: "The night is pitch black, come and make my pale face fit into place, ah, please!" ("Spanish Harlem Incident," 1964); "I return to the Queen of Spades and talk with my chambermaid. She knows that I'm not afraid to look at her." ("I Want You," 1966); "We are covered in blood, girl, you know our forefathers were slaves." ("Precious Angel," 1979). Sounes, writing about Dylan's 1978 tour, says, "It was not lost on the band that all these girlfriends were black. 'Bob is really into black culture. He likes black women. He likes black music. He likes black style,' says [guitar player] Billy Cross. 'When he asked for musical attitudes, they would always be black.' When [percussionist] Bobbye Hall was invited to Bob's suite for dinner, she was surprised to find a banquet of soul food. 'He ate soul food after every show. He seems to be infatuated by going out with black women. He was infatuated with that whole black thing, even eating the food.'"

It's likely that Dylan in 1988 learned "The Lakes of Pontchartrain" from an album by Irish folksinger Paul Brady. Brady's album is called *Welcome Here, Kind Stranger*, the key phrase in the Pontchartrain ballad. It seems worth noting that these words are like a rephrasing of a key line in a Bob Dylan song (and, perhaps, in the story of his life): "'Come in', she said, 'I'll give you shelter from the storm.'"

The songs, Dylan told us in *Newsweek* in 1997, are his lexicon, the source of his religiosity and philosophy. A lexicon is a dictionary, or the vocabulary of a particular person or group of people. Shortly after seeing the Concord and Mountain View concerts, I wrote that "I wasn't completely surprised to hear Dylan sing 'Man of Constant Sorrow' at Concord, because 'Rank Strangers to Me' [from his newly released album] is the Dylan performance that speaks most powerfully to my heart this year, and every time I hear the lines

> They've all moved away, said the voice of a stranger
> To that beautiful shore by the bright crystal sea

I think of 'Man of Constant Sorrow':

> Your mother says I'm a stranger
> My face you'll never see no more
> But there's one promise, darling,
> I'll see you on God's golden shore."

The recurrence of this word and image "shore" struck something in me as I listened to Bob Dylan in spring 1988. "Stranger," of course, is another word and image from this lexicon that links "Rank Strangers" and "Constant Sorrow," and it could also be heard at Concord in Dylan's beautiful rendering of "The Lakes of Pontchartrain": "All strangers there no friends to me, till a dark girl towards me came" and "'You're welcome here, kind stranger, our home is very plain but we never turn a stranger out, on the lakes of Pontchartrain.'" Such recurrences, whether delivered and received consciously or unconsciously, do contribute to the overall impact of a concert performance (and the cumulative impact of a series of performances heard via albums and at concerts and on concert tapes). It's intriguing that "My face you'll never see no more" also recurs in "Pontchartrain": "So faretheewell my creole girl, I'll never see no more." How does this resonate (consciously or unconsciously) with the fact that the next song in the Concord acoustic set, "Boots of Spanish Leather," starts, "I'm sailing away my own true love, I'm sailing away in the morning"? I think we feel the narrator's unspoken anguish at the possibility that he'll never see her again. And maybe on some deep level that word "morning" brings us back to these powerful lines from "Constant Sorrow": "I'm bound to ride that morning railroad/Perhaps I'll die on that train."

"Boots" (first-ever concert performance) is quite moving. And then the mood changes abruptly and meaningfully ("trying to adjust the moods of the different songs can be tricky sometimes") with a surprisingly powerful "Driftin' Too Far from Shore." "Driftin'" at

Concord is an example of Dylan leading his band so successfully, with his voice and his presence and his rhythm guitar playing, that the entire ensemble performance becomes an expression of one man's personality and spontaneous creative intent. The sound is very different from the two-guitar solo acoustic set we've just been listening to, but the narrative flow of the concert is uninterrupted – the juxtaposition of sounds and images and words and melodies and rhythms and situations continues to enthrall us and stir us up in powerful ways that charmingly violate any expectations or ideas we may have had about who this artist is and what he probably wants to say and achieve tonight. "I didn't know that you'd be leavin', or who you thought you were talkin' to ... I tried to reach you, honey, but you're driftin' too far from shore." This could be addressed to the "you" of "Boots of Spanish Leather," though Dylan at Concord doesn't sing the first of these sentences from the "official" album version (and, now, website lyrics) of the song. He doesn't seem to remember the words to the verses of this song, so he ad-libs slurred "dummy" lyrics suitable to the meter and mood ... but in any case, the important thing is that it *sounds* so wonderful! The drums, the guitars, the voice blend into a single, very expressive, nonverbal voice. Indeed, at moments like this (including each of the marvelous acoustic performances at Concord, and the earnest reading of "In the Garden" that ends the first electric set and opens us for the revelations of the next few songs), we listeners have an opportunity to meet the new, June 1988, evolution of the performing artist whose name is on the marquee tonight. He clearly has something to tell us. There is a feel to the overall sound of each song that seems equivalent to the ambitious self-expression found in this artist's early writings and performances. Dylan might not be able to answer our questions about what it is he's trying to say. But he says it with such conviction, such charming and inventive artistry, that we find ourselves finding meaning here, recognizing ourselves, our world, our feelings in these songs and performances. For the performer and the audience, the gateway to a new kind of audience-artist relationship is opening. In this case, it's the gateway to Bob Dylan's Never Ending Tour, a new art form and format which, he says, he was inspired to create or search for after watching the Grateful Dead perform in the summers of 1986 and 1987.

As he did at the start of the fall '87 tour, Dylan varied his set lists considerably, Grateful-Dead-fashion, at his first 1988 shows.

The second concert, Sacramento, only included two songs that had been played at the first concert. The third concert included nine songs from the previous shows, and eight that were new to the tour. Nine more songs were introduced at the next show, so that forty different songs were played in the first four concerts of 1988. By the fifteenth show, sixty-two different songs had been played. And in spite of a few predictable slots – "Subterranean" first every night, "Rolling Stone" closing the show (before the encores) every night, "Maggie's Farm" the last encore most nights, and "Silvio" the first or second song in the second electric set almost every night after its introduction at the ninth show – the set lists continued to vary significantly night after night, with few repeating sequences. The last ten shows of the year, from Sept. 22 to Oct. 19, offered three different songs in the number two position, five different songs in the #3 slot, five different #4s, and five different #5s. "Highway 61" closed the first set nine times during those last ten shows, followed by "One Too Many Mornings" three times and by an acoustic "Gates of Eden" four times. The acoustic sets at those ten shows featured nine different songs, although the acoustic set at the last four shows of the year (all at Radio City Music Hall) did repeat the same three songs in the same order almost every night. Altogether, thirty-three different songs were played during the last ten shows of 1988 (not including a post-tour Dylan appearance when he did six acoustic songs at a benefit concert in December). And Dylan managed to surprise and delight his fans at the 66th show of the year, Upper Darby on October 13, by singing "Bob Dylan's 115th Dream" ("I was riding on the Mayflower, when I thought I spied some land ..."), a song he'd never played live before, and then ending the show with "Every Grain of Sand" – his fourth performance of this major work during 1988, a song he'd hadn't sung on stage since 1984.

The leader of Dylan's 1988–89 band, G. E. (George Edward) Smith, had been the frontman of the *Saturday Night Live* television show band since 1985. He played lead guitar for the "blue-eyed soul" duo Hall & Oates from 1979 to 1985, and can be heard on their #1 hit singles "Kiss on My List," "Private Eyes" and "I Can't Go for That." Bass player Kenny Aaronson had also had the experience of playing in a group with a #1 record, Stories (their hit was "Brother Louie," summer 1973). Aaronson joined Dylan's band only a few weeks before the 1988 tour started, after Dylan decided original bassist Marshall Crenshaw's six-string bass "did not fill the sound out enough." The third bandmember, Christopher Parker, also a New Yorker, was an experienced recording session drummer who played with Smith in the *Saturday Night Live* band. This was the smallest backing band Dylan had ever toured with. Clinton Heylin calls them "a tough, punchy, no-frills band." Andrew Muir, in *Razor's Edge: Bob Dylan & the Never Ending Tour* says, "They looked and sounded like a band of rock and roll gangsters from the wrong side of the tracks."

At Concord, and the other three Bay Area shows that opened the 1988 tour, Dylan and the band were joined onstage by Neil Young. He played guitar on all of the electric songs, all four nights. That is, he could be seen playing – few of us who were at the shows could actually hear him playing; nor is there much evidence of the distinctive sound of Young's electric guitar on the recordings of the shows, though I hear an attractive solo that sounds very much like it could be his near the end of "You're a Big Girl Now" on the Concord tape. One friend of mine swears he hears Young's guitar on the Berkeley "Gates of Eden." In any case, Young's enthusiastic presence onstage (and his playing, as heard in the monitors if not the PA) may have helped spark the particularly spirited band and vocal performance of "Like a Rolling Stone" at Concord (leagues above the Rock and Roll Hall of Fame all-star jam version).

Bob Dylan, in rehearsing the songs he was likely to include in his 1988 tour, paid uncharacteristic attention to songs he was singing at the very start of his career, in 1961. The first song of his acoustic set at each of the first four 1988 shows is one he recorded in 1961 for his first album – "Man of Constant Sorrow" at Concord and Mountain View, "Baby, Let Me Follow You Down" at Sacramento, and "San Francisco Bay Blues" at Berkeley. Three weeks later, in Mansfield, Massachusetts on July 2, he sang another song from that album, "Pretty Peggy-O," early in the first electric set. July 14, on the outskirts of Chicago, he opened his acoustic set with "Song to Woody," also from his first album. June 25, the acoustic set opened with "Trail of the Buffalo," a song that can be heard (like "San Francisco Bay Blues") on a recording of Dylan performing at the home of some friends of Woody Guthrie's very early in 1961. June 22, 1988, he opened his second set with "Wild Mountain Thyme," another song that turns up on an early 1961 recording of Dylan performing for friends. Other songs performed on the 1988 tour that he was probably singing as early as 1961 are "Barbara

Allen" and "Wagoner's Lad." We can infer that Dylan in spring '88 devised a strategy for "getting back there" to the meaning of his own work without emergency assistance from Jerry Garcia. Remember what he said in 1993 he heard in U2: "Just more of a thread back to the music that got me inspired and into it. They are actually rooted someplace and they respect that tradition. They work within a certain boundary which has a history to it, and then they can do their own thing on top of that. I don't know how anybody can do anything and not be connected someplace back there." Hence this 1988 gambit. Listen to Dylan sing (and emphasize, stretch out) the word "I" in the lines "I am a man of constant sorrow" and "I bid farewell to old Kentucky" and "I'm bound to ride that open highway" in spring 1988, and I think you can actually hear a person getting connected, and discovering and creating a platform on which to do his work as a performer.

9.

I saw (attended) ten of the seventy-one shows Bob Dylan and his new band played during their 1988 tour of North America. I enjoyed all of them thoroughly, and felt deeply enriched every time. But as I said back in chapter zero, the primary source material for this study of one performer's work must be – for the sake of accuracy and some possibility of common ground between reader and author – recorded performances rather than recollections of concerts attended. And the 1988 shows, as recorded performances, offer few examples of this artist doing his very best work. Yes, "Gates of Eden" from June 13th is extraordinary, and "The Lakes of Pontchartrain" from June 7th and "Two Soldiers" from June 9th and various other 1988 acoustic "cover" song performances are quite wonderful. But there don't seem to be as many such moments scattered among the tapes of the shows as I would wish. And it is not easy for me to find a full recorded show from 1988 about which I can wax as enthusiastic as I did in chapters four and five about Dortmund and Munich and other fall '87 tapes.

1988 was the start of something exceptional: Bob Dylan's Never Ending Tour (now in its fourteenth year). Like almost every new environment Dylan has created for himself or found himself in as a performing artist, the "Interstate '88" band and tour concept was an experiment. Its longevity (not with the original players, but as a format and as an approach to the task of being Bob Dylan, live performer) bespeaks its success at meeting the needs of the singer and of his audiences. Like a long-running Broadway show, it evidently has pleased somebody. But the success of the artistry is another matter ... and my particular interest in this study. The Never Ending Tour has produced a remarkable number of great performances, great works of art, over the years. But not quite as many in its maiden year as I had expected to find, based on my memories of seeing the shows and of listening to the tapes back then.

What I'm trying to say, I guess, is that these books have been (and will continue to be) an argument for and exegesis about Bob Dylan's greatness as an artist, specifically a performing artist, and my approach has tended to be to focus on examples of that greatness as they turn up in the course of this chronological survey ... but 1988, although a turning point, was not a bumper year for greatness. It was a year when almost any of the shows was a true pleasure and very rewarding for the Dylan fans who happened to be there. But listening to the recordings (tapes, CDs, etc.), one finds a lot of very good (though seldom "great") performances alongside a lot of disappointingly routine stretches (depending on the mood the listener is in, these can be quite enjoyable; but seldom are they examples of the artist being particularly awake and present within his song and performance). Dylan is comfortable with his band this year, and that means he's able to be as reliable an entertainer as live performers are expected to be. But for connoisseurs of Bob Dylan's "accidental" art, good entertainment is not satisfying. We prefer moments of transcendent awakeness, those moments when, to quote the man again, "songs are heroic enough to give the illusion of stopping time" and "to hear a song is to hear someone's thought, no matter what they're describing."

The difference between "comfort" and "heroism" is split nicely on those few 1988 nights when Dylan and his band work together so well that they manage to create a sound and mood unique to that particular concert, as if the entire show were a single thought we are privileged and thrilled to be able to hear, a single moment of seemingly stopped time lasting well over an hour. By way of example, I call your attention to the 16th show of 1988, July 1st in the Jones Beach Theater, Wantagh, New York.

What is striking about this July 1st show is the consistent feeling of connectedness between Dylan and the band, song after song, all night. This results in and is expressed in the unusual (for 1988 electric sets) freedom and confidence of the vocals. Too often in 1988, Dylan sings as though he's trying too hard to sound like Bob Dylan, giving words and phrases a little extra spin, and unfortunately not because he's connected to the sentiment of the lines he's singing or the story he's telling. No, it often sounds like he's just doing what he thinks he's supposed to do, not really trying to get close to us.

The second and third songs of the June 30th show, also at Wantagh, "Just Like Tom Thumb's Blues" and "You're a Big Girl Now" are to my ears clear examples of the sporadic musical disconnectedness and inauthentic vocals that may be encountered on too many of these '88 tapes. It's remarkable that Dylan can sound so wooden on these particular songs. In the first case, the tempo and feel of the playing seem way off, which of course helps explain the awkwardness of the singing. This was "Tom Thumb"'s first appearance on the tour (or at any Dylan concert for more than two years). According to bass player Kenny Aaronson (as quoted in Heylin's biography), "On the road, every so often before the show G.E. would come back and go, 'Fellows, Bob wants us to do this tune and here's how it goes.' And G.E. would show it to me and Chris Parker right before the show." Dylan has made some great recordings by asking musicians to back him live in the studio on a song they've never heard before. If his terrific results on those occasions are a function of the power of his presence, one has to wonder why there are so many performances on this tour when that power seems absent. In the case of "Big Girl," Dylan and band had performed the song at seven shows already this month, so the stiffness of the singing and playing cannot be explained by unfamiliarity. Maybe overfamiliarity (comfort) is the problem. Or there may be other factors causing the performer to go in and out of connection with his band and his songs. The June 30th show does eventually come to life with the fifth song – a surprisingly bright "Masters of War," which gets a new musical feel and even some new lyrics ("though I'm no smarter than you"). Things go well after that.

On July 1st, Dylan and Smith and Aaronson and Parker start

off with arguably the best "Subterranean Homesick Blues" of the tour. Most nights, this song suffers from its placement in the opening slot ... Dylan sings words and sometimes whole lines off-mike as he warms up to being on stage. The band doesn't so much play the song as provide a standard rock and roll shuffle accompaniment, presumably as instructed by Dylan at an early rehearsal. They play fast, Dylan sings a lot of words fast, and it's usually a good example of showmanship replacing interaction and respect for the material. But July 1st is a happy exception. Every word of the song is audible, and singer and rhythm section sound like a team, conscious artists creating something together. The resultant performance is nothing particularly memorable, certainly not comparable to the original 1965 performance, but a credible statement of intent by singer and band which kicks off a flow of songs and music that is very satisfying, and as close as we get all year to a concert-length expression of who Bob Dylan feels himself to be and what his songs and his body of work mean to him at this moment in his life.

"Simple Twist of Fate" shines like a jewel in its setting between "Subterranean Homesick Blues" and "Driftin' Too Far from Shore." The fourth song, "Absolutely Sweet Marie," is another high point. The band truly *nails* this one from the opening notes, and the singer responds with a vocal performance that actually is comparable to the *Blonde on Blonde* original. This is an instance of Dylan's '88-style emphatic phrasing sounding connected and authentic and even rich in nuance and presence. And it's clearly the result of his being inspired by what the rhythm section is doing, and thus being able to lean into the song so that it comes to life rather ecstatically.

The last two songs of the 7/1/88 first electric set are a particularly well-realized "Ballad of a Thin Man" and an equally alive "It's All Over Now, Baby Blue." Listen to that man sing "great lawyers and scholars" and "on your sheets"!! It could only be one singer who's ever lived. And only at this specific moment in his trajectory. We connoisseurs live for such instants.

The acoustic set begins with an unusual choice: "Mama, You Been on My Mind," written in 1964 and not released on a Dylan album until *The Bootleg Series* in 1991 (and performed five times in 1988). Dylan sings it well at the Jones Beach Theater and follows it with another 1964 love song, "It Ain't Me Babe" – also a very fine performance. The quality of this July 1st acoustic set, which continues with a powerful, heartfelt "The Lonesome Death of Hattie Carroll" and concludes with the fourth 1988 "Barbara Allen," makes me wonder if subtle changes from night to night in the chemistry of the relationship between Dylan and electric set bandleader and acoustic set co-guitarist Smith could be a factor in the noticeable fluctuations in the extent to which Dylan sounds present in his singing, and connected to the music being made, from show to show and even from song to song in 1988. This kind of fluctuation is normal for him on most of his tours. However, until 1988 his live acoustic performances were explorations of a dynamic in which his (usually rhythmic) guitar playing and his playful, emotive voice spoke to and stimulated, influenced, each other. The introduction of a second guitar player (with responsibilities very different from the tasteful highlighting of Bruce Langhorne's and Charlie McCoy's second guitars on the 1965 recordings of "Mr. Tambourine Man" and "Desolation Row") must certainly have changed the dynamic of these no-longer solo acoustic performances.

In listening to recordings of Dylan shows over the years, there have been times when it has seemed to me that an unusually powerful and fresh vocal performance of, say, "A Hard Rain's A-Gonna Fall" has resulted from Dylan being inspired by the particular rhythmic riff he (seemingly unexpectedly) has just fallen into in his guitar playing. This sort of thing may occasionally happen in the Smith-assisted performances, though I haven't found many '88 examples and it's difficult for me, with my untrained ears, to guess who's playing what or to what extent what I'm hearing is just Smith "covering" Dylan's playing by strumming or playing patterns in the appropriate chords.

On this July 1st tape, it does seem to me that the interplay between voice and guitar(s) is an important element in the excellence of "Mama, You Been on My Mind" and "It Ain't Me Babe," although the power of the performances is primarily located in the vocals. But then Dylan delivers his finest vocal performance of the night on "The Lonesome Death of Hattie Carroll" and the contribution of the guitar or guitars seems quite minimal ... that is, to provide accompaniment without getting in the way of the singer's passion. It sounds as though the fiery vocal just builds on itself, that this particular evening Dylan reconnects with and is genuinely inspired by the song's rhythmic language ("emptied the ashtrays on a whole other level") and the power of the story these words tell – is in fact suddenly feeling the presence of this woman and drawing the strength of his singing directly from her. G.E. plays a nice solo or two between verses, but the important thing – which perhaps Smith does deserve some credit for – is that Dylan feels very at home with his song tonight.

"Barbara Allen" is not exceptional this evening, but it contributes to the impact of the whole show by giving us another side of Bob Dylan, and even a rather different Dylan-voice, just when we might have been lulled into thinking we know who this artist is and what he wants to accomplish tonight. What he wants to accomplish is to put on a good show, and play music he loves. So he starts the next set with "Silvio," his latest single ("Driftin' Too Far from Shore," played earlier in the show, another song that the crowd doesn't know and that he enjoys playing and identifies keenly with the "sentiment" of, is the B-side of that single).

The second electric set continues with "In the Garden," another song-choice intended to assert this performer's right to be true to himself regardless of who his fans think he should and shouldn't be. You can hear in his voice, his voices, that he's having a great time going from protest song to traditional ballad to uptempo Grateful-Dead-style rocker to the story of Jesus Christ (sung with love and gusto) to a signature song and greatest hit he can still sink his teeth into, "Like a Rolling Stone." The drumbeat that kicks off "Rolling Stone" a few seconds after the dramatic closing notes of "In the Garden" can be felt as a moment of joyful irony when you let Bob Dylan get you on his wavelength, his July 1, 1988 mindset. Every song, every transition, has a message, and the artist on a good night like this one delights in rising to the challenge of thrilling an audience without feeling like a prisoner of their expectations. So his encores are a greatest hit from the acoustic protest era, "Blowin' in the Wind," followed by a Christian era rocker/hit, "Gotta Serve Somebody," wrapped up as usual in '88 with his perennial declaration of independence, "Maggie's Farm." "I try my best to be just like I am." He does. And in this work of accidental art, he succeeds gloriously.

I recently told my friend Gary Schulstad of my difficulty coming to terms with my mixed feelings about what I'm hearing now listening to the 1988 shows, and he wrote back: "From what I remember of the '88 Dylan performances I attended, I empathize with what you are going through. There seemed to be an energy in the music that wasn't really directed to the audience." Well said. That word "energy," quite applicable to what I'm calling Dylan's emphatic (or overemphatic) 1988 singing style, helps me make a connection that eluded me until now. In 1985, Dylan said of his 1974 tour of America, "I think I was just playing a role on that tour. It was all sort of mindless ... an emotionless trip. The greatest praise we got on that tour was 'incredible energy, man' – it would make me want to puke." Dylan's exaggerated, "energetic" approach to singing on the 1974 tour does have something in common with some of his 1988 singing; and I would guess that in both cases it arose from a part of himself that had doubts about his ability to give the people what they must want and that therefore decided he had to push the words of the songs out forcefully in order to get them across successfully. In 1974, he was back on tour and on stage after a seven-year hiatus; in 1988, he was trying to make a personal comeback after a year when he'd felt he'd "reached the end of the line" and "couldn't do his old songs" onstage. Such circumstances naturally make us push harder, which can have good results, but can also be a kind of obstacle in itself. Interestingly, one week ago as I write this, Dylan brought up the topic of his dissatisfaction with the 1974 tour again, in an interview (about his new album, *"Love And Theft"*) with Robert Hilburn of the *Los Angeles Times*. Dylan: "I always felt that if I'm going to do anything in life, I want to go as deep as I can." Hilburn: "Have you always lived up to that goal? Have you ever felt you were just a superficial artist?" Dylan: "Sure, I think the tour I did with the Band in 1974 was superficial. I had forgotten how to sing and play. I had been devoting my time to raising a family, and it took me a long time to recapture my purpose as a performer. You'd find it at times, then it would disappear again for a while."

If we apply this 2001 recollection of 1974's seven-week tour (and cogent self-observation) to 1987–88, it seems reasonable (based on what I hear in the show-recordings) to suppose that the voice in Dylan's head in October '87 telling himself "I'm determined to stand!" was a decision to recapture his purpose as a performer, and that the strangely uneven 1988 results are another painful portrait of an artist finding it at times, then watching it disappear again for a while. I said in the last chapter that listening to Dylan sing the word "I" in "Man of Constant Sorrow" at the start of the 1988 tour, we can hear an artist getting connected to something and discovering and creating a platform on which to do his work as a performer. I've also referred to the '88 tour, in this chapter, as an experiment that was successful as measured by the longevity of the format and the enthusiasm with which Dylan has toured the world as a performing artist and bandleader ever since … and unsuccessful artistically in the short term as measured by what can be heard on the show-recordings. What happened, what got in the way of Dylan's purpose as a performer to go as deep as he can into whatever he does, was, I hypothesize, the result of fear of failure, fear of not being loved, leading to trying too hard to be safe up there on that stage, leading to singer/performer being lulled to sleep by the safeness and lack-of-aliveness of his working environment. Particularly in the electric sets, but also in the acoustic sets, Dylan tried to get songs across in 1988 by shouting their words. This was damaging to his voice, as well as being an obstacle to being melodically and emotionally present within the songs themselves. So by the end of the tour, as Clinton Heylin has written of the four October shows at Radio City Music Hall, "his voice was in very poor shape, and he shouted his way through songs, stripping them of nuance and subtlety."

Dylan seldom spoke between songs in 1988, but at that opening show in Concord, there was a surprising moment just before the encore when he said, "I want to thank you people for being so *nice!*" This was not formulaic (indeed was not repeated night after night or ever again), but sounded like a warm, spontaneous expression of sincere appreciation, as though the speaker really hadn't expected such kind treatment (the applause after the last song? the attentiveness of the audience throughout the show?). The fact that Dylan uncharacteristically refused to play an encore at the end of the next concert feels closely related, as though the sensitivity that made him so appreciative on June 7th made him feel wounded when the audience appeared inattentive on June 9th. At this June 9th show he was also unhappy about harsh reviews in the San Francisco newspapers that asserted that the audience he'd called "nice" at Concord were actually "exasperated" that he didn't play more "familiar classics" and that so many of the songs he did perform were "unrecognizable." These newspaper comments led to Dylan's next between-song soliloquy, at the June 11th show (still in the San Francisco area) after singing "I'll Remember You": "I don't think that's an obscure song, do you? Was that an obscure song? I don't think so …"

Two months later, near the end of a concert at the Santa Barbara County Bowl on August 7th, Dylan spoke to the crowd again: "Sometimes I feel that I should be down there and you should be up here."

Listening to a tape of the August 2nd show at the Greek Theater in Hollywood, a particularly heartfelt performance of "I'll Remember You" caught my attention. Obscure or not, and in spite of several lyric errors in the first verse, the song takes on new life and rare beauty this night. Captivated by the sweetness and fresh-ness of both the music and the vocal, I found myself wondering for the first time why a lover would say, in a song praising a beloved partner, "There's some people that you don't forget, even though you've only seen them one time or two." Could the "you" who to me was "the best," the one I'll remember "at the end of the trail," actually be a one-night stand? The question and the special flavor of this performance turned the song on its head for me, and for the first time it struck me that he could be addressing a very immediate "you," the audience in front of him now. I tend to think of "Seeing the Real You at Last," another song from *Empire Burlesque*, as being addressed to Dylan's live audience, because most of the many times I saw him perform it in 1986 he would point an arm and finger at the crowd while singing the chorus. But "I'll Remember You" had always hit my ears as a song to a very special romantic partner, until this August 2, 1988 version recently transformed for me the possible "message" of "Didn't I, didn't I try to love you? Didn't I, didn't I try to care?" and "Though I'd never say that I done it the way that you would have liked me to, in the end, my dear sweet friend, I'll remember you." I want to thank you for being so nice, indeed.

Bob Dylan's often troubled love affair with his live audience ("A million faces at my feet, but all I see are dark eyes") surely is central to the weaknesses and too infrequent strengths of his 1988 tour. A performing artist's urge to please can take away his creative freedom in subtle ways. The essence of creativity is awakeness, aliveness, presence in the moment. But the "safe" structures stage performers invent so they can more reliably do good work in the face of everchanging external and internal conditions can often lull them to sleep, rob them of their aliveness, of the source of their power to stop time, their power to awaken something in the other players and in themselves and in their audiences through spiritual attraction.

Dylan's dissatisfaction with the results of his energetic efforts to reach out to audiences in 1974 is documented in his 1985 and 2001 comments on that tour. The only indication we have that he wasn't too sure at the end of 1988 that his new band and approach to touring had allowed him or would allow him to recapture his purpose as a performer is his strange impulse in February 1989 to call the Grateful Dead asking to become a member of their band. What was it he wanted? We can't be certain, because the Dead said no, and after taking a few months off to record *Oh Mercy*, Dylan reassembled his 1988 band and resumed his Never Ending Tour in May 1989.

In the winter 1988–89 issue of *The Telegraph*, the editor, John Bauldie, quotes a tour insider he spoke to at a midsummer show as saying: "Bob wants to go on playing shows all the time. He wants an audience to follow him around from place to place, like the Dead. That's what he wants the fan club [the "Entertainment Connection" advertised on the inner sleeve of *Down in the Groove*] for – to encourage that kind of following." On another page of John Bauldie's tour diary in that issue, another manifestation of Dylan's new ideas about the importance of audience involvement is described: "A funny thing. At each show the security men work really hard for about 40 minutes to keep people out of the aisles and away from the stage, and then suddenly on a prearranged signal they get up, pack up their chairs and walk away, leaving approach to the stage free. Lately it's been happening on the second verse of 'Silvio' [first song of the second electric set], and the audience are 'allowed' to rush the stage. In fact, at the June 25 show nobody moved, and the security men had to wave people down, to encourage them to cluster at Bob's feet at the front of the stage." This practice continued for the next few years, reportedly because Dylan likes to be able to see people standing, and responding to the music, while he's performing.

Bauldie's editorial in the next issue (spring '89) apologizes to readers for his "negative" review in a U.K. music magazine of the recently released *Dylan & the Dead*: "It took a bit of heart-searching for me to go slagging Bobby off in public, but there are some things that I dislike so much that I can't help but say it right out loud … I think that it's a rotten record, and that it's such a shame that it stands as official testament of live performance since 1984. Especially after the 1988 shows, which were so terrific. My favorite at the moment is the Manchester concert, with its sparkling 'Visions of Johanna.' Give me that track alone and you can stuff the *Dylan & the Dead* record."

We all (everybody I talked with and saw commentary by) thought the '88 shows were terrific at the time. Note that Bauldie is referring to both the shows he saw (eight in late June and early July) and the tapes he's been listening to. I'm sympathetic with his enthusiasm for the Sept. 3 performance of "Visions" in Manchester, New Hampshire, but I find the rest of that recorded show a typically (for 1988) bleak listening experience, dull at best and embarrassing at worst (I'll cite the badly slurred vocal and shapeless, characterless band performance on "Like a Rolling Stone" as an example). This brings me to the awkward issue of the essentially subjective nature of all art criticism and commentary, including, of course, the study you are presently reading. Dylan raises this issue when he asks, "I don't think that's an obscure song, do you?" and when he speaks disparagingly of people praising his "emotionless" 1974 tour performances as "incredible energy, man." I also believe he expresses his sensitivity to and contempt for criticism (of himself and especially of his work) when he says, "The judge, he holds a grudge, he's gonna call on you … but he's badly built and he walks on stilts, watch out he don't fall on you" in his 1966 song "Most Likely You Go Your Way (and I'll Go Mine)."

So, like John Bauldie, I'm uncomfortable with the role of judge, especially when honesty and sincerity require me to be negative about certain works of the artist whom I came here to praise. I could be wrong, of course. Or I could change my view at some future time of relistening, as I've changed my view years later about certain excellent Dylan albums and songs that I'd failed to appreciate on first encounter. I suppose I could also change my mind about my enthusiasms, though I don't like to confront that possibility (and happily it hasn't happened to me much, so far). The truth is, all history of art which we're taught in schools or which we absorb otherwise is based on individual subjective judgments that have become consensus judgments and have thereby created the canons of "great" literature and visual art and music. Big responsibility. "Am I sure?" I do ask myself this, and spend a lot of time listening to the performances like "Gates of Eden" 6/13/88 that I find myself praising enthusiastically herein, to be as sure as possible of my opinion. This is pleasant work. Repeated listening to performances I've decided to dismiss as mediocre is not so rewarding. And I find certainty about mediocrity more elusive than certainty about greatness.

Consensus helps, of course. Early in the process of writing this volume, I struggled with my displeasure at almost everything I heard on the tapes of the Dylan/Dead summer '87 performances ... but I was comforted by the almost universal agreement among Dylan commentators about the poor quality of these shows. Such consensus is not yet available to me regarding my judgment that most of the 1988 shows described by John Bauldie in 1989 as "terrific" are in fact mediocre. Mediocrity, in any case, is the absence of excellence, so the crux of the matter is: can we trust our own abilities to detect excellence in such subjective realms as art appreciation and listening to recordings of live musical performances?

Probably not. But we can trust that if we go on record with our views, they will be disputed, leaving observers to wonder, "Whom should we believe?" The history of human art and culture, I repeat, is based on such processes. Let me share with you a slightly self-serving example of how this functions in the realm of Dylan scholarship. The reader will recall that I did find one performance to be very enthusiastic about from the Dylan/Dead concerts. Long after I wrote my resultant praises of "Queen Jane Approximately" as performed in Eugene 7/19/87 and included on the otherwise unfortunate *Dylan & the Dead* album, I was delighted to read an essay (in a Dylan symposium in *Mojo* magazine, June 2001) by Richard Williams, author of *Bob Dylan, A Man Called Alias* and long-time music critic on London's broadsheets, dedicated to expressing his enthusiasm for this particular performance ("In a humdrum year, one transcendent moment," reads the tag line above the article). Williams describes the Eugene "Queen Jane" as "a Dylan moment to put alongside all the precious ones from an earlier time," and ends his essay with this paragraph:

> When it came out, I wrote something in *The Times* about the track's "wrecked majesty" and, ten years later, got slapped on the wrist by Michael Gray in the third edition of *Song & Dance Man*. "This was wishful thinking," he wrote. "Wrecked, yes;

majesty, no." Which only goes to show how easily preconceptions can hinder genuine perception, and how people who spend too much time listening to the words so often miss the music.

Reading this, I was of course pleased to see a fellow listener/scholar going out on a limb to defend and praise a beloved and "obscure" performance that I also admired and had recently found myself praising publicly. Agreement is heartening, even though, like Dylan, I'm committed to not being disheartened by disagreement. Preconceptions do indeed hinder genuine perception, as Richard Williams notes, and I find it ironic to realize that – although I tend to be critical of fans who are unable to appreciate live Dylan performances because their expectations are so shaped by their familiarity with and attachment to the way he sounded as a performer/recording artist back in the past – the greatest hindrance to my appreciation of these 1988 show-recordings is that I am looking in them for, and failing to find, the sort of excellence and quality of presence and inventive interaction between singer and band that I've become accustomed to in listening to recordings of Dylan's Never Ending Tour shows from the 1990s ... the future, which he was still struggling to invent, seemingly unsuccessfully, during these 1988 performances.

Six weeks after ending his 1988 tour on October 19th in New York City, Dylan contributed a six-song acoustic performance (with G. E. Smith on second guitar) to a benefit concert in Oakland, California organized by Neil Young on behalf of a school for disabled children. Young introduced Dylan at this Bridge School Benefit as "my favorite songwriter in the world for many many years," and Dylan then began his set with two songs he didn't write: Jesse Fuller's "San Francisco Bay Blues" and Woody Guthrie's "Pretty Boy Floyd." Again, selections from his 1961 repertoire (although "Pretty Boy" was also the most recently released Dylan recording; *A Vision Shared*, the Guthrie tribute album with Dylan's 1987 version of the song, had been in stores since August 24).

The next three songs played by Dylan and Smith at their Bridge Benefit appearance were "With God on Our Side," "Girl from the North Country" and "Gates of Eden," all songs that had been included frequently in acoustic sets at the end of the tour. The sixth song, "Forever Young," had been played in concert only once

before in 1988 in an acoustic version (it was also performed three
times in '88 in an electric version). The tape of the benefit performance shows that Dylan's voice had recovered significantly during
his six weeks off; unfortunately, it also suggests again that the
two-guitar acoustic set format was not very stimulating for Dylan as
a performer in 1988. These are again lackluster, uninspired performances, interesting solely because this was only the third time in
his career that Dylan is known to have performed "Pretty Boy
Floyd" on stage and because, as he had at the October shows,
Dylan added to "With God on Our Side" a verse about the
Vietnam War that he didn't write – the Neville Brothers had added
it when they recorded the song on an album produced by Daniel
Lanois earlier that autumn. Dylan learned it when he visited a
recording session for that album (*Yellow Moon*) after playing a show
in New Orleans in late September.

Altogether, Dylan performed 87 different songs at his 1988
shows. Many of these were unexpected and intriguing selections,
including "cover" songs as disparate as "I'm in the Mood for Love"
(from a 1935 film), "She's About a Mover" (1965 pop/rock hit,
sung with the song's author, Doug Sahm, at a show in Alberta),
"Hallelujah" by Leonard Cohen (performed in Cohen's hometown,
Montreal, and again at a show in Hollywood), Chuck Berry's
"Nadine" (performed in Berry's hometown, St. Louis), "Eileen
Aroon" (a traditional Irish ballad), "We Three (My Echo, My
Shadow and Me)" (originally done by '30s and '40s black vocal group
the Ink Spots), and two Johnny Cash songs, "Give My Love to Rose"
and "Big River" ("Bob Dylan told me he heard the opening lines
of 'Big River' on his radio when he was a teenager in Hibbing,
Minnesota, and he says they seemed to him 'just words that turned
into bone'" – Nicholas Dawidoff. Elsewhere in Dawidoff's 1997
book *In the Country of Country*, he writes: "I recently asked Bob Dylan if
he thinks it might become boring for Cash to sing the same songs
every night for so long, and he scoffed at the notion. 'They're just so
automatically perpetual,' Dylan says. 'They always existed and they
always will exist. Who would get bored singing those?'").

As for unexpected *Dylan* songs introduced to his live repertoire
in '88, I've already mentioned "Subterranean Homesick Blues,"
"Absolutely Sweet Marie" "Driftin' Too Far from Shore," and
"Bob Dylan's 115th Dream." The latter was performed at all of the
last six concerts of the tour, but the lyrics aren't always intelligible

on the tapes, and Dylan seldom seems present enough in the song or its story to convey any of the humor that is at the heart of this 1965 talking blues. Which makes me suspect that he knew his 1988 mission to rediscover America, and himself, had gone astray, gotten lost somewhere, presumably making him all the more determined, deep in his music-loving heart, to keep trying.

In two earlier chapters of this book I mentioned that "it sometimes takes Dylan more than six shows to find his voice, and his confidence as an artist and bandleader, at the start of a new tour." Very ironically, I now find myself thinking 1988 would be a much better Dylan-year if only the other sixty-five shows had more of the flavor and presence one can hear in the first six shows of 1988 (Concord, Sacramento, Berkeley, Mountain View, Park City, Denver). It's as though, this time around, once he did find his voice and stage-confidence, he lost the freedom and aliveness and power-of-spiritual-attraction that are central to his success as a performing artist and that have resulted in his very many great works of accidental art. This of course is just one listener's view, and I encourage others to find (and defend, be faithful to) their own truths and genuine perceptions regarding the quality and value and high points of the 1988 tour and its show-recordings. After a lot of listening, I'm surprised by my own ambivalence about such arguable high points as "Visions of Johanna" in Manchester Sept. 3, "Wagoner's Lad" in Upper Darby, Oct. 14, and "Every Grain of Sand" in Hollywood, Aug. 2.

The 9/3/88 "Visions of Johanna" was Dylan's first performance of the song in twelve years, and only his third performance of it since 1966 ... and his first-ever "electric" live version of "Visions." The uptempo arrangement is bright and fun to listen to, because Dylan seems to be enjoying experimenting with a new way of approaching a major work. At times, I agree with my friend John Bauldie's description of the track as "sparkling," and understand why he was so charmed by what can be heard as a friendly and fearless deconstruction of the song (I myself was thrilled and charmed by Dylan's 1976 spontaneous electric deconstruction of "Tangled Up in Blue," when I encountered it on a tape of the May 23 Fort Collins show). But this 1988 live "Visions" can grate on me, like so many 1988 performances, on repeat listenings. It is certainly not an example of a performer/singer going as deep as he can. At times, it just sounds to me like an uninspired vocal on top of an uninspired band performance. That this is too common on the '88 tapes is demonstrated by the next performance of the 9/3/88 show: "Shelter from the Storm" sung too fast and with no feeling on top of metronomic drumming and a band performance that does indeed sound like it might have been made for television.

In his book *A Life in Stolen Moments*, Clinton Heylin writes that the 10/14/88 acoustic performance of the traditional folksong "Wagoner's Lad" (sung in the first encore slot, as it was at the four concerts that followed) "features a particularly beautiful vocal by Dylan." It's a pretty song, and a pleasure to hear Dylan attempt it. And some days I hear beauty in this performance, other days very little. I find myself responding in this contradictory manner to many of the '88 acoustic performances. Although they could be very striking if you were at the concert or when first encountered on tape, they mostly fall short of the standard of excellence set by Dylan in this kind of performance on other tours – which I interpret to be a matter of the singer failing to find his Muse or any sort of inspiration very often in the format of the 1988 acoustic performances.

My 1977 edition of Webster's dictionary defines "ambivalence" as "simultaneous attraction toward and repulsion from an object, person, or action." That makes it an appropriate word for my reaction to Bob Dylan's performance of "Every Grain of Sand" in Hollywood, California on August 2, 1988. Again, he shouts his way through the song; but in this case, since the form of this song is a sort of oracular declamation, this singing style results in an unexpectedly powerful and fresh performance. Hence the attraction. The repulsion arises from my doubts (ambivalence in the secondary definition of "continual fluctuation between one thing and its opposite") about the singer's sincerity in his delivery of these sensitive, spiritually autobiographical lyrics that depend utterly on their listener's willingness to suspend disbelief regarding the speaker's sincerity. Suffice to say, this is a performance that anyone interested in Bob Dylan's life and work will find of interest. Whether they will find it thrilling, or ultimately unsatisfying, or even troubling, probably depends, based on my experience with it, on their state of mind at the time of listening.

8/2/88, though not as consistently enjoyable as 7/1, is worth seeking out among the 1988 show-recordings. Along with its powerful "Grain" and the aforementioned fine "I'll Remember You," it offers a quite pretty and pleasing "You're a Big Girl Now" and climaxes about halfway through in a memorable acoustic performance of "Trail of the Buffalo." It's not that Dylan tells the story here with great conviction, but – as with some of the other 1988 performances of "Trail" and "Eileen Aroon" and "The Lakes of Pontchartrain" – that the sound of his voice, and its resonance with the accompanying guitars, is so appealing, so full of strength and even joy, as though at this moment the performer is at one with his purpose and is expressing it in his voice and through his sense of the drama and pacing of the song he's singing.

For an example of the freedom and aliveness I say can be heard in the early 1988 shows, let me mention "Just Like a Woman," the first song in the second electric set in Denver, June 15. Here we can hear Dylan trying out his forceful/energetic singing style and feeling out his relationship with his new band and the sound he's directed them towards. At moments this sounds like "Just Like a Woman" as if sung by Johnny Rotten of the Sex Pistols. The effect is both comic and exhilarating. One imagines that in another year, when Dylan might have been moved to lead the band further into the unknown and fertile territory suggested to him by what he hears himself and them doing, this could have become something quite remarkable and successful on its own terms, rather than the interesting portrait of a singing style in progress that it is.

For an example of Dylan's occasional power-of-spiritual-attraction before he decided to lay back and let G. E. Smith just be the leader he naturally was of the band he'd put together: in addition to "Gates of Eden" on 6/13/88, there's the very next performance at that Park City, Utah show, a unique and indeed remarkable "License to Kill." As with "Gates," the power of the performance is in Dylan's excellent vocal, his unusual presence within every phrase of the song. And this presence is made possible and supported by the responsiveness of the band's accompaniment, which is full of space for what Dylan is doing, and sensitive to and expressive of the particular spirit he's breathing into the song today. You can hear his voice and the drums responding to each other, augmented by articulate lead guitar figures that clearly are spontaneous responses to the vocal phrases immediately preceding them. One imagines Dylan took charge of the stage and the music during that powerful "Gates of Eden" and then this naturally carried over into the next performance, again producing a very strong and awake piece of music.

Why is this the exception rather than the rule this year? I suspect because both Dylan and the band fell back into a sort of default relationship created during rehearsals and then perpetuated by Dylan's lingering uncertainty about how to achieve the sort of audience–artist relationship he longed for after watching the Grateful Dead and their crowd. "You'd find it at times [his purpose as a performer] and then it would disappear again for a while." Soon it would reappear and stay for a very long time indeed.

IV. "Nobody Breathes Like Me"

December 1988 – August 1990

10.

On December 6, 1988, two days after the Bridge School Benefit concert and seven weeks after the release of *Traveling Wilburys, Volume One,* Roy Orbison died of a heart attack. That pretty much ended any short-term consideration of a Wilburys tour or concert. In mid-January, Dylan reportedly rehearsed with Smith, Parker and Aaronson at Montana Studios in New York City, even though their first shows of the year would not be until the end of May.

February 6, 1989, the album *Dylan & the Dead* was released. On February 12th, Dylan made a surprise appearance at a Grateful Dead concert in Inglewood, California, playing guitar on eight songs and also sharing vocals on three, the encores, "Stuck Inside of Mobile with the Memphis Blues Again," "Not Fade Away," and "Knockin' on Heaven's Door." According to biographer Howard Sounes, "Bob insisted he play only Grateful Dead songs. Unfortunately he did not know the words and he made a mess of five of their songs before the band forced him to sing his own." Sounes says Dylan called the Grateful Dead office the next day and said he wanted to join the band ("He made it clear that he was serious"). He quotes Bob Weir: "I think we would have [taken him], if it

171

hadn't been for that one guy [a band member who voted against it]. We would have picked him up as a sort of temporary band member."

So it didn't happen. But Bob Dylan came very close, at the beginning of 1989, to pulling off the most dramatic expression of his desire to free himself from his audience and his myth since his very public embrace of Jesus Christ as his Savior in 1979 (and subsequent tour asking his listeners to do the same). The 1970 album *Self-Portrait* and even "going electric" in 1965 can be seen as expressions of the same impulse. "There must be some way out of here!" It's the exact opposite of "I'm determined to stand!" – but Dylan has often acknowledged his tendency to contradict himself. Before I knew of Dylan's Feb. '89 phone call, I wrote in chapter 3 of this book that Dylan in 1988 "fantasized about somehow becoming the Grateful Dead" the way he dreamed in high school of joining Little Richard. Creating "Bob Dylan" in the first place, the voice, the fictional history, the persona, took a lot of imagination and courage ... and for Bob Dylan with his actual history as of the end of 1988 to dissolve himself into being a musician member of America's most popular and idiosyncratic touring band would have been a related act of imagination and self-invention (or deconstruction). And surely would not have been a good fit, musically or otherwise, and not particularly beneficial to the Grateful Dead and their sense of purpose and identity. Dylan clearly coveted the Dead's audience, and was still having a hard time being at peace with his own audience, or his ideas and feelings about them and what he imagined they expected of him. How tempting it must have been for him to have a chance to gain one audience and escape the other in one bold act. Perhaps the boldness of the act (again like the 1979 conversion) was its most seductive aspect.

In any case, the roving gambler (as Dylan would later characterize himself, by opening concerts with that song) had another card up his sleeve: the strongest batch of songs he'd written in more than five years. In March 1989 he began recording them in New Orleans with his new producer, Daniel Lanois. Lanois had coproduced two albums for U2, and when Dylan played some of the new songs for his friend Bono of U2, Bono suggested, according to Dylan, that "Daniel could really record them right." Lanois, a Canadian living in England, was on an extended working visit to New Orleans in summer 1988, and when Dylan and his band played a show in the

Big Easy in late September, Lanois "came to see me," Dylan later recalled, in an interview to promote the Lanois-produced album, *Oh Mercy* (released in September 1989). "We hit it off. He had an understanding of what my music was all about. It was thrilling to run into Daniel because he's a competent musician and he knows how to record with modern facilities ... He managed to get my stage voice, something other people working with me never were quite able to achieve."

This last comment is very suggestive. It sounds as though (in 1989) Dylan thinks of his stage voice (presumably meaning what he hears and feels himself doing when he's up there) as his true voice as an artist, attainable most nights on the road but often elusive (it seems to him) in the recording studio. It also sounds as though he tends to think (understandably) that whether or not his "stage voice" is captured on a recording is a function of technological considerations and of the producer's and recording engineer's knowledge of or approach to the equipment. No doubt this is true to some degree, but it is the premise of this series of books and, I believe, the consensus of a large community of listeners, that Bob Dylan's stage voice – and many remarkable examples of great and enduring vocal artistry – can be heard on recordings made for the most part by amateurs with relatively simple recording equipment smuggled into concerts and used surreptitiously ("accidental art"). There are significant variations in the technical quality of these surreptitious recordings, of course, but again I believe that the consensus of the community of listeners is that the primary factor affecting the value of a particular (recorded) Dylan concert performance is the state of mind of the singer, the performing artist. Dylan acknowledges this to some extent in the interview quoted above (with Edna Gundersen of *USA Today* newspaper) when he says: "Daniel just allowed the record to take place any old time, day or night. You didn't have to walk through secretaries, pinball machines and managers and hangers-on in the lobby and parking lots and elevators and arctic temperatures." Thus, Lanois's achievement was not just based on knowing how to record with modern facilities but also on knowing how to free a singer from the feeling of being imprisoned or oppressed by modern facilities and the distractions that go with the territory.

I like *Oh Mercy* very much, and consider it quite worthy of the status it is granted by many listeners and commentators as a solid example of, let's say, the second level of excellence among Dylan's albums, slightly below the exalted first rank (i.e., *Blonde on Blonde*, *Highway 61 Revisited*, *Blood on the Tracks*, *John Wesley Harding*, etc.) but still as likely to reward repeated listenings and to endure as a work of art beyond its creator's era as such albums as *Another Side of Bob Dylan* or *The Times They Are A-Changin'* or *Planet Waves* or (the reader is invited to fill in the blank with another beloved if not superlative example of Bob Dylan's craft) ... and certainly far above *Knocked Out Loaded* or *Down in the Groove* or *Dylan & the Dead*, his album releases in the three years leading up to this one.

Oh Mercy, like, say, the amateur recording of Bob Dylan's September 1987 concert in Munich, Germany, is a (very aesthetically gratifying and stimulating) portrait of a moment when this artist truly felt inspired to *perform*. We have to move our minds outside of time a little to identify this moment. The unity of place and time that characterizes the plays of Sophocles and Euripides (according to Aristotle) is apparent in a concert recording, an auditory snapshot of a singer or a band on stage in a particular theater on a particular day for a certain number of minutes. *Oh Mercy*, on the other hand, was recorded over a period of six weeks in what Lanois called Studio on the Move ("it's more a state of mind than a specific address"), a portable recording studio set up wherever he and his artists decided to work. For the very first *Oh Mercy* sessions in early March '89, the Studio on the Move was located in an apartment in EMLAH Court on St. Charles Avenue in New Orleans where Lanois and the Neville Brothers had recorded their album *Yellow Moon* a few months earlier. "Where Teardrops Fall" was probably recorded here. But soon Lanois and Dylan decided a change of venue was appropriate, and on March 7 Lanois relocated the Studio on the Move to a big blue house at 1305 Soniat Street in New Orleans. The rest of the album and some portentous outtakes ("Series of Dreams," "Dignity," "Born in Time," "God Knows") were recorded here between March 7 and 24. But atypically, Dylan did some vocal overdubs (occasionally with new and revised lyrics) on some of these songs, and these were recorded at 1305 Soniat between April 3 and April 12, 1989.

The moment that *Oh Mercy* captures so powerfully also includes some days in summer 1988 when most of these songs were probably written (Lanois reports that "Dylan came in [to the sessions] with songs completed," although "Man in the Long Black Coat" was written in the studio and other songs, notably "Shooting Star," were rewritten and restructured during the sessions; Dylan has said, "Yeah, those songs had come to me during that last year"). "I was thinking of a series of dreams," Dylan wrote (and sang) sometime during this extended moment, "where nothing comes up to the top. Everything stays down where it's wounded, and comes to a permanent stop. Wasn't thinking of anything specific, like in a dream when someone wakes up and screams. Nothing too very scientific. Just thinking of a series of dreams." And living a series of dreams. And finding ways, with the help of a "thrilling" new collaborator, to share those nonlinear dream-perceptions in an album of performed song-pictures as vital and alive and true to his artistry as a particularly good night out on the road.

Richard Williams (in his *London Times* review of *Oh Mercy*) has again articulated my own experience of a Dylan performance, by writing: "Throughout *Oh Mercy*, Dylan's delivery is relaxed and confident. He sounds like a Bob Dylan you could talk to [as opposed to other recent albums where "he sounds uncomfortable in his own skin"]. How did Lanois pull it off? At a guess, by enfolding the notoriously nervy Dylan in a sympathetic working environment." Williams went on to point out, in a helpful insight, that Lanois's use of portable equipment in a converted house "to escape the prefabricated studio-as-factory atmosphere ... was how Dylan and the Band recorded the seminal *Basement Tapes* and *Music from Big Pink* in a Woodstock mansion twenty-two years ago."

Nothing too very scientific. "This last record here came out of nowhere, really," Dylan told Adrian Deevoy in October '89, "There certainly wasn't any plan on my part to make any *statement*."

And, as often happens for me with the concert tapes: plan or no, I love the statement he did find himself making. Even the sequence is impeccable. "We live in a political world ..." Is this the only Dylan album that opens with the word "we"? Yeah, and maybe the first D. song that does since "Tears of Rage." How surprising that Bob Dylan, who has an allergy to being thought of as the voice of any generation, in 1989 feels like making a statement about the human condition to his audience, whoever they are, using an inclusive personal pronoun, as if he really does feel like he's speaking for someone, an "us." Unlike several of my peers (Michael Gray calls "Political World" "a bore" and says "there's no heart in it"; Clinton Heylin describes Dylan as having achieved a breakthrough in his songwriting in the *Oh Mercy* songs – "Dylan seems to be taking a single thought, shattering it and following each shard part of the way" – but says, "On 'Political World' the trick fails because the idea itself cannot sustain the song"), I enjoy "Political World" almost every time I hear it, and consider it very successful at fulfilling its task as opening song of this album/performance (like "Subterranean Homesick Blues" and "Gotta Serve Somebody" and "Tangled Up in Blue," it reintroduces the singer/songwriter to his listeners: "Here I am, and this is who I am this time!").

I like the *sound* of "Political World" – the sound of the singer's voice, certainly, and the feel of the musical accompaniment, starting with the 25-second synthesizer-bass & drums-guitars intro. For me the rising and never-relieved rock and roll tension of the instruments and the vocal together is very effective at setting up the entire 39-minute *Oh Mercy* experience. It's a very bold opening, in fact, creating an expectation in the listener/observer (every time he or she listens) that something wonderful is about to be presented and shared. Tension/release. There's no release in the song, no musical or lyrical bridge, or chorus. So the "message" of the song is underlined again and again and release of the masterfully built-up tension is postponed to occur during other tracks ... and those tracks don't disappoint. As "It's Alright, Ma" is a belated payoff for "Subterranean Homesick Blues," and as "Slow Train" and "Precious Angel" and "When He Returns" are for "Gotta Serve Somebody" (and "Idiot Wind" and "If You See Her, Say Hello" for "Tangled Up in Blue"), so "Ring Them Bells" and "Man in the Long Black Coat" and "Most of the Time" and ultimately "Shooting Star" are payoffs and delicious releases for tension built up in the album's opening track, a tension sustained, arguably, in a more metaphysical way ("When's he gonna start being **Bob Dylan**?") through the next two early tracks, "Where Teardrops Fall" and "Everything Is Broken."

When Heylin says (in his book *Bob Dylan: The Recording Sessions*), "the idea itself ('We live in a political world ...') cannot sustain the song," he helps us understand why Gray was bored and why the song does not seem to have had much impact on the "we" Dylan's speaking for, even though similarly unsubtle litanies made their author a legend in another era. For Dylan, the observation "we live in a political world" does indeed sustain his interest and passion throughout the song's eleven verses. You can hear this in his voice, feel it in the earnestness of his performance (whether he planned to make a statement or not, he can't hold himself back here, not when the track he's singing to is such a splendid and stimulating realization of what he was hearing in his head when he wrote this tune). But the repeated phrase ("... political world") doesn't work for Gray or Heylin or probably for very many listeners because it's in a kind of private language that genuinely resonates for its author but isn't an effective summation for many of the rest of "us" of what's out-of-kilter about this world or civilization we find ourselves living in. I think by "political world," Dylan means a human world that is dominated by the lust for and manipulation of institutional power ... and therefore empty of other values. The first time he sings, "We live in a political world," he follows it and explains his phrase by saying, "Love don't have any place." Something wrong with a "world" in which the latter statement is true. The next two lines, "We're living in times where men commit crimes/And crime don't have a face," I interpret as being a reference to crimes committed against the poor and powerless of the Earth by faceless corporate and governmental decision-makers (crimes that don't *seem* to be crimes like a murder or robbery committed by a person standing in front of the victim). There are moments in these verses quite worthy of Dylan the social commentator of "It's Alright, Ma" and "Masters of War": "As soon as you're awake, you're trained to take/What looks like the easy way out." In other words, you go to work and participate in activities with dire consequences for distant others in order to "make a living," as you've been trained to do. Because the Buddhist monk/peace activist whose writings I resonate with was exiled from his country (Vietnam) and saw his young students killed by both the Communist rebels and the Catholic government because he and they were advocating "peace," I recognize a succinct wisdom in: "We live in a political world/Where peace is not welcome at all/It's turned away from the door to wander some more/Or put up against the wall."

What Dylan expresses so passionately (but not resonantly for every listener) in this song is familiar to those of us who've read his interviews over the years. In the 1985 interview included in the box set *Biograph*, he told Cameron Crowe: "The truth about anything in this society, as you know, is too threatening. Gossip is King. It's like 'conscience' is a dirty word. Whatever is truthful haunts you and don't let you sleep at night." Compare this with "We live in a political world/Wisdom is thrown into jail/It rots in a cell, discarded as

hell/Leaving no one to pick up the trail." Or with these verses from
the early 16-verse outtake version: "Truth is the outlaw of life/It's
hunted and slain, and there's no one to arraign/Or put under a
doctor's knife." "Conscience don't have a clue/Climb into bed, talk
out of your head/You're not even sure that it's you."

So Dylan is telling/sharing his truth in "Political World," and
the more I listen to it the more I'm struck by its language (along
with the overall sound and the singer's timing and phrasing). "We
live in a political world/Where mercy walks the plank/Life is in
mirrors, death disappears/Up the steps into the nearest bank." This
is rich, inspired language. "Mercy" is clearly compassion, executed
by the pirates who run this world because it interferes with the
profitability of death. So we can understand the album's title as an
expression of compassion with compassion itself, and its harsh fate
in our "political" world.

Commenting on how this 1989 protest song starts (and thus
starts the album) with the word "we," the Dylan album-opener that
first came to my mind was "The Times They Are A-Changin'." That
song does not contain the word "we," although the feeling of the
word is implicit in the balladeer's opening phrase "Come gather
round people" and is more strongly felt by the song's listeners when
the speaker tells "mothers and fathers throughout the land" that
"your sons and daughters are beyond your command" ... because
the structure of the song and its language suggest that the speaker is
as one with those sons and daughters who are asking "you" to get
out of this new road "if you can't lend a hand." Because the implicit
"we" is so strong on this album, and at this historical moment, there
is an enormous emotional payoff when Dylan sings "When the Ship
Comes In" much later on the record (another powerful anthem that
strongly implies that there is a "we" community that is on the ship
and that is being spoken for here), because in the last verse of that
song the speaker/singer finally confirms that he does indeed see
himself as one of the ship's crew when he uses the first person plural
pronoun to say (to the "they" who are surrendering), "We'll shout
from the bow, 'Your days are numbered!'"

From such subtleties the relationships between artists and audiences are built. And one would underrate Bob Dylan to think it is
only by accident that a song that repeats the phrase "we live in a
political world" eleven times (heightening the claustrophobic quality
of this awareness with every verse and every repetition) is followed

immediately on his album by the words, "Far away where the soft winds blow/Far away from it all/There is a place you go ..." Clearly, the message is: there is some way out of here; there is another world, another place you can go.

The nature of that place is intentionally or accidentally masked by the title of the second song (and the final phrase in the verse just quoted), "Where Teardrops Fall" ... because "teardrops" as a word belongs to the language of love songs, and so the easy assumption by the listener is that this must be a, possibly autobiographical, man–woman love song. And the "place" must be their trysting place. But none of the other language in the song confirms this, although the peaceful beauty of the song's music, in contrast to the claustrophobic tension of the previous track in which we were intimate with the same voice but in a different mood (a mood of sympathetic urgency in the first song, one of blessed and delicate and richly textured relief in the second), could suggest a love song.

The transitions on this album are always stimulating and pleasing, particularly the transitions between the different voices and moods of the same vocalist, and the related differences in the sounds of each track, each recorded song and performance. Therefore, just as the phrase "far away" is suggestive as the next words after a song about being trapped in an unpleasant world, it might be worth noticing that the last words of the previous song were: "... shout God's name/But you're not even sure what it is." The sound of the new song and of the voice should be enough to help us recognize that the intimate friend addressed here, as in many Dylan songs, is a spiritual rather than a human love object. "You are there in the flickering light." The strongest clue might be the line "Thinking of you when the sun comes up," which can bring us back to "I believe in you even on the morning after/Oh, when the dawn is nearing/Oh, when the night is disappearing/Oh, this feeling's still here in my heart" ("I Believe in You," 1979).

In this context "We banged the drum slowly/And played the fife lowly" in the third verse could be a kind of communal invocation of the holy spirit, immediately leading to the I/Thou of "You know the song in my heart" and the humble, prayerful "You can show me a new place to start." It's a beautiful song, though, like "Political World," it has been scorned by some commentators.

The late Bert Cartwright, in the 1992 edition of his book *The Bible in the Lyrics of Bob Dylan*, rightly says there is something "spiritually haunting" about "Where Teardrops Fall," and provides some interesting insights into how biblical language that Dylan is surely familiar with may have influenced the wording of the first line of the fourth verse. The entire verse is:

> I've torn my clothes and I've drained the cup
> Strippin' away at it all
> Thinking of you when the sun comes up
> Where teardrops fall.

Cartwright comments:

> "I've torn my clothes" is a common Hebrew expression of profound grief as is illustrated in 2 Samuel 3:31: *Then David said to Joab and to all the people who were with him, "Rend your clothes and gird on sackcloth and mourn before Abner."* The phrase "I've drained the cup" possibly alludes to Psalms 75:8: *For in the hand of the Lord there is a cup, with foaming wine, well mixed; and he will pour a draught from it, and all the wicked of the earth shall drain it down to the dregs.*

Dylan's interest in the aural as well as lyrical transitions between the songs (or movements) on this album is particularly evident in the little saxophone concerto that surprisingly and very pleasingly concludes "Where Teardrops Fall," following the line, "I just might have to come see you …" This is a pleasure to the listener – similar in form to Dylan's long harmonica solos at the ends of many of his best recorded song-performances – regardless of what one supposes the song to be about; and when one tunes in, consciously or intuitively, to the spiritually haunting aspect of the song, it certainly becomes a powerful evocation of what Dylan in "Every Grain of Sand" referred to as "the pool of tears beneath my feet in the hour of my deepest need."

Even if one feels one has been hearing a man–woman love song, this saxophone passage is so fulfilling, so rich in beauty and feeling, that it is striking (and, again, surprising) that the next sound one hears is kind of silly, a boogie riff reminiscent of hit television themes like "Peter Gunn" and "Batman." From the sublime to the ridiculous? Yes, but. But this remarkable composer/performer/album-builder had a moment earlier conveyed his listeners very skillfully from the seemingly ridiculous ("Roses are red, violets are blue") to the sublime ("Time is beginning to crawl") and now we are inclined to trust ourselves to his whims, and just let him call the shots. "Roses are red ...", it occurs to us, is poetic "filler" used in amateur versifying like Valentine messages, and thus just what a serious poet might want to say to express a subjective mind-state in which time is beginning to crawl (and so he can't think of anything fresher to say here). This is songwriting as performance, juggling unlikely and awkward objects in real time before our eyes (and ears) and not just getting away with it but creating powerful new meanings and aesthetics in the act, so cleverly that spontaneity seems brilliantly premeditated. This is actually the Bob Dylan we've always loved.

And this third song, "Everything Is Broken," deftly manages to be less ridiculous than its boogie riff and seemingly predictable "list" structure suggest ... and, thanks to the charm and particular energy of the singer's delivery, might even sound sublime, depending on the mood and mind-state the listener happens to be in when he or she encounters it (again; albums, unlike concerts, are made to be experienced over and over).

What is delightful about "Everything Is Broken" is, once more, the vocal performance and the sound of the track (its *feel*), and the stimulating effect of this sound and this vocal performance and this message alongside these other songs and *their* sounds and vocals and messages. On *Oh Mercy*, Lanois not only manages to get Dylan's "stage voice," but also succeeds in reawakening, or anyway making a safe space for, Dylan's remarkable intuitive gift for album-building. The two probably go together. Dylan's stage voice and his ability to create wonderfully unitary assemblages and art objects like *The Freewheelin' Bob Dylan* and *Highway 61 Revisited* and *Blonde on Blonde* are expressions of his performer instincts, his sense of audience and his keen ability to create and communicate in a milieu separate from any fixed ideas and concepts about who's observing and what they expect or need from him. The performer creates his listener like a lover invents and creates his or her beloved in the act of and at the moment of lovemaking. It's an inspired activity. Bob Dylan's artistry, his songs, his albums, his concerts, have always been muse-driven in the sense that his best results in every medium have always come when he's been able to allow himself to trust and follow and be guided by intuition, accident, and inspiration. His great albums have all been created at moments when, for whatever reasons, he felt himself standing on a stage in the recording studio (and at his typewriter or notebook) with "a million faces at my feet," a world-stage outside of time, allowing him to whisper sweet nothings in the ears of, and do his best to charm and surprise, a very worthy and intimate audience unrestricted by space or time. Feeling himself in this relationship to his imagined or felt listeners inspires him, and when this performer is inspired, he often breaks new ground in his chosen art forms – he gets extraordinary results.

Not to say that "Everything Is Broken" is extraordinary, but that the particular charms of this recording and performance, following the two songs that come before it and preceding the three blockbusters that come next, do make a meaningful contribution to the extraordinary achievement of *Oh Mercy* as a whole, as the modest and delightful absurdities of "From a Buick 6" contribute in their way, and thanks to their location in the listening sequence, to *Highway 61 Revisited*.

The particular energy of Bob Dylan's overdubbed (i.e. sung to a previously recorded track, not live in the studio while the musicians are playing) vocal on "Everything Is Broken" is the sound of happiness (in sharp contrast to the literal message of these lines). Because of the existence, and availability to fans and students, of an early take of this song with quite different lyrics, we know Dylan has recently rewritten these verses (even the chorus line has evolved, from "everything broken" to "everything is broken"; and it seems the working title of the song when it was first attempted in March was "Broken Days"). I don't think Dylan is ad-libbing the new lines as he's singing this album version of the song, the way he ad-libbed much of "Gotta Serve Somebody" at the fall '87 shows (Lanois to an interviewer: "Dylan's a very committed lyricist; he would walk into the studio and put his head into the pages of words that he had and not let up until it was done"). But it's not easy to tell, because the singer at this moment is truly present with the fun he had following the flow of language suggested by the song's premise (start with the repeated word "broken" and fill in the blanks, guided by considerations of meter and rhyme and of overall theme and narrative message). So he sings as though he were inventing these clever (and cheerfully disposable) lines at this moment.

It's not a great song but it is an exceptional performance, an opportunity for the listener to experience the joys of writing, inventing, rapping, collaborating with the Muse and the universe. Words come fast, sometimes, and often surprise and delight their speaker/

author as they arrive. "Everything Is Broken" begins, "Broken lines," which could almost be self-referential, since the form of this song is a pause, or break, after every two words. The next phrase is "broken strings," retroactively changing "lines" in the listener's mind to the sort of lines that belong in a group with strings, maybe fishing lines or clotheslines. Continuing in this group, the next phrase (beginning the second line of the song) is "broken threads." The need for a rhyme determines that the next broken item is "springs." This is particularly satisfying, to the listener and the composer, when the fourth line of the verse turns out to be "People sleeping in broken beds," because broken springs are traditionally (in recent centuries) the most common and unpleasant element in broken beds.

The third line of the verse is "Broken idols, broken heads." The first part of this has its origins in the first draft of the song, "Broken Days," where Dylan sings towards the end, "Broken idols, broken heroes/Broken numbers, adding up to zeroes." Why "Broken idols, broken heads"? Dylan has described the *Oh Mercy* compositions as "stream-of-consciousness songs" (speaking of how he wrote them). If Dylan lifted his eyes from his scribbled-on pages of words in the Studio on the Move in April '89 and wondered why his mind followed "idols" with "heads," I'm sure he, like me, heard the phrase "idol with the golden head" come up in his mind ... and probably more quickly than me recognized it as the title of a 1957 song by the rock and roll group the Coasters. When you listen to him sing "Everything Is Broken" on *Oh Mercy*, you can share his amusement and sense of wonder at this process. My sense of Dylan as a songwriter, in the '60s and in this case in the '80s, is that he'll notice an internal rhyme ("threads" "heads") sometime after he's produced it, and notice an appropriate image match ("broken springs" "broken beds") once it's already in place, and feel good about what he has almost unconsciously given birth to. Later, people will attribute all sorts of conscious intentions to his choices of words, and that will sometimes flatter him, sometimes irritate him. Mostly, though, I believe it's a joy for him when a place to start (in this case a single word, "broken") results in a flow of language and a song to sing that satisfies his musician and performer needs and instincts. In the album version of "Everything Is Broken," he expresses as a performer his delight in the very appropriate sound of the track these New Orleans musicians have laid down in collaboration with him for his song, and demonstrates the playful spirit aroused in him by the way this flow of language (jotted down months before, then recorded in March and rewritten in April) has gathered itself into a song to sing, now and on many future stages – "my songs were not written with the idea in mind that anyone else would sing them, they were written for me to play live & that is the sort of end of it."

In "Broken Days," there is a verse that starts, "Broken lives hang by a thread/Broken bones in a broken bed." In "Everything Is Broken," this metamorphoses into the just-described verse, with thread now plural and also broken, and into the rather dire "Broken bodies, broken bones" of the third verse, which is marvelously followed by "Broken voices on broken phones." Not a great song, perhaps, but certainly a great songwriting experience, and thanks to this singer's gift for being present in a performance, an experience we all can share now (the fun of the writing, and the fun of singing these words to this accompaniment, at this moment in this house in New Orleans).

One last thing I want to point to in "Everything Is Broken" is the deft manner in which the personal pronoun "you" changes its identity between the first bridge and the second bridge. In the first bridge – "Seem like every time you stop and turn around/Something else just hit the ground" – it clearly means "one," you or me or anybody. In the similarly worded second bridge – "Every time you leave and go off someplace/Things fall to pieces in my face" – the inclusion of the word "my" indicates that "you" is now a specific other person, probably a lover (possibly a personal assistant). So for this moment, "Everything Is Broken" becomes a possible love song, instead of the complaint about the state of the world ("Take a deep breath, feel like you're chokin'") it can seem to be in its album position two tracks after "We live in a political world/Love don't have any place." Amusingly, taken as an autobiographical statement, this second bridge directly contradicts the repeated boasts in the album's sixth track, "Most of the Time" ("I don't even notice she's gone") ...

Returning again to Dylan's 1988 essay for the Hendrix exhibition, the triumph of *Oh Mercy* is that as a whole and track by track it serves as a splendid demonstration of what he meant when he wrote: "my songs are different & i don't expect others to make attempts to sing them because you have to get somewhat inside & behind them & it's hard enough for me to do it sometimes & then obviously you have to be in the right frame of mind. but even then there would be a vague value to it because nobody breathes like me so they couldn't be expected to portray the meaning of a certain phrase in the correct way without bumping into other phrases & altering the mood, changing the understanding & just giving up so that they then become only verses strung together for no apparent reason."

Nobody breathes like Bob Dylan. He seemed to be referring to this same basic principle of how his songs come to mean what they mean when he said to Paul Zollo (in a 1991 interview in which he was asked to talk about his songwriting and comment on specific songs) about "Ring Them Bells": "It stands up when you hear it played by me. But if another performer did it, you might find that it probably wouldn't have as much to do with bells as what the title proclaims." In other words, it is the nuance and totality of the vocal (or vocal-and-instruments) performance that gives the words of a song their meaning or semblance of meaning, their message, their sentiment.

"Ring Them Bells," the fourth track on *Oh Mercy*, is a superb performance, a terrific song which one can easily imagine having become the anthem of a historical moment (and a million personal moments) if some other performer had happened to rebreathe it at the right time as skillfully (and luckily) as Peter, Paul & Mary did "Blowin' in the Wind" and the Byrds did "Mr. Tambourine Man." It is an excellent example of a singer/performer getting inside and behind a song and portraying the meanings of certain phrases in the "correct" way (i.e. a way that is powerful and effective for the listener, and that ultimately allows him or her to hear these verses as being strung together for an intuitively evident reason that is very satisfying and stimulating and uplifting). And if we listen carefully, it's not hard to see how this is accomplished by the way the singer breathes.

In every verse of "Ring Them Bells," there is a breath structure as well as a meter and a rhyme scheme. In the first three verses, and the last, there is no pause after the first line or the third line and a pause (a breath) after the second and fourth lines. There are then pauses after the fifth and sixth lines and no pause after the seventh line (turning the seventh and eighth lines into one double-length line, which rhymes with the sixth and the seventh (in the first verse, this double line is "And time is running backwards and so is the bride").

The fourth, bridging, verse becomes a bridge by changing this breath structure along with changes in the rhyme scheme and the lengths of lines. There are pauses at the ends of every line, and also short (and very meaningful) pauses in the middles of the first three lines and the fifth after the repeated phrase "Ring them bells" (which only occurs twice in each of the first three verses, with no breath after it in those).

Of course, there's more to this matter of how Bob Dylan breathes than the easily observed pauses for breath and absence of pauses. Especially because he's singing to his own rhythmic piano playing on this song, there is a powerful yet subtle respiratory pulse to the performance that is remarkably expressive. In the first verse, this is present in every word, but most noticeable in his phrasing of "sanctuaries" (the first two syllables lightly and firmly stressed, as though it were sank/tchew/airies), and the depth and width of the words "deep" and "wide," and the emphasis on the word "time" near the start of the seventh line and the open grace of the word "bride" at the end of that line. In the fourth verse, it is present in the unusual shape he gives the repeated word "bells" so that it seems to rhyme with itself.

Dylan's distinctive breathing of "Ring Them Bells" climaxes (as it should) in the three evocative lines that end the song:

> Oh the lines are long
> And the fighting is strong
> And they're breaking down the distance between right and
>   wrong.

We actually hear him gasping for breath while he sings this, with an urgency and intimacy that unmistakably communicate his sincerity, his conviction, his concern, his regret. ("Listen to the distance that Dylan puts here between right and wrong by his intake of breath between those crucial words." – Christopher Ricks, in *The Telegraph*, 1994.)

Ultimately it is up to each listener to have an idea about what the song "means," what the bells might be saying and why the singer is calling on all the saints, and others, to keep ringing them. One thing that is said fairly clearly ("so the people will know"; "so the world will know that God is one") is that the bells convey knowledge, spiritual awareness, and (presumably) comfort. Mercy.

"Ring Them Bells," to me, is a very pretty song, a careful and moving and earnest performance that manages to express some of the pain and beauty of being alive and awake (open to feelings) in the body and consciousness of a late-20th-century man, a man like so many others who has read the Bible, and some poetry, traveled a little, and has found himself hoping that symbols of human faith like monasteries and bells might somehow have the ability to offer relief, if only by being seen or heard, to the many who are suffering here.

Increasingly, and especially since the release of *"Love And Theft"* a few months ago as I write this, I feel sure that most of Bob Dylan's songs are written in a "stream-of-consciousness" manner (as he has said at least twice about the *Oh Mercy* songs and once about *"Love And Theft"*) in which language and images and phrases flow freely rather than being directed by some kind of conscious intent to make a *statement* ("My approach is just to let it happen and then reject the things that don't work," he said in 2001). This throws a monkey wrench into the natural tendency of commentators like me to interpret songs – that is, to attempt to determine the author's precise intent via analysis of the text. And Dylan's declaration that "nobody breathes like me" and thus another singer "couldn't be expected to portray the meaning of a certain phrase in the correct way," although it does imply that there is a "correct" way, does seem to deny that the meaning of a song can be grasped simply by reading (or hearing, in the absence of the author's intonation) its lyrics. No, he says, it depends significantly on the way the singer or speaker breathes.

But since I love "Ring Them Bells" so much, and am so genuinely interested in gaining understanding for myself and shedding light for others on the question of how this artist's great works of composition and performance come into existence, and what they signify and add up to as a body of work, as an enduring contribution to human experience, now and henceforth, time out of mind, I cannot resist sharing with you what I have learned from my study of the text of "Ring Them Bells," while acknowledging that although this may tell us something about the consciousness through which these thoughts and words streamed, still the "meaning" of the song depends completely on what I or you or other listeners experience as we hear these words sung by this artist who breathed in this particular way that early winter morning in New Orleans in 1989.

The first words of the song, after the excellent piano invocation, are "Ring them bells ye heathen from the city that dreams." I first heard this as "you hear them" rather than "ye heathen" and still find it difficult to get that first phrase out of my mind as I listen. I'm fairly sure he does sing "ye heathen," as all the published lyrics indicate, but I also believe his failure to lean into the word as he might have at another moment in his life is expressive of an accepting and empathetic, albeit ironic, view of nonbelievers at this moment of composition and performance (presumably two different moments, but they become one in the act of singing into the studio microphone). I've searched for a biblical or other use of the phrase "the city that dreams" that I might not have been aware of, and although I was amused to find instances on the Internet of both present-day Jerusalem and New Orleans (!) being given that moniker by someone, the only use of a related phrase that I found (via *Bartlett's Quotations*) that strikes me as something Bob Dylan might have once encountered, and that might thus have helped the phrase bubble up in the stream of his consciousness when he wrote these lyrics, is a well-known poem by Matthew Arnold ("Thyrsis," 1866) that refers to Oxford, England as "that sweet city with her dreaming spires." Thus (speculating about the subconscious, mind you, not any conscious linkage or intent) "ye heathen from the city that dreams" could be nonbelieving university intellectuals, who are still urged to "ring them bells" because we need all the help we can get.

After this verse, the persons beseeched to ring bells are Saint Peter, sweet Martha and Saint Catherine. Sweet Martha is easily identified, especially in the context of that verse's lyrics, as the sister of Lazarus and friend and contemporary of Jesus Christ. But looking in my one-volume encyclopedia for Saint Catherine led me to the unexpected conclusion that she and Peter were chosen (by the unconscious mind, presumably) not for the characteristics of their sainthoods but for the bell-holding edifices that bear their names. St. Peter's Church, Rome, is "the principal and largest church of the Christian world." St. Catherine's Monastery is located at the foot of Mount Moses in Sinai, Egypt and does indeed look like a fortress ("Ring them from the fortress"). Dylan has traveled in this part of the world more than once, and it seems likely that he has seen St. Catherine's. It also seems likely to me that the mysterious and charming "from the top of the room" is (in characteristic Dylan form) a workable replacement for "from the top of the hill" or something like that, either because the rhyme that came up for "hill" wasn't to his liking and then the pleasing "for the lilies that bloom" (itself possibly derivative of Christ's "consider the lilies of the field") arose and sought a retroactive rhyme ... or perhaps Bob vaguely remembered that St. Catherine's is at the foot of a hill, not the top, and cared enough to revise the lyrics (not in the studio but at the time of first writing; the circulating early sessions recording of "Ring Them Bells" has exactly the same lyrics as the finished version).

In the spirit of *"Love And Theft"* (and of course Dylan's "folk process" technique of theft of tunes and titles and phrases goes back to his earliest work as a songwriter), it is not surprising to learn (as I did from Michael Gray's *Song & Dance Man III*) that there is an old Negro spiritual called "Oh Peter Go Ring-a Dem Bells." My sense of it is that both "Ring Them Bells" and "What Good Am I?" reflect Dylan rediscovering "Chimes of Freedom" in 1987 at the prodding of the Grateful Dead and subsequently finding himself wishing he could write another song like that ("Tolling for the aching ones whose wounds cannot be nursed/For the countless confused, accused, misused, strung-out ones and worse").

"Ring them bells sweet Martha/For the poor man's son" certainly sounds to me and perhaps to most listeners like a reference to Christ. I was surprised to find that the phrase "poor man's son" does not seem to occur in the Bible, nor, oddly enough, is it in *Bartlett's*. But via an Internet search I found it in Shakespeare (*The Merchant of Venice* and *King John*). It is worth noting that Bob Dylan, who has been a highly successful coiner of phrases, is also a very skillful phrase-borrower. See, for example, most of the lyrics of *Empire Burlesque* and of *"Love And Theft"*.

Of course there are also freshly minted phrases in "Ring Them Bells." The wonderful couplet "Oh it's rush hour now/On the wheel and the plow" always sounds to me like a description of our historical moment, an acknowledgment of the triumph of technology. In the next verse, "the shepherd is asleep ... and the mountains are filled with lost sheep" (partially borrowed from the Bible) is an evocative portrait of modern man out of touch with his spiritual guides or Caretaker. Some commentators have asked whether Dylan (since this is the "poor man's son"/ "God is one" verse) is here expressing "impatience with Christ for not returning immediately to remedy a 'world on its side.'" Um, yeah his subconscious mind might be, but please also note that in the Book of Ezekiel, the Lord tells Ezekiel, "My sheep were scattered, they wandered over all the mountains" and asks Ezekiel to prophesy against the shepherds of Israel who have been feeding themselves and not the sheep. A footnote in the *New Oxford Annotated Bible* says these shepherds are the kings of Israel who had misused their people and scattered them. This suggests an interpretation of "the shepherd is asleep ... and the mountains are filled with lost sheep" that is obviously very consistent with this album's opening message of "We live in a political world...."

The next track on *Oh Mercy*, improbably, is just as powerful a performance and as good an example of Bob Dylan's genius as a creator of fiercely original and poignant, unforgettable songs. As noted before, producer Lanois says "Man in the Long Black Coat" was "written in the studio and recorded in one take." It is a very impressive piece of writing. The song opens with an evocative description of a scene that at first feels very peaceful and in which every detail immediately seems significant ("Crickets are chirpin', the water is high/There's a soft cotton dress on the line hangin' dry") but soon incorporates a bit of violent weather (even though "window's wide open"): "African trees bent over backwards from a hurricane breeze." The equivalent AABB lines in the first half of the last verse are again descriptive, mostly of nature: "There's smoke on the water, it's been there since June/Tree trunks uprooted 'neath the high crescent moon." These are very effective bookends, since the repetition of "the water" confirms we're observing the same place, as do the uprooted tree trunks which are certainly consistent with trees bent over backwards from a hurricane breeze. For another nice touch, "it's been there since June" suggests that the dramatic events described in the song occur at the time of the first verse's landscape and that their fallout is still present and visible (and tangible – "feel the pulse and vibration") by the time of the closing scene, apparently months later.

The image of "the man in the long black coat" is so striking (and repeated in all five choruses) that it lures the listener to focus on this figure and wonder about him (who is he? what does he symbolize?) even though the primary subject of the song is the devastating loss experienced by its viewpoint character, presumably the husband of the "she" who "went with the man in the long black coat." He doesn't speak in the first person, but we are inside his mind as he reviews the data: "Somebody seen him" "Somebody said ..." "Not a word of gooodbye, not even a note" and bewails the mystery, not of the "man in …" but of her abrupt departure: "She never said nothing, there was nothing she wrote." He is justifiably distressed, though he tries to find understanding by also reviewing pop psychology ("there are no mistakes in life, some people say") and the sermons of the local preacher regarding the errors men (and women) make trying to follow their consciences. But still, "It ain't easy to swallow, it sticks in the throat." So one assumes (consciously or unconsciously; the song reaches its listeners on both levels) that the "somebody [who] is out there beating on a dead horse" in the last scene is the abandoned husband, still futilely asking, "Why?" It's a song about loss, a brilliant and powerful song on a big subject, and since the death of a loved one is probably the most universal, and devastating, experience of loss, it is appropriate that the man in the long black coat sounds as though he might be Death … not that I'm saying he is, in this narrative, but that the universal power of the song lies in its ability to employ the metaphor of a man whose wife has run off with a mysterious stranger (whom, it is said, she approached and asked to dance) to stand for any person's experience of devastating, and inexplicable, loss. And as the "somebody" beating on a dead horse in the last verse is the husband, so we can be sure "the soft cotton dress on the line hanging dry" is the wife's, is what's left of her in her former home on the day she left without a word of goodbye. The day of the hurricane.

What I referred to as "a powerful yet subtle respiratory pulse" in "Ring Them Bells" is not subtle in "Man in the Long Black Coat." The first thing any listener notices in this vocal is the way Dylan gives the narrative and the song a unique and bizarre shape and rhythm by leaning into every fourth or fifth word as if it were the whole point of the story and he doesn't want you to miss it. "*Crickets* are chirpin', the *water* is high/There's a *soft* cotton dress on the *line* hangin' dry …" In the third couplet of this verse – "Not a *word* of goodbye, not *even* a note/She'd *gone* with the man in the *long* black coat" – this has the intriguing effect of making "gone" rhyme with "long." In the next couplets (start of the second verse) he manages to emphasize just the syllable "out" in "outskirts" and five words later just the "in" part of "into." This highlighted "out" and "in" followed by a highlighted "stopped" does indeed feel like breathing. It's hypnotic, and no, nobody else breathes or sings quite like this. The tune is in waltz time, and at times Dylan, like the partner who "leads" in dancing, seems to be emphasizing the "one" of "one, two, three" by leaning into particular words. It feels as though he's conducting the music, the band, with his voice, while simultaneously calling attention to key elements in the story he's telling. His gift for phrasing puts a unique and rather spooky character into the (leaned-on) word "dust," which is then echoed meaningfully in the preacher's word "must" in the following verse. The singer is having a ball with his phrasing throughout the song, and somehow the pulse he creates by stressing every fourth or fifth word seems to give him the space for this; he takes charge of the story, the flow of language, and as a result gains enormous freedom to be present inside each vowel and consonant, to tell more of the story and paint more details into each scene via tiny expressive gestures of phrasing and breathing. The pulse isn't subtle nor meant to be, but the vocal effects it makes possible certainly are. None of this technique could possibly be communicated in transcription or a musical score, so we can understand Dylan saying he doesn't expect others to attempt to sing his songs ... An example of how hard this song would be for any other singer to do "without bumping into other phrases & altering the mood, changing the understanding" is the vocal sleight of hand whereby the word "sometimes" manages to finish the phrase "and it's true sometimes" while simultaneously starting the phrase "sometimes you can see it that way" with a different nuance in each case, so that "it's true sometimes" is friendly and affirmative and "sometimes you can see it that way" is skeptical and close to hostile. We'll encounter more of this sort of trickery in the next performance, "Most of the Time."

I find it intriguing that "Man in the Long Black Coat" was (reportedly) recorded in one take. Listeners often speak of *Oh Mercy* (approvingly or critically) as an example of a producer's "sound" dominating an artist's album. John Bauldie: "It often seems as if it's as much a Daniel Lanois record as a Bob Dylan record." Clinton Heylin: "That *Oh Mercy*'s alluringly subterranean sound was more a product of Lanois's sensibility than Dylan's seems indisputable. One listen to Lanois's own album *Acadie* should clinch the matter."

But surely the track on *Oh Mercy* that most conveys the "swampy" sound and feeling of Lanois's *Acadie* and of the Lanois-produced Neville Brothers album *Yellow Moon* is "Man in the Long Black Coat." This is most striking in the haunting 69-second musical introduction to the track, which derives much of its sound and mood from Dylan's harmonica passages. According to the album sleeve, the only musicians playing on this song are Lanois on dobro (a resonator guitar often used in bluegrass and sometimes in folk blues), Lanois's production assistant Malcolm Burn on keyboards, and Bob Dylan on 6- and 12-string guitar, and harmonica. Certainly Burn and Lanois as players and Lanois's unusual studio set-up and the New Orleans locale are common links between *Oh Mercy* and *Acadie* and *Yellow Moon* ... but if indeed "Long Black Coat" was recorded in one take (one wonders if one of the two guitars Dylan is credited with having played might have been overdubbed), surely the unique and beautiful sound of the instrumental track must be primarily an expression of the personality and will power and presence of the *de facto* musical director of the take, who can only have been Bob Dylan during a live, one-take-only performance. He was attracted to the blend of music Lanois had been exploring during his Louisiana residency, and had been at a *Yellow Moon* session and had probably already heard some of *Acadie* in some form, and very likely what he'd heard helped inspire his recent writing of this song. And then there's the fact, evident to any listener, that the "feel" of this track is already present in Dylan's harmonica playing during the first moments of the take. So I argue (thus disputing Heylin) that the sound of "Man in the Long Black Coat," and by extension *Oh Mercy* as a whole, while certainly characteristic of Lanois, can best be perceived as a collaboration between two (or three?) powerful personalities with strong and original (and convergent) musical ideas and ambitions at this particular moment in their lives and creative careers. I've spoken before of Dylan's evident ability to "use the unwieldy gravitational pull of his presence to awaken the collective genius of a handful of musicians, in service to the music and the artist/bandleader's internal vision." Dylan as a creative artist works with the elements available to him and attractive to him at the moment, and often succeeds in inspiring his co-workers (the players he's with) to rise to the occasion in spite of or because of his usual inability or unwillingness to articulate what he wants them to do. I believe Aaron Neville was alluding to this sort of musical co-creation when he said (to a British music paper) about watching Dylan record *Oh Mercy*: "He certainly knows how to achieve that intense chemistry that makes his work so unique."

"The songs on this specific record are not so much songs but rather exercises in tonal breath control," Dylan wrote in the liner notes to his 1965 album *Highway 61 Revisited*. So now we know what "Most of the Time" and "Queen Jane Approximately" have in common, apart from being the opening song on the second side (and sixth track) of a Bob Dylan album. In both performances, tonal breath control and judicious use of rhyme allow the singer/writer to vary the lengths of verse-lines erratically while conveying a very pleasing sense of regular, graceful meter and song structure. As a result, the flow of language in both is quite engaging, almost intoxicating. In "Most of the Time," this flow of performed language is a humorous and elegant exploration-in-depth of the personality of the speaker, a fictional character who boasts of his ability to "hold his own" and "deal with the situation" at the same time that he denies that there is a situation ("I don't even think about her") and insists unconvincingly that he's "halfways content" and that he doesn't "hide from the feelings that are buried inside," whatever they might be. He is a person who has been through a loss as difficult as the one suffered by the narrator of "Man in the Long Black Coat," and at times it seems he'd like to see himself as being as humble as that other narrator on this album who can ask, "What good am I?" – even though he is in fact being used here by the songwriter and vocalist as an example of the perils of the disease of conceit ("I can handle whatever I stumble upon/I don't even notice she's gone"). In the first verse he sounds like a drunk bragging of his ability to hold his liquor ("Most of the time/I'm clear focused all around"). Hilariously, he boasts, "I can keep both feet on the ground/I can follow the path," not realizing that the first assertion makes the second impossible. But that's okay, because most of the time his head is on straight. And he's not afraid of confusion, no matter how thick.

Throughout this song, Dylan uses his unique way of breathing to bring this character to life (the different stresses he puts, and doesn't put, on the recurring title phrase; the emphatic pause for breath after "think" in "I don't even think about her"). The song turns on (and probably originated from) its author's perception that this familiar phrase, "most of the time," can have contradictory meanings. At the start of each verse it means "usually" or "more often than not." But the way he sings it at the end of each verse it means "but not always" ("Don't even remember what her lips felt like on mine ... most of the time."). Dylan is not necessarily speaking for himself in this song, but like any novelist or short story writer or actor, he is drawing partly on his own personal experience to get inside the skin of a fictional character. Mose Allison, a singer quite gifted at the sort of ironic delivery Dylan achieves in this performance, once said, "Many of my songs suggest a character who is often described as 'laid-back,' 'cool,' or 'philosophic.' I am not that character, although I certainly understand and sympathize with him." This last sentence, I believe, is what Dylan would or could say about the characters portrayed in "Most of the Time" and many of his other inventions.

"Most of the Time" is a "big song," a major work, the sort of listening experience that brings people back to an album again and again. This is also true of "Ring Them Bells" and "Man in the Long Black Coat," and in each case the song's appeal is as much based in its music as in its words. Songs are music and words working together, and it's a mistake to assume that the words come first and to think of the music as accompaniment and support for the lyrics. Songwriters report that very often the words and the music come to them simultaneously, or as a germ of an idea that is both melodic and lyrical and that then gets completed in a process of music suggesting and asking for certain words, and vice versa.

In fact, "Most of the Time" is an example of a very pleasing musical and melodic effect being heightened and fleshed out by the words of a song, specifically the repetition of the title phrase "most of the time." These four words, repeated three times in each verse – except the bridging fourth verse, where they only appear twice – are a riff in themselves, as central to the song's musical impact as the teasing melodic riff (played on the bass guitar) that runs through the whole performance. The sound of the lyrics is also an important part of the satisfying musical crescendo that occurs in the second half of the last verse and is then repeated in the fulfilling instrumental passage that ends the song. The lyrics I'm referring to here are the five "I don't"s ("I don't cheat on myself," etc.), a mirror for the five "I can"s of the first verse ("I can make it all match up," etc.), and the way Dylan breathes the phrases and words that follow these "I don't"s. The song reaches an emotional climax at this point, one that is located more in the music than in the words – very likeable music that seems to circle back on itself, and to become richer and more meaningful every time it returns, every time the guitars (Dylan and Lanois on guitars, Tony Hall on bass) and percussive instruments (Willie Green on drums, Cyril Neville on "percussion," with some contributions from Malcolm Burn on keyboards) complete another musical loop.

What you as a listener feel when you listen to the 52-second instrumental passage at the end of "Most of the Time" is the true "meaning" of this song, and the effectiveness of the entire track's musical expression is what calls us back to it again and again, as was true of "Queen Jane Approximately" and "Just like a Woman" and so many of Dylan's earlier recorded treasures. Of course, the singer's vocal performances are very much a part of the musical pleasure of all these recordings. All the more reason why it may be the words we remember most clearly. But it is often the song's music that penetrates us most deeply, and certainly the quality of the musical experience, as much as the quality of the lyrics and the verbal content, is what makes "Ring Them Bells" and "Most of the Time" and "Man in the Long Black Coat" great songs and, on *Oh Mercy*, great and memorable performances.

Each of the songs on this album is strikingly different in form and sound and essential character from all the others, as though part of the songwriter's and performer's intent is to demonstrate his versatility and, more significantly, to put together a sonic and narrative collage that truly stands for who he is – what he feels and is interested in and attracted by and committed to – at this moment of performance and invention and creative expression. "What Good Am I?" immediately and very effectively creates an atmosphere as different from the soundscapes and vocal personas of "Most of the Time" and "Man in the Long Black Coat" as those tracks are from each other.

The listener's first reaction to this song is likely to be surprise at how naked the speaker is willing to be, not just with me the person listening, but also with himself, the person he's clearly directing these hard questions to. "What good am I if I know and don't do? If I see and don't say, if I look right through you?" "You" in this context is not himself, although the form of the song is soliloquy. Rather, the "you" he's thinking of is any of the lowly, the powerless, the suffering of this Earth – "the luckless, the abandoned and forsaked" of "Chimes of Freedom." He wants to speak of and for these persons again, and of his and every man's relationship with them. To do so, he turns "Blowin' in the Wind" inside out, so instead of the third person of "How many times must a man look up, before he can see the sky? How many ears must one man have, before he can hear people cry?" he asks, "What good am I if I know and don't do? If I see and don't say, if I look right through you? If I turn a deaf ear to the thunderin' sky?" In effect, by making an example of himself, Dylan challenges the listener, any human, to ask himself or herself these questions. It's a powerful device – and a riveting performance. Again, compare "Yes, 'n' how many times can a man turn his head, pretending he just doesn't see?" to "What good am I if I'm like all the rest? If I just turn away when I see how you're dressed [i.e. in poverty]? If I shut myself off, so I can't hear you cry, what good am I?" It's the sort of song, and performance, that may speak more resonantly for and to a mass audience a hundred years from now than at its time of release.

"Disease of Conceit," the eighth track on *Oh Mercy*, is another riveting vocal performance. In this case, there can be no question that the person singing is speaking – again, quite courageously and nakedly – from his own personal experience. In 1979, Dylan wrote, on the same topic, in the clearly autobiographical "Trouble in Mind": "Here comes Satan, prince of the power of the air. He's gonna make you a law unto yourself, build a bird's nest in your hair. He's gonna deaden your conscience till you worship the work of your own hands. You'll be serving strangers in a strange, forsaken land." In March 1991, he told Elliott Mintz – in response to Mintz's comment that some people might come away from hearing this radio interview saying, "Gosh, I don't know why he isn't more proud of what he's done, what he's written" – "Pride? No, pride goes before a big downfall, you've heard that, we've all heard that. What is there to be proud about?"

"Disease of Conceit," like 1985's "Trust Yourself," is a straightforward slice of Bob Dylan's personal philosophy, not taken from the Bible (though it certainly resonates with Ecclesiastes' "Vanity of vanities; all is vanity") but from his own life experience. Notice, in this album that keeps returning to the theme of compassion, that the song starts, "There's a whole lot of people suffering tonight." Dylan's interest in the "disease of conceit" is not to condemn anyone, but to bemoan the pain caused by this affliction that "comes right out of nowhere," "comes right down the highway," "steps into your room." The clear implication is that although "the doctors got no cure," the singer believes awareness is the medicine that can help (as in, "ring them bells so the people will know") and that he as a singer of broadsides has a responsibility to spread the word. The song is gracefully structured with the chorus at the start of each verse, the chorus being: "There's a whole lot of people ["hearts" in verse two] gerund tonight/From the disease of conceit," repeated so that the second gerund rhymes (internal rhyme) with the first ("breaking"/"shaking" "dying"/"crying" "in trouble"/ "seeing double"). As is often the case in skillful songwriting, the exceptions to this form only contribute to its elegance: "in trouble" not being a gerund, "suffering"/"struggling" not quite rhyming in the first verse, and of course the fourth of the five verses being a bridge, four lines instead of eight, with no "whole lot of ..." chorus at the start but instead the tagline inverted: "Conceit is a disease." This structural elegance makes it easy for the singer to tear into each line the way the disease "rips into your senses." He is fierce, eloquent, obviously sincere (you can hear it in his piano playing as well as in his voice) in his testifying, his empathy, and his regret. Songs like this are his way of ringing them bells.

"What Was It You Wanted," the next track, presents a different mood, a different sound, another different aspect of this same relaxed and confident and intimate voice, another side of the *Oh Mercy* Bob Dylan, the Dylan of this particular inspired moment.

It's a very special song. In 1965, Dylan wrote, "I am about to sketch You a picture of what goes on around here sometimes." In "What Was It You Wanted" he (again) does exactly that. The narrative of the song (the lyrics, brilliantly supported by the music and the vocal performance) is a three- (and four-)dimensional expansion of two lines from his 1973 song "Nobody 'Cept You": "Everybody wants my attention/Everybody's got something to sell." It's true. I've seen this, when I've been backstage with Dylan (in 1966 and 1980), and so has anyone who's watched *Don't Look Back* or *Renaldo & Clara*; and I've been approached by many friends and strangers who imagine that because I write books about Dylan, I have some kind of access to the man and can convey to him or "his people" their requests. It has been Bob Dylan's fate to receive more such entreaties than most celebrities, even presidents of the United States. There's always someone who wants something from him more complicated and urgent than an autograph, so a normal scene in his life is him trying to be polite and attentive, or kind and dismissive, without committing himself, to a new face in a seemingly endless succession of faces, as hilariously portrayed in this five-minute sketch. "Are you the same person that was here before?" How would he know? It becomes a blur of supplicants, as described in this song and in poet Anne Waldman's account of being in Dylan's hotel room in 1978:

> Supplicants moaned and scratched at the door. Wild and hungry beasts, the "fans" were always out there. Then suddenly the knocking and motion would subside, only to start up again a few intervals later, girls calling softly and seductively to the beloved. Messages were slipped under the door at an alarming rate. Flowers, baskets of food, excellent champagne were delivered at frequent intervals. Delivery boys were busy and tipped generously, hopping in and out of the elevators with trained alacrity. The phone kept ringing with invitations and further seductions. It seemed to amuse and annoy him by turns. ... I leafed through a pile of works and the accompanying notes and cards. Take me into your world they were all saying. I am young. I am talented. I am good.

The music is perfect, exhilarating. Again, those who imagine Daniel Lanois has somehow superimposed his "sound" onto this Dylan album should take note of the fact that the cornerstone of this track's wonderful soundscape is Dylan's own harmonica playing, perfectly and intuitively complemented by Lanois's guitar, Malcom Burn's bass, Mason Ruffner's third guitar (Dylan is playing one, too) and Willie Green's drums and Cyril Neville's percussion. Lanois deserves a lot of credit for his own playing and his very successful supervision of the sessions, but this is because in both cases he is doing such a good job of supporting and following the lead of bandleader/maestro Dylan, who expresses exactly what it was he wanted to say in the words and music of this song, and how he wanted it to sound, in every harmonica note he blows herein.

As for the way the singer breathes, his vocal timing here is every bit as expressive and full of sly humor and poignancy as his harp playing. Back in chapter 5 I brought up the subject of how in the Arab world it is said a good singer is one who creates an environment of enchantment with his or her vocal performance. In Arabic music, there are a number of recognized tools for accomplishing this, and among them are *ghunna* (nasality) and *bahha* (hoarseness). An attentive observer will find excellent examples of Dylan's use of hoarseness to create an emotional and musical environment, and thus cast a spell on his listeners, in the opening lines of "What Was It You Wanted" and throughout the performance. Few American singers breathe like this.

Earlier in this book – again, chapter 5 – I quoted Bob Dylan on the subject of how some of his songs have come through him:

> Then of course, there are times you just pick up an instrument – something will come, like a tune or some kind of wild line will just come into your head and you'll develop that ... Whatever it brings out in the voice, you'll write those words down. And they might not mean anything to you at all, and you just go on, and that will be what happens.

When I quoted this 1968 interview earlier, I didn't tell you what he said next: "Now I don't do that anymore. If I do it, I just keep it for myself. So I have a big line-up of songs which I'll never use." The fact that some of the versions of the *Oh Mercy* songs recorded before the officially released album versions have leaked out (to circulate in the community of Dylan fans and students) gives us a rare chance to watch this songmaker at work. We get to hear a rough draft of "Shooting Star." Dylan probably would have kept "Shooting Star" for himself and never used it – or used it in different form a year later, as in the case of "God Knows" and "Born in Time" – if the song had not suddenly taken on new life (probably at the April overdub sessions) for its author/performer, bringing out something quite different in the voice and some lively new words to be sung and written down, arising from the same wild line which at the earlier recording sessions, or perhaps at a still earlier writing session, had developed into the disappointing narrative dead ends heard in these early recordings (there are two, and they're almost identical lyrically, suggesting these are words he wrote before entering the Studio on the Move, although there are times in these early takes when Dylan definitely sounds like he's trying to improvise lyrics and not quite getting a flow of words going).

The early lyrics:

> Seen a shooting star tonight
> And I thought of you.
> There was something reaching out to me
> Something coming through
>   [mumble]
> Something I thought I'd do
> Seen a shooting star tonight
> And I thought of you.

> Seen a shooting star tonight
> Against the grain
> Up in the hot rod sky
> Across the prairies and plains
> I's looking up and dreaming
> Like I sometimes do
> Seen a shooting star tonight
> And I thought of you.

The third verse, the bridge, is lyrically the same as the album version ("Listen to the engine ...") and is followed by this last verse:

> Seen a shooting star tonight
> Across the flatland roads.
> I's a thousand miles away
> From where the end of time explodes.
> Looking up and wondering
> As the dawn was breaking through ...
> I seen a shooting star tonight
> And I thought of you.

Listening to these performances, and even just reading these words on paper, it's fairly obvious that the singer/author isn't actually thinking of someone. But listening to the album version of "Shooting Star," one can't help but feel the presence of a very real "you" whom the speaker is remembering and thinking of at this moment. This gives the song most of its power.

As for watching the songmaker at work ... "Many of these songs were written in some kind of stream-of-consciousness kind of mood," Dylan said of *"Love And Theft"*, "and I don't sit and linger, meditate on every line afterwards. My approach is just to let it happen and then reject the things that don't work." In the early drafts of "Shooting Star," we see and hear some things that didn't work and were rejected to make room for a more successful stream of associative writing to begin flowing from the same starting point.

But since the bridging verse in the early version did offer a nice flow of language, and presumably because no new bridging verse arose as easily and magically as the new second verse arose from the new first, the original bridging verse was retained – awkwardly since it's not about the "you" and "me" who are now central to the other verses, and because Dylan seems to sing it a little overaggressively to compensate for his own uncertainty about how this apocalyptic

outburst (change of pace is appropriate in a bridge) fits with the now
sweetly meditative verses where the speaker thinks of the two halves
of a lost relationship ... a friendship interrupted by death or a marriage broken by divorce. My own guess is that after unsuccessfully
inviting the song to be about prairies and plains and looking up and
wondering, it suddenly occurred to him that a shooting star is a
symbol of impermanence and therefore loss, and that this prompted
him to try making "I thought of you" be about his ex-wife. The lines
"You were trying to break into another world/A world I never
knew" evoke for me the lines "This time I'm asking for freedom/
Freedom from a world which you deny" from "When the Night
Comes Falling from the Sky" (*Empire Burlesque*), which has an
"ex-wife" flavor because of the line "when you were gambling for
support." In any case, one can argue that the "last fire truck" and
the "last time you might hear" and the other three "lasts" in the
"Shooting Star" bridge are also about impermanence as expressions
of awareness that "you" and "I" may not be here much longer.
Which awareness, whether the song is addressed to someone who
died or to a relationship that died, can be heard in the powerful last
lines (before the chorus) of the song's last verse: "Guess it's too late
to say the things to you/That you needed to hear me say."

Certainly, as most commentators have mentioned, it's a wonderful last song for an album. The very soothing opening notes of
the track seem to reach out to every feeling aroused in the course of
the nine preceding songs. There's a further sense of completion in
the fulfilling sweetness of the vocal phrases "and I thought of you"/
"and I thought of me" in the first verses. The "tomorrow will be
another day" cliché in the last verse is a nice bookend for the memorable "roses are red" of "Where Teardrops Fall" and also an interesting contradiction of "the last radio" and "last time you might
hear" in the preceding verse. Best of all, anyway, is the harmonica
solo that ends the song and the album and certainly manages to
summarize and acknowledge any feeling that may have arisen in
any listener while listening to this song or to all ten of these
performances.

"Dignity," a song recorded during the March-April 1989 *Oh
Mercy* sessions but not officially released until late 1994 (when the
1989 vocal performance was included on the album *Greatest Hits
Volume 3* with a partially rerecorded backing track), is another
example of the very fine results sometimes produced by Dylan's

songwriting approach of "just letting it happen" (this time he didn't "reject the things that don't work" because there weren't any, even if he did keep the song for himself for five years). When the flow of language is this inspired and the impact on the listener of subtle choices of words and images as brilliant and unexpected and deeply intelligent as this, it is natural to think of Dylan's songwriting here as "meticulously assembled" and "beautifully thought-out" and "thrillingly well-crafted." These quotes are from Michael Gray's comments on "Dignity" in *Song & Dance Man III*, and I certainly agree with the spirit of what Gray is saying in his enthusiastic assessment of the song (and I appreciate many of the specific insights Gray shares in his essay on "Dignity" – for example, the ramifications of and impact on the listener of the choice of "Prince Philip" as the name of the character who met the narrator at the home of the blues and "said he wanted money up front, said he was abused by dignity"). But the particular thing I'm pointing to here is process, the mysterious matter of how the songs come into existence. Particularly after contemplating *"Love And Theft"*, I believe that when Dylan says, "I don't sit and linger, meditate on every line," he is sincerely reporting that in his experience his songs are not thought out or carefully assembled, or crafted in the usual sense of the word; mostly they just flow out of him and then he wonders where that came from, and lets himself be guided by what just came out towards what might come next (thus, "stream of consciousness songs").

Gray in his essay notices and acknowledges the flowing stream of "Dignity" 's narrative and language. The full paragraph containing the phrases quoted above is:

> What is so liberating and invigorating about "Dignity" is that while it is free-spirited and ineffably relaxed, fluid as mercury and malleable as clay on the wheel, it is at the same time meticulously assembled, as beautifully thought-out and thrillingly well-crafted as a major tap-es-tree.

Quite right. But in the interests of clarity about the great songwriter's surprising process, I want to modify this to read "it at the same time appears meticulously assembled ..." My point is that, as he tells us in various interviews, Dylan doesn't think these things out while he's writing, instead he lets himself get into a mind-state where the language and narrative flow, where he's guided ... and the fact that the result can seem so well-crafted and deliberate is a tribute to the skillfulness of his unconscious mind and a credit to his performer's discipline of following his Muse and just letting the music and language happen (not allowing his conscious mind to intervene) (*not* thinking it out, but just trusting in the guidance of some higher power, and reserving the right to edit later – in the case of songwriting and recording; on stage, where Dylan and his voice feel most at home, there is no chance to edit later).

It is possible, for example, that when Dylan began writing this song, his only notion was to describe various people ("fat man, thin man" "wise man, young man") looking for dignity in various places – "a blade of steel" in the first line and, happy but probably unplanned echo (performer's instincts), "a blade of grass" at the start of verse two – and then only as he reached for a bridging effect (break the pattern) in the third verse and heard the lines that poured forth ("Somebody got murdered on New Year's Eve/Somebody said dignity was the first to leave") did it occur to him (prompted forcefully and irresistibly by his unconscious mind) that the song could also be a murder mystery, with "dignity" the name of a person, the prime suspect, and thus the narrator a sort of detective tracking down the culprit (searching for Dignity as the fat man and wise man had been looking for his lower case, more abstract and less dastardly counterpart – another happy echo, again possibly quite spontaneous, in which case the craft of the author was primarily his agility at following the clues provided by his unconscious or Muse or intuition).

Gray in his book reports that "Nigel Hinton [another U.K. Dylan scholar] declares 'Dignity' to be his favourite of all the 'big' songs of the last twenty years: more loved than 'Brownsville Girl,' 'Angelina' or even 'Blind Willie McTell.'" Hinton wrote, in a letter Gray quotes:

> What I particularly like about it is the consistency of its conceit: Bob Dylan as Sam Spade, or any one of those hard-bitten, cynical L.A.-based private dicks, conducting his B-movie, film noir hunt through the corrupt world in search of the missing character, Dignity. I like the array of characters – all those sons of darkness and sons of light – typical of the wonderful supporting actors who people those films. And I love the little familiar scenes from the movies – the murder at the New Year's Eve party, the wedding of Mary Lou ... and

the continual echo of films – the drinking man in a crowded room full of covered-up mirrors could come straight from *Citizen Kane*.... The song even ends in the kind of despairing, enigmatic way that the best film noirs do – standing at the edge of the lake, knowing that everywhere leads to dead ends and that the case won't get solved. It's a black and white masterpiece.

Since we know Dylan to be familiar with and fond of this sort of movie, and since we ourselves are familiar with his gift for language and his sense of humor and his storytelling skills and his performer's sense of and appreciation for song structure and timing and cadence, it is not such a mystery how this song could flow out of him once its narrative and structural premises presented themselves, once the floodgates were open, and instantly become a rich, complex, deeply satisfying invention that seems meticulously assembled and beautifully thought-out even though probably all he was doing was trying to write it down fast enough.

When good songs come to Dylan, they do seem to come in batches, as in the case of the *Infidels* songs and outtakes in 1983 and the *Shot of Love* songs and outtakes in 1981. So it's interesting to speculate on how they encourage and influence each other and can be seen as extensions of the same creative moment, expressions of the same set of favorable conditions for songwriting. "Dignity" probably didn't but easily could have originated as a discarded line from "Political World," a song in which abstract nouns and human virtues often are spoken of as though they were persons: "Wisdom is thrown into jail, it rots in a cell" "Mercy walks the plank" "Peace is turned away from the door to wander some more." Similarly, in the 1989 version of "Born in Time," the second bridge climaxes with the declaration, "I'm broken." – so one wonders if this could have been the origin of "Everything Is Broken," which in its early "Broken Days" version is unambiguously a song about a man-woman relationship.

"Born in Time" is the only out-and-out love song among the *Oh Mercy* batch. The title phrase ("When we were born in time" on the 1989 take; "Where we were born in time" when it was rerecorded a year later for *Under the Red Sky*) means whatever the listener can make of it (of course). I hear it as a reference to the moment when (or place where) you and I became "we" – lovers, an item, a romantic union. There's an evocation of this moment in the first bridge, "Oh babe, now it's time to raise the curtain." The melody is quite pretty, full of affection and a sort of love-intoxication; Dylan breathes it with a lot of feeling. In the second bridge, he offers a wry yet seemingly heartfelt variant on "beauty is in the eye of the beholder": "You were snow, you were rain/You were striped, you were plain/Oh, babe, truer words have not been spoken." This would sound like nonsense to me were it not for LSD trips I took many years ago, and love-intoxication moments I've experienced since then.

"Series of Dreams" was recorded on March 23rd, 1989, according to the booklet in *The Bootleg Series, Volumes 1–3 [Rare and Unreleased] 1961–1991*. It was remixed and some guitar and keyboard overdubs were added and some vocal edits made (splicing together two vocal takes with differing lyrics, one probably from the April '89 sessions) in January 1991, thus justifying the album's title date (the other 57 selections on the compilation were recorded between 1961 and 1985). So the extended moment of invention and performance that is expressed in the *Oh Mercy* batch of songs (ten on the album and four known outtakes) was extended still further, with two "big" songs, "Dignity" and "Series of Dreams," completed and officially released in 1994 and 1991 ("God Knows" and "Born in Time" were recorded again and released on *Under the Red Sky* in 1990).

"Series of Dreams" is a major Dylan song and an important statement. Like "Dignity," it's two statements at once, charmingly playing hide and seek with each other. In "Dignity," of course, the two are "life is just a Sam Spade movie" (a picture of what goes on around here sometimes) and an expression of "the heartfelt yearning for a more dignified world" (in Michael Gray's words). In "Series of Dreams," as in most Dylan songs, it's entirely up to the listener or community of listeners to decide for himself or themselves what the statements are. Again quoting Gray, he says of "Dignity," "As with so much of Dylan's finest writing, its credible possibilities are open and the opposite of limiting."

One of the statements "Series of Dreams" makes, certainly, is "life is like thinking of (remembering, contemplating) a series of dreams" (another picture of what goes on around here sometimes). John Burns, in a 1998 essay in the Dylan magazine *The Bridge*, has this to say about the song's other major statement: "Listening to 'Series of Dreams,' one cannot fail to be struck by the way in which it seems to offer something like an artistic credo, and by the way in which its central metaphor opens up our understanding of Dylan's achievement." He then quotes the second halves of verses two and three:

> Wasn't making any great connection
> Wasn't falling for any intricate scheme
> Nothing that would pass inspection
> Just thinking of a series of dreams
>
> Wasn't looking for any special assistance
> Not going to any great extremes
> I'd already gone the distance
> Just thinking of a series of dreams

Burns goes on to say: "Of course we all know how dangerous it is to accept at face value any of Dylan's pronouncements on his art, because he is so obviously unwilling to let himself be analysed or categorised, even by himself. Yet it also seems to me that if we are to get some kind of grip on Dylan's music, then seeing it as a 'series of dreams' is a very good place to start."

Wow. I don't agree that "one cannot fail to be struck" because I'm not sure I noticed this until Burns opened my eyes (as I went years not noticing that "Chimes of Freedom" is a description of being caught in a thunderstorm). But I'm inclined to agree with and endorse the rest of what he says here. And I would add that this aspect of the song's "message" might well be the result of Dylan's summer 1987 reconnection with his own earlier work as a result of conversations with Jerry Garcia and other members of the Grateful Dead. "I can't remember what it means – is it just a bunch of *words*?" Presumably sometime that summer he found relief in the realization that in "Desolation Row" and "Just Like Tom Thumb's Blues" and "Mr. Tambourine Man," he'd been "just thinking of a series of dreams."

And then when this song started coming out of him, with at first just the message of, "I want to tell you what it feels like to recognize my and our everyday reality experience in the distorted time sense and juxtapositions of dream-consciousness," he helped the flow of words come by acknowledging a double assignment: find language for a song-picture of dream-consciousness, and simultaneously take a stab at answering those familiar questions about

"What do your 1960s songs mean? What were you trying to do?"
As he often does in interviews, he answers with a list of negatives,
trying to clear up misunderstandings (i.e., "I don't sit and linger,
meditate on every line afterwards"):

> Wasn't thinking of anything specific …
> Wasn't making any great connection/Wasn't falling for any
>   intricate scheme
> Wasn't going to any great trouble
> In believing it's whatever it seems.
> Nothing too heavy, to burst a bubble
> Just thinking of a series of dreams.

These last four lines are from one of the circulating takes of
"Series of Dreams" from the March–April 1989 sessions, the one
that has almost entirely different lyrics for the second verse. Here
Dylan says, twenty-four years past 1965, that he wasn't trying to
burst anyone's bubble, he was just describing what he observed –
"believing it's whatever it seems." Or, as he said it back then:

> And if my thought-dreams could be seen/They'd probably
>   put my head in a guillotine/But it's alright, Ma, it's life, and
>   life only.

After *Oh Mercy* came out, producer Lanois told an interviewer:
"We had four or six songs that we recorded and didn't use. One
track, 'Series of Dreams,' was a fantastic turbulent track that I felt
should have been on the record but … he had the last word." Some
biographers and commentators have suggested Dylan held back
"strong" songs like "Dignity" and "Series of Dreams" from *Oh Mercy*
because, after having some difficulty writing new songs in 1985–87,
he wanted to have a few excellent ones available for whenever they
might be needed. Others have taken the opposite view that he kept
these songs off the album because he didn't realize how good they
were. But because *Oh Mercy* seems to me to hang together so well as
an album and as a dignified and inspired series of dream-
performances itself, I tend to believe Dylan avoided including these
two powerhouses here because his ears and intuition told him they
would unbalance the record and distract the listener from other
new songs that worked together, in the sequence he was finding
himself guided to, very well indeed.

Another strong possibility, suggested by Dylan's past actions regarding songs he knew to be powerful but didn't release right away, is that the sound he had in mind for "Series of Dreams" was very important to him, and while he and Lanois and the players were able to approach it in the 1989 recordings, Dylan wasn't satisfied until he heard the results of the January 1991 remixing and overdub sessions. Bob Dylan's great successes as an artist, in the recording studio and on stage, have often resulted from pursuing a musical vision, a sound he heard in the back of his mind and wanted to realize in his work, as well as a lyrical vision. This again is an expression of a performer's instincts, always regarding songs as music and words working together. When this is successful, a phrase in a song's narrative ("In one [dream] I was running, and in another all I seemed to be doing was *climb*") may be expressed as powerfully in the overall sound and feeling of the music as in the lyrics. The listener receives and feels the entire package at once.

Ironically, the superb and powerful final version of "Series of Dreams", released on Dylan's box set *The Bootleg Series* in 1991, suggests that what Dylan aspired to and dreamed of when working on this song, as a writer and recording artist, was the grandiose sound and feeling achieved by producer Phil Spector in his early 1960s work but specifically as updated and realized very successfully by Dylan's producer Daniel Lanois and his partner Brian Eno in the wonderful (and very commercially successful) 1987 U2 hit records "With or Without You" and "Where the Streets Have No Name." Dylan aspired to something he thought Lanois might be able to give him and that certainly would have been very appropriate to this song. The insistence and claustrophobic tension of the backing track of the finished "Series of Dreams" would have been overwhelming on "Political World," I suspect, and might have made it an unpleasant listening experience instead of the delight I think it is, but these – as finally realized in the 1991 remix – are perfect for the twin messages of "Series of Dreams" and all of its imagery and language. So Dylan was strong enough to hold to his musical vision even at the price of frustrating Lanois, who felt the track as recorded "should have been" on *Oh Mercy*. The final song when released as a single in 1991 was not the international hit record Dylan may have dreamed of, but it is a remarkable achievement that can stand with his better recordings. The performed line "Like in a dream, when someone wakes up and *screams*" might someday stand beside Edvard Munch's painting *The Scream* (which could have been a conscious or unconscious influence on Dylan here) as an evocation of the experience of the individual human being in our modern era. Similarly, the pace of the music and imagery in "Series of Dreams" evokes for me Charlie Chaplin's great 1936 film *Modern Times*. And, neatly enough, one of the subtexts of the song seems to be its author's relationship with modern times via his work and how he did and didn't arrive at his essential oeuvre: "Wasn't making any great connection/Wasn't falling for any intricate scheme/Nothing that would pass inspection [i.e. close critical analysis]" ...

Echoes of other songs that arose from Dylan at this same creative moment can be heard in the repeated bridging lines "And the cards are no good that you're holding/Unless they're from another world" (versus "Shooting Star" 's "You were trying to break into another world") and the line "In another [dream] I witnessed a crime," which resonates with "men commit crimes" in "Political World" and "somebody got murdered" in "Dignity." But the strongest correlation I hear is that "What Was It You Wanted," like "Series of Dreams" but less overtly, is another in Dylan's long series of attempts to find narrative language that will break through conventional time perceptions and capture the timeless quality of actual experience. In "Series," which of course attempts to describe the out-of-time feeling of events perceived and participated in in a dream, this is partly accomplished by the narrator primarily speaking in the past tense ("I was thinking of ... Wasn't making ... Wasn't falling," etc.), while other statements are in the present tense: "nothing comes up" "everything stays down" "someone wakes up" "there's no exit" "the umbrella is folding" "the cards are ..."

In "What Was It You Wanted" Dylan paints a subjective picture of a world (presumably his normal backstage or on-tour reality) where strangers and himself are constantly appearing, disappearing, reappearing, as if in some complicated folk dance sequence ("Could you say it again?" "I'll be back in a minute" "You can tell me, I'm back" "Would you remind me again?" "Was there somebody looking, when you gave me that kiss?"...) accompanied by mind-bending references to the fact that he's both speaking to the person and singing on a record (which in turn might be the music being danced to): "Has the record been breaking? Did the needle just skip?" "We can start it all over, get it back on the track" "Is the scenery changing? Am I getting it wrong?" "Is the whole thing going backwards? Are they playing our song?" I find this hilarious, and quite consistent with the perceived reality of "dreams where the time and the tempo drag/And there's no exit in any direction/'Cept the one you can't see with your eyes" and "Dreams where the umbrella is folding/Into the path you are hurled." "Are you the same person that was here before?" Indeed. And am *I*? "Wasn't looking for any special assistance ..."

Dylan's breathing, particularly his emphatic pauses for breath, are again very central to how he gets (and gets us) inside and behind the sentiment of "Series of Dreams." He sings, "Into [pause] the path you are hurled/And the cards are [pause] no good that you're holding/Unless they're [pause] from another world." "In one [pause], the surface was frozen/In another [pause], I witnessed a crime/In one [pause], I was running, and in another/All I seemed to be doing [pause] was *climb*." This is very engaging, and the effect is built upon in the next three lines, with breaths after "looking" "going" and "already" until we're hanging on the narrator's every phrase, as surely as in "Pretty Boy Floyd."

So Dylan was rebuffed in his effort to join the Grateful Dead. But that certainly gave him great impetus to go forth and reinvent Bob Dylan (singer/songwriter/performer) once again. With considerable flair.

11.

In 1989, Bob Dylan toured from late spring to mid-autumn, beginning May 27 at a castle in Andrarum, Sweden, and ending November 15 at a performing arts center in Tampa, Florida. There was one break in the tour, September 11 to October 9. Otherwise, Dylan and his band worked steadily, playing twenty concerts a month, for a total of 99 shows. It was the most shows he'd done in a year since 1978, when he played 115 in a tour that ran from February through December.

The 1989 tour didn't have a name until Dylan referred in that October interview to "the Never Ending Tour," which fans immediately accepted as a name for his ongoing tour with roughly the same band that had begun in early June 1988. The 1988 band (Smith, Parker, Aaronson) backed Dylan at the first three shows of 1989 and at the fifth through the eighth. At the fourth show, and at every show beginning with the ninth (June 10, 1989), Kenny Aaronson, who had to return to the U.S. for health reasons, was replaced on bass by Tony Garnier, who had played with G. E. Smith in one of his former bands. In late July, Aaronson tried to get his job back, but was told by Dylan, "I'm not sure if I wanna change the band right now." In the long run, Garnier outlasted Parker and Smith, and is still playing bass in Dylan's touring band in April 2002.

So 1989 was when Dylan started scheduling and performing close to one hundred shows a year (after only 71 in '88), as he has done every year from age 48 to age 60. Why does he choose to live his life this way, on the road nearly eleven months a year, most years? I recently read a comment from a thespian that I think sheds some light on the call of performing. Jeffrey King, an actor with the Oregon Shakespeare Festival, was asked, "What led you to become an actor?" He replied:

> When I was a senior in high school, I got into a drama class because the physical education class I wanted to be in was closed. In the drama class I started to feel a kind of release, a contact with something really deep, a feeling of being a conduit. The only way I knew to continue to follow that feeling was to act. And still that's the reason I do it, to experience that kind of heightened and widened awareness. It feels like having been introduced to an experience that was so necessary and essential in my life, I just followed it.

This resonates nicely with Dylan's remarks in a 1981 interview:

> What I do is more of an immediate thing: to stand up on stage and sing – you get it back immediately. It's not like writing a book or even making a record ... What I do is so immediate it changes the nature, the concept, of art to me. It's like the man who made that painting there [points to a painting on wall of hotel room] has no idea we're sitting here now looking at it, or not looking at it, or anything. Performing is more like a stage play.

At the first 1989 show, Dylan performed the whole concert wearing a hooded anorak (with a cap on under it) that completely covered his head and upper body. He wore the same outfit at the next three shows, until (in Clinton Heylin's words), "on the second night in Dublin, Dylan finally abandoned the hood, performing for the remainder of 1989 in full view of the paying customer." During this European leg of the '89 tour (twenty-one shows in May and June in Sweden, Finland, Ireland, Scotland, England, the Netherlands, Belgium, France, Spain, Italy, Turkey, and Greece), Dylan also kept the stage as darkly lit as possible, and performed from the darkest parts of center stage he could find. In Patras, Greece, he interrupted a song to ask that the lights be turned down, and played the rest of the show in virtual darkness (the audience booed). So we can assume that although Dylan was determined to stand (and had told his manager to book him as many shows as possible), he still had mixed feelings about being looked at while he did his work.

The recordings of the first two concerts of the tour show them to be kind of ragged (although they do have the virtue of including three songs Dylan had never sung on stage before). In the summer 1989 *Telegraph*, John Bauldie quotes his friend Felix Canares, who said he had "a strange feeling all through the Stockholm show [the second 1989 concert], like anything could happen. I was really worried that he wouldn't survive the show in a way – that he'd do something totally bizarre. He seemed to be so confused, started this really bad version of 'Times Are A-Changin'', and his harmonica playing was terrible, really embarrassing. He mixed up everything, started several songs in the wrong places ... His singing was very low, rough voice, he wasn't even singing into the mike ... He was really drunk, or influenced by drugs."

The third show, however, in Helsinki, Finland, May 30, sounds terrific. Dylan's vocals and his harmonica playing are exemplary, and his rapport with the band, and with co-guitarist Smith on the acoustic songs, seems much improved over many of the 1988 shows. Helsinki is a tape worth pursuing (imagine a version of "All Along the Watchtower" noteworthy just for the excellence and inventiveness of the harmonica parts) and, along with Athens (the last show of the European leg, June 28), a solid example of the spring '89 tour at its best. The Never Ending Tour was starting to do what it would do well for at least another thirteen years: provide thrilling live concert experiences and produce occasional works of accidental art able to please and speak to listeners miles and years away from the space-time location of the original performance. Dylan and his band would achieve this, like the Grateful Dead before them, by constantly going on – going on from the nights of confusion and poor sound and overindulgence, to the next towns and the next shows and better conditions – going on from a year of rival bandleaders awkwardly getting to know each other and struggling to find ways to work together, to subsequent years of frequent instances of happy and inspired collaboration.

The three songs included in the first two shows that Dylan had never sung on stage before were all covers: "You Don't Know Me" (a country song co-written by Eddy Arnold that was a pop hit for Jerry Vale in 1956 and for Ray Charles in 1962) May 27 and "When Did You Leave Heaven?" and "Hey La La" May 28. "When Did You Leave Heaven?" is the 1936 Guy Lombardo hit Dylan had included on *Down in the Groove*. "Hey La La" is a country song co-written by Ray Price and recorded by Ernest Tubb in the early 1950s. At Helsinki in the number two slot, where he had introduced "You Don't Know Me" and "Hey La La" at the earlier shows, Dylan sang for the first time on stage a song he can be heard singing on one of the 1967 "Basement Tapes" home recordings, "Confidential to Me." This was a 1956 pop hit for r&b singer Sonny Knight, which Robert Zimmerman probably heard on the radio when he was fifteen.

A small but significant part of Dylan's work as a performing artist is writing set lists before concerts determining what songs he might play tonight and in what sequence. Related to this is deciding before a tour what songs to refamiliarize himself with and rehearse with his band and co-guitarist. The 1988 tour was given much of its flavor and character by Dylan's decision to include in most shows old folk songs he'd recorded on his first album in 1961, or that he'd been playing in performances around that time, or similar selections. Sometime before the 1989 tour started, Dylan seems to have made a conscious decision to broaden his choice of songs to cover at this year's shows in order to embrace and explore another aspect of "the music that got me inspired and into it." He continued to sing "Eileen Aroon" and "Barbara Allen" and (occasionally) "Two Soldiers" and "Trail of the Buffalo" and "The Lakes of Pontchartrain," but now he also added to his shows, during the electric sets, a broad variety of country songs and rock/pop/r&b songs he'd heard and probably played in his youth, most of them united by the fact that few in the audience were likely to be familiar with them or even to be able to guess what sort of song this is and why he's singing it tonight. An exception (a song probably familiar to many European Dylan concert attendees) was his performance in Cava de Tirreni, Italy, of "Pancho and Lefty" (written by Townes van Zandt, and popularized by Willie Nelson and Merle Haggard in 1983).

Other cover songs considered and rehearsed for this tour

(according to drummer Christopher Parker in a 1989 interview) included the Who's "I Can See for Miles," the Beach Boys' "God Only Knows," Vanilla Fudge's slow rock version of the Supremes' "You Keep Me Hanging On," Rodgers and Hart's "Where or When" (a hit for Dion & the Belmonts in 1960), the Coasters' "Poison Ivy," Buddy Holly's "Everyday" and "Love's Made a Fool of You," Patsy Cline's "Walking after Midnight," Robert Johnson's "Little Queen of Spades," Johnny Cash's "Ring of Fire," Hank Williams's "Lonesome Whistle" (which Dylan had attempted at the sessions for his first album), and Jimmy Work's country standard "Making Believe." Of these, only "Making Believe" was actually performed on the Europe '89 tour, on which Dylan did sing Hank Williams's "A House of Gold," Thomas A. Dorsey's gospel standard "Peace in the Valley," Ricky Nelson's 1958 hit "Lonesome Town" (sung regularly by Dylan at his 1986 shows), and "The Water Is Wide" (a folk song Dylan and Joan Baez sang together at seven of the 1975 Rolling Thunder shows).

The inclusion of many unfamiliar and unexpected covers in the early shows of tour '89 helps to give these shows a feeling of freedom (anything can happen!) similar to the freewheeling and unpredictable fall '87 Dylan shows with Petty & the Heartbreakers. In both cases, the fact that the set lists and the structuring of the shows were so much looser than on Dylan's U.S. tour with the same band the previous year was a reflection not only of Dylan's wish to apply what he'd learned about show-structuring and song-sequencing by watching the Grateful Dead, but also of Dylan's ideas about European audiences and the freedoms available to him because of their open-mindedness. In a transatlantic telephone interview on the eve of a European tour in 1981, a journalist asked him, "Are you looking forward to coming back to London?" Dylan replied:

> Oh, sure. It seems like they appreciate different things in Europe than they do here. Here they take a lot of things for granted. We've been playing some new songs that nobody has ever heard before. I think people in England react more spontaneously to the stuff that I do than the people here. You sit here for so long and they take you for granted, you know.

This tells us something about what Dylan wants and needs from his audiences. "It's the crowd that changes the songs," he said to Adrian Deevoy in 1989 on the topic of the improvisational nature of his shows.

Even though Dylan could barely be seen by the Helsinki crowd under his big hood on the darkened stage in May 1989, he presumably could see and hear and feel them – and listening to the tape of this show you can feel him responding to their presence (and to his ideas about their ability and willingness to react spontaneously) as he expresses himself very freely through his band and his voice and his harmonica playing on "Confidential to Me" and "Ballad of Hollis Brown" and "Just Like a Woman" and "All Along the Watchtower" and "To Ramona" and "Mr. Tambourine Man" and "The Times They Are A-Changin'." Yes, he's playing harmonica again after not doing so throughout 1988, and he seems to be playing his band as an instrument again after some apparent difficulty with that aspect of his performing artistry at many of the 1988 shows.

"My love for you will always be/Confidential to me! Our love is a precious secret ..." Hearing the conviction with which Dylan sings these lines in Helsinki in 1989, two things come to my mind. This quote from Howard Sounes's biography: "The wedding of Bob [Dylan] and Carolyn Dennis took place in Los Angeles on June 4, 1986. The certificate was filed with the county registrar as a 'confidential marriage.' There was not even a hint in the press. 'We were [all] sworn to secrecy never to mention it,' says [personal friend] Ted Perlman." And one of my favorite "lost" (unrecorded) Bob Dylan compositions, "Let's Keep It Between Us," which he sang (accompanying himself on piano) at all of his shows in November and December 1980.

The next performance at Helsinki, "Ballad of Hollis Brown" (a 1962 song Dylan performed once on the 1988 tour – for the first time since he sang it at Live Aid in 1985 – and seven times in Europe in May–June 1989) makes me think of the compassion/empathy theme in *Oh Mercy*. Except for the first and last verses, the song is written in the second person: "Your brain is a-bleedin'/And your legs can't seem to stand." It's a song in which the singer/writer puts himself (and the listener) inside the mind of a killer/suicide, a madman, a tragic figure. "What good am I if I see and don't say?" What young Bob Dylan saw and said in 1962, he is still saying on stage almost three decades later. "You looked for work and money/And you walked a rugged mile." The way the singer breathes in this particular arrangement and performance of the song is worthy of note. It's simple and very effective. No one else does it quite like this.

"Just Like a Woman," the next performance after "Ballad of Hollis Brown" at the Helsinki show, provides a good example of Dylan successfully playing his band as an instrument and expressing himself freely through his voice and harmonica. Other particularly fine examples of him expressing himself very freely through voice, harp, and band at Helsinki '89 are "Mr. Tambourine Man" and "The Times They Are A-Changin'" – even though in these cases the "band" is just himself and G. E. Smith on two acoustic guitars.

When the 1989 European shows were first announced, the concert after Helsinki was going to be in Leningrad. But that changed. John Bauldie had a conversation in a bar the day before the Glasgow show with Dylan's assistant tour manager. Bauldie asked, "How come Leningrad was cancelled?" "It was the government," he was told. "They said we couldn't go. Everyone was real disappointed. When we got word of the tour, we said, 'Oh Europe, OK.' But then they said, 'You're playing Leningrad.' And this made it real exciting for all of us – it became the main purpose of the trip, Leningrad, yayay! But then they said, 'Er, Leningrad's off.' Oh dear. 'But, you're going to Istanbul!' And then it was, 'Istanbul's off.' Oh. 'But you got two shows in Leningrad!' Yayayayay! And then, last week, 'Leningrad's off and Istanbul's off,' and everyone was real disappointed. But now it looks like Istanbul's back on. Yayayay!"

Dylan's own excitement and fulfillment at playing to a responsive crowd in Istanbul, one of the great historic cities of the world, can be heard and felt in a magical 17-minute sequence of performances from that June 24 concert: "Mr. Tambourine Man," "Don't Think Twice, It's All Right," and "Knockin' on Heaven's Door." The magic here is not so much in the singing but in the music, with the vocal functioning as another instrument dancing with and alongside the guitars and the harmonica. These four instruments together (eventually joined by bass and drums halfway through the third segment) make extraordinarily expressive music, always magical and occasionally ecstatic, this night in "the largest and most splendid European city of the Middle Ages," called Constantinople until eleven years before the birth of Abraham and Beatty Zimmerman's son Robert. The moment at which the closing melody notes of "Don't Think Twice" turn out to be the opening melody notes of "Knockin' on Heaven's Door" is thrilling, and so is almost every harmonica re-entry, particularly the ones near the ends of each of the three segments of this love song to Istanbul and to the life of a performer.

The ninth show of Tour '89, and the second show with Tony Garnier replacing Kenny Aaronson on bass, was at Statenhal in The Hague, the Netherlands, on June 10. After opening *all* of his 1988 concerts with "Subterranean Homesick Blues" (and almost all of the first eight 1989 shows – the exception being Stockholm, where he opened with "The Times They Are A-Changin'"), the roving gambler finally shuffled the deck by opening at The Hague with "Most Likely You Go Your Way (and I'll Go Mine)." During the remaining twelve shows in Europe, Dylan opened with "Most Likely" seven times, "Subterranean" twice, "Times" once, "Hey La La" once, and "Tangled Up in Blue" once (the only time he played it on this European tour).

As is often the case with opening songs at Dylan shows, "Most Likely" gets fairly scrambled at The Hague. Dylan comes in late with his vocal, constructs a first verse out of lyrics from three differ-ent verses, and awkwardly improvises the second verse (one line is appropriate: "Can't be this way every time!"). After the bridge, Dylan lets the band play the last verse without benefit of his vocals (sounds good) and eventually does sing the last verse. The sound of his voice is unusual and attractive here and throughout the show, notably in the next song, another powerful electric "Hollis Brown." John Bauldie, who attended this concert, wrote in *The Telegraph*, in a piece called "Diary of a Bobcat": "In The Hague, Dylan doesn't really seem to care that he's messing things up for too much of the time. He's in one of his 'funny' moods again. Is he drunk? The more I think about it, the more it seems to me that he was drunk, not long before, but that he's swallowed or sniffed something else to pull himself together for long enough to do the show." And from Bauldie's next diary entry: "Further consideration of the show in The Hague, a show which is, a little to my surprise, I must confess, spoken of with enormous enthusiasm by some long-term Dylan watchers, prompts more serious discussion as to whether, or how much, Dylan takes drugs. Is this, like '78, a coke-fuelled tour? Or a whisky-and-brandy tour? Or both? ... Outside the hall, I bump into my friend Nigel, the electrician. 'Things seemed a little "loose" at

times last night,' I observe. 'Rotterdam,' he replies. 'No, The ...'
'We stopped in Rotterdam. Scored some great hash. The Americans really enjoyed themselves afterwards.' "

One of these Americans was surely Victor Maymudes, Dylan's close friend and dope-loving traveling companion in the 1960s, whom he had rehired as his road manager in 1988. In any case, some sort of intoxicant seems to give an unusual edge and presence to many of Dylan's vocals at The Hague (and again, three nights later, at the show in Frejus, France).

It is characteristic of the Europe '89 concerts that a recorded show becomes notable for one unusual (and very striking and memorable) song selection and performance. The Hague is a good show, but its other high points (including a soulful "Mr. Tambourine Man," a spirited "Shelter from the Storm," and a particularly pleasing electric "I Don't Believe You") are overshadowed by a remarkable electric (i.e. full band) performance of "Trail of the Buffalo." This was the first of only two electric "Trail of the Buffalo"s that Dylan has ever performed, as of this writing. What makes it so special is not just its rarity but the intensity of the sound and feel of this musical performance, chiefly as a result of the interaction between Smith and Dylan's electric guitars – Dylan playing an inspired rhythm guitar part and Smith offering melodic lead lines played in a very appealing tone, and occasionally doubling or answering Dylan's rhythm lines. Bass and drums offer appropriate support and Dylan's voice also responds to and further extends the great mood the guitars are creating. Hot stuff. Here the techniques and rapport Dylan and Smith have developed during their acoustic duos spill over into and result in an exceptional band performance. The Rotterdam hash is probably helpful, too, and it occurs to me that tonight Dylan could be singing the song partly from the point of view of Garnier or Parker or even Smith or Aaronson as workers recruited for a fateful summer of hard traveling by a swift-talking "well-known famous drover" who, of course, is Bob Dylan. "Yes, I will pay good wages, an' transportation too ..." (Though he doesn't actually sing this line and occasionally finds himself improvising: "Well I couldn't drink the water, could not sleep or drown ...")

At Frejus, a small city in the south of France, on June 13, 1989, Bob Dylan sang as his first encore an especially attractive version of his 1963 song "Boots of Spanish Leather." Perhaps inspired by the grace of the interplay between his and G. E. Smith's acoustic guitars, he sang this true account of a difficult moment in a youthful love affair as if he were reliving it, and wrapped up the story and performance with a wonderfully sweet and expressive harmonica solo. This should be reason enough for the recording of this concert to be a sought-after work of "accidental art." But the next performance that night, though not as pretty or as well-realized, has the distinction of being Bob Dylan's only known performance (to date) of a familiar gospel song recorded by Elvis Presley early in his career, Thomas A. Dorsey's "Peace in the Valley."

"Well, I'm tired, and so weary," Dylan sings (though he's so tired the word sounds more like "tried"), "but I must travel along ... till the Lord come and take me away." He's not sure of the next words, so he slurs and improvises: "Well, I survive till the night, but the night so bright, but the night as bright as the day." (The words Dorsey wrote here are, "Where the morning's so bright, and the Lamb is the light, and the night is as bright as the day, oh yes." These lyrics might have stuck in Dylan's mind, but his teacher Elvis also fudged them when he sang this song late in the night at the session where he recorded his sixth #1 record, "All Shook Up." Elvis sang something like: "Well, the morning's so bright, and the lamp is alight, and the night, night is as black as the sea, oh yes.") Dylan, well supported by his band who've clearly rehearsed this number, continues passionately: "There will be *peace* in the valley for me one of these days. There will be peace, peace in the valley for me, oh Lord I pray. There'll be no trouble, no trouble and pain, no problem releasing from the higher gain." This last line is also improvised, and the second time he sings this chorus he sings, "no trouble and pride" – evoking for me his sincere awareness of the suffering caused by the disease of conceit. Dorsey's original line, which Elvis sings, is: "There'll be no sadness, no sorrow, no trouble I see."

Alcohol and road-weariness seem to interfere with the quality of Dylan's singing of "Peace in the Valley" at Frejus, but it is still fascinating and moving to listen to this aural snapshot of him being washed by feelings about his relationship with Elvis ("I thank God for Elvis") and his relationship with the Lord ("This is the flat-out truth: I find the religiosity and philosophy in the music, I don't find it anywhere else") at this weary moment on stage near the end of a concert and in the middle of a tour. Indeed, Elvis's death in 1977 (and its reminders for Dylan of his own mortality) was a primary link in the chain of events leading to Dylan's Christian conversion in 1978–79. It's moving to hear him sing hoarsely, "And the beasts from the wild, they will be led, led by a child ... and I'll be changed from this creature that I am!" and then to hear his gentle and emotive harmonica playing for 40 seconds at the close of the performance.

And then it's intriguing and amusing to hear Dylan and his band segue from "Peace in the Valley" into "Man Gave Names to All the Animals," a song Dylan wrote in his own "gospel" era. It's on the set list because Dylan remembers that it was a hit in 1979 in France. Such footnotes can be meaningful in the life of a songwriter and recording artist and performing artist. Thomas A. Dorsey, composer of "Peace in the Valley," led Ma Rainey's backing band on her tours in 1924–28 ("Where Ma Rainey and Beethoven once unwrapped their bedroll/Tuba players now rehearse around the flagpole" – Bob Dylan, 1965) and recorded a million-selling record ("It's Tight Like That") with another Dylan hero, Tampa Red, in 1928, and went on to found the National Convention of Gospel Choirs and Choruses. He is credited with coining the term "gospel music."

Two weeks after singing "Peace in the Valley" in Frejus, Dylan found himself in Greece, on the Hill of the Muses (Philopappos) in Athens, singing and playing guitar and harmonica with Van Morrison for a British film crew collecting footage for a BBC-TV documentary to be called *One Irish Rover, Van Morrison in Performance*. This resulted in one of Dylan's finest spring 1989 performances: his harmonica accompaniment to Morrison's Philopappos rendition of "Foreign Window," a song from Van's 1986 album *No Guru, No Method, No Teacher*. In the television programme, this is introduced by part of an audiotape interview with Morrison in which he talks about songwriting in words very similar to the 1968 Dylan comment I quoted in chapters 5 and 10 ("some kind of wild line will just come into your head ..."):

> A line will come into your head, and out of nowhere. And you'll wonder, "What is this? Why am I saying this? Why is it coming in my head? I think I'll write that down." And then that line will lead to another line that will lead to your verse and lead to your chorus, and that will lead to your song.
>
> I'll give you an example: "I saw you from a foreign window, bearing down the suffering road." I'm reading about Lord Byron, and then there's a line about Rimbaud. So one line

might be about something and another line might be about something else, you know, but the song itself is about suffering. It's about someone who is having to either travel in other countries or live in countries other than where he would like to be, and he feels like there's entanglement, and this is causing suffering, and that's basically what the song's about. But it's not about any one person, or any two people. It's an idea, leading to redemption through suffering. When I was singing it with Dylan, it just occurred to me that part of it could be about him; and I didn't realize it until that second.

In spite of Dylan's various efforts to hide his face from onlookers at his concerts this spring, the 48-year-old singer's face looks very attractive in this Greek footage. The three Morrison/Dylan performances included in this documentary, "Crazy Love," "Foreign Window," and "One Irish Rover," are another opportunity for anyone interested to spend some fairly intimate moments with the "real" Bob Dylan. In tight close-ups ("hold" shots such as Dylan favored as a director in *Renaldo & Clara*), we watch him listening intently, and with evident respect and appreciation, to a peer's songwriting and performance at the very moment that he is participating in these song-performances himself, singing a faint (because he's not sure of the words of these songs he probably first heard an hour or two earlier) harmony vocal, and playing expressive and inventive second acoustic guitar on "Crazy Love" and "One Irish Rover" ... and playing marvelously responsive and expressive harmonica lines alongside and between Morrison's vocals on "Foreign Window."

In these shots we can watch Dylan thinking as a musician and as a music lover. We can see him getting smitten with the lyrics and musical feel and "message" of "Crazy Love" as though he'd just written or discovered it himself. In this case, his participation in the song is minimal, almost inaudible, though the expressions on Dylan's face do add to Van's excellent performance. The background – the Hill of the Muses overlooks the Acropolis, with the Aegean Sea between them – also enriches this film portrait of two rather similar roving performers crossing paths. In each of the other two performances, Dylan clearly communicates his enthusiasm for and sensitivity to the song's musical and lyrical sentiment (and adds significantly to each performance) by way of his harmonica playing (on "Foreign Window") and his guitar accompaniment (developing and extending a riff implicit in Morrison's playing on "One Irish Rover"). It is fascinating to watch Dylan, a singer and songwriter who tours the world supported by and interacting with other musicians, function as a sideman musician himself (and to watch him so closely we can see him thinking). His innate respect for the art of the song and of the collaborative performance is evident, and in a sense we are given an intimate glance at his artistic process and values, as he seems to accompany Morrison as he himself wishes to be accompanied and joined in the art of song-presentation when he's singing and playing (with G.E. or with his band). Dylan's love of music and of this form of communicating with the world come through quite charmingly, and he does indeed make strong and meaningful statements of his own, always respectful of and in service to the song and singer, through his harmonica and guitar contributions.

Still in Athens, on the night of June 28, 1989, at Panathanaikos Stadium, Bob Dylan and G. E. Smith and Tony Garnier and Christopher Parker played the last concert of the Europe '89 leg of the Never Ending Tour, with a guest appearance by Van Morrison on two of the nineteen songs, two of the five encores, "Crazy Love" and "And It Stoned Me," both songs from Morrison's superb 1970 album *Moondance.* "And It Stoned Me" had also been performed by Van and Bob for the BBC film crew on the Hill of the Muses, but wasn't included in the documentary. Perhaps a copy will emerge someday.

Athens, Dylan's 21st show of spring '89, two nights after the "turn down the lights" concert in Patras and four nights after the memorable evening in Istanbul, is arguably the best single show of the twenty-one, not a transcendent masterpiece but a solid and pleasing portrait of a man in motion ("I saw you from a foreign window/You were trying to find your way back home/You were carrying your defects/Sleeping on a pallet on the floor/In the palace of the Lord," as Morrison put it), doing his life's work on the stages of a hundred nations, experiencing a kind of heightened and widened and very immediate awareness by standing up on stage and singing to the people in the room, feeling like some sort of conduit, a performing artist.

The Athens concert gets off to a good start with a few assertive drum hits from Christopher Parker at the start of "Most Likely You Go Your Way" that provoke the rest of the band into following inventively and moving the arrangement they've been playing for the last week into new territory, something like a 12/8 time signature (as with "Gates of Eden" at Park City in '88). Dylan responds with a rather inspired vocal, happily shouting every line of the song (that he can remember tonight) so it fits snugly within the exotic rhythmic riff Parker is creating (supported by Dylan on rhythm guitar, Garnier on bass, and Smith on melodic lead, all clearly enjoying themselves as the singer is). A pleasant mood of barely controlled chaos is established. "I just can't do what I've done before!" But in fact he can and he does, using this song as a doorway through which to become himself with his band and onstage. The shot of energy seems to sustain singer and band all through an excellent 100-minute performance.

The second song, "You're a Big Girl Now," demonstrates very well that Bob Dylan has a sense of purpose at this concert: moved and impressed a few hours earlier by the music and the performing of Van Morrison, who is in the audience tonight, he now wants to respond by making the best presentation he can of the music of Bob Dylan. In this performance of "Big Girl," and especially in the two heartfelt harmonica solos Dylan plays after the fourth and fifth verses, you can hear his confidence in his band and their ability to speak for him, and his satisfaction with the beauty and intelligence of the music he and they are making together.

"Ballad of Hollis Brown" follows, and is again a very impressive (and fresh) musical creation. With the fourth song, "Shelter from the Storm" in its new uptempo arrangement, one cannot help being struck by the versatility of this band. And of this singer. Some of the shows in Italy this past week, particularly Livorno on June 22, were marred by the extreme hoarseness of Dylan's voice, but tonight he seems able both to make the hoarseness disappear when he wants his voice to be sweet and tender ("Big Girl," "Hollis Brown") and to use the hoarseness to his advantage, both to communicate feeling (in "Shelter") and to bring out the humor of his songs' lyrics – he does this skillfully on the fifth and sixth songs, "Ballad of a Thin Man" and "Highway 61 Revisited." On "Thin Man," he sings: "No one has any respect/They just expect/You to sign over your check" rhyming two hoarse "ect"s with a hoarse "eck" before spitting out "To some tax-deductible charity organization." Funny stuff. Yet later in the evening he can give us as tender a rendition of "The Lakes of Pontchartrain" as one might hope for.

By the end of the electric set, Dylan has offered two songs from

Blood on the Tracks, two from *Highway 61 Revisited*, one from *Blonde on Blonde* and one from *The Times They Are A-Changin'*. A dozen years of work, well represented, and here presented as though each song is clearly relevant to the human situation – in Athens and anywhere else – in 1989. Which it is. It is indicative of the depth of this performer's art that I have to tell you that as terrific as "Shelter from the Storm" is at Athens (I particularly like the way the backing music drops out momentarily to transform "I'm living in a foreign country/But I'm bound to cross the line/Beauty walks on a razor's edge/Someday I'll make it mine" into a dramatic monologue), you'll also want to hear the same song as performed at Milan on June 21, 1989. It's the same arrangement, but in Milan it has a motion to it, a rock and roll feel, that is unique and very appealing. Either performance could be your favorite, or you might find you like them equally, for different and perhaps mysterious reasons.

The acoustic set at Athens begins with "Don't Think Twice." It's the seventh time Dylan and Smith have played this song during the spring '89 tour, and a good example of how musically alive their acoustic collaboration has become. With Dylan's guitar taking the lead, the two find themselves at times here getting into an exploration of the song's rhythmic core that is as vibrant and fulfilling as Dylan and Morrison's guitar exploration of "One Irish Rover" at the BBC filming the day before. Dylan responds with an excellent "fast blues style" vocal performance, and several extended harmonica passages that are delightful – further evidence of what an effective and versatile instrument for self-expression the harmonica has become for him at these spring '89 shows. It is as though picking up the instrument on stage again after a year off, and listening at the early May mixing sessions to all the fine harp playing he did on *Oh Mercy*, have both stimulated him to a renewed confidence in his ability to speak his musical heart and serenade his Muse through this simple instrument. He plays harmonica on eight of the Athens songs, the six acoustic performances and "Big Girl" and "Shelter." Dylan played harmonica a lot throughout the Europe '89 tour, in many different ways and sometimes in unexpected places: there are a number of playful and colorful harmonica explorations in the second half of "Most Likely" at the start of the Rome concert.

The next song at Athens is one of those striking spring '89 rarities I spoke of earlier: the only time, as of this writing, that Dylan has ever performed an acoustic version of "Every Grain of Sand" in concert. It's a very good performance, and mostly what makes it special is not the vocal (although Dylan puts a lot of feeling in it and makes some very aesthetically satisfying use of hoarseness, like a painter experimenting with alternate shades of familiar colors) but what could be called the shadow of the vocal, the singer's expressive and earnest harmonica playing at strategic moments, notably before the start of the vocal and after its conclusion. In these harmonica passages it is easy to believe we are hearing the frail, questing voice referred to in this song's portentous opening lines: "In the time of my confession, in the hour of my deepest need…. There's a dyin' voice within me, reaching out somewhere …"

The ninth Athens song is "Mr. Tambourine Man," which Dylan has played at sixteen of these spring shows – and particularly well at Helsinki, The Hague, Istanbul, and now Athens. This is why, given the opportunity, a connoisseur of the performing arts will attend a series of shows in the same season by the same performer. He or she may play Hamlet or Ophelia every night with the same skill and intent, and yet each of the performances may be a unique and enriching work of art, not at all interchangeable with the others and not to be missed if one appreciates such artistry and can somehow arrange to be there. The Athens "Tambourine Man" is one of the best Dylan performances of any song on this tour. And the version of "Blowin' in the Wind" that comes next at this 6/28/89 concert is almost as good. Why are these old chestnuts, these "greatest hits," suddenly so alive? I don't know, but unfortunately the same cannot be said for "Like a Rolling Stone" or "I Shall Be Released" or "Maggie's Farm" at Athens or other spring '89 shows. Dylan sings these and the band plays them fairly mechanically, as though he and they are just doing their job – a job they enjoy, but not necessarily one that's particularly meaningful to them at this moment. On some other Dylan tours, of course, "Like a Rolling Stone" has been the high point, the summation of the whole evening, for Dylan as well as for the audience … and on some, "Tambourine Man" and "Blowin'" have been fairly routine performances. But in Athens in spring 1989 at the end of this tour of Europe, Dylan seems to be saying with every line of "Mr. Tambourine Man": "I'm Bob Dylan, and very happy to be the author of this song that you are clapping along to so joyfully. You are my tambourine man as I am yours, and in this 'jingle jangle' evening I happily come following you."

The clarity and confidence of the single guitar notes (Bob's?) that arise out of the strumming (G.E.'s?) at the start of this "Mr. Tambourine Man" offer some hint of the powerful and intimate-yet-anthemic performance that is to come. As the vocal starts (hoarse but quite beautiful), the audience begins clapping along and a fine groove is soon established between handclaps and guitars. At these shows, Dylan omitted the song's third verse ("Though you might hear laughin', spinnin' ...") and replaced it with a two-guitar instrumental break. Again, high strong single guitar notes ring out, sounding like they really have something to say. The joyous tension of the performance is ratcheted up another notch, and suddenly Dylan shouts and pleads, with gleeful urgency, "Take me disappearing!!" His presence in this last verse, especially the first few lines, is surprising. And then this is trumped by the remarkable two-minute harmonica solo that completes the performance, in which the harmonica player lovingly and eruditely explores the meaning of every note of this song's melody and every word of its lyrics. This is the sort of harmonica-and-guitar-and-voice performance that caused many people to fall in love with Bob Dylan's persona and music in the first place, and it's not a replay of anything but very much an expression of what the singer and player is feeling and experiencing at this moment in his life. He sounds like he's feeling the same very special kind of freedom now on this Athens stage that he felt and wanted to sing about when he first wrote this song.

"Blowin' in the Wind" at Athens inspires the same sort of audience clap-along as the previous song, and again Smith and Dylan's guitars sound very responsive to and well-synched with the rhythm line the crowd is providing. And again Dylan sings his song in a very awake voice that sounds full of purpose (and keenly aware of the unchanging relevance of the questions the song is asking). Again, he sounds inspired by the interplay between his guitar and G.E.'s, and grateful to have found a format where he can explore very personal and subtle musical impulses in his acoustic guitar playing onstage, and to have arrived at a moment in time when this format is really opening doors for him and allowing him the confidence to create spontaneously. And again his harmonica playing – two extended solos, one after the second verse, another a whole verse in itself at the end of the song – is as eloquent and heartfelt and rewarding as any Dylan fan, past or future, could ask for ... or dream of.

The second electric set at Athens starts (as it so often did in 1988–89) with "Silvio," and continues with "I Shall Be Released," and ends with "Like a Rolling Stone." The third song in this set is Hank Williams's "A House of Gold," which Dylan had sung in concert for the first time ever thirteen days earlier, in Madrid. Although written by Hank himself (to the tune of one of his earlier hits, "Lost Highway," which he didn't write), "A House of Gold" is as much a gospel song as "Peace in the Valley." The message is strong, practically a sermon:

> People steal, they cheat and they lie
> For silver and gold and what it will buy
> But don't they know on Judgment Day
> Silver and gold will melt away?
>
> I'd rather be in a deep, dark grave
> And know that my poor soul was saved
> Than live in this world in a house of gold,
> Deny my God and doom my soul.

Clearly, it's the message conveyed in the lyrics that led Dylan to put this song on his set list tonight (along with a desire to keep himself connected to his own musical roots). Interesting that Madrid, where he first attempted this cover, was the next show after the one where he sang "Peace in the Valley." Something was on his mind. He also, of course, put "Every Grain of Sand" on his set list for Athens, as though there was a side of himself he needed to go public with before leaving Europe and completing this tour or this leg of the tour. And very interesting that three days after the Athens show, on July 1st, 1989 in Peoria, Illinois, Dylan would sing his most direct statement of faith, "I Believe in You," for the first time in more than seven years.

None of these ("Silvio," "I Shall Be Released," "A House of Gold" and "Like a Rolling Stone" at Athens) are particularly inspired performances. But as always, each performance illuminates the others, and the excellence of the Athens concert is best appreciated by listening to the whole show and feeling the flow of the performance, and thus connecting oneself with the context in which each song was sung and played. "I'd rather be in a deep, dark grave" comes after "I see my light come shining"; and "live in this world in a house of gold" is followed by "Once upon a time you dressed so fine ..." What is this singer/concert-maker trying to say to us? And to himself?

After the two electric sets, and the four-song acoustic set between them, the last segment of this concert is the encores – five of them, two acoustic songs, then two songs sung by guest artist Van Morrison (Dylan singing with him, though not always on-mike), and finally, as at 16 of these 21 shows, "Maggie's Farm" to declare the evening over ("I ain't gonna ... no more"). The acoustic encores are done well, and with feeling; "Maggie's Farm" is almost a throw-away, as usual; Morrison's guest songs are well sung, and it's fun to hear Dylan joining in, sometimes enthusiastically, on every third or fourth word. A meandering end to a fine show and to an uneven but increasingly promising tour. Two "travel days" between the end of a European leg and the start of a North American one is certainly evidence of a "never ending tour" mind-state setting in ("You can pick and choose better when you're just out there all the time and your show is already set up [and] you don't have to start it up and end it").

In the course of these Europe '89 shows, Dylan sang two of his own songs that he had never performed publicly before: "Congratulations" from *Traveling Wilburys, Volume One* and "Tears of Rage" from *The Basement Tapes*. The first "Congratulations" (at Glasgow, June 6) is not well sung, although I like the way he uses his harmonica in the course of the song. The other "Congratulations" (at Birmingham, June 7) is much improved; no harp but a very spirited vocal performance (better than on the album). Two of the Wilburys, George Harrison and Jeff Lynne, were at the Birmingham show, and the placement of the song on the set list as next-to-last encore suggests that this was intended to be a joint performance. But – perhaps due to a communication error – that didn't happen. "Tears of Rage," which Christopher Parker has said he and G. E. Smith had asked Dylan to play at rehearsals sometime, was debuted at Patras, June 26. In this case, Dylan's southern Europe hoarseness is an obstacle, and he doesn't find a way to deliver the song's melody via his singing (and, perhaps as a result, the band's playing is rather tentative). The performance is unsatisfying – but breaking the ice was important, Dylan would go on to include "Tears of Rage" at seven shows later in 1989 and at ten more shows in 1990.

12.

On July 1 in Peoria, Illinois, Bob Dylan started the second leg of his 1989 tour. He opened the concert boldly with his second-ever public performance of Townes van Zandt's "Pancho and Lefty" (not half as good as the song's debut in Italy June 21 – Dylan in '89 tended to sing his first song of the night rather tentatively, more focused on getting used to being in front of an audience than on delivering a song's "message" or even articulating its lyrics clearly). This was followed with his first-ever concert performance of Van Morrison's "One Irish Rover," a song he'd learned four days earlier during the BBC filming on the Hill of the Muses. The third song at this first North American show of 1989 was "I Believe in You" (which Dylan had last performed in Lakeland, Florida on November 21, 1981; he sang it at every one of his concerts in 1979, 1980 and 1981, and then didn't sing it for seven and a half years). It's a memorable performance – well worth seeking out, although the rest of the Peoria show is not especially noteworthy, except that "Stuck Inside of Mobile with the Memphis Blues Again" sounds particularly good coming right after "One Irish Rover" and "I Believe in You," as though Dylan were consciously creating a collection of

233

song-statements and performances as resonant with each other and as full of the joy and mystery of being himself right now as his album *Blonde on Blonde*, where "Stuck Inside of ..." first appeared, and where it fit in as perfectly as it does at Peoria on July 1 as the third part of this very expressive impromptu trilogy on the subject of being in love with God and life and the absurdity of it all.

"One Irish Rover" was a relatively recent Van Morrison composition. Like "Foreign Window," it's from his 1986 album *No Guru, No Method, No Teacher*. I was very struck with it the first two times I heard Dylan sing it, at concerts in southern California Sept. 8 and 10, 1989. After trying out his own arrangement of his peer's song in Peoria, Dylan performed "One Irish Rover" at twelve more '89 shows. It got better as he and the band grew into it more, but the Peoria performance is quite satisfying, especially the one-minute "duelling guitars" instrumental passage at the end.

The opening lines of the song are clearly a songwriter/poet talking to his Muse, or to that part of himself that romanticizes his own life experiences: "Tell me a story/Now that it's over/Wrap it in glory/For one Irish rover." These last two lines are the chorus, repeated throughout the song. Of course, when Morrison sings the song, he's describing himself in the title phrase; and when Dylan sings his version, this is unchanged. Bob Dylan, just back from a tour of twelve European countries including Ireland, playing a show in the midwestern U.S. where he was raised by his Jewish parents, is describing himself, with a flourish and a hint of ironic pride, as "one Irish rover." This works because the author of the performance sees himself as an international being, connected to many true homelands through music and song, "walkin' a road other men have gone down."

"I Believe in You" from the Peoria Civic Center Arena, 7/1/89, is memorable because there's an earnestness and a grace to the performance that is impressive even though the vocal is uneven – sometimes fiery and full of conviction, other times slurred and unconvincing. What we feel is not so much the strength of the singer/performer's faith, but the sense of purpose in this music which he seems to be conducting with his heart, a feeling that he is very conscious of making an offering here (to a Higher Power, not to the audience) and that he cares passionately about the quality of the offering, that is, the beauty and grace of the music as a whole, as if that were much more the conveyor of the message than the words of the song. So the *sound* of his voice may be more important to him than his phrasing or his presence with the story he's telling. The performance is memorable because it seems such a strong example of Dylan working with a small combo of musicians to create genuine (and new) Bob Dylan music. Not necessarily spontaneously – in fact, this performance seems quite well rehearsed – but with a keen awareness that the time is now, we have an opportunity (a moment of inspiration) and we have to seize it. One imagines that some of the fine small combo performances on Dylan's early albums were created with this sort of urgency and commitment (and silent leadership). I also imagine that I can feel Bob Dylan's heart beating as I listen to this performance of "I Believe in You." G. E. Smith really shines here: the inventiveness and responsiveness of the parts he's come up with and of his solos in the second half of the performance … and the tone of his guitar, which contributes significantly to the ensemble sound and thus to the realization of Dylan's auditory vision of what he wants and needs this song to be on this occasion. Interestingly, Dylan concludes the vocals of both "One Irish Rover" and "I Believe in You" (and leads into each song's closing instrumental passage) by repeating the song's title phrase five times. In the latter case, he shouts "Yeah!" before the second and fourth "I believe in you."

From a "mind out of time" perspective, a Never Ending Tour can have many opening nights (can also be considered an Always Beginning Tour). Milwaukee, July 3, 1989, the third show of the North American leg and the 24th Dylan concert of the year, seems to me a place where the Never Ending Tour as we know it starts to take shape … a beginning in spirit, if not on the calendar.

In preparing his set lists for his first U.S. shows of the year, Dylan did not play it safe. It seems to have been more important to him to challenge himself, to write scripts that would keep him and his band awake and on their toes. Only seven of the fifteen songs performed at Peoria were ones he'd included at his previous show, in Athens. Two of the new eight were songs he hadn't yet sung in 1989; three others were ones he'd only sung once during the twenty-one shows in Europe.

At the second North American show, at Poplar Creek Music Theater in the suburbs of Chicago, July 2, Dylan sang twelve songs he had not sung the night before in Peoria. Five of these were songs he hadn't performed yet in a 1989 concert; three more were songs he'd performed only once in the previous twenty-two shows.

Continuing in this vein, for the third show of this leg, Milwaukee, July 3, Dylan wrote a seventeen-song set list that included only four songs he'd played at the previous show and only seven he'd played at either of his last two shows. He sang five songs he hadn't yet sung in a 1989 concert. One of these he'd never played live before; another one he hadn't performed on stage since 1961.

The Milwaukee show, like Peoria and Poplar Creek, opened with a cover song. At Poplar Creek, it was "Everybody's Movin'," a rockabilly song Dylan had played twice in 1988 – both times as an encore. The Milwaukee opener was a scrambled version of "Early Morning Rain," a song by Gordon Lightfoot ("every time I hear a song of his, it's like I wish it would last forever," Dylan said in 1985) that Dylan sang on his 1970 album *Self Portrait* but had never performed live before. This mini-trend of opening with unexpected cover songs ended July 3. Dylan opened his next seven shows with "Most Likely You Go Your Way (and I'll Go Mine)"; after that he opened with "Subterranean Homesick Blues" twice, then back to "Most Likely" three times, and then on July 21 he opened a New Jersey show with his first-ever live performance of "Trouble" (from *Shot of Love*).

Milwaukee 1989 foreshadows much of the Never Ending Tour in that it is an unspectacular yet excellent show in which Bob Dylan is clearly working at creating opportunities to express himself. Listening to a recording of the show, we can feel his keen interest in being true to his own musical instincts and impulses. And we can hear him squandering a few of the resultant opportunities mysteriously, and seizing others gleefully.

As connoisseurs of the Never Ending Tour know well, seized opportunities and squandered ones can occur in the course of the same song-performance. One imagines the notion to add "Early Morning Rain" to his live repertoire came to Dylan in an airport somewhere between Athens and Peoria. So it's not mysterious that he found it difficult to acquire and memorize the song's lyrics in the next day or two. What is disappointing is that in singing the lyrics he does remember (half the first verse combined with half of the second, a largely improvised middle verse, and all of the original last verse – the one that includes the phrase "stuck here on the ground," a phrase he inserts into two other verses in the course of this performance), Dylan never manages to evoke any of the strong feelings this song evidently stirs in him. I say "evidently" because of the beauty and depth of feeling in the music and the instrumental sound he and his band achieve here. In 1969, Dylan told Jann Wenner that the sound he was aspiring to when he went in to record his album *John Wesley Harding* was "the sound that Gordon Lightfoot was getting [on his recordings] with Charlie McCoy and Kenny Buttrey." I take this as an indication that when Dylan said later "every time I hear a song of [Lightfoot's] ... I wish it would last forever," he was referring to his appreciation of the song's sound as well as of its lyrics and its melody. In any case, the music Smith, Parker, Garnier and Dylan make in the course of this Milwaukee "Early Morning Rain" inspires Dylan to a marvelous and very evocative bit of self-expression in the form of his harmonica solo after the last verse and leading into the lovely instrumental passage that closes the performance. The harmonica player/bandleader is soaring ... not stuck on the ground at all.

The second song at Milwaukee is a ragged "Driftin' Too Far from Shore," a song Dylan played at thirteen shows in 1988, but only at this one in 1989, and never once since then (as of this writing, June 2002). I believe he put it on the set list in Milwaukee and all those times in 1988 because he likes the song and feels it can open him up in some way during a show. And perhaps also because he recently had a conversation, by phone or in person, with a female friend to whom he now wishes to say, "I tried to reach you, honey, but you're driftin' too far from shore." And I guess he hasn't performed it since this show because he got tired of having to sing dummy lyrics through every verse of a song he doesn't know the words to (except for the chorus, which he loves and sings here with gusto) and that he can't familiarize himself with on the road because it's from a 1986 album and so is not included in his book *Lyrics 1962–1985*.

Next in the electric set July 3 is "John Brown," a song Dylan sang four times in the spring '89 leg and nine times in 1988, and which he will go on to perform eight more times during this 1989 tour and another thirteen times in 1990. I'd never particularly liked this song, lyrics or music or as a whole, so I was not too pleased when he rediscovered it after 24 years and played it three times with the Grateful Dead in summer 1987 and eleven more times with the Heartbreakers in the fall, then made it a staple of the first three years of the Never Ending Tour. Why did he place it on this

Milwaukee set list and on so many others? It's certainly not a "greatest hit" or a Dylan song people in the audience are hungry to hear. As of 1989 it had never been on a Dylan record (it was going to be on a never-released 1963 album called *Bob Dylan in Concert* and did eventually get included on *Unplugged* in 1995). So the set list writer must have known it would be as unfamiliar to almost everyone in the Milwaukee crowd as "Driftin' Too Far from Shore" ("Hey," says the set list writer, "that was a song from one of my two most recently released studio albums; what do you mean, 'unfamiliar'?") or "Confidential to Me" or "Hey La La."

My guess is that Dylan in preparing his set lists is trying to balance a variety of strong considerations: to include a reasonable number of songs he thinks the audience wants to hear (but not too many – that would feel stifling to him), to have an appropriate mix of "rockers" and "slow songs," to pace the show according to certain notions of drama and musical dynamics that satisfy his aesthetic sense as a concert performer and that will stimulate him and his band to do their best, to select songs that will make this show fun for him and the other players and for the imagined audience. He does sometimes read his own press, reviews or previews of shows in local newspapers, so he is aware that he is still thought of by much of the public as a "protest singer," some kind of historical/cultural figure (a "legend") who symbolizes the antiwar/counterculture spirit of the 1960s. I think that this is why "Masters of War" has been regularly played on his concert tours since 1978, because he would try to think of a song other than "Blowin' in the Wind" and "The Times They Are A-Changin'" that would fit this mass audience image of what you might hear if you paid to see '60s protest legend Bob Dylan in concert (and, preferably, that could be done during the electric sets, and as a crowd-arousing rocker) … and "Masters of War" seemed to fit the bill. So when the Grateful Dead encouraged him to resurrect "John Brown," and then when Petty and the Heartbreakers demonstrated that it could be performed with a satisfying rock crunch, I think Dylan filed it in his set-list-writing mind as "another 'Masters of War'" … another antiwar Bob Dylan "protest" song suitable for inclusion in his present-day electric sets. And he must also have found that he liked the song, enjoyed performing it, maybe because it's a story song (like "Barbara Allen" or "Joey" or "Two Soldiers") and one that doesn't require too much concentration on the part of the singer/storyteller, or maybe because he liked the way it would feel coming out of his mouth on stage to his band's accompaniment, the drama of some of its images and musical/lyrical language. Another possible explanation of Dylan's affection for "John Brown" is that he's never forgotten his pleasure when legendary American journalist (and friend of the working man) Studs Terkel told Dylan, during a 1963 radio interview, that he'd heard Dylan sing this and requested that he perform it again, referring to it (twice) as "a powerful one" and comparing it to the traditional antiwar song "Johnny I Hardly Knew You" (which had been in Dylan's repertoire at the start of his performing life, in 1960).

At Milwaukee in '89, Dylan performed both "John Brown" and "Masters of War." Both are better-than-average versions of these too frequently performed selections, in both cases because Dylan's vocals are not oversold, as often happened on these songs in '88–'89, and because the band, following the singer's lead, succeed in playing attractive, fresh and engaging music on songs that often ended up sounding bombastic. "John Brown" at Milwaukee does suffer from some lyric errors (swallowed words and phrases, and lines from different verses jumbled together), making it difficult to follow the story song's narrative (particularly for the majority of the audience who'd never heard this song before). Since there were similar problems with the first two songs at this show, this makes me wonder if some kind of intoxication was a factor in this concert's weaknesses and strengths, a question that would often arise during the next few years of the Never Ending Tour (as of course it had throughout Dylan's performing career up to this time).

In 2001, Dylan told interviewer Robert Hilburn: "Every time I sing 'Masters of War,' someone writes that it's an antiwar song. But there's no antiwar sentiment in that song. I'm not a pacifist. I don't think I've ever been one. If you look closely at the song, it's about what Eisenhower was saying about the dangers of the military-industrial complex in this country." The song is indeed a sermon denouncing war profiteering rather than a denunciation of war itself, although the undesirable effects of wars are cited ("fear to bring children into the world") ("young people's blood flows out of their bodies and is buried in the mud") to make the speaker's case against "you [who] fasten the triggers for the others to fire." Similarly, "John Brown" can be heard as an inquiry into the causes of war and resultant human suffering, rather than as an attack on war itself. In fact, if Dylan had included it in his 2001 rant to Hilburn ("A lot of my songs were definitely misinterpreted by people who didn't know any better, and it goes on today"), he could have said, with some justification, that "John Brown" is actually about the disease of conceit. The mother's *pride* at having her son be a soldier in a "good old-fashioned war" is referred to throughout the song along with her interest in how impressed her neighbors will be as a result. So although Dylan told Hilburn, "I believe strongly in everyone's right to defend themselves by every means necessary," "John Brown" doesn't question that principle but points out that this young man who was maimed beyond recognition in a "war on a foreign shore" wasn't defending himself or his country, but rather "couldn't help but think that I was just a puppet in a play" largely written by his mother's pride and her sense of what would impress the neighbors.

So did he sing "Masters of War" and "John Brown" so often because they let him feel he was giving the public what they wanted and because he got some masochistic satisfaction out of being misunderstood? ("I've always said the organized media," he told Hilburn of the *Los Angeles Times*, "propagated me as something I never pretended to be ... all this 'spokesman of conscience' thing.") I don't know, but the *Oh Mercy* empathy theme does come through clearly when Dylan sings in Milwaukee, "But the thing that scared me most, when my enemy come close, I could see that his face looked just like mine!"

During the fourth, fifth and sixth songs at Milwaukee (and at the first two North American shows the two nights before that), new bassist Tony Garnier played upright acoustic bass and Dylan played acoustic guitar. So songs 4–6 at these shows, the second half of the first electric set, were an experiment, a forerunner of the fully acoustic band sets that would become a standard feature of the Never Ending Tour starting in 1990. This experiment was abandoned after July 3, although Dylan did play his acoustic guitar on songs 4–6 (while Tony stayed on electric bass) at three shows later in July. The difference in the sound of the songs because of this early July experiment (only G. E. Smith left on an electric instrument; drums still in the mix, but now sometimes played with brushes) is not immediately obvious to the untrained ear (to my ears, anyway). But the stimulus of changing the instrumentation and trying something different may have a lot to do with the aliveness of the vocals and the music in these three songs, this third night of the blue-eyed prodigal son's return to American theaters.

Indeed, when Dylan sings the phrase "I'm back in the rain" during the fourth song at Milwaukee, "You're a Big Girl Now," I find myself imagining that he's consciously referring to the fact that he's back in the States, back in the wash of mixed emotions that he feels performing before a crowd of American "Bob Dylan fans" (and whoever else might come to a show like this, for whatever reason).

It's a particularly sweet performance of this song which is already a Never Ending Tour regular (played at twenty-six 1988 shows, and at ten shows in spring '89). Why Dylan keeps putting this one on the set list is no mystery. *Blood on the Tracks* is his most acclaimed post-1960s album, so he can reasonably suppose that playing something from that album is one way to keep the customers satisfied. He also seems very happy with his band's arrangement of this song (the distinctive opening guitar chords make it a "signature" piece) and feels confident of it as a love song and sweet-and-slow selection to include in any electric set. It's a crowd-pleaser he likes and feels comfortable singing, so of course he keeps including it. On 7/3/89 he sings it quite tenderly, and with a clarity of articulation that had eluded him in the three previous songs. When he sings the title/chorus phrase, the "you" he's speaking to seems to be right in front of him ... thus one naturally thinks he could be addressing his audience ("I'm just like that bird, singin' just for you/I hope that you can hear, hear me singing through these tears").

So it occurs to me, listening to this fine performance of "You're a Big Girl Now," that being onstage in an outdoor amphitheater in the Midwest in July could easily turn Dylan's mind to where he thought, for a few days back in February, he'd be performing right about now, summer '89: big outdoor American venues in front of huge crowds as a member of the Grateful Dead. He came *that* close to walking away from his long-term relationship with his own audience and so, feeling good about these people in front of him listening to him tonight and the thing he and they have together and realizing how close he came to throwing it all away, suddenly he can feel and picture himself singing to them through these tears. Thus the song takes on a new and immediate significance (not surprisingly, because Dylan has often realized and demonstrated that any man/woman "I"/"you" song can also be about the relationship between an individual human and God or about the relationship between a singer/performer and his audience).

"Ah, but what a shame, if all we've shared can't last!" G. E. Smith follows the last vulnerable words of this verse ("I can make it through/You can make it too") with an inspired and inspiring guitar solo that can stand beside other impressive instances over the years of Mike Bloomfield or Robbie Robertson or Fred Tackett reading Dylan's heart and mind during a performance and becoming an eloquent vehicle for everything the man is feeling and longing to say right now. It's a precious moment. And when the solo and the instrumental break are over, Dylan responds with a marvelously wry and appropriate (it's the lightness of how he says it) delivery of "A change in the weather is known to be extreme" – we can feel the weather changing inside him as he's standing there listening to Smith and himself, and looking at the audience, and thinking with both pleasure and regret of how extreme his abandoning his solo identity and becoming a member of the Dead would have seemed to his public, if he'd pulled it off. "Ah, but what's the sense of changing horses in the middle of the stream?" He's singing the words as they're written in his script/songbook, but it's as if he's speaking on behalf of his audience in this alternate July '89 that could easily have been a reality. "I'm going out of my mind, with a pain that stops and starts," he sings, as if trying to describe and explain his own ambivalence and his Locarno "I'm determined to stand!" experience to the jilted lovers he imagines standing in front of him, while simultaneously describing his own pain and regret in that alternate reality if he had in fact gotten away with his intended escape.

The last words of this verse ("ever since we've been apart") are then followed by a rich and expressive harmonica solo which, it seems to me (as it often does), is a very personal, indeed naked, weather report on what it feels like to be Bob Dylan right at this moment. Not painful or ambivalent, actually. Based on what I hear in this harp solo, he is in fact feeling very good about himself and his work (and, by extension, his audience) at this moment, very moved by the fullness of what he's hearing and feeling, and ready and keen to give his audience and himself a gift, an expression of gratitude as much as a plea for reconciliation. The band takes it from there, responding to this earnest and expressive long harmonica solo with

keen sensitivity, closing the song well with a little instrumental bene-
diction built around a solo in which Smith's guitar sounds like a
harmonica.

Imagine yourself standing in the audience at this moment,
hearing the band, including Garnier on string bass and Dylan on
acoustic guitar and harmonica, starting the next song with a very
pretty bit of harmonica playing ... and suddenly realizing that the
melody they're playing is "I Dreamed I Saw St. Augustine"! Wow.
It's the first time Dylan has played it in 1989, and in fact will be his
only performance of this song this year. He was saving it for just the
right moment, it seems, though in fact he probably wrote it onto the
set list hours earlier, thinking it would sound good in the middle of
the string bass/acoustic guitar/electric guitar/drums set. A gift
indeed. To himself and to us. Listen to the unusual flavor he gives
the word "accordingly," and to the way he breathes between "was"
and "amongst" in the phrase "I dreamed I was amongst the ones
that put him out to death." Moments like this are what the Never
Ending Tour is all about. For him and for us.

Dylan sings "I Dreamed I Saw St. Augustine" in Milwaukee
July 3, 1989, very deliberately and clearly, with a lot of affection
(not for the saint, but for this little song he wrote twenty-two years
ago). Again, he sounds like he feels good about himself, as a songwriter and performer, and very good about the people listening to
him do his work tonight, as though (I conjecture) he did indeed
have a moment of regret at the possibility that he might have
separated himself from them by "changing horses in the middle of
the stream." One does get the feeling that the appearance of rarely
performed songs like this (and "I Believe in You" July 1, and "Tears
of Rage" and "Pledging My Time" July 2) on his set list is an effort
to challenge himself as a performer, Grateful-Dead-style, to create
something totally new and deeply meaningful at this show, by
making a new meta-song out of the elements available in the songbook in his head and in the talents of himself and his musicians, and
by leaning on and trusting the private language cultivated over the
years between himself and his listeners.

The sixth song at Milwaukee, "Highway 61 Revisited," is a
familiar touchstone (he had performed "Highway 61" in this #6
spot, last song of the first electric set, at twelve shows already in the
past two months ... and 26 times in 1988), made pleasantly fresh by
the decision to perform it on acoustic bass and acoustic rhythm

guitar, with electric lead guitar and drums. Dylan starts it off on acoustic guitar, a few clear, exploratory notes ringing out before the drums and the rest of the band join in. The vocal that results, though fun at times, is not particularly inspired and the song still closes with the same already overfamiliar (and tiresome) lead guitar riff, but all this is forgiven when "Highway 61" is followed by "In the Pines," a song recorded by Leadbelly in 1944 and last performed by Bob Dylan at his first non-club show, at Carnegie Chapter Hall in New York City, November 4, 1961. This is a new addition to the Never Ending Tour repertoire of songs Dylan performed at the start of his professional career, his effort to keep himself connected to the music "back there" "that got me inspired and into it."

In a preview of the sort of song scholarship that informs Dylan's 1997 song cycle and album *Time Out of Mind*, this 1989 "In the Pines" is not the Leadbelly version Dylan sang at Carnegie Chapter Hall, but bits of the Leadbelly version about an unfaithful lover (instead of "black girl," Dylan in Milwaukee sings "dark girl," linking this song to "The Lakes of Pontchartrain," which he last sang at his Athens show five days before) added in to what is primarily the version of the song recorded by bluegrass pioneer Bill Monroe in 1952. "The longest train I ever seen," Dylan sings at the start of his acoustic set in Milwaukee, "Was on that Georgia line. The engine passed at six o'clock, the cab passed by at nine." He starts the next verse with a Monroe line that sounds like it could easily be from one of several songs on Dylan's 2001 album *"Love And Theft"*: "I asked my captain for the time of day/He threw his watch away." After this verse and the "In the Pines" chorus, there's an earnest harmonica solo, making a bridge to the Leadbelly-based "Dark girl ... where did you sleep last night?" verse, which here concludes with the Monroe lines "You caused me to weep/And you caused me to mourn/And you caused me to leave my home." Then the chorus, another harmonica solo, and some guitar picking wrap up the performance, which can certainly be heard as an essay on American history and culture as measured by the distance and relationship between Leadbelly and Bill Monroe, with young (and, later, not-so-young) Bob Dylan as the observer. In the pines, freight trains pass and lovers cheat, and songs are written and performed. "I asked my captain for the time of day ..."

Any thought that the singer who slurred and swallowed and

misplaced lyrics during the first three songs might be under the influence of intoxicants at this Milwaukee concert disappears when we hear him sing in the middle of the acoustic set (song #8) every word of verses one, two, three and five (ninety-two long lines in all) of "It's Alright, Ma" with clarion diction and almost flawless articulation. He is so present with the song's language that he recovers instantly from his one (understandable) error: "For them that think" instead of "For them that defend" at the start of a verse that does include the phrase "For them that think" a few lines later. He skips the fourth verse ("For them that must obey authority ...") only because that's the way he's chosen to shorten the song for these five performances (July 2, 3, 5, 6 and 8, 1989). Of course, skipping this verse does mean he omits the line "one who sings with his tongue on fire," as if he feared he couldn't live up to it this week. He does sing very well, though, delivering the song with the clarity and presence of a spoken word performance, without losing a note of its melody. He apparently leaves most of the guitar playing to G.E., letting his partner provide the riff while he focuses on getting the words right. It's a stirring performance, and certainly another loving gift to anyone who's come out to see him tonight.

But the greatest gifts are still to come: an exceptional (very sweet, very loving) performance of "To Ramona" and, immediately after it (start of the second electric set), an unusual (twice in '89, thrice in '88, once in 1990) and quite delightful "Just Like Tom Thumb's Blues."

This wonderful Milwaukee '89 performance of "To Ramona" has a timeless quality about it, as though it has "always existed and always will exist," as Dylan said of Johnny Cash's songs. The entire performance, harmonica, vocals and two acoustic guitars, is so magical that the one tiny lyric error ("your magnetic movements still captures" instead of "capture") is painful because it momentarily breaks the spell, the feeling that this is a true story and Ramona a real person whom he and we can see before us at this moment, the feeling that there is something extraordinary about the singer/musician's presence in this performance, as though a lifetime love affair with music and song and performing is being consummated right here right now, every word and every harmonica note filled with great love for this song and for the person (and people) he's singing it to. "Ramona, come closer ..."

In 1980, Bob Dylan said, "You really are still that person [who wrote the song] someplace deep down. You don't really get that out of your system. So you can still sing it if you can get in touch with the person you were when you wrote the song ..." I say Dylan sees himself as and aspires to be a "mind out of time" as a songwriter and performer because of statements he has made in interviews and writings over the years about the tyranny of time and the liberation an artist experiences when his work frees him (and the observer/listener) from that straitjacket. I believe the fulfillment Dylan finds in performing (which he has also spoken of often over the years), the sort of conduit that he sometimes feels himself becoming on stage, is that of a consciousness interacting with other consciousnesses in a manner that is "so immediate" it seems to be outside of time as we know it. A place where he can forever talk to Ramona, and successfully convey to her how her magnetic movements perpetually capture the minutes he's in. This performing artist/mind out of time can create "To Ramona" on stage on a good night as genuinely and miraculously as at the moment when he wrote the song, or the moment when he recorded it for his 1964 album *Another Side* ... because he still is that person, always is, when he can get out of time and get in touch with the 23-year-old songwriting Dylan and album-making Dylan someplace deep down inside him.

And I further assert that the performer got to this remarkable space from which he sings this luminous 7/3/89 "To Ramona" by singing "St. Augustine" and "In the Pines" and "It's Alright, Ma" (and "Driftin'" and "Highway 61" and "Big Girl" and "John Brown" and "Early Morning Rain") with his band and his accompanist in this amphitheater tonight. The sequence in which he performed them may also have been a factor in his getting in touch with and arriving at this very special place. So the set list writer certainly deserves some credit. As do the other musicians, and the audience. Each word, each line of this performance ("Everything passes!" "Everything changes!") is thrilling, filled with the essence of Dylan's unique artistry. The music is just as pleasing. The instrumental break in the middle of the song sounds like a band performance, because one of the acoustic guitars (probably G.E.'s) is accompanying the other with a sort of bass line. The harmonica-solo-with-guitars that so evocatively follows the last words of the song ("I'll come and be cryin' to you") builds to an evident climax that sets the audience to clapping and cheering, and then continues in a series of mini-climaxes that eloquently convey the rest of what the story's speaker wants and needs to say to this attractive country girl in her moment of sorrow and confusion.

The Milwaukee '89 "Just Like Tom Thumb's Blues" is a perfect example of what Dylan was trying to explain when he said in 1966 (in the *Playboy* interview), "My songs are pictures, and the band makes the sound of the pictures." Again, a seemingly timeless state is achieved (as in many of Dylan's favorite works of art, such as Cezanne's paintings and the film *Les Enfants du Paradis*), and we (future listeners to this show as a work of accidental art) find ourselves enjoying an example of the essence of Bob Dylan's artistry ... this time primarily as a result of the sound the band makes throughout this performance. True, the vocals are marvelous, but it is clear that this is a function of how good Dylan's voice sounds against this sonic backdrop, how free and playful he feels singing to music that is so expressive of what this song means to him, music he experiences as precisely the sound of this poem-picture. To start with, Parker, Garnier and Smith (and Dylan) have found a way to make a splendid and compact version of the delicious musical figure that opens the original 1965 album recording of this song, even though the recording studio band included two keyboard players. And that's just the beginning of a 1989 work of music that is as fluid an example of the "wild mercury sound" Dylan has talked about getting on his mid-1960s albums as are the 1965 album version of "Tom Thumb" and the two 1966 live versions with the Band that have so far been officially released: Liverpool and Manchester.

"Silvio" comes next, and to my surprise I enjoy it. I like the quick segue from the luminous instrumental passage that ends "Just Like Tom Thumb's Blues" into the opening riff of "Silvio." In this context, the first words of the song, "Stake my future on a hell of a past/Look like tomorrow is coming on fast," can only be heard as a direct reference to having written the likes of "To Ramona" and "Tom Thumb" and to standing here right now creating a new art form and finding a new purpose in life (both called the Never Ending Tour) based on being the singer/performer of these songs and anything else the legendary Bob Dylan chooses to include in his stage shows. He wants to use these elements to create new montages every night, fresh and fulfilling works of art that surprise and stimulate and speak to and for both himself and the paying audiences, as he's watched the Grateful Dead do in their shows and sets.

Just imagine … (he ponders) going from "Early Morning Rain" to "Driftin' Too Far from Shore" and from "You're a Big Girl Now" to "I Dreamed I Saw St. Augustine" and from "Highway 61 Revisited" to "In the Pines" to "It's Alright, Ma," all in the same hour-plus and never to be put together in quite this sequence or with this particular spin and spirit again!

After the last verse of the song, the band gets into a nice groove on the chorus, as Dylan sings this chorus ("Silvio, silver and gold/Won't buy back the beat of a heart grown cold/Silvio, I gottta go find out something only dead men know") twice, repeating its last four words four times after each run-through (accompanied by G.E., who uses his falsetto and manages to make himself and Bob sound like the return of the 1986–87 Queens of Rhythm). After the fourth repetition following the second chorus, Dylan uncharacteristically (for this song) interjects an extemporaneous "Every, every day!!" before singing "Only dead men know" four more times and then repeating the chorus again as a lead-in to the band finale. Because this is a song where Dylan wrote music to lyrics provided by the Grateful Dead's primary lyricist (Robert Hunter) and because of the way Dylan's mind works as indicated by him playing his song "Dead Man, Dead Man" at some of the concerts he performed with the Grateful Dead, I'm certain Dylan is particularly aware of the Dead and what they mean to him while he performs this song, and I suspect his "Every, every day!!" outburst is an allusion to the familiar GD line "I need a miracle every day!" And when he repeats, "Only dead men know," I believe he is including in this mantra his sense that Dead men (the players and their audience) know something about the creation of a kind of live music that he now aspires to, and so he is honoring and acknowledging them and in a friendly way challenging himself as he sings these repetitions and presents "Silvio" as just the right piece of the puzzle to follow "Just Like Tom Thumb's Blues" in Milwaukee (and to follow "It Ain't Me Babe" in Peoria, and "Pledging My Time" at Poplar Creek).

The song that follows "Silvio" (and the segue is very pleasing) on July 3 is "When Did You Leave Heaven?" I find this a very attractive performance, easily the best of the four times he has performed this so far in 1989. It still doesn't offer the "spine-tingling presence" of lover speaking to genuine loved one that I wished for but found missing in the *Down in the Groove* version. But Dylan in

Milwaukee sings the song with great tenderness and gets an equivalent tenderness from his band, a sweet evocative sound that can also be heard in his harmonica solo (soon after the first "I am only human ... and you are so divine," a line he includes twice in this performance). My friend Bev Martin, who was at this concert, recently wrote to me: "The Milwaukee show was at Summerfest, a huge festival with lots of beer and a partying audience pumped to rock. He knew it and threw them the occasional bone, but his heart was in the slower stuff. The whole performance was hung over with a feel of nostalgia and melancholy, tinged with regret ... bubbling up from some fountain of sorrow. It was subtle and lost on the crowd, but beautifully clear on 'Early Morning Rain,' a conversational 'John Brown,' 'Big Girl Now,' 'It's Alright, Ma,' 'St. Augustine,' 'Ramona,' and an out-of-the-blue one-off of 'In the Pines.' Before the encores he stepped back and was doing back bends and stretches and hair fluffs, as if to shake himself out of the mood."

Bev's recollection fits what I'm hearing in this lovely performance of "When Did You Leave Heaven?": a rich (and melancholic) affection not for the "angel" being addressed but for the song's melody ... possibly a journey on the timeless wings of American song to a childhood moment when Bob Dylan had not yet heard Leadbelly or Bill Monroe or Little Richard or Hank Williams or Woody Guthrie, but was already feeling the first stirrings of a lifetime love affair.

"Heaven" ends with another tight (well-rehearsed?) segue ... into "Like a Rolling Stone." But it's a false start, and in a few seconds the "Rolling Stone" intro is deftly replaced with the opening notes of "Masters of War." Clearly Dylan changed his mind at the last moment – probably because he wanted to give the audience another rocker before ending this part of the show, but it's also possible that he wanted to preserve the excellent flow he and the band had gotten into. He knew he was on a roll, inspired to lean into each new song as if it were all one big statement, and when he heard the first notes of "Like a Rolling Stone" he realized either that it wasn't time for the "closer" yet or that this wasn't the right song at the right moment to keep the juice flowing, so he got Tony's attention and passed the word that "Masters" should be next. And it works: "Masters" is bright and fresh, and then when "Rolling Stone" follows, the spirit of the night stays alive in the singer and his band (and, presumably, in the crowd, always an important part of the equation), and we get a spirited, better-than-average "Like a Rolling Stone" – not great, which seldom seemed an option for this early '89 incarnation of the song, but certainly a crowd-pleaser, and probably a more satisfying conclusion to the pre-encore montage, a more fulfilling work of performing artistry for the artist and us listeners, than it would have been if he hadn't followed his hunch and inserted "Masters of War" between "Heaven" and "Stone."

So the back bends and stretches and hair fluffs could have been to shake himself out of a mood, or an attempt to keep a certain mood alive. In any case, the encores are good, with "Mr. Tambourine Man" not equal to the best of the previous month's performances of this one but still quite pleasing and full of love for the song and respect for the people out there who want to hear it. When he sing-shouts "I'm ready to go anywhere!", it sounds like a spontaneous reaffirmation of his commitment to the life of a performer. "Knockin' on Heaven's Door," the second encore, is rich in such moments of unexpected aliveness, notably the excitement in his vocals early in the song, seemingly in response to a fine beat set up by his rhythm section (and possibly by an audience clap-along as well). The sound of his voice is very full and appealing here. It's a "greatest hit," but Dylan seems inclined to put a lot into it this time. Even "Maggie's Farm," which often sounded dismissive in '88–'89, is more spirited and a little fresher in rhythm and vocal presence than at most of these shows. This suggests that on a Never Ending Tour the singer-bandleader's experience of being stimulated by a series of songs – a fresh creation – at the start or at the heart of his show can awaken something in him that will help him bring a freshness even to the most routine parts of his act. This is why he's ready to go anywhere, because he never knows when he'll find himself unusually awake and full of creative juice out there somewhere. "Just like so many times before …" Often he's praising the Muse when he repeats this phrase. At one point in Milwaukee he shouts a broken and loud and heartfelt "*Yeah!*" after singing it. The message to the audience is: "We're doing this together, knockin' on heaven's door (just like so many times before), following the tambourine man and going under his dancing spell, refusing to work on Maggie's farm no more. Not because I say so, but because we share a love and enthusiasm for the power of music and the joy of live music and of the singer-band-audience experience." Bob Dylan is saying this even as he conducts his band in playing the riff from "To Ramona" at the end of "Maggie's Farm" and of the night's festivities.

(In view of the Milwaukee set list and the ongoing question of why certain songs are included in the shows, this dialogue from the 1969 Jann Wenner interview with Dylan is of interest: Wenner: "Are there any albums or tracks from the albums that you think now were particularly good?" Dylan: "On any of my old albums? Uhh ... as songs or performances?" Wenner: "Songs." Dylan: "Oh yeah, quite a few." Wenner: "Which ones?" Dylan: "Well, if I was performing now ... If I was making personal appearances, you would know which ones, because I would play them.... I like 'Maggie's Farm.' I always liked 'Highway 61 Revisited.' I always liked that song, 'Mr. Tambourine Man,' 'Blowin' in the Wind' and 'Girl from the North Country' and 'Boots of Spanish Leather' and 'Times They Are A-Changin'' ... I liked 'Ramona' ..." A moment later he acknowledges that of the rock and roll songs, he "probably liked 'Like a Rolling Stone' the best," as a song and as a recorded performance.)

13.

In 1977, Allen Ginsberg visited and interviewed Bob Dylan while Dylan and Howard Alk were finishing the editing of their film *Renaldo & Clara*. Dylan, after referring to Bosch, Van Gogh and Da Vinci ("I consider myself like Da Vinci"), said, "We try to make something better out of what is real. If we want to be successful as an artist, we make it better and give meaning to something meaningless." Ginsberg asked, "What's your idea of 'better,' your direction of 'better'?"

Dylan replied: "You can make something lasting. You wanna stop time, that's what you wanna do. You want to live forever, right, Allen? Huh? In order to live forever, you have to stop time. In order to stop time, you have to exist in the moment, so strong as to stop time and prove your point. And if you succeed in doing that, everyone who comes in contact with what you've done – whatever it might be, whether you've carved a statue or painted a painting – will catch some of that; they'll recognize that you have stopped time. They won't realize it, but that's what they'll recognize, that you have stopped time. That's a heroic feat! ... We have stopped time in this movie. We've grasped that time."

I quote this now because while Dylan is speaking as a film-maker and thinking of himself in relation to other visual artists ("If film was around when Da Vinci was operating, he'd have made films ..."), this is also clearly a clue to his private aspirations as a performing artist, his ambition to be what I call a "mind out of time." Later in the conversation, Ginsberg asked, "Does Renaldo [a singer, the character Dylan plays in the film] have a soul, or is he a succession of disparate illusorily connected images, like ordinary mind?" Dylan responded: "At the beginning he's locked in, he's wearing a mask you can see through, he's not dreaming. Most likely he will become what he's dreaming about. Renaldo's dream almost killed him." Ginsberg: "It's at the end of the movie, when he's putting make-up on – 'What you can dream about can happen.'"

Dylan: "Exactly! You got it! Renaldo has faith in himself and his ability to dream, but the dream is sometimes so powerful it has the ability to wipe him out. Renaldo has no ordinary mind – he might not even have a soul. He may in actuality be Time itself, in his wildest moments."

Speaking of wildest moments, Dylan's presentation of himself (the way he played the part of "Bob Dylan") on stage in summer and fall 1989 seemed quite striking to some observers. Bev Martin, in the letter I quoted in the last chapter, said of the July 1 concert: "The Peoria show took place only two days after his last show in Greece. We were expecting him to be jet-lagged or tired. The opposite was true. It was a fierce, intense performance, with G.E. working to keep up with him, multiply repeated lines, and some real, not just for-show, harp solos. I still remember that image of him right out of the chute standing on his toes and with his legs prancing like a horse pawing to race." Andrew Muir in *Razor's Edge* quotes *Newsday*'s Stephen Williams on the July 23 Jones Beach concert: "He slammed through his 90-minute set like a small gale passing through the beach. [Dylan's] no-nonsense posture – he'd lean forward sometimes, his guitar neck pointed at the wings like a machine gun – supplemented his aura of aggression." "It was a posture he adopted for most of 1989," Muir adds.

"He took the stage like a wild man" – Muir's valuable book quotes Dylan aficionado Peter Vincent describing the first night of Dylan's Oct. 10–13, 1989, residency (series of shows in the same place) at the Beacon Theater in New York City – "stalking back and forth and tearing into the first song ["Seeing the Real You at Last"] at a furious pace. He slowed slightly for the second song, the debut of 'What Good Am I?', but there were no niceties like pauses for applause; one song segued into another while the musicians flogged themselves to keep up. Without good peripheral vision this would have looked like a solo electric appearance, as the band were hovering at the edge of the stage, eager to keep as far away from Dylan as the leads on their instruments would allow."

Oh Mercy had been released on September 22 (to a waiting world that hadn't heard an album of new songs written by Bob Dylan since 1985), and so, after playing 51 shows in the U.S. and Canada in July, August, and early September, Dylan and his band took four weeks off to catch their breaths and make room for a few days of rehearsals focused on the *Oh Mercy* songs (four of which they debuted at the Beacon shows).

"In order to stop time, you have to exist in the moment, so strong as to stop time and prove your point. If you succeed in doing that, everyone who comes in contact with what you've done will catch some of that." The Beacon shows, as recordings, are not my idea of Dylan at his very best as a performing artist (like, for example, New Orleans Nov. 10, 1981 or Stockholm June 9, 1998). They have, like most shows, their weaknesses as well as their strengths … but they can be considered a rare instance of Dylan consciously setting out to play his strongest hand and demonstrate to the world who he is and what he can do at this moment in his life, this year with this band.

Does he stop time? He certainly did for many who were in the audience at one or more of these shows. Peter Vincent reports that "Queen Jane Approximately" at the third Beacon show, October 12, 1989, "may have been the single greatest performance by Dylan I have ever had the good fortune to attend, and no one in the band was willing to let it go … It seemed like they were going to keep playing 'Queen Jane' all night, endlessly finding new variations on the song's themes. Everywhere they went with the music seemed totally and absolutely right, a combination of power and spontaneity the like of which I have practically never encountered." Clinton Heylin agrees, calling the Oct. 12 "Queen Jane" "one of the two or three greatest performances of the Never Ending Tour." Inspired by their experience exploring the music of "Queen Jane" together, Dylan and the band go on to deliver an especially powerful "Most of the Time" (the first encore at three of the Beacon shows) and to offer unusually good (for 1989) versions of "Like a Rolling Stone" and "Maggie's Farm."

Like so many of the high points of Dylan's work in 1989, the Oct. 12 "Queen Jane" is an example of him leading his band via his harmonica playing. The performance starts and ultimately concludes with quite remarkable examples of Dylan expressing himself through his harmonica. For me, the astonishing musical journey Dylan and the band take each other (and their listeners) on during "Queen Jane Approximately" October 12, 1989, seems to start with a particularly beautiful and inspired harmonica-and-guitars passage at the end of "Boots of Spanish Leather" four songs earlier that night.

Since Dylan defines the work of the artist as "trying to make something better out of what is real," it's noteworthy that every one of his four Beacon concerts begins with "Seeing the Real You at Last" … and that the next song at each of these shows is "What Good Am I?" (calling attention to the fact that the "you" he's talking to in "Seeing the Real You at Last" could be himself, as the "you" of "Like a Rolling Stone" sometimes is).

Dylan's unusual stage presence during these New York City shows climaxed appropriately in his exit at the conclusion of his residency. Towards the end of "Leopard-Skin Pill-Box Hat," the second encore that night, he started to play harmonica sitting on his heels at the edge of the left side of the stage. After a few minutes, he jumped down into the audience, walked up the aisle still playing the harmonica, and then disappeared through one of the exit doors to the street, while his confused band continued to play for a while. Now you see (the real) me, and now you don't. There must be some way out of here … Let me also note, as further evidence of Dylan's impulse to make a statement, albeit an ironic or ambiguous one, with these four shows and thus particularly with the last of the four, that on Oct. 13, the final Beacon concert, he wore a gold lamé suit, simultaneously evoking Elvis Presley and another of Dylan's peers, Phil Ochs (who dressed in such a suit on the cover of one of his last albums to make his own ironic/ambiguous – and possibly slightly bitter – comment on his role as a public person). Let it also be noted that some observers report that before jumping off the stage, Dylan leaned down and (uncharacteristically) shook hands with members of the audience.

After the Beacon shows, Dylan and his band (G. E. Smith,

Tony Garnier and Christopher Parker) played 23 more shows in October and November 1989, all on the East Coast of the United States except for three in Illinois, Michigan and Ohio. After debuting "Most of the Time," "Everything Is Broken," "What Good Am I?" and "Man in the Long Black Coat" at the Beacon, they introduced two more *Oh Mercy* songs, "Disease of Conceit" and "Ring Them Bells," in the course of this autumn tour. Another notable aspect of this leg of the Never Ending Tour is that Dylan played piano at twelve of the shows – usually on "Disease of Conceit," but other songs he played piano on were "Gotta Serve Somebody," "When You Gonna Wake Up?" and "Ring Them Bells."

Between November 15, 1989 and January 12, 1990, Dylan's Never Ending Tour took an eight-week break. Presumably this gave the bandleader some time to be at home in the Los Angeles area with his wife Carolyn and their three-year-old daughter Desiree (and, it is suggested in one recent biography, perhaps a slightly younger child as well). On January 6, Dylan began to record his 36th album (32nd if you don't include "greatest hits" packages and other compilations), *Under the Red Sky*. Work on the album would continue in March, but in the meantime there were concerts to give on three different continents.

The midwinter 1990 leg of the N.E.T. began rather spectacularly with a five and a half hour public rehearsal in front of a paying audience of 700 people in a club in New Haven, Connecticut called Toad's Place. Dylan and the band played fifty songs, including three from *Oh Mercy* they hadn't debuted before ("Political World," "Where Teardrops Fall" and "What Was It You Wanted") and a few covers he hadn't sung publicly before (Joe South's "Walk a Mile in My Shoes," Bruce Springsteen's "Dancing in the Dark," the traditional "Hang Me, Oh Hang Me," Muddy Waters's "Trouble No More," Big Bill Broonzy's "Key to the Highway," Moon Martin's "Pay the Price" and Kris Kristofferson's "Help Me Make It Through the Night").

The next two shows were at Pennsylvania State University and Princeton University. Then Dylan played two concerts in Brazil, in front of close to 100,000 people at each show. A few days after the second Brazil show, Dylan began a four-night residency at the Grand Rex Théâtre in Paris. While in Paris, he received a high award, "Commander of Arts and Letters," from the French

Ministry of Culture. The short European tour concluded with a six-show residency at the Hammersmith Odeon in London.

The Hammersmith residency of February 3–8, 1990, according to many reports, was a tremendously rewarding experience for most of those in attendance, as was true of the Beacon residency the previous October. How does a transcendent experience for concert-goers (and thus a very successful work of intentional art for the performer), translate into the "accidental art" form of archivable amateur audio recordings? This is a big question. "Queen Jane Approximately" from 10/12/89 is an impressive and very stimulating work of art, but probably not, for most who hear it in recorded form, one of the very greatest performances of the Never Ending Tour, as it was for the two experienced and trustworthy observers quoted earlier who happened to be present at the creation.

The very high praise accorded the 1990 Hammersmith shows by the experienced Dylan observers who were there (" 'The best since '75,' said many, 'since '66,' said others; I joined in this daft game, to a slightly lesser extent, by affirming it 'the best I'd seen him since 1978' " – Andrew Muir) tended to be for the residency as a whole, or in some cases for the sixth show in particular. But if we turn our attention to the recorded "accidental art" version of one performance that did get singled out for high praise by some commentators, "Dark as a Dungeon" from Feb. 6, I think it's fair to say we find an intense, moving performance worthy of repeated listenings, but not in itself conclusive evidence that the performer was doing some of the best work of his career at these six shows. Maybe you had to be there. That, of course, is the general rule for performed art. What makes Bob Dylan's "accidental art" worth chronicling and well worth seeking out is that here and there in the body of work (43 years of live performances, as I write this in June, 2003) are quite a few recordings that seem to have the power in themselves to transport the listener to the concert hall and place him or her inside the skin of the singer, the musicians and the audience in that room far away in space and time where this musical art was being improvised, invented, breathed into existence.

Not that the point is the re-creation of anyone's experience, but rather the opportunity here and now via a recording to have a powerful and unique and deeply rewarding experience of human artistry. One can find this again and again amidst the 16 years so far (and more than a thousand recorded shows) of Never Ending Tour

Dylan performing at the World Eucharistic Congress in Bologna, Italy, on September 27, 1997. Dylan and his band performed three songs at this event before Dylan met briefly with the Pope. *(John Hume)*

CW Post College, Brookville, New York, January 30, 1998. *(John Hume)*

Wembley Arena, London, May 27, 1998. *(John Hume)*

Dylan with Eric Clapton, performing together at a benefit concert at Madison Square Garden, New York, June 30, 1999. *(LFI)*

Dylan on stage with Paul Simon, June 1999. *(LFI)*

Berlin, May 23, 2000.
(John Hume)

Vicar Street, Dublin, September 13, 2000.
(John Hume)

June, 2001. *(Bernd Muller/Redferns)*

Bournemouth, May 5, 2002. *(John Hume)*

Newport Folk Festival, August 3, 2002. *(Ebet Roberts/Redferns)*

Brighton Centre, May 4, 2002. *(Harry Scott/Redferns)*

Melbourne, February, 2003. *(Martin Philbey/Redferns)*

A photo shoot during Dylan's August 2001 visit to Telluride, Colorado.
(Ken Regan/LFI)

performances. Instead of saying, "you had to be there," we can say with some sincerity, "it's not too late to go there." In saying this, we're just thinking of a few particularly powerful works of accidental art that we as individual listener-appreciators have found to be reliable conveyors of the genius of Bob Dylan as a singer and song-creator and bandleader and maker of timeless music. Someone who's been able to exist in the moment so strong as to stop time in a way that can be experienced and recognized by anyone who comes in contact with what he's done (provided they have ears to hear: "It's for myself and my friends my stories are sung").

There is no machine, mechanical or human, that can reliably find all or most of the great works of this sort of art that are available in the form of show recordings from a particular month or year of an artist's work. I resign the task which my subconscious persists in telling me I have assumed by undertaking this chronicle or study. The best I can do is find something now and again that I truly believe in and am repeatedly and reliably enriched by. Um, there will be another such example cited before the end of this chapter you're now reading and I'm now writing. But don't ask me, or don't let me ask myself, to identify in these pages the relative merits of any particular batch of shows – i.e. for example the three momentous residencies, New York, Paris and London of 10/89 – 2/90 – when experienced as archived audience recordings ("accidental art") ... My subconscious would have me shovel the glimpse into the ditch of what each one means (or how it rates) and cares not to come up any higher, but would rather get me down in the hole that he's in – and it's dark as the dungeon way down there. By the way, this 2/6/90 performance of "Dark as the Dungeon" does, in its opening moments, make a fairly convincing case for the origin of the memorable opening phrase ("Come gather round people, wherever you roam") of "The Times They Are A-Changin'."

On March 2, almost three weeks after the 28-day first 1990 leg of the N.E.T. ended in London, Dylan made an interesting and, I think, not very successful experiment. With his son Jesse behind the video camera, he rerecorded a major song from his 1989 album *Oh Mercy* which he had been performing on stage since October: "Most of the Time." The assignment was to create a video to promote the song and thus the album via MTV and other "rock video" media. If Dylan had not chosen to re-record the song (accompanied by the bass player, drummer, and slide guitar player he was working with in the recording of his album then-in-progress, and produced by one of the producers of that album), then the video, to be a film of him apparently singing and playing the song, would have had to have been him lip-synching (pretending to sing, on camera) to the *Oh Mercy* recording.

So he undertook a new "live in studio" performance. Like any spontaneous Bob Dylan live performance (in studio or on stage or just among friends), this new version could have been breathtaking, time-stopping, exceptional. But it isn't, in my opinion. The 3/2/90 performance completely lacks the irony (and presence) of the *Oh Mercy* performance, and thus asks us to take the speaker literally when he says, "Most of the time, I don't even notice she's gone." So what? It's as though, as was the case with recording the *Saved* album in 1980, singing the song onstage for a couple of months has somehow made it more difficult for him to get inside it in a studio, to sing the lyrics and lead his band from the mind-state or feeling-state he was in when he wrote this song. A good experiment, but once again the accidental art (the superb Oct. 12 Beacon perform-ance recording, which draws so much power from the sublime two-man and four-man band performances of the endings of "Mr. Tambourine Man" and "Boots of Spanish Leather" and "Like a Rolling Stone" and of every note of "Queen Jane Approximately" that all build up to this wonderful 10/12/89 "Most of the Time") is the keeper, the work of art that will live forever … alongside the original March 1989 performance, still the heavyweight champion for its author's singing and his conducting of the band, his breathing into life of an unforgettable song.

So how about the album Dylan began (with producers Don and David Was) a few days before his marathon Toad's Place show and the start of the winter tour in mid-January, and continued working on in various sessions in Los Angeles in February, March and April of 1990? *Under the Red Sky* would be released September 11, 1990, one year after *Oh Mercy* and exactly eleven years before the release of *"Love And Theft"*. It sounds, particularly because of the title track, like an album made by a songwriter who's spending a lot of time this winter with his two very young children and who has had occasion to wonder, as the father of five grown children, why he's never really written any children's songs as his mentor Woody Guthrie did so memorably.

"Wiggle wiggle wiggle …" the album starts, after eight jolly and solid drum hits (and eight more accompanied by sparkling electric guitar interplay) to get things off with a flourish, a childlike and attention-getting throat-clearing, a careful and effective piece of punctuation (those drum hits, not the opening lyrics) from a master of the grammar of song and the psychology of album-building. "Wiggle wiggle wiggle in your boots and shoes" – listen to Dylan's *performance* of "Wiggle Wiggle" and of the album's second song ("There was a little boy and there was a little girl, and they lived in an alley under the red sky"), and you can hear clearly how much he loves his small children and therefore life itself, his life right now ("This is the key to the kingdom, and this is the town … This is the blind horse that leads you around") ("Wiggle like a big *fat* snake!").

Like *Oh Mercy*, but in a quite different way, *Under the Red Sky* is a very successful and evocative (and time-stopping) portrait of an extended moment in its author's life, the life of a performing artist, a guy just about to leave for or just back from Brazil, Paris and London. "He been around the world and back again / Something in the moonlight still hounds him," he sings later in the album on his wry self-portrait, "Handy Dandy" (a few days after recording this, he would sing "I've Been All Around This World" – also known as 'Hang Me, Oh Hang Me" – four times during his first three shows of 1990).

And like "Political World" on *Oh Mercy*, "Wiggle Wiggle" does a splendid job of reintroducing Bob Dylan to his listeners: "Here I am, and this is who I am this time!" If it confuses or even alienates some of those listeners, that's never been a problem for him. "I try my best to be just like I am," he once told us. How he does this, again and again, so successfully (almost endlessly revealing other sides of Bob Dylan) is explained well by the co-producer of *Under the Red Sky*, Don Was, in the following remarks (from an October 1990 interview, in response to the question, "Was there a certain kind of sound Dylan was looking for?"):

> He likes the sound of older records – Sun Records. We spent a lot of time talking about what it was that gave them that kind of grain. In the end, I think he likes ambience. he likes to be able to hear the room. And he's absolutely right. The closer you put the mikes and the cleaner you record something, the less you accentuate the room – you drain it out. But the excitement and the vibes live in the room, not two inches from the drumhead, and I think he's pretty hip to that.

But it's very difficult to go in and recreate that sound, and you don't want to make a retro album – he certainly doesn't – but … You know, the great thing about him is that he's willing to take any kind of risk as long as he's trying something new. That was the only rule in making this record. Just don't repeat – not only don't repeat yourself, but don't repeat anybody else. You know, if you make records for 30 years, you're going to fall flat on your face every so often – everybody does, but he's constantly trying to expand. I think that's the great thing about him.

To appreciate *Under the Red Sky*, it helps to approach it as a sound sculpture (with the sound of the words, as always, an important adjunct to and element of the sound of the music). It is a rich and expressive, deeply satisfying sound sculpture, and recognizing and appreciating this can actually help the listener get new insight into what makes *Bringing It All Back Home* and *The Freewheelin' Bob Dylan* such inspiring and enduring works of art. Yes, there are a few great songs (and song-performances) on those albums, but they also are very successful creations as a whole, listened to from start to finish. Bob Dylan as songwriter and performer/bandleader has successfully created an overall feeling (or, as in the case of *Bringing It All Back Home*, two contrasting, almost contradictory and wonderfully interrelated, overall feelings) on each of these albums, and thus made a memorable and endlessly stimulating and attractive statement through the album as a whole, as well as through individual songs. He did this (does this, since the music-making is in the present tense each time we listen) by being willing to take any kind of risk and by constantly trying to expand his palette and his means of expressing what he's feeling and thinking. He does this by caring about and being sensitive to ambience. Each of his albums can be said to have a different ambience, and in every case that ambience is a significant part of the album's statement and of what makes it attractive and satisfying to those who love this particular work of art.

I acknowledge that in these last sentences I'm using the word "ambience" to mean something different (dictionary definition: "a surrounding or pervading atmosphere") than what Don Was meant by the word. He was using it as a technical term used in the world of recording to refer to, as he said, being able to hear on a recording something of the character of the room or place where it was recorded. In an almost metaphysical leap, this is what Bob Dylan was referring to when he told Sam Shepard (see Chapter One): "It's like that place made James Dean who he is. If he hadn't've died there he wouldn't've been James Dean." Bob Dylan likes ambience. He's sensitive to it and respectful of it, and extremely good at communicating it through the sound of a recorded song like "It's Alright, Ma" or "Bob Dylan's Dream" or "Born in Time." His impressive ability to create a unique ambience (a surrounding or pervading atmosphere) on a recorded album or at a concert is an extension of his genuine respect for place, as if this place (this room or this stage, at this moment in time) has the capacity to make the song-performance what it is and will be for its listeners. "He wouldn't have been James Dean." Place as inseparable from aesthetic presence and value, significance. "Where we were born in time," indeed.

"But, Professor" (somebody raises his hand in the back of the room) "I think I read that *Under the Red Sky* was recorded in a couple of different studios/places, like *Oh Mercy* was." Good point. So let's acknowledge that the unique ambience/atmosphere of a record is not entirely a function of the sound of the room(s) where it was recorded (when that is captured by "unclean" recording techniques). Rather it is a function of an aesthetic consciousness that is sensitive to places and their sounds and qualities and that therefore sees a work of art, a record album or a concert, as a sort of place, one with a unique sound and texture, and so is willing to take any kind of risk that might help him create a new (and fulfilling) sound-place for the listener to occupy while in the presence of these songs. Please insert "Unbelievable," track 3 of *Under the Red Sky*, and its sound and the sound of its language and message, right here. Thank you. "It's unbelievable it would get this far." ("He's constantly trying to expand.")

The sound of "Wiggle Wiggle" and then "Under the Red Sky" and then "Unbelievable" is the sound of this album, and it is a wondrous invention. As was the case with, say, the seven "electric" songs that make up side one of *Bringing It All Back Home*, you can't identify a specific precursor to this *Under the Red Sky* sound in the rock and roll or rhythm & blues or rockabilly of Bob Dylan's youth (it's not a repeat of something), but you can easily recognize the sort of records and the sound and feel that inspired him, that he's reaching towards (and evoking for himself) in this sound sculpture. Wow.

The sound of the drumming. The feel of the rhythm section. The sound of the guitars. The sound of Bob Dylan's voice and every moment (went by so fast you're not sure what hit you) of his vocal phrasing. Al Kooper's keyboard playing is pretty cool, too. And the way all this stuff works together, the overall sound, the movement of all this musical machinery (lyrics, narrative, rhythm and melody, the sounds of instruments and voice, and the interactions between the sounds and minds of the instruments – notice the miracles every time the harmonica comes in during the band performance on "Unbelievable"!). It's breathless. It's thrilling. On an uptempo track like "Unbelievable." And it's breathless in a different way and just as thrilling and filled with astonishing beauty on a slower track like "Under the Red Sky." This is fantastic music. Again, a brilliant accomplishment, the result of all kinds of subtle and heroic risk-taking on the part of the songwriter/performer, and excellent and sympathetic support from the producers (notice that the album has three producers and one of them is Bob Dylan under an assumed name evocative of childhood, "Jack Frost").

I'll tell you a secret. The lyrics for "Unbelievable" as printed on the CD insert that comes with the album show the fourth line of the second bridge (after "Once there was a man who had no eyes/ Every lady in the land told him lies/He stood beneath the silver skies") as "And his heart began to bleed," but what I hear Dylan actually singing on the recorded performance is, "And his heart beat with glee" ... which is also a good description of what I hear expressed in the sound and the music of this album, a heart beating with glee. And it also makes sense to me that the songwriter/ co-producer might choose to obscure or conceal this line when approving the lyrics for publication on the insert by replacing it with a line that's also true to his sense of the song and that happens to rhyme more directly with the last line of the bridge, "Everything is criticized when you are in need." The (open) secret, then, is the glee throughout this record. It's an ambience. It's a surrounding and pervading atmosphere, a sound, a unique sound, created by Bob Dylan with some very able collaborators (on "Unbelievable," Waddy Wachtel on guitar, Al Kooper on keyboards, Don Was on bass, Kenny Aronoff on drums, Don Was and David Was co-producers, and Ed Cherney engineer and mixer). The sound of the language also contributes to this wonderful sound:

It's unbelievable, it's fancy-free
So interchangeable, so delightful to see
Turn your back, wash your hands
There's always someone who understands
It don't matter no more what you got to say
It's unbelievable it would go down this way

So Bob Dylan tells us, "it don't matter no more what you got to say," but inevitably some of his fans and critics react to this new record by being distressed that the once-great lyricist could write and perform a song called "Wiggle Wiggle" and could end his album with the seeming nonsense of "Cat's in the Well" ... and by spending some time trying to determine what the gnomic songwriter is really saying in the song "Under the Red Sky" ... and by criticizing the album as a whole for "not having anything to say." An erroneous accusation, in my opinion. *Under the Red Sky* has a lot to say, and says it very well. In any case, Dylan as songwriter anticipated these reactions, and told Edna Gundersen in a September 1990 interview that the song "Under the Red Sky" is "intentionally broad and short, so you can draw all kinds of conclusions."

The point of this kind of art is not what the songwriter performer is trying to say, but rather creating words and music and an ambience that empower listeners to experience the work of art as something meaningful and moving and nourishing for themselves (drawing their own conclusions). The technique for doing this is to let the composition and then the performance flow through you with freedom and aliveness and trust in the creative process and the collective music-making process. As a songwriter does this, interesting resonances occur. "Once there was a man who had no eyes." "This is the blind horse that leads you around." The songwriter doesn't plan these thematic resonances between songs. But he may learn from them.

Incidentally, Don Was, in the before-quoted 10/90 interview with Reid Kopel (for the Dylan magazine *The Telegraph*), said of "Under the Red Sky," "That's the only time I really ever asked him about a lyric and he told me about it. He said, 'It's about my hometown.' So I thought about it, and it's such a great little fable. These people have all this opportunity and everything and they choose to be led around by a blind horse and they squander it. It's beautiful and so simple, and he sang it one time through and it was perfect."

Earlier in the same interview, Was said, "It's actually about people who got trapped in his hometown. I think it's about Hibbing and about people who never left."

I don't hear this in the song. I think what Dylan shared with Was (in response to Was telling him that he thought the song was "about ecology"; Dylan then told him, "I can't believe people read this much into it") was something he found himself thinking about or picturing when the song first came through him. Singing partly to his children, he not surprisingly found himself thinking of his own childhood. And, I suggest, it might not have been like it was even him thinking it. These phrases just came into his mind, along with this evocative melody. And then he decided to leave the song broad and short, so listeners could draw their own conclusions. The important thing, anyway, is he thereby gave himself something to sing that he could really throw his heart, and his artistry, into. What a great performance this album track is! And there will be more fine performances of this song in Dylan concerts in years to come.

I said earlier that *Under the Red Sky* (the album) is a portrait of a moment in the life of a performing artist, and only backed this assertion by quoting a line from "Handy Dandy" that says, "He been around the world and back again," and by suggesting that finally spending some time at home with his children was a big influence on the form and language and spirit of these songs. A further point that needs to be made is that the life of a performing artist was almost the entirety of Bob Dylan's life at this time (99 shows in 1989, and only one four-week break between May 27 and November 15), and that a lot of what happens in such a life takes the form of realizations during performances, small and large insights and discoveries in the course of singing songs and playing with a band and speaking to oneself and a live audience through music. *Under the Red Sky*, I suggest, is the product of these musical and aesthetic experiences and discoveries. This is what the artist hears and wants to hear at this point in his long and very intimate relationship with music and song. That's his idea of a self-portrait. The *feel* of "Born in Time" (this winter 1990 version) and the *feel* of "Cat's in the Well" and the distance between them and the implications of their coexistence, this Dylan voice and this Dylan voice, placed where they can be seen as parts of the same assemblage, like pictures hanging on the same wall.

"People can learn everything about me through my songs, if

they know where to look," Dylan told Edna Gundersen in 1990. "They can juxtapose them with certain other songs and draw a clear picture. But why would anyone want to know about me? It's ridiculous." The implication is that his intention in writing and performing the songs is to enable people to learn about themselves through what they hear in them, as he himself has experienced as a listener ("I find the religiosity and philosophy in the music. I've learned more from the songs than I've learned from rabbis, preachers, evangelists, all of that"). Not that he has something to teach, but that he has a lot to give, and music – song – is his vehicle: "Handy Dandy, he got a basket of flowers and a bag full of sorrow." "In the lonely night/in the blinking stardust of a pale blue light/You're coming through to me in black and white/When we were made of dreams ..." And listen to those drums on "Wiggle Wiggle" and "Unbelievable" and the way Dylan sings to them (Kenny Aronoff's drumming, and the sound of his drums, is wonderful on almost every track of this album)!

When I say "Handy Dandy" is a wry self-portrait, I don't mean he's talking about himself, but that he's enjoying painting a picture of a performer (which he is) as seen by those struck by him, as Dylan is struck by some of his likely models for this painting, probably Frank Sinatra or Prince (who had at least two girls in his orchestra/band at this time) or Jimmy Cagney ("He finishes his drink, he gets up from the table, he says, 'Okay boys, I'll see you tomorrow'"). Marvelous singing, and what fun that this is all done to the progression of "Like a Rolling Stone," with Al Kooper on organ again. "There's something that happens when he starts playing with Al Kooper," Don Was reports. "Those guys have got chemistry. They play differently when they play with each other than they do when they play alone. They interact in a certain way and make a certain sound. Oh man, all I ever wanted to do was be in that band and there I was!" Right, and he was probably looking at Bob and thinking, "If every bone in his body was broken, he would never admit it." That adolescent admiration of the "handy dandy," be it James Dean or whomever, is part of the self-portrait aspect of the song.

It's a magnificent album, really, and I love every performance on it. Oh, there have been times over the years when I've had my doubts about "10,000 Men" or "2X2," but as with a good concert, each performance in sequence opens doors in listener and singer and musicians and, because the whole is greater than the sum of the parts, the parts are elevated in dignity and expressive power just by their connectedness to that whole. So I find myself getting into the groove of "10,000 Men," the easy flow of the language, the surprising shouts and whispers of the vocal, the irrepressible *Under the Red Sky* humor that chugs along throughout (and catches my attention at different moments every time I listen). Of course, it's fun to hear Bob Dylan singing the blues and playing piano with Stevie Ray Vaughan and Jimmie Vaughan and David Lindley on guitars. (Don Was: "When Bob walked in, Stevie walked up to him and said – I don't think they'd ever met before – 'Hi, I'm Stevie Ray Vaughan.' But Stevie didn't have his hat on, and Bob just went, like, 'Yeah, sure,' and kept going. He didn't believe him. And then he saw Jimmie and David Lindley and he flipped! He realized that it *was* Stevie Ray Vaughan, and he went back and said, 'Aw man, this is …' He was very warm and very excited about having Stevie Ray on the record.") And having superstars Elton John and David Crosby on piano and background vocals on "2X2" – Dylan's second "by the numbers" song, apparently a songwriting exercise like seeing what phrases arise to follow the repeated word "broken" – works well because they and the rest of the band do a good job of fulfilling what seems to be the song's role on the album: to sound like several different genres of "ordinary" fringe pop music rolled into one, a sweet slab of coolness to balance the wonderful heat of "Unbelievable" and "Cat's in the Well." One more mysterious and rewarding report on what the performing artist was hearing in the back of his mind as he and his muse chased each other around the world.

Oh, and I should say that another "hot" track, of a very different sort, is "T.V. Talkin' Song." Those cats (Bruce Hornsby on piano, Kenny Aronoff on drums, Randy Jackson on bass, Robben Ford and Bob Dylan on guitars) are *cooking*! Laid-back cooking, so there's plenty of room for the singer to "talk," but they still create such heat and excitement in the music that the urgency of the singer's message (or the message of the other speaker whom the singer is cleverly quoting, distancing himself while certainly sounding like he personally believes and endorses every word of the man's polemic) is perfectly supported, just as if the talkin' blues song form Dylan learned from Woody Guthrie and frequently used in his early songwriter/performer days was always intended to be backed by a combo like this, making just this flavor of music.

It's another splendid and unique song/performance, one of ten that lean up against each other on this boldly original and (dare to say it) remarkably successful album. Along with the eloquence of (and infinite variety in) the sound sculpture, the album benefits from a nonstop flow of Dylan language and humor: " 'It's all been designed,' he said, 'to make you lose your mind; and when you go back to find it, there's nothing there to find.' " (Triple internal rhyme, by the way.) And how about the resonance between the climactic line of "Under the Red Sky" – "One day the little boy and little girl were both baked in a pie" – and this line from "T.V. Talkin' Song": "The man was saying something 'bout children when they're young being sacrificed ..."? As for what I make of the troubling "baked in a pie" image in "Red Sky," it makes me think of the Grimm fairy tale "Hansel and Gretel" about a little boy and a little girl who come very close to being baked in a pie (or anyway an oven). The line of the song that precedes this, "Let the wind blow low, let the wind blow high" sounds to me, because of the way the singer delivers it, like an acknowledgment of the power of fate, so I imagine that after Dad hears himself telling his little girl that someday she'll have a diamond as big as her shoe, it occurs to him that he doesn't want to hide from her that there are other things that happen in fairy tales (and in grown-up lives). Yes, the man in the moon could visit, but also the river could go dry. And further, the question might arise, do we fail to have empathy or compassion for the four and twenty blackbirds baked in a pie in the nursery rhyme because they're *not* a little boy or a little girl?

The segue from "T.V. Talkin' Song" to "10,000 Men" is quite satisfying. Nice that on a CD we can hear these back to back without having to turn the record or cassette over first. But it figures that the segues or transitions on a deliberate sound sculpture would be pretty pleasing. "Under the Red Sky" to "Unbelievable" is fabulous. The 26-second outro of "Wiggle Wiggle" (after "big *fat* snake") followed by the memorable drum-hit-and-keyboards opening of "Red Sky" is also pretty terrific. And the transition from the band's conclusion to "10,000 Men" to the elegant opening of "2X2" by itself is enough to explain why these two works of music (and language) are vital to the sound sculpture as a whole. At the Toad's Place club show/rehearsal, Dylan told the audience, "We're just working on the endings tonight, that's all we're doing." So you know song endings are important to him. On *Under the Red Sky*, every ending seems to have something to say, and adds to the listener's pleasure in the album. And then Dylan manages a very wonderful ending to the album itself, when he wraps up the exhilarating proto-rocker (Bob and the Vaughan brothers and the six other players, including two horns, sound like they've just invented the medium) "Cat's in the Well" by singing/saying, "Goodnight, my love, may the Lord have mercy on us all." Of course I imagine he's particularly speaking to his young daughter, but it's kind of a nice (and unusual) way for him to address an album's listener, isn't it? And of course the band follow with an appropriate rock and roll finale, just as if this were a concert or a club show. Not overstated. Just delicious.

Speaking of which, I have a note here to mention that "Born in Time" communicates the deliciousness of romantic/sexual love (particularly falling in love), and as such represents the other side of the story told in Dylan's 1997 album *Time Out of Mind* ("this kind of love, I'm so sick of it!"). Not that the pain or destructive power of love is completely overlooked in "Born in Time" (I suspect that's the implication of "You can have what's left of me" and "You hang the flame, you'll pay the price" and also, with a nice edge of ambiguity, of "You won't get anything you don't deserve.") But then, this awareness of the agony and the deliciousness going together is not new to Dylan love songs ("I like the cool way you look at me/ Everything about you is bringing me misery" – "Buckets of Rain," 1975).

Dylan's voice on "Born in Time," his phrasing and the sound and texture of his voice and its interplay with the band (Jackson, Aronoff, Ford, Hornsby, Crosby, and Paulinho Da Costa on percussion) is one of the high points of *Under the Red Sky*. It's an album full of high points, most of them related to the sound sculpture, but some of them snatches of lyrics, like these from "God Knows": "God knows the secrets of your heart/He'll tell them to you when you're asleep." It's a good line, made all the more penetrating by Dylan's delivery of it and his interaction with the band – which again creates a delightful one-of-a-kind sound on this track. I'm also very fond of the way Dylan sing-speaks, "God knows it could snap apart right now/Just like putting scissors to a string." He could be talking about the exquisite musical tension that holds the whole album together. Another intra-album resonance: "The river went dry" on "Red Sky" and "God knows there's a river/God knows how to make it flow." Dylan plays piano on "God Knows" and on "Handy Dandy" and "10,000 Men" and "Cat's in the Well." He's credited with playing accordion on "Born in Time." Also of interest from the CD insert pages: this album has a dedication, "For Gabby Goo Goo." (The daughter who turned four while this album was being recorded is named Desiree Gabrielle Dennis-Dylan.)

I have written elsewhere that "*Under the Red Sky* is like *Oh Mercy* in that it is only superficially related to anything Dylan has ever written or performed before. What an artist! Thirty years on and he's still breaking new ground." This accords with Don Was's observations after working with the man that "he's willing to take any kind of risk as long as he's trying something new. He's constantly trying to expand." In this respect, as a modern artist, Dylan is comparable to Miles Davis. I emphasize this because many Dylan commentators and admirers seem blind to the risk-taking aspect of his work and therefore get caught in criticizing him for trying something new.

This happened, of course, early in his career – "Positively Fourth Street" ("You got a lotta nerve to say you are my friend") was his response to an "Open Letter to Bob Dylan" published in a folk music magazine in 1964 by an early supporter who felt he'd lost his way as an artist by writing and recording non-political songs like "To Ramona" and "It Ain't Me Babe." In 1980, Dylan at a concert told a story about Leadbelly, a fable clearly related to the criticism the teller was getting for not playing enough of his "old songs" in concert now that he had a new batch of songs related to his Christian conversion: "At first he was just doing prison songs, and stuff like that ... He'd been out of prison for some time when he decided to do children's songs. And people said, 'Oh wow! Has Leadbelly changed?' Some people liked the older songs, some people liked the newer ones. But he didn't change. He was the same man."

In the thirteen years since the release of *Under the Red Sky*, Bob Dylan has recorded and released only four albums (a larger part of his creative energy has gone into his live performances during these years), each of them extraordinarily good, and each of them only superficially related to anything Dylan has ever recorded before (or written before, in the case of the two albums featuring songs he wrote himself). He's constantly trying to expand, and we as listeners often have trouble accepting the results. (I found it difficult to appreciate *Another Side of Bob Dylan* myself in 1964. Changed my mind later, of course.) In the last 17 years, as I write this, Bob Dylan has released only four albums of new, self-written songs. *Under the Red Sky* was one of them. And it's as rewarding and original and as worthy of respect and attention as any of the others from this period, including the two masterful albums of "cover" songs, *Good As I Been to You* (1992) and *World Gone Wrong* (1993). What an artist!

Sometimes a good artist is just a good sport, and of course great artistry is not necessarily the result. In early to mid April 1990, possibly simultaneous with some of the vocal and instrumental overdub sessions where *Under the Red Sky* was completed, Bob Dylan and George Harrison and Jeff Lynne and Tom Petty wrote and recorded the second Traveling Wilburys album (called *Vol. 3*). Dylan (now referred to as "Boo Wilbury" – not "Lucky" anymore) wrote four of the eleven songs on the finished album and contributed to a co-written song – significantly more songwriting than any of the other Wilburys managed on this occasion.

Dylan is also very present on this album as a singer. He sings the lead vocal on two songs and sings lead on a majority of the verses on two other songs, and on one or more verses of four other songs. But all this Dylan presence doesn't make *Vol. 3* a Bob Dylan album. Rather, it's a collaboration that aspires to spontaneity and the sound of friends having a good time together, but doesn't quite achieve it. This seems to be no one's fault, but simply the result of circumstances not being favorable at this moment. Drummer Jim Keltner, who played on the sessions for both albums, has been quoted saying, "It was Roy Orbison's presence that made the other Wilburys rise to the occasion" at the time of the first album's creation. "The second album was really deflated," Keltner added, "It was just sad [because of Roy's death and absence] and the enthusiasm wasn't there."

Dylan as I say was a good sport in his approach to the collaboration – the songs he wrote could indeed have been fun for these four singer-players to record together as Wilburys if everyone had felt more ready to have musical fun. But such moments can't be scripted or controlled. What is impressive is Boo Wilbury's evident willingness to give as much as he could to the collaboration. Neither Dylan nor any of the other Wilburys can be faulted for not being able to breathe joy and bright inventiveness into these well-intended sessions. I do regret, though, that the song Dylan wrote for these sessions that didn't end up on the album, "Like a Ship," squanders such a likeable melody and "feel" by opening with the bad poetry of "Like a ship on the sea/Her love rolls over me." Bad poetry because the simile doesn't work: ships on the sea don't roll over anybody or anything. On the other hand, the opening of "If You Belonged to Me" (including the marvelous harmonica/drum/guitar intro) flows just as freely, but with more pleasing results: "Waltzin' around the room tonight/In someone else's clothes/You're always coming out of things/Smelling like a rose." The rest of the verse flows right into a *non sequitur* – "You hang your head and your heart is filled/With so much misery/You'd be happy as you could be/If you belonged to me" – but it's sung with such conviction and charm (and subtle playfulness) that I find myself believing the singer and smiling – so I call this good poetry. Good Wilbury poetry, anyway. *Vol. 3* is quite enjoyable if you hopscotch from Dylan song to Dylan song, "She's My Baby" to "If You Belonged to Me" to "7 Deadly Sins" to "Where Were You Last Night?", maybe throwing in his opening vocal on "Inside Out" between the first two. The Wilburys as a quartet may have been a little downhearted this season, but a pale shadow of the glee that animates *Under the Red Sky* can be heard here and there in Boo Wilbury's contributions to *Vol. 3*, and it's almost enough to turn things around.

The Never Ending Tour started up again May 29, 1990 in Montreal, with the same band but a significant new twist in that the acoustic sets were now "acoustic band" sets, with Garnier on standup bass and Parker playing with brushes or just maintaining a backbeat. One of the songs the acoustic band performed at this show was "Desolation Row," the first time Dylan had sung it in concert since fall 1987. Acoustic band sets (as opposed to solo or Smith/Dylan duo sets) would remain standard at N.E.T. shows for years to come (until summer 2003 as I write this).

From Montreal, Bob Dylan and his band (Garnier, Smith, Parker) traveled slightly west and began three weeks of shows in the midwest of Canada and the United States: Kingston, Ottawa, London and Toronto, Ontario; Davenport, Iowa; East Troy and La Crosse, Wisconsin; Sioux Falls, South Dakota; Fargo and Bismarck, North Dakota; Winnipeg, Manitoba. The majority of these shows were less than 500 miles from Hibbing, the town where Robert Zimmerman had grown up. After two shows in Winnipeg, Dylan and band flew to Europe for more shows, in Iceland, Denmark, Norway, Finland, Germany, Belgium and Switzerland.

Altogether they played 25 shows between May 29 and July 9. After a month off, the barnstormers resumed their travels on August 12, 1990, back in Canada for four shows in Alberta and two in British Columbia. Between Alberta and B.C., they played a show in a rural winery above the Columbia River gorge in George in the state of Washington. With a posse of friends from Northern California and from various parts of the Pacific Northwest, I drove from George to Victoria and Vancouver, and then to Portland, Oregon for four Bob Dylan concerts in four days.

You can't expect all the shows to be good, of course, since circumstances affecting the work conditions and spirits of the musicians vary so much from night to night on a road tour. So I thought it was fortunate for me and my friends that the weakest show was the first of the four we caught (though one member of the posse insisted it was the best, simply because the third song that afternoon was Dylan's first and, so far, only performance of Otis Redding's song "(Sittin' on) The Dock of the Bay"), and that Dylan and his band seemed to get better each night until, by the fourth show, they were terrific, spectacularly good. A reverse sequence would have been disappointing. But the sequence of "shaky," "good," "equally good or even better," and "superb!" was high drama and immensely satisfying. If I could pay to go back in time and follow those barnstormers through those three states and provinces again and re-experience that sequence of concerts, I would eagerly do so. What an adventure! As with Dylan's heroes or recent role models the Grateful Dead, the band is on the road and the audience is too, and then they meet at the concerts, band and audience both bringing their road-experiences and their resultant moods with them to the rendezvous points, the shows, the moments at which and inside of which the music is created.

And for better or worse, recordings are made, usually by random outside-the-law audience members, accidental art, in an attempt to capture the moment in a retrievable format, to give some kind of permanence to this very ephemeral and very often profoundly fulfilling art form.

You and I have arrived, dear friends, at the Arlene Schnitzer Concert Hall in Portland, Oregon, U.S.A., August 21, 1990 in the course of this narrative entitled *Bob Dylan: Mind Out of Time* due to the following circumstances: I listened to the CDs and tapes I have of autumn 1989 Dylan shows for many months, expecting and hoping to have the sort of transcendent listening experience I have recounted earlier in this book and in the previous volumes in this series, the sort of "thrill" Dylan himself has frequently spoken of his gratification at being able to deliver via his chosen art form ("Being on the road to me is just as natural as breathing. It's rewarding to thrill the crowd. That's all I can tell you about it." and: "My motivation is to go out and thrill people night after night"). But I couldn't find that thrill, possibly because of circumstances affecting the quality (receptivity) of my own listening, or possibly because my expectations are high and the recorded concerts I was auditioning weren't actually artworks, in this format, that could meet or even exceed those expectations. The man does a lot of good work. But the great work, due to the nature of the medium, is only here and there, now and then, and possibly only located via good luck, favorable and fortunate conditions and circumstances.

I am in the process of confessing, I suppose, that the most useful insights in these exegeses of mine come about primarily as a result of the opportunity to observe myself in the process of being awakened, thrilled, given aesthetic fulfillment, while listening to what seems to me a particularly good piece of "accidental art" (not excluding Dylan's non-accidental art in the form of performances and recordings like those that comprise *Under the Red Sky* and *Oh Mercy*). So I must seek the tapes that will sound great to me to be able to write informatively about this performing artist. Otherwise, how can I presume to try to answer the question Dylan himself implied in his comments to Allen Ginsberg quoted earlier in this chapter – has this artist stopped time? And if so, how has he done so? And what is that like to experience as a listener or observer?

So I listened to the Toad's tapes and found them fascinating and rewarding, as most Dylan appreciators would and do, but I didn't, at this moment in my life, feel as though time had been stopped for me. That's not a criticism. Hey, it's just a rehearsal, anyway, and what a thrill to be present in a small club for such an artist's five-hour rehearsal! And for whatever reason, I also didn't quite feel it in the recordings I have from the much-loved (by those who were there) Hammersmith 2/90 residency.

So I sought out a tape I remembered being very pleased by twelve years ago, Dylan and band in Berlin, July 5, 1990. I listened and found it a good show, but not the sharp blow to my skull (instrument to bring me to my senses) I suppose I was looking for.

So I recalled how much I'd been impressed by this Portland '90 show when I was there, though I don't remember ever spending time with it in years past as a recording and getting thrilled once again. But I was looking for something, this year I mean, and lo and behold, this turned out to be it. Portland 1990!! THIS (he proclaimed) is what I mean by great art and what I think Dylan is referring to when he says he aspires to the "historic feat" of "grasping that time and stopping it"!! Hey, everybody, listen up! This is greatness. This is what a few of us human creatures (in this case a singer-songwriter-bandleader and his band, four other musicians) were capable of creating, in the forms and contexts and media available late in the 20th century. This is an opportunity for us as listeners to have the sort of out-of-time experience made possible by the best work of an artist determined to function as a mind out of time.

A few months before the Portland show. Dylan wrote a letter to the editor of a small magazine called *Sister to Sister*, in which he expressed his interest in escaping the prison called "time":

> Life on the road is not what it used to be. But what used to be may not have existed anyway. All of Europe used to be a desert. What they say about shifting sand is not unfounded. Everything is happening by the clock. Without clocks there wouldn't be any useful idea of time. My soul is unaware of any time, only my mind. My poor mind which is so bombarded with dates, calendars and numbers has been deceived into believing there is such a thing as time, woe is me. Hasn't everybody at some point of their life asked, "What time is it?" It's no time. The sun comes up and the sun goes down. That's what time it is. That's why it's taken me so long to write you this letter.

August 21, 1990. Bob Dylan had played Portland's Arlene Schnitzer Concert Hall before. It had a different name then, Paramount Theater; Dylan and his then band played five "gospel tour" shows at the Paramount, three in January 1980, and two in December 1980. It's a smaller-than-average theater, small enough to give a performer-bandleader with a good crowd the feeling that he's playing in a club, a feeling that can be very stimulating to Bob Dylan as a bandleader.

Also stimulating to Dylan's genius as a music maker and baton-less conductor on this evening was the presence of a new musician in the band, Austin, Texas guitar player Stephen Bruton.

Evidently G. E. Smith had been asking for a larger raise than Dylan was willing to give him, and threatening to leave if he didn't get it, and as a result Dylan decided to try out a few possible replacement lead guitarists by adding them to the band (which still included G.E.) for a few shows. Dylan had played with Bruton before, during recording sessions in Mexico City in 1973 for the *Pat Garrett & Billy the Kid* soundtrack. Portland was Bruton's third night in a row playing with Dylan and Smith and Garnier and Parker, and the extraordinary musical rapport amongst the ensemble that can be heard on the 8/21/90 recording no doubt has to do both with the newness of these five playing together and with the fact that by the third show, each musician is beginning to feel at home with this new circumstance and the musical opportunities presented by playing with just this particular combination of musical skills and instincts and personalities.

Most of all, I think, the wondrous music this team is creating at this show is a reflection of the mind-state of the singer/rhythm guitarist/bandleader/harmonica player – Bob Dylan, the author of this magnificent work of accidental art, this recording which stops time and leaves me as a listener breathless and thrilled, over and over again. I think Dylan finds himself unexpectedly awake, inspired to give his best, showing off as it were to the new kid on the block, this very intelligent and spiritual and musically wise and responsive and likeable new guy in the band. And also of course showing off to the seemingly very alert and responsive audience packed into this relatively small concert hall. Dylan is finding himself unusually awake and alive as a musician, and he's loving the experience. You can't plan it. You just have to respond to it, with delight and enthusiasm and wonder, when you find yourself in the midst of it. I believe this is what he lives for, and why he chooses to spend so much of his life playing music with a band on the road. "He's been around the world and back again … and when he says, 'Strike up the band,' they *hit it*!" (Lines from "Handy Dandy," a joyful song about being or appearing to be a bandleader.)

The show starts, and the magic starts, with "Subterranean Homesick Blues" – only the tenth time it's been played this year and the first time in the last thirteen shows. Because it's no longer the standard opener, or because of the aforementioned special circumstances of this show, Dylan and the band fall into a new groove with the song here. Something has happened in the rhythm section, and

I suspect it's being sparked by Dylan's rhythm guitar playing, driving the bass and drums and setting up some fine call-and-response with both the other two guitar players. The vocal still doesn't have the *mutrib*-like clarity of diction I hunger for in a live version of this song. Instead it's more like a breathless attempt to keep up with the tempo and maintain the mind-state of this musical performance, in some ways more an exploration and update of Chuck Berry's "Too Much Monkey Business" than ever. Good rock and roll. And a good way to kick the evening's door open.

Because it's the second song on the set list he wrote a few hours before, Dylan sings "I Want You" next (the first time he's performed it since the last show of the Hammersmith residency in February). Time stops. Time stops because these five musicians (one of whom sings, plays guitar, plays harmonica and conducts the others in some mysterious but very effective fashion) have built an edifice that will stand forever, as long as recordings survive and there are listeners with any rudimentary understanding of these musical languages, the "garage band" rock and roll plus harmonica language, and the language of spontaneous music-making as a way of singing praise to the Divine from which all blessings flow. Again, this is *it*. And just the beginning of an absolutely extraordinary flow of music that will extend itself through the next four song-performances. Great art.

According to my theory of how this show came to be so good, "Subterranean Homesick Blues" this night went beyond the ordinary opening-song-at-a-Dylan-show function of giving singer and band a chance to arrive at the concert, to accept and embrace the reality of being here, in front of this crowd, playing together in real time ("What time is it?" It's show time! All bluffs are now called, you gotta show what's in your hand and play like your life depends on the outcome). "Subterranean" went beyond that "arriving at the show" function by delighting Dylan with the fresh rhythmic groove his ensemble was finding, and by the sonic and musical possibilities being realized and invented spontaneously by this new three-guitar (not counting the bass) line-up, two leads and one rhythm, or, as appropriate, two rhythm guitars and one lead, or occasionally three lead guitars interacting at once, depending on what the performance and the song dictate or suggest.

As a band performance, and a demonstration that we're a rockin' band and we're here to knock you people's socks off tonight, this "Subterranean" is very successful. And, to the gratification of the bandleader who said at Toad's, "We're just working on the endings tonight," it arrives at a particularly elegant ending – not the kind of ending you "work on," but the kind that demonstrates impressive musical intelligence and presence and collective consciousness, by being so playful and redolent and resonant and surprising while also seeming to resolve deliberately and emphatically every musical and emotional theme that's been raised in the course of the song. You work on the endings at rehearsals and warm-up shows in hopes of getting to the place where you can be this confident and free and inventive and convincing during the endings at real shows, because the basics are there already and you know you can lean on them while also taking the opportunity to wail, to express the spirit of the moment through your instruments and through the music you all find yourselves making together.

So, according to my theory, Dylan sees and hears during this opener that something's happening, and is given an inner or hormonal signal that "tonight's the night," and that the opportunity is now here for these five players (and therefore him) to reach beyond themselves. It's not like he thinks about it. It's like he takes a deep breath and opens himself up to the spirit of this night, this show, and lets it direct him and his band, like a skipper letting the wind fill his boat's sails.

"I Want You" sounds terrific from the get-go, multiple guitars playing the evocative and recognizable opening notes of the song with keyboard richness against a bright and easy rhythm backup, as though Dylan were proudly reminding the delighted audience that he's the author of the *Blonde on Blonde* album, whose second side began with these very notes. Immediately, in an example of Dylan seemingly conducting his band through sheer mental power and presence, the guitars drop back while bass and drums play on with the same quiet brightness, creating a perfect and wonderful space for the entrance of the harmonica (later than and quite different from its entrance on the original recording). Guitars return, sustaining the bright, relatively quiet *Blonde on Blonde* feel, and again a perfect space is constructed, this time for the entry and arrival of the vocal. Dylan's voice sounds luminous, even though he swallows the word "guilty" at the start of the first line. The word "I" is swallowed (omitted) in the third line ("The silver saxophones say I should refuse you"), and this has the happy, though probably unintended, result of calling attention (for the listener familiar with the song, who finds his mind yearning for that "I") to the marvelous triple-rhyme structure of these verses, with the third rhyme in the middle of a line instead of at the end (internal, and in this case also a near-rhyme, since it's "sighs" and "cries" that "I" unmistakably rhymes with, when it's not omitted).

The *sound* of Dylan's voice is very special, a connoisseur's delight, throughout this Portland '90 "I Want You." In particular, his singing of the repeated title phrase during the chorus is very striking, different every time and always so expressive (especially when he sighs "Oh!" after "Honey, I want you" at the end of the second chorus) that we cannot doubt the urgency and self-mocking anguish of the speaker's desire ... which suggests that what is really being expressed at this moment is how much the singer desires what his muse is tempting him with right now, to be able to make the ful-filling music, on this stage with these players tonight, whose promise is already so dazzling and desirable to him this early on. He wants it. And when we hear him speak-sing, "I wait for them to interrupt" and "doesn't matter," desires we didn't even know we had are sated. The last words of the vocal – "Ah, I want you" (with "Ah" and "I" united in a single bit of phrasing) – are more of the same. This is followed by an instrumental break (band taking a verse in place of the last verse of the original song) that is more routine than inspired ... but even this seems to have been just right when the harmonica re-enters and duets with the band quite soulfully to the performance's end.

It doesn't seem possible (except that, according to one of my theories, the bandleader fervently desired this to happen), but things get significantly better with the next song, "You're a Big Girl Now" (already a Never Ending Tour chestnut, played at 26 shows in 1988, at 25 shows in 1989, and nine times in the first two 1990 legs – but this was the first and would be the only performance of the song during the August-September shows).

Beauty in music is intangible and always in the ear of the beholder, yet it is essential. It is difficult to think of a great work of music – composition or performance – that isn't rich in moments of what most of us would call beauty, maybe even "breathtaking beauty." The brief passages of harmonica-and-band music at the end of the 8/21/90 "I Want You" have this quality, and I suggest that most listeners to the recording of this show will find themselves mesmerized by these earnest and expressive passages, still uncertain what they've just been through but instinctively treasuring the experience and perhaps longing for it to go on and on ... which in a sense it then does as the audience wraps the last notes of the performance in their warm applause and seconds later the familiar G. E. Smith/Bob Dylan "Big Girl"-live signature chords arise, a musical phrase that has played many roles at different shows over the past two years, but that I believe for most listeners to this tape is now immediately about extending the beauty and sensitivity of that tender but glorious climax of "I Want You" into the tender and almost painfully evocative opening of tonight's "You're a Big Girl Now."

Wow. It's like a large promise is being made, which Dylan's performance and Dylan's band's performance immediately fulfill, sustaining the beauty of those last notes of the previous song through all the new colors of this one. It's odd how fresh these signature chords G.E. has played so many times (and has occasionally made tiresome) suddenly sound – and not so odd, as the vocal enters and we suddenly realize how *real* this work of music is for this singer and these players tonight, and how important it is to Bob Dylan as singer and bandleader and harmonica player to grasp the moment through it right now and thereby make this musical/emotional moment live forever.

As quoted earlier in this chapter, Dylan told an interviewer about a month after this performance, "People can learn everything about me through my songs, if they know where to look. They can juxtapose them with certain other songs and draw a clear picture." Hmm. In his concerts, Dylan the performer and set list writer does this for us, juxtaposes one song with another or several others. He does this for musical reasons or entertainment reasons, having to do with pacing and his sense of what will be stimulating to the audience, to him, and to the band. Yet as a result, we audience members (including listeners to the recordings) hear "I Want You" juxtaposed with "You're a Big Girl Now" and consciously or unconsciously we draw pictures. More importantly, these juxtapositions may lead us to draw pictures of ourselves and, in Dylan's words, "a picture of what goes on around here sometimes."

"But why would anyone want to know about me? It's ridiculous," Dylan told the interviewer. The answer is that we are so struck sometimes by the way he makes something better (or anyway very good) out of what is real that we want a glimpse of the reality he was transforming in this case (as travelers visit Monet's gardens and neighborhood to honor and investigate what they've seen in his paintings). Of course, while painters and singers and poets naturally draw on their life-experiences as subjects of their artworks, those artworks stand on their own and affect us as observers without benefit of footnotes or photographs of the afternoon sun on this particular cathedral. The painting or the song is itself a photograph and its beauty and its innate meaningfulness speak for themselves.

I bring this up because I can't resist mentioning here that exactly two weeks before this performance, according to Howard Sounes in *Down the Highway*, Bob Dylan's second wife, Carolyn Dennis-Dylan, filed for a dissolution of their marriage. "You're a Big Girl Now" is a powerful song arising from and describing a time when the songwriter's first marriage was entering a difficult "dissolution" period ("I'm going out of my mind with a pain that stops and starts"). And "I Want You," which is juxtaposed so intimately with "Big Girl" in this concert, is about the speaker's sexual desire, evidently a primary source of the conflict that led to the first marriage's dissolution. So it seems fair to say that the two songs, while not necessarily about "Bob Dylan," are both about being a man. "She breaks just like a little girl" has always sounded like a man's observation, and its sequel phrase "you're a big girl now" also does. I can report that the Portland '90 vocal performance of "Big Girl" doesn't sound to me like an expression of great pain ... rather, if I may say so, one of respect, for the forces from within and without that rule our lives. I also hear it as an acknowledgment of the beauty of it all, of being alive and feeling these complicated feelings. I can't imagine that the changes underway in Dylan's personal life were not part of the time he was grasping in this performance. Going back to the meaning I find myself hearing in Portland '90's "I Want You," Sounes's biography does not point at sexual misbehavior as a problem leading to the 1990 request for dissolution; the problem, he says, was that Dylan was seldom home, was on the road performing most of the time. In this sense, the very audience he was singing to at this show was "the other woman," or at least the act of playing with a band and making music and performing shows was. So who is he addressing this time, when he sings, "I'm ... singing just for you"? It doesn't matter. Just speculation and gossip (for which I apologize).

What matters is the experience the listener has as a result of this performance. Everyone who comes in contact with it (hears it), I believe, will recognize that something very powerful has been accomplished here. That something, I am certain, is what Dylan was referring to when he spoke to Ginsberg of "stopping time" in a work of art. It's like the "hold shots" Dylan favored in the film he directed, *Renaldo & Clara* – camera lovingly freezing a certain face or image, while the rest of the world stays in motion, so the viewer can go deeper and deeper into the expression on this person's face or contemplate deeply the significance of this object and how it looks in this context. What time is it? It's no time, it's timelessness, when five inspired musicians improvising together cause time as we know it to hide itself, to set us all free. The vocals in "Big Girl" again benefit from a special sound the singer's voice has and projects tonight. They feel deliberately restrained. And then the guitars – particularly Smith's soloing – in the instrumental break after the words "make it too" seem to let out all the feelings that were held back in those verses, band speaking articulately for Dylan as though it were his conscious aesthetic choice to express his passion first by obviously withholding it and then by releasing it in these fiery guitar lines.

Smith sounds unusually good. His playing is always skillful and often impressive, but tonight, surely because of the chemistry amongst this new set of players and thus between Dylan and Smith as well, he has more heart, he seems less the consummate professional bandleader and more the responsive musician bandmember. And the result overall – because of Stephen Bruton's presence and Smith's seemingly renewed enthusiasm, and sometimes also because of Bruton's playing, notably his inspired rhythm guitar figure behind Dylan's heartfelt and rather magnificent harmonica solo at the end of "Big Girl" – is great Bob Dylan music.

One slab of great Bob Dylan music after another, as "Big Girl" segues smoothly (Dylan's "thank you!" sounds full of awareness of and pride in the quality of the performance just finished) into "Masters of War." This particular "Masters of War" (a song Dylan had included in all of his last 32 shows, always in the second half of the first electric set) is a showcase hard rock performance as good as Neil Young and Crazy Horse at their live best. And good for the same reasons: the interplay between rhythm and lead guitars, and the ability of the rest of the rhythm section to support and respond to this. Yow! This is "I'm determined to stand!" music. As Dylan awkwardly tried to tell the audience at a couple of shows two months earlier, it's not a song about war in this version ("Some people say it was the first anti-war song, it's always felt like a NO-war song to me!"). It's a song about believing in your own vision and not taking shit from anyone. A song of self-assurance. Dylan has been singing and playing it so regularly, I think, because he finds it both thrills the audience and charges up his and his band's confidence and energy and readiness to rise to any challenge. The message is not in the words. It's in the sound of the music, which is white hot, untouchable, on this song, this night. Listening to the tape, it's easy to imagine a whole concert hall full of people pumping their fists furiously. That isn't what was happening, but that's what it feels like. Rock bandleaders live to create sound paintings like this one. For Bob Dylan, with Bruton and Smith accompanying him, it's an opportunity to demonstrate again that what he brought out in Mike Bloomfield and Robbie Robertson, he can bring out in other guitar players. The last couple of minutes of this 8/21/90 "Masters of War" are particularly incandescent. And how marvelous that this performance is immediately followed by another ensemble music showpiece of a very different structure and mood (self-assurance martial rave-up to back-porch celebration of contentment, affection and freewheelin' musical companionship): "I'll Be Your Baby Tonight."

Writing about a Dylan/band 1988 performance of "Gates of Eden" seven chapters back, I said, "everything depends on the musicians' and vocalist/bandleader's responses to each other.... The triumph of this 1988 tour and of the Never Ending Tour it evolved into is the creation of a creative environment in which moments like this can and do happen." In the case of Portland '90, this moment is not one song but a sequence of songs: the unforgettable first electric set of "Subterranean Homesick Blues"/"I Want You"/"You're a Big Girl Now"/"Masters of War"/"I'll Be Your Baby Tonight"/"Gotta Serve Somebody." The "moment" in which Dylan and his collaborators succeed in stopping time is also the entire concert, every song including the twelve that follow the six just named (a four-song acoustic band set, a second six-song electric set, and two encores).

You wanna know what "stopping time" means? Listen attentively to this 8/21/90 "Baby Tonight," and notice how unique and fresh this work of music is. This is certainly an example of Dylan as intuitive bandleader creating a memorable (and, if musicians hear this recording, an influential) sound comparable to the first side of *Bringing It All Back Home*, and to all of *Highway 61 Revisited* and *Blonde on Blonde* and *John Wesley Harding* and *Blood on the Tracks* and *Oh Mercy* and *Under the Red Sky* and *Time Out of Mind*. The man has a gift. And it has to do with how strong he exists in the moment sometimes. Repeating the *I Ching* comments I quoted in chapter 6, "This is the echo awakened in men through spiritual attraction. Whenever a feeling is voiced with truth and frankness, whenever a deed is the clear expression of sentiment, a mysterious and far-reaching influence is exerted. ... The root of all influence lies in one's own inner being; given true and vigorous expression in word and deed, its effect is great." ("In order to stop time, you have to exist in the moment, so strong as to stop time and prove your point. If you succeed in doing that, everyone who comes in contact with what you've done will catch some of that; they'll recognize that you have stopped time.")

Like the way Bob Dylan sings, "And I'm back in the rain/You are on dry land/You made it there somehow" in "Big Girl" in Portland 1990, the way he sings, "You don't have to worry anymore/I'll be your baby tonight" at this same show is remarkably, charmingly present without being dramatic, and is extremely engaging. I find myself noticing (for the first time?) that every verse of this song has an overtly reassuring message: "You don't have to worry anymore." "You don't have to be afraid." "You won't regret it." "Do not fear." In this wonderful Portland '90 version he says, "You don't have to be afraid" a second time, because he spontaneously repeats the song's second verse after the fourth verse (then ending the song by repeating the title phrase, as if he particularly means it this night). Fine singing. And rich, satisfying, appropriately idiosyncratic music. The sound of this performer's inner being.

Again, the segues between movements of this six-part Portland '90 first electric set concerto are very striking and lend drama and significance to both the song that's ending and the one that's just getting started. Not that it's easy to add drama to this powerhouse blues-rock (with a distinctly jazzy aura) rendition of "Gotta Serve Somebody." But this segue, like the aforementioned Portland segue between "I Want You" and "You're a Big Girl Now," is another brilliant example of a seldom-acknowledged aspect of Bob Dylan's artistry and genius: his appreciation for, and occasional mastery of,

transitions – musical transitions, as long as one recognizes that
language is music and so lyrical transitions (chains of images and
word-sounds) are manifestations of the same artistry and instinct
and genius. When these segues are successful, they convey a sense of
connectedness amongst the parts of a whole that has the effect of
creating what I've referred to above as a concerto, "a piece for one
or more soloists and orchestra with three or more contrasting movements." The segues unify the movements (in the listeners' minds)
into "a piece," and this is a significant part of what gives albums like
Blonde on Blonde and *Highway 61 Revisited* (and other Dylan albums;
see the next two chapters) their special power for many listeners.
Furthermore, it is one of the secrets of the success of a composition/
performance like "Desolation Row" that the song is made into such
a powerful whole, such an affecting "piece," by the segues between,
for example, the image (and musical sound) of leaning your head
out far enough to hear Dr. Filth and his nurse and his sexless
patients all blowing on pennywhistles ... and the image and performed musical sound of "Across the street they've nailed the
curtains/ They're getting ready for the feast" and so forth. The
segues point to and make us feel the wholeness of the piece. To our
considerable satisfaction and pleasure.

This 8/21/90 "Baby Tonight" to "Serve Somebody" segue is
not a tight, overlapping transition like many of the fall '87 segues. It
doesn't need to be. The silence after the very elegant and grace-
filled ending of "Baby Tonight" (in which Dylan repeats the title
phrase with perfect timing in relation to the music, singing/speaking
with marvelous expressiveness and presence) ... this silence is rich
with meaning ("a pregnant pause," as we say), and so is the fierce
guitar chord that breaks the silence and announces and introduces
the "Gotta Serve Somebody" riff and rhythmic bedding. It all works
perfectly to help us hear these two songs as part of a larger tapestry,
one that communicates something in its wholeness outside of and
beyond the sum of its impressive parts. Call it "The 8/21/90 first
electric set," or call it "Johnny-to-somebody" (from the first and last
words of this six-song sequence).

This way of making statements with song-sequences and
sets-taken-as-a-whole is something Dylan was excited to see and
hear the Grateful Dead doing in their shows that he watched in
1986 and 1987. It's an aesthetic he has always practiced and
enjoyed exploring (as demonstrated on his *Live 1966* album), and it

was a thrill for him to see the Dead use it so well in their concert construction and execution, and to see their audience acknowledging and appreciating consciously this aspect of performed art. Dylan already had the inclination and the gift, but he was encouraged hugely to observe the Dead and their audience exploring and appreciating this aesthetic so openly and energetically. So he found himself setting out to stop time again (and forever) in this fashion on what would become the Never Ending Tour.

Getting back to the Portland '90 "Gotta Serve Somebody": as perfect a climax as it is to this six-song excursion/invention, it also stands on its own as a rock and roll *tour de force*, a riff-based improvisation (including the vocal performance, though this time only a small proportion of the lyrics are improvised) comparable in quality to the searing performance of "Political World" that opens the *Oh Mercy* album. Hot stuff. Timeless. Eternal.

And it all holds together so well. At times the vocals are a rhythm instrument, offering the other musicians something solid to jump off from. And at times the vocalist seems to take a solo, just as the guitarists do (as if they were horn players in a good jazz band on a particularly inspired night). The guitar leads in this performance are so pretty, so expressive, so wonderful, one can't help wondering if that's Smith (does sound like him, at his best) or Bruton ... but it doesn't really matter, whichever guy it is, he'd have to give a lot of credit to the other guy (and to Dylan's rhythm guitar playing too). This fine music is very much a collective creation, five players so in touch with their muse and so responsive to each other there's no stopping them, no keeping them from this rendezvous with genius. Nor are these five guys alone. As Duke Ellington tells us in *Music Is My Mistress*, the autobiography of a composer/performer/ bandleader: "The audience is the other side of the realm that serves the same muse I do." "When one is fortunate enough," Ellington wrote, and he could have been talking about this Portland '90 show, "to have an extremely sensitive audience, and when every performer within the team on stage feels it, too, and reacts positively in coordination toward the pinnacle, and when both audience and performers are determined to not be outdone by the other, and when both have appreciation and taste to match – then it is indeed a very special moment, never to be forgotten." And this is what Bob Dylan is talking about, in this version of this song this night – he knows he is serving somebody and acknowledges that he doesn't always know whether it's the Devil or the Lord (and implies that you may not always know either), but he is a human being and he is in service, and this is his anthem of expressive acknowledgment. A *tour de force*, as I said already.

The climax of "Gotta Serve Somebody" is given extra flavor as Dylan hisses "S- S- S-" leading into the word "Serve." The band is already playing "finale" notes, bringing the performance to a dramatic and satisfying conclusion. The audience claps and cheers enthusiastically; and in the next second after the band wraps up the song, we hear amplified acoustic guitar notes reaching out into the room, cutting through (and ending) the applause and loosely reaching towards the start of the next song (as though Dylan's instructions to his guitar tech ahead of time had been to hand him his new guitar while the finale of the last electric set song was still going on, so that he'd be able to keep his own intuitive musical flow going almost nonstop if he wanted to). "Thank you!" he shouts and slurs, and then quite clearly speaks the following remarkable sentence:

"I'd like to dedicate this next song to all prisoners of war … today, and every other day."

This is remarkable to me because as a contemporary of Dylan's (and of his 1990 audience), I know that the phrase "prisoners of war" at this moment in America is usually heard as a reference to American soldiers captured during the Vietnam War two decades earlier, some of whom, it is rumored, may still be held and still alive. Something of a "flag-waving" patriotic cause in late-twentieth-century America, and not one one expects to hear Bob Dylan embracing (but he does love to tease his audience, to declare independence from their assumptions about his views, in this way). And then, listening to the recording (I can't claim to have had this awakening while I was in the audience that night), I hear Dylan and his acoustic band deliver a particularly fine rendition of "John Brown" and slap my head like I'm an idiot for never grasping this in quite this way before: this is indeed a song of empathy for "prisoners of war" – young people waking up to find themselves soldiers, trapped in a foreign and very hostile environment, at constant risk of losing their lives or (as in this case) their ability to walk or talk or see. With no opportunity to even try to escape. Prisoners indeed. "I thought when I was there, Lord, what am I doing here?? Tryin' to kill somebody, or die tryin'." "I couldn't help but think, through the thunder and rolling stink, that I was just a puppet in a play …"

It's an absolutely inspired moment, Dylan's seemingly spontaneous spoken introduction to this song – like some of his early
triumphs, a play on words that turns out to be profoundly right (and
clever and communicative) and in tune with the times and with the
unchanging essence of the human situation. Of course, Dylan may
have thought the previous day or sometime in the previous months,
reading something in the newspaper about POWs, that in fact all
those poor soldiers, Americans or Iraqis (the first American-Iraqi
war was already brewing in August 1990), are prisoners of war right
now. "Um, isn't that what my song 'John Brown' is about?" Or the
"wild line" may have just come into his head without any fore-
thought, in the heat of this fortunate night with a very sensitive
audience and a magnificently awake band somewhere out on the
endless highway. Yes, any poor souls still held in Vietnam or somewhere, but also *all* prisoners of war, today and every other day,
that's whom I'd like to dedicate this song, this performance to. With
feeling. With sincere compassion. "Don't you remember, Ma, when
I went off to war, you thought it was the best thing I could do?"

It's a great performance (of a song I've just learned to like a lot
better) – and, oddly, a powerful rock and roll performance, even if
this is the acoustic band set and set-up. The musical fire that was so
present in "Gotta Serve Somebody" and "Masters of War" appropriately burns through this performance too, despite the subtle
change in the form of the instruments. (Drums, of course, just as
acoustic, but also just as loud – played with sticks, not brushes, for
this song – as they ever were. In fact, Christopher Parker's playing
at the end of the song, the way he manages to make the clapping-
along-to-the-beat of the audience another musician to play off of,
is breathtakingly good. Fine musicianship, inspiring and inspired
by both the sensitive audience and the so-hot-tonight singer/
bandleader. Um, imagine what it must be like to play drums behind
a singer who thinks he can stop time! Not so bad, if, as I hope is true
for Christopher Parker, you realize that through your collaboration
with him you've stopped time yourself, made an indelible – and
very aesthetically pleasing – mark. Tonight and many other nights.

"Thank you!" Dylan shouts as the audience erupts into appreciative applause at the end of this fabulous performance. "That's an
old song. Here's a new one. A new one to us [Meaning, 'We five
haven't played it together before']." And he starts singing, "I'm out
here a thousand miles from my home ..." Wow. So this night in

1990, he follows his autumn 1962 empathy-for-the-kid-in-uniform story song/"protest song" with "Song to Woody," his February 1961 tribute to his mentor, the greatest "protest song" writer ever. Two portraits, if you will, of the artist as a very young songwriter. "Old" songs in terms of the headliner's chronology, but otherwise timeless. And both made new this night by the muse-serving singer and his muse-serving band and audience.

The band does a fine job of supporting Dylan on "Song to Woody" (played twice before this year, in London Feb. 6 as a Smith/Dylan duo and in Berlin July 5 as an acoustic band song), but what is particularly striking about the Portland version of this song is that the singer is in such good voice and puts so much feeling into his singing and into the long harmonica passage that concludes the performance.

The next song, "The Lakes of Pontchartrain" (its second and final appearance during 1990), is again distinguished by the sound of the singer's voice, and by the rich texture of the music created by this string band – each song tonight a new painting, offering fresh colors and portraying a new scene and story that in turn feel like part of a bigger story told by all the songs together, by the flow of melody and rhythm and sonic invention that drives and supports these narratives. "Pontchartrain," a song about falling in love (with a dark girl) and about the virtue of fidelity, is followed pointedly, this month of the beginning of the end of the singer's second marriage, by "It Ain't Me Babe."

"It Ain't Me Babe" in Portland is a performance enlivened by the interaction between the various guitars and enriched by another long sweet harp solo at the end; but otherwise it seems surprisingly listless on a night like this, when every other song-performance is full of life and awakeness and love for performing ... even the next two songs, "Rainy Day Women" and "All Along the Watchtower."

So we come to the beginning of the second electric set, the eleventh of 18 songs performed at this 8/21/90 show, and we come to a moment that I and perhaps many of my friends and readers have feared would someday come: I am about to cite a particular concert performance of "Rainy Day Women #12 & 35" as an example of Bob Dylan's genius, of his unique and enduring artistry as a singer/songwriter/bandleader/performer. "Oy vay, it's come to this!" I mutter, because I have a long-standing aversion to Dylan and his bands' live performances of this song. It tends to be a sleepwalking throwaway. But oddly, on a night when "It Ain't Me Babe" is almost a throwaway, "Rainy Day Women" seems to me (when I can get past my automatic aversion) a very fresh and, yes, inspired invention. Structurally, it's quite short, three semi-improvised verses and choruses (with an excellent instrumental break between the second and third verses) leading into an unpredictable, funny, very hip and very musically smart and pleasing harmonica solo (played with the band).

In this case, it's worth recounting the lyrics as actually sung (or my best guesses as to what he's saying) – because it may offer some insight into Dylan-the-performer's process and technique, and thus bring us a bit closer to being able to understand how he does what he does (stopping time, or whatever it is).

Verse 1: " [inaudible words, almost certainly "They'll stone you"] when you're trying to keep your feet [feels as though he's thinking, "keep your beat," making this line about the performers while the next one's about the audience]

"Stone you when you're trying to get your seat
"Stone you when you see [or "say"] that it's the end
"Stone you and then they'll be back again
"I would not feel so all alone
"Everybody … get stoned."

Verse 2: " [mumbled and slurred words] breakfast table
"Stone you when you are young and able
"Stone you when you say you'll be back
"Stone you when you [mumble] Cadillac
"I would not feel so all alone
"Everybody must get stoned." [this line sung by a far-off chorus of voices, not including Dylan's]

Verse 3 (after an instrumental break/jam almost as celebratory and spontaneous as the original Nashville recording): "They'll stone you [mumble, mumble] back for more
"They'll stone you when they [mumble] close the door
"Stone you when they'll say that it's for good
"Stone you just like they said they would
"I would not feel so all alone
"Everybody must get stoned!"

A few measures after these last words, Dylan begins a series of harmonica jabs and sucks (fragments, really) that stimulate and lead the band in the creation of a very nice musical capstone to this surprisingly brief and fulfilling performance (what he's doing is expressing to the band and the audience and himself how he feels about this music they're all making now). As happens with performances like this, the song seems to have a whole new meaning as of this moment, and that meaning is something like, "You don't have to feel so all alone, because music is your friend, and it understands what you're going through and will always be here for you, whether you get stoned (in either sense of the phrase) or not."

So what might we be able to learn from contemplating the lyrics the singer sang (or didn't sing, or gestured in the direction of singing) to this song, this night? Something about how improvisation works, and how Dylan works with it to create his freewheelin' and very impressive performed art. Of the six couplets in the three verses quoted above, only three employ rhymed phrases found in the original recorded version ("it's the end"/ "back again," "breakfast table"/ "young and able", "good"/ "said they would," and of these only one could possibly be lyrically identical to the original (the "breakfast table" one; "possibly" because we can't tell what he's saying, he slurs a set of words together as if deliberately trying to hide them, to conceal or leave ambiguous their message). Two of the other three couplets contain, at the end of a line, one phrase that is used in this position in one of the original song's lines ("your seat" and "the door"). The other couplet introduces a rhyme that is new to the song, although one of its rhyming phrases is present in both the original song and elsewhere in this new, improvised version: "be back." So Dylan in this improvisation sounds like he's singing words as related to the original ones as the melody of a jazz "interpretation" of a tune is related to the melody of the song's original or best-known form. Deconstruction, if you will. Getting into the essence of the work of art and running forward musically exploring possibilities suggested by that melodic theme or that batch of language. This can seem undisciplined (and certainly there is a possibility that the performing artist and some of his bandmates are stoned, on alcohol or marijuana or both, at this show) and disrespectful, but in truth, in the case of first-rate jazz and first-rate live Dylan music, it is an expression of a rather demanding musical discipline and what it primarily expresses is deep respect for the original composition, its melody, rhythm, structure, language and essential identity, its success in creating something so tangible that these players and their leader can take it apart spontaneously and rebuild it on the spot, as a kind of tribute to and exploration of the song's breadth and depth, like John Coltrane honoring Richard Rodgers' and Oscar Hammerstein's "My Favorite Things" and demonstrating its remarkable plasticity and beauty and the enduring power of this work of art.

Which is not to say that I'm struck by the beauty or plasticity or enduring expressive power of "Rainy Day Women." I'm not. But I am very struck by what this singer and these players achieve in this particular performance of the song. They reclaim it and reinvent it. They reduce it to almost meaningless fragments, and then seem to have no difficulty making these fragments speak, as music and as lyrics. They demonstrate that music is or can be a collective, seemingly telepathic, expression of the moment in which it is performed, a representation in chords and beats and words and harmonics of an individual's or of a group of individuals' true experience of life in this vale of tears, on this ball of dirt spinning around a ball of fire. They demonstrate the open-endedness of song and of the art of performing songs as an ensemble. "I would not feel so all alone," indeed! If even this hoary old chestnut, this warhorse of a set-list habitué, can be this fresh and joyful, then none of us is quite as imprisoned by time as we might seem to be.

Please note that in this Portland '90 "Rainy Day Women" there is no evidence of Dylan striving to sing or remember the "original" or standard lyrics of the song. The first line he sings is not close to or arguably a misremembering of the song's first line, which ultimately shows up here in slightly different form as the third line of the third verse. So it's not just an alcohol-mangled version of the song's lyrics, but rather a seemingly conscious effort to sing the song's words and lines in a thoroughly different sequence, with the intent that lines and couplets (pairs of rhyming lines) will be spontaneously rewritten as often as not, just to see what happens, just to exist so strong in the moment that you give it a chance to speak through you, to speak for itself using a reshuffled set of old lines and images as a script, a jumping-off place. The "breakfast table" line is the only verse-starting line this night that was used as the starting place for one of the original five verses. There's a method, an odd discipline, in this seeming sloppiness, is what I'm suggesting.

Back in chapter 5 of this volume, I made the outrageous suggestion that Dylan's slurred and mumbled words during a particular performance ("Joey" 9/30/87) are somehow a part of his "singing freely and spontaneously and sincerely, a peculiar byproduct of his concentration on creating an environment of enchantment with his performance. I further suggested that "the singer's strange diction," the sound of his voice here, "is the vehicle by which his particular mood and intent, unique to this performance and this moment, are communicated to the other musicians so that the end result is a collective creation with a spirit all its own." This is again the case with "Rainy Day Women" 8/21/90. At times Dylan's voice here seems to me to be a rhythm instrument holding the band together, conducting it as if it were an orchestra. Listening to this performance again and again, I never fail to be impressed and delighted at how the sound of his voice and the music he's making through the band all lead up so perfectly to the free, fragmented harmonica solo (and harmonica/band duet) that concludes the performance. I hear profundity. I hear great creative and expressive power. I wouldn't have expected to find these in a performance of this song, but that's just my personal prejudice. The performing artist works with the elements available to him at the moment of creation. And often surprises himself in the process. "They'll stone you, and then you'll go back for more!"

When the first thundering chords of "All Along the Watchtower" arise right out of the closing moments of "Rainy Day Women," I again feel an aversion that comes from having heard this arrangement of this song at too many concerts (and on too many concert tapes or CDs) ... but I can't deny the power and brightness (and even, humor) of the segue. Let us not talk falsely now. This segue is the sound of the artist being himself, and enjoying what he's doing. (And winking broadly as he changes song-costumes.) Heard this way, it pleases me very much. And, I believe, will please others who seek out this work of accidental art ("accidental" only in its recorded form; the artwork's effect on the live audience was entirely conscious and intentional, even if intoxication may have been one of the many elements employed to achieve this result, to grasp this time).

Again. Dylan sings "Watchtower" in a very free manner in which he seemingly gives himself permission to hurry or swallow or slur words and phrases ... he's not inventing new lyrics on this one, but he is singing some lines so quickly they can't be deciphered unless you're already very familiar with them. The opening words, "There must be some way out of here," are almost inaudible (sung fast and possibly off-mike) so that a newcomer (if there are any such in this crowd) might reasonably wonder what it was the joker said to the thief. This sort of singing continues throughout the performance and oddly, when listened to closely, it seems to me a very effective and expressive vocal. For example, "You and I we've been through that" sounds genuinely sincere, one comrade talking to another, which is quite affecting when you are the listener who's just been acknowledged and included in this way.

Meanwhile the music – though I spoke of "the first thundering chords" – is rather light and easy, not half as thundering or bombastic as became standard on this song when it resided unchangingly in the #3 position at Never Ending Tour concerts from August 20, 1992 to May 3, 1997. In fact, it's a lighter sound for this song than was already becoming standard when it was played at all but four of the 1990 shows prior to Portland. This new lightness – a middle road, because the performance retains some of the structural excitement and power of the derived-from-Hendrix approach Dylan had come to favor on this song, yet manages some of the friendly and light musical flavor achieved earlier in this show on "I'll Be Your Baby Tonight" – is clearly another expression of Dylan's enjoyment of the possibilities presented by tonight's new band line-up. There's only one additional player, another guitar, but the changes in the chemistry of the interaction between the musicians is substantial, mostly because the bandleader feels refreshed by the change of situation, and his response to it directs and affects everyone. He also feels the self-confidence, because of the quality of the musical experience he's having with this line-up and this crowd so far tonight, to throw away the script – the one in his mind which called for putting a surefire crowd-pleasing loud rocker at this point in the second electric set – and follow the music wherever he finds it leading him. The music is his muse, and it directed him to allow or encourage "Watchtower" to take on another flavor or "feel" tonight.

The third and fourth songs of the second electric set, August 21, 1990, are "I'll Remember You" and "What Good Am I?" The former had been sung and played at eleven shows in 1990 before this, and the latter had been included at ten 1990 shows prior to

Portland (the 48th Dylan show of the year). These songs are from albums Dylan released in 1985 and 1989. The first songs in this set were from albums released in 1966 and 1968 and were both hit records on their own (for Dylan in 1966 and for Jimi Hendrix in 1968). The last two songs of this set will be similarly balanced: one newer, less famous song from an album released in the past decade ("In the Garden," 1980) and one older, revered hit song from the 1960s ("Like a Rolling Stone," 1965).

If we continue this sort of analysis (just to be aware of the sort of elements the set-list writer is juggling), we see that this show's 18 songs include six that appeared on the 1967 album *Bob Dylan's Greatest Hits*, two others that were hits, "All Along the Watchtower" (Hendrix's cover got to #20 in the U.S.) and "Gotta Serve Somebody" (Dylan's single got to #24 in 1979, his last top 40 hit as of this writing), one cover ("Pontchartain"), five more Dylan songs from the 1960s and one from the 1970s and three from the 1980s. A fair representation, for the performer and for the audience, of 30 years of work so far (including one song from the man's first album and one from his most recent release). What was it you wanted? he might reasonably ask. But instead he asks the musical question that this list of mostly Dylan-authored tunes might seem to answer, What good am I?

As I write this (September 2003), Bob Dylan's most recent work of authorship is in the theaters (a collaboration, but he wrote the bulk of the screenplay and dialogue) – a film called *Masked and Anonymous*. The title is certainly a good expression of how the private man Dylan wishes to be seen by the public. Of course, the public's impulse is contrary: to see through the mask (the stage name "Dylan" is a kind of mask), and hear the songs as true reflections of the author's life and experience. Dylan is well aware of this, and has played an ongoing game with the world and his public in this respect, expressed for example in his 2001 comment to an interviewer about *"Love And Theft"*: "I've never recorded an album with more autobiographical songs." What was it you wanted? "Step right up," he teases, "buy an album or a concert ticket or a movie ticket and maybe you'll get it." Or maybe you won't. Or maybe you'll get more in touch with the masked and anonymous side of yourself …

"This is the way I really feel about things," Dylan told the interviewer in 2001 to clarify or defend his use of the word "autobiographical." The virtue of Dylan's fine Portland '90 performances of "I'll Remember You" and "What Good Am I?" – as with so many examples of his live artistry – is that they powerfully communicate how the singer/bandleader really feels about things. Real feelings are expressed, whether or not we listeners know anything about their immediate origins in the artist's life experiences. We the listeners also have feelings, and are moved when we come upon their counterparts in a song, a novel, a painting, a film, or a musical performance. Shock of recognition. This occurs without any knowledge of the autobiographical details affecting the artist's process of creation, his choice of words and of sounds and of melodies and of rhythms/punctuations. We get the end-product, the result, and can be strongly affected and pleased by it. Something intimate has been transmitted, shared. We may not know its origins, but in any case we make it our own, we find it meaningful and enriching and fulfilling.

So as the reader may have guessed, I'm back to the topic of "Why would anyone want to know about me? It's ridiculous" because again (yes, I'm a member of Dylan's public and yes, I'm caught in the game) I hear these next two performances as expressions of feelings related to the biographical circumstance that two weeks before this show, Dylan's second wife had begun the legal process of divorcing him, like his first wife (and the mother of his other children) more than a decade earlier. And I think the fact that we now have this information can offer some insight into the process whereby the performer reciting the script (singing the set list) consciously and/or unconsciously makes his performance a unique expression of the emotional moment he finds himself in at this hour on this stage with these players and in front of this crowd.

"I'll Remember You" ("when I've forgotten all the rest"), we may reasonably presume, is a song written for Carolyn Dennis by Bob Dylan during their courtship. The song was recorded in January 1985 (with Carolyn's mother, Madelyn Quebec, singing a second vocal part). Dylan and Dennis were married in June 1986; their daughter was born five months before that, and therefore conceived in April of '85. According to the Sounes biography, Dylan and Dennis had dated "on and off" (she was married to someone else during part of this time) since 1978.

It's a love song, a sort of tribute (as, for example, "Love Minus Zero" is), and that's how I hear it in this August '90 performance. What is noteworthy about this particular version is that Dylan and

his band play the rhythmic riff the song is based on at a new tempo,
brighter and a little faster, giving the song a new feel, a cheerful,
almost celebratory quality. What is being celebrated, I surmise, is
the enduring nature of the relationship and of how "I" feel about
"you" regardless of changes in outer circumstances. It's a song
Dylan had performed fairly often in recent years (at 18 shows in
1988 and 22 times in 1989), perhaps because for him it was an
expression of affection for a wife he cared for though his constant
touring meant he seldom saw her ... but I think also because he
enjoyed performing this song with a band, and thought of it as the
sort of American song (in the tradition of Irving Berlin or Cole
Porter) that could become or be considered a "standard" – another
side of Bob Dylan that he was proud of and wanted to represent at
his shows. I also speculate that lyrically and musically he found it a
song with a pleasing plasticity, the ability to reshape itself spontaneously at the moment of performance in response to a great variety
of different moods and expressive impulses. (When I speak of
reshaping itself lyrically, I don't mean he would change the lyrics,
but that the same words and phrases could carry different messages
and feelings depending on the intent of the singer/performer.)

There is a lovely freshness to this Portland "I'll Remember
You," a special spirit in it that builds to a surprising yet very natural
series of climaxes, all of them releases for the tension built up by the
repetition of the wonderful riff that propels this particular performance. The first of these climaxes follows the vocal bridge between
the second verse of the song and its last verse. After the last words of
the bridge, "when the rain was blowing in your hair," Dylan
exclaims, "Ahh ... Yeah!!" (echoing his own "Yeah!" a line earlier,
after the line "Didn't I try to care?"). Then early in the last verse
there's something climactic about his singing of the lines "It was you
who cut right through/It was you who understood." He emphasizes
the word "cut" (which is an improvisation – the original lyric is
"came right through"). This "cut right through ... understood"
mini-climax is immediately followed by another powerful moment
when the band goes into a kind of rhythmic change-up behind the
lines "Though I'd never say/That I done it the way/That you
would have liked me to" ... after which the guitars build nicely, in a
loose garage-band fashion (which points to something that was
often missing in these G. E. Smith years – he's just not a garage-
band kind of guy, though Bruton's presence this week seems to have

opened a door for him), to a return of that bright guitar riff, along-side and under the closing words, "In the end, my dear sweet friend/I'll remember you ... Ah, babe!"

Immediately after this, with that riff still continuing to build and release tension, something delightful happens, another climax: one of the guitar players, Smith or Bruton, plays a little melodic piece that often turns up at the end of a verse in this song, but plays it in an unusual high sweet tone (could there suddenly be a mandolin on stage?) that is particularly striking, almost sounding like a bagpipe solo. This by itself would serve to sum up the whole song, but then a suddenly inspired Dylan jumps in with fragments of an expressive harmonica solo, playing call-and-response to the guitar riff, until the guitars wrap things up in a delicious little garage-band-style ending that you just know Dylan would have happily rehearsed for days to arrive at, except that in this case he didn't need to, it happened naturally as an expression of this night's particular magic and of the singer/bandleader's feelings of affection and anguish at this biographical moment. Phew. Sweet stuff.

But, we might ask since we're playing this game, where does the evident joy in this performance of "I'll Remember You" come from at this biographical moment? The answer certainly is that the man loves his work, and feels (and often expresses) joy when it's going well, when he and the other musicians on stage are interact-ing well with each other ("reacting positively in coordination toward the pinnacle," as Ellington put it) and with the music and with the felt audience, creating something together that is thrilling to be part of. And where the biographical moment fits into this picture is that this – playing music, the endless highway, the never ending tour, the life of a committed performer – is what the man has chosen instead of life at home with his female companion and child. A diffi-cult choice, presumably, but one he feels reaffirmed in tonight, when his creative work, the life he's chosen, is going so well. "There's some people that you don't forget, even though you've only seen 'em one time or two ..." Tonight, I suggest, "I'll remem-ber you" means "I won't lose you. The love I feel for you (wife and child I see so seldom) will continue to be present with me as it is right now, as long as I'm true to myself and my calling." So the joy of this good night of performing is not unrelated to the "message" of this song. "In the end, my dear sweet friend, I'll remember you." "My dear sweet friend" can be his music, and his faraway wife, and the Divine (inseparable from the issue of being true to himself and his earthly calling). The joy comes from the immediacy of reaffirmation in the face of personal difficulties and doubts, reaffirmation that yes, he is doing what the higher power that both he and Carolyn believe in wants him to do. Doubts disappear on a night like this.

The Portland '90 "What Good Am I?" is a messier but equally marvelous example of a performing artist consciously or unconsciously or both at once communicating the way he really feels about things ... and, arguably, stopping time in the process.

This rendition of "What Good Am I?" is messy in (and perhaps successful because of) the way it plays free with the lyrics and structure of the original song (i.e. the album version). Dylan starts the song with what was once the third verse, following it with the original second and fourth verses. He then ends with a variation on the same verse he opened with tonight. So the original first and last verses are omitted, both replaced by the repositioned former middle verse. The second time around, this newly significant verse (it opens and closes the song, clearly the key to any message the singer intends to deliver) contains two borrowed lines, one from each of the verses left out of this performance. This is so elegant, it makes me fairly sure Dylan sat down with the song and actually rewrote it (lightly) on paper sometime before this performance. He did this, I believe, because the title of the song made him think of it (as he wrote the set list and, pointedly, put it after "I'll Remember You") as an opportunity to express and explore his feelings of remorse at this biographical moment. ("But the audience doesn't know he's just been served with divorce papers." "That's okay; the way he thinks of it, his job is to breathe life into the songs, with his voice and his band, and then let the audience hear that aliveness, and thus the stories of all of our lives, in the songs.")

If you're attached to the message this song conveyed via its *Oh Mercy* form and performance, you could be disappointed that that message (akin to those of "Chimes of Freedom" and "Blowin' in the Wind," as I wrote three chapters back) is not conveyed very well in this version. Instead of "What good am I if I'm like all the rest?" the song starts, "What good am I while you softly weep/And I hear in my head what you say in your sleep ..." This verse was apparently thrown into the album version to introduce the possibility that the person the singer is speaking to is a woman, a lover. This sort of ambiguity has served Dylan very well as a song-crafter. He opens various doors, and lets the listener decide at the moment of listening what sort of story is being told (which door to walk through). "What good am I?" is a very humble question for a lover to ask in the context of how he treats his loved one. The nakedness and vulnerability of this title for a possible love song creates a tension and gives the song some added power, makes it attractive and intriguing. This is a device, a skillful one, and tonight Dylan the performer turns it around by singing in fact to a love partner instead of to "the countless confused, accused, misused, strung-out ones an' worse."

"What good am I, while you softly weep?" he opens, and then concludes the song with "If I just turn my back while you silently die, what good am I?" (followed a moment later by a brief and intense guitar solo by G. E. Smith that surely does speak for the singer/song-creator at this moment). There's a lot of grace also in the song's introductory passage – bass, drums and guitars playing tender and dramatic, almost-familiar notes that say something powerful's coming, though we in the audience can't guess what until the harmonica enters, sounding just like a continuation of the "I'll Remember You" closing harp solo we heard seconds ago and then resolving into the melody notes of the title and chorus phrase of "What Good Am I?" Musical grace, leading into tender and almost urgent vocals. There's a restraint in the vocals that only serves to make them feel more passionate and almost out of control in the self-castigating "where must I have been?" soliloquy. It's a very moving performance, full of great moments, but for me the instant when time truly stops is the quick segue to the next song: "Thank you!" and then those signature opening chords of "In the Garden." Unmistakably, a statement is being made, one that the singer/ bandleader's heart is totally in at this moment. His singing is impressive and very moving on both "What Good Am I?" and "In the Garden," and it occurs to me after many affecting listens that "In the Garden" tonight is sung in honor of Carolyn and the special space of fellowship which she and he have shared in their mutual love and respect for the hero of this narrative. For a few minutes of song, his love for Him and for her are one. And we listeners don't have to know anything of this to be moved by the passion in these performances.

And then, marvelously, "In the Garden" segues nonstop into "Like a Rolling Stone." Another passionate performance. In the context of what has been evoked for me by the songs leading up to this show-climax, from "I'll Remember You" through "What Good Am I?" to "In the Garden," I notice that as ever the song can be heard as addressed to a particular woman ("Miss Lonely") that the speaker has been infatuated with ... but most of all, I realize as I have before, he's addressing himself at this moment: "How does it feel to be on your own?" Singer and band rise to the occasion, as they have all evening. "You're invisible!" the masked and anonymous singer announces sympathetically, "You've got no secrets to conceal."

Maybe he doesn't, but after "Rolling Stone" rolls to a very satisfying conclusion, and over the opening notes of the first encore, "Blowin' in the Wind," Dylan manages to give us the feeling that he is (playfully, humorously) sharing a secret, when he tells the audience (repeating a line he's used at a few other shows in the past month or two), "Joan Baez used to always tell me, 'You keep singing this song, boy, you're gonna be a star.'" A fine reading of "Blowin' in the Wind" follows (rich in examples of Bob Dylan breathing like nobody else does), and then Portland '90 concludes with an enjoyable and not overstated "Highway 61 Revisited." Bob is in such a good mood, he even shouts something (could be, "Take it away!") over the closing notes of the song and the concert.

Stephen Bruton stayed with the band for another five shows (in Colorado, Iowa, Indiana and Minnesota) and also joined them for two shows in mid-October (where he is reported to have played electric mandolin). G. E. Smith did leave the band after a five-show residency at the Beacon in New York City in October. He was replaced for the rest of the year by Cesar Diaz and John Staehely. In 1991, the Never Ending Tour continued, with John Jackson and Ian Wallace now playing guitar and drums, respectively.

"'What time is it?' It's no time." It's August 21st, 1990, eternally.

V. "Gonna Keep on Walkin'"

January 1997

14.

This chapter was written in September 1997 and is included here because although the chronological part of this volume only runs from August 1986 to August 1990, I believe that from a "mind out of time" perspective – Bob Dylan's preferred perspective – Dylan's growth as a performer and artist in these years cannot be properly portrayed without acknowledging the two great works of intentional art and composition that were already present in him at this time as wishes and intentions (a gleam in his eyes, and thus some kind of guiding light) and that he would execute and release in 1997 and 2001, *Time Out of Mind* and *"Love And Theft"*. So I am including here the essays I wrote about these albums when I first heard them (and will doubtless have more to say about them as performances in future volumes in this series).

[The essay that follows first appeared in *Crawdaddy!*, under the title "Sparkly-Eyed Master of the Highlands." When it was reprinted in *On the Tracks* soon after that, I included at the start a "Note to the Reader," which said: "This review was written in mid-September, listening to the advance tape weeks before the album came out. I swear, I wrote paragraph 4, where I say the character who speaks in these songs is like Dylan but 'is no more him than Hamlet is Bill Shakespeare,' 2½ weeks before the *Newsweek* interview came out, in which Bob says, 'I'm not the songs. It's like somebody expecting Shakespeare to be Hamlet.'"]

"I see nothing to be gained by any explanation." Well, you never did. But in context, I agree wholeheartedly. Even the softest touch always means so much, and explanations, especially between lovers, usually aren't as helpful. Nevertheless, this essay about Bob Dylan's brand new album *Time Out of Mind* takes off from the easy observation that, like all of Dylan's best and most significant artworks, it reaches its listener, serious fan or journalist or man-on-the-street or whomever, as a parcel of riddles. Like a major, ground-breaking work by Pablo Picasso at the moment of its unveiling. What is it? What's it about? What will it come to mean to us? What new world or way of perceiving the world does it possibly announce or introduce? And how about all the contradictions? Is it really about a woman he's trying to forget but can't stop thinking of, as every one of these eleven songs seems to assert? And so forth. Lovely, challenging questions. Superb music. And some of the better lyrics Bob Dylan has ever offered us – yes indeed, unquestionably. But ahem. I been listening and listening for four days now, and I'm still contemplating this koan, and expect I will for decades should I live so long. And having puzzled over more contradictions than I care to itemize (reminiscent of the 1966 contradiction between the biographical fact of BD's recent marriage and the journey-through-the-realm-of-the-one-night-stand subject matter of *Blonde on Blonde*), I find myself already living with an answer or "explanation" that so satisfies me I want to blurt it out.

Is the author of these songs living through such passionate love-conflict currently … or was he when he reportedly wrote this whole song cycle two years ago? Who could the woman have been? Or is it all some pointed metaphor? I'll tell ya how it seems to me.

Moby Dick is a fiction, even though Herman Melville had indeed shipped out on some whaling voyages. So is *Time Out of Mind* a fiction. A brilliant treatment by the lyricist for a film to be shot in a recording studio. The story? Isn't it obvious? It's about an imaginary protagonist/everyman who is anguished by the loss of love (and equally by the love object's refusal to depart from his daily thoughts). She is a great beauty. He is (still) fascinated, anguished, confused. Confused not only about her intentions but mostly by his own reactions. And the great beauty of the song cycle itself is its ability to articulate and share those reactions: "Gon' walk down that dirt road/Until my eyes begin to bleed/'Til there's nothing left to see/'Til the chains have been shattered and I've been freed." Great God almighty, free at last! Yes, but: "Gonna keep on walkin' 'til I hear her holler out my name." What a fucking brilliant piece of writing and music and performance this is. It all is. Bob, you finally wrote your novel. And um, it ain't no tarantula but a tall oak tree, a masterpiece.

Blood on the Tracks is a clever and extremely powerful fictionalization ("Tell it like a story happening to invented characters," he mighta told himself) of real life. *Blonde on Blonde* is an impressionistic fiction full of real-life moments but not bound to any autobiographical time-line. In both cases the listener is as convinced of the reality of the created milieu as he or she would expect in a good novel or movie. *Time Out of Mind* (great title; the essence of each of these major Dylan works is the ability of the author's mind/heart to transcend ordinary time limitations and to confer this ability or power on the listener. "Take me disappearing ..." ... and reappearing, again and again) is apparently a fiction about a character who has a relationship with an ex-wife and/or former or current lover that is not necessarily unrelated to the playwright/lyricist's own experiences but who is no more him than Hamlet is Bill Shakespeare or Mr. Tagomi is Philip K. Dick. Just time out of mind, okay? A created universe. A story to sing. That may in turn become a metaphor for all sorts of other matters in his (author's) or our (listeners') lives. But stories and fictions have their own (non-metaphorical) internal logic, after all. You could even call it an aesthetic. Or a "sound."

We expect autobiography of the singer-songwriter or the blues singer because that's the premise of the form. "I asked for water, she gave me gasoline." Howlin' Wolf is not of course saying this specifically happened to him. But that's how it felt, and he imagines his listener knows what he's talking about. Truth or invention? No problem. We very willingly suspend our disbelief.

And identify with Prince Hamlet as he stalks the stage and tries to make peace with his ghosts and lady friend and circumstances. What a fine nonsequential (timeless) drama Mr. Dylan has constructed here. And how masterfully he (and each of these musicians under the spell of his presence, his conviction) performs it here. Wow. "They" may not have said it couldn't be done, but they did have their doubts. What a great goddamned record. Consciously and openly dipping at the same well as Hank Williams and Robert Johnson and Elvis Presley and Howlin' Wolf. And tipping a hat to the Rolling Stones (at least once in the lyrics and probably more than once in the music, as if to acknowledge that the rock process and the folk process are the same in this poetic era). Good story, good images, great music and great words. My God. Frankly I think even his fans (some of 'em) underrate this man's artistry. He works hard. And he sure has fun when he finds a way to let loose and invent and bear down and rant and rave. And groove. And laugh at life. And tell it like it is.

If you ever liked anything he did, it came from where this album came from. Get a grip. "Still tryin' to get to heaven before they close the door." He's just as earnest and as brilliant as he ever was. How's your listening?

By the way, although the title phrase, "time out of mind," can be traced to Shakespeare (*Romeo and Juliet*) or Cervantes (chapter 1 of *Don Quixote*), the most likely source in this case (ironic, given the banter about reading women writers) is Edna St. Vincent Millay, "Dirge Without Music" (1928): "I am not resigned to the shutting away of loving hearts in the hard ground. So it is, and so it will be, for so it has been, time out of mind."

Gosh. Now I've been listening for two weeks, not steadily but in the cracks of my typically busy late-1990s everyday life. Waiting, since I wrote the above, for a day when I could truly clear my own schedule and just talk with you (whoever may be reading) about these thoughts and feelings that keep coming to me in response to the arrival (and presence) in my life of *Time Out of Mind*. "And I don't know" (he said lustily) "how much longer I can wait."

This entire album is one song. I would argue strongly that every one of these songs fits into the meta-work at least as brilliantly and consciously as the individual pieces that make up *Blood on the Tracks*. Whew. Does this ambitious work have a message? Yes, absolutely. But exactly as in the glory days three decades back, that message is specific to every listener. Fill in the blanks yourself. Try to resist filling 'em in! The music and the language of this album are so seductive you'll find them speaking to you even as your conscious mind resists and maybe (as has happened to a few friends of mine already) dreams up some clever arguments as to why this isn't really your cup of tea. Smells funny. Well, friends, isn't that the way the folkies felt in 1965? Isn't that the way lots of true-fans-till-now felt when *Slow Train Coming* came? How about that Bob Dylan?? He's upset the applecarts of his faithful once again! True, only a few of my friends are grumbling; more of those who are listening to this pre-release circulating tape and commenting on the Internet or over the phone are enthusiastic. But most of us, I think, are at some moment or other genuinely and rather personally challenged by what *Time Out of Mind* is saying to us during this first month that we've taken the beggar into our homes and minds. Hey, my apples are rolling down my inner street in different directions! Thanks, friend.

In my lifetime and cultural milieu, the arrival of a major new album by Bob Dylan has been a shared event, something to talk about, something that connects us or (in some cases) disconnects us. A few quotes from my mail (already!, becuz of the Internet) that I like and heartily endorse: "My initial impression is that *Time Out of Mind* is a major Dylan album, which deserves to be treated at the same level of seriousness and artistic accomplishment as, say, *Blonde on Blonde* or *Blood on the Tracks*" – Stephen Scobie, British Columbia. "The album is also like a website full of hyper-text-links to the history of blues and folk, with lots of references all the way" – Johnny Borgan, Norway. "Every second line sounds like a fucking classic to me. Fascinating alternation between moving lines and hilarious ones ... surely this is his most humorous album since *Another Side*" – Imre Salusinszky, Australia. "It seems to put me someplace, if I listen to it without being interrupted, that I can't really put a handle on yet. It's not bad it's not good it's not depressed or even overjoyed. But definitely somewhere out there, kinda a strange mood that I can't describe" – David Johnson, Iowa.

Thanks, friends. And then there's Greg Kot, whose review in *Rolling Stone* I must take issue with, even though he praises the album and does articulate some good insights (i.e. ones I agree with). I don't like the idea that some of the millions who read *RS* and naturally look to it for a sense of "how is the world reacting to this new Dylan CD?" will have their experience of the album, this new moment of intimacy with a powerful contemporary artist, shaded by what this reviewer hears (and hey, he's got a right, the songs are constructed so we're encouraged to make of them whatever we will, a kind of Rorschach test) as the message of *Time Out of Mind*. I can't deny that the lyrics Kot quotes are evocative and memorable and accurately quoted. I just have to deal with my own irrational suspicion that every rock critic/journalist wants to establish his or her superiority to this Bob Dylan guy whenever they write about him. So anyway, Kot says, "On *Time Out of Mind* Dylan paints a self-portrait with words and sound that pivots around a single line from the album's penultimate song, "Can't Wait": 'That's how it is when things disintegrate.'" Later, he closes his review by describing the voice of Bob Dylan 1997 as "a voice that is confident of only one thing: 'When you think you've lost everything, you find out you can lose a little more.'"

Okay. And I can't really disagree when Kot says of the persona speaking in *Time Out of Mind*: "He projects the unease of someone adrift in a world that he ceases to understand and that has ceased to understand him." It's just that I would like it better (and this has to do with my ideas of what journalism should and shouldn't be, which ideas are out of step not just with *Rolling Stone* but with almost all commercial magazines and newspapers) if the reviewer would say something like: "Dylan brilliantly and imaginatively and with very skillful wordplay creates a new, 1990s 'outsider' character who feels adrift in a world that he ceases to understand and that has ceased to understand him. Kinda like I feel these days, and maybe you too." I am defensive, in other words, about the possible implication in the review that Dylan himself is out of touch and not as confident a voice as he was back in the good old days. I disagree! (I recognize I'm disagreeing with something I thought I read, not necessarily what the writer is saying.) To me, the most striking thing about *Time Out of Mind* is the enormous artistic confidence of the songwriter, bandleader, and singer. Wow. If this is how it is when things disintegrate, I'll have some of what he's having.

And anyway, the line which I would audaciously claim the album pivots around, is the six words that begin the last couplet of the epic poem that closes the song cycle, to me an obviously intentional sequel to the first eight words of "All Along the Watchtower": THERE'S A WAY TO GET THERE. Yeah, the character in the songs often reports that he's disoriented and distressed. But he also announces, in the first words of *Time Out of Mind*, "I'm walking," further asserts in the second song, "gonna keep on walking," and finally ends with the playful, gently self-mocking assertion that he's going to somehow figure out how to get to this place he keeps longing for. And, trumping that, he adds that he's already there in his mind, "and that's good enough for now." Is this the statement of a depressed man? Hell no, it's the proclamation of a happy man who even feels free enough to talk about and make fun of his own depressive moments. I woulda always said that a general message to be found in Bob Dylan's works is: "Personal freedom brings happiness." How delightful that he still says so, and how unsettling that we still need to hear it. And how marvelous that, on the evidence of this work of art, Mr. D. now feels so friendly towards and respectful of his imagined audience once again. Kot does say something in his review about Dylan seeming to be speaking not only to a distant lover but to "a long-departed audience." Good insight. I believe most Dylan love songs can be partly understood as being spoken to the persons he's actually speaking (singing) to, his immediate or projected audience (i.e., "It Ain't Me Babe," "Seeing the Real You at Last"). But I'm still fighting my strange defensive battle against the possibility that the words "long-departed audience" could be read as confirmation that *Rolling Stone* in its pop youth culture wisdom regards Bob Dylan as something of a has-been. Sorry. And so I just want to say that Dylan's immense playfulness and intelligence here, and his freewheelin' references to the history of blues and his own history as an artist, as if the people listening were sharp enough and attentive enough to pick up on all this stuff (even the sly little vocal and rhythm-section tricks) ... this is the very essence of the self-confident artist, as defined for our era by Bob Dylan in 1965 and 1966. Let's save our pity then, for the audience if it's so over-the-hill that it wouldn't know a real Dylan album from a fake one if it tripped over it. Um ... This is not an expression of depression. Like good uptempo blues performances, this album and this song-cycle are an expression of joy in the face of hard times.

He's not just saying he needs a shot of love. Slyly, he offers one, paradoxically wrapped in statements like, "I'm sick of love! I hear the clock tick." The lyrics can't help but suggest that the speaker is saying he's sick of life. Shocking stuff. And yet, that's not the felt message.

Listening to this album is like getting fairly close to the singer (first few rows) at almost any show (or every other one) in the last few years, and seeing the joy on his face and in his movements. He's having *so much fun*. On that stage. And here, on this digital-recording stage. This new installment of the diary of the poet-observer-lover-performer. Yeah, I did say the form is fiction. An invented story. That's the (very impressive) writing technique. But the *performance* of this fiction speaks with the kind of immediacy and authenticity that first endeared most of us to this artist. As autobio-graphical as "Desolation Row" and "It's Alright, Ma" and "Hard Rain." The man has stayed true to his method, and speaks to us from his heart from start to finish of this opus. And maybe you can't paraphrase the message you hear, but you sure can *feel* it. If you dare to listen and open your heart to this ragged and dirty charac-ter. (As my friend M. Matos pointed out on first listen to the first four songs, "Ragged and Dirty" is the theme song and probably proper name of this kind of music. "This kind of love! I'm so sick of it." But not this kind of music. I get the strong sense that I'll be happily listening to this album for the next six months, steadily walking in deeper, and finding new surprises. As David in Iowa said, the kind of music that puts you someplace, somewhere out there. "I'm already there in my mind. And that's good enough for now." Somehow this reminds me of the *feel* of "Mr. Tambourine Man." The jingle-jangle morning. The highlands. My heart's in 'em both, especially when I listen to this particular ragged clown.)

Some comments that I imagine will be helpful to anyone wrestling with the truth/fiction riddle or other questions related to the iden-tity of the characters and speakers in the *Time Out of Mind* songs:

> Bob Dylan to Jonathan Cott, Sept. 1978: "I've heard it said that Dylan was never as truthful as when he wrote *Blood on the Tracks*, but that wasn't necessarily truth it was just perceptive. Or when people say Sara was written for 'his wife Sara' – it doesn't necessarily have to be about her just because my wife's name happened to be Sara. Anyway, was it the real Sara or the Sara in the dream? I still don't know." Cott (in response to a comment about "Is Your Love in Vain?"): "Is that the kind of woman you're looking for?" Dylan: "What makes you think I'm looking for any woman?" Cott: "You could say that the song isn't necessarily about you, yet some people think that you're singing about yourself and your needs." Dylan: "Yeah, well, I'm everybody anyway."

One of the things that "everybody" seems to have done in recent years, which resonates loudly and with fine, non-preachy humor in this group of songs, is to stop imbibing alcohol and other intoxicants. A couple of years ago, around the time this album is believed to have been written, its author boasted to friends that he'd been "clean and sober" for two years now. This (rather universal) biographical circumstance is illuminating in reference to lines like (from the end of "Not Dark Yet") "Every nerve in my body is so vacant and numb./I can't even remember what it was I came here to get away from." Sounds like a bar song, sketched from memory perhaps, like 1978's "I think we better talk this over/Maybe when we both get sober." And lines like "I can't wait, wait for you to change your mind/It's late, and I'm tryin' to walk the line ... The air burns, and I'm tryin' to think straight." So many fine lines (that keep me searching for a heart of gold in the highlands).

Oh hell. Had I space enough and time, I could talk about this album for weeks. True, he does sing, in the luminous closing lines of "Highlands": "There's less and less to say." Yet, again paradoxically, I find myself with so much to say about this album. Probably because its author seems to have so many things to say to me here and now, as on other beloved and now-legendary BD records. For example, in this same verse there's a particularly luminous line which strikes me as the one moment on the album that could be heard as a commentary on his career: "The sun is beginning to shine on me/But it's not like the sun that used to be." As he sings it, the first part sounds very positive, relieved, and the second part sounds like a good-humored and quite humorous mocking of his role as ex-hero. Funny how "Days That Used to Be" is the name of the song Neil Young (who of course gets a namecheck on this album) wrote as a kind of letter to Bob Dylan. After "used to be," Bob says, "The party's over/And there's less and less to say/I got new eyes, everything looks far away." Sounds like the voice of his generation (persons born in the 1940s), doesn't he?

I do wanna share with you some of the evidence that backs up my assertion that this entire album is constructed as a conscious song cycle. For example: the first words of the album, "*I'm walking*," are quickly echoed in the second song ("gonna walk down that dirt road") and in the first words of the third song, "I'm walking through the summer nights." And this repetition is not careless but quite agile, images and moods building on themselves almost impressionistically from song to song. The whole image of the speaker walking is dramatically turned around in the chorus image of that third song, "You left me standing in the doorway crying." Fourth song: "I try to get closer but I'm still a million miles from you." Movement and distance continue to be central in song five: "I've been walking through the middle of nowhere/Trying to get to heaven before they close the door." By the way, notice how this line could evoke a well-known Bob Dylan song, "Knockin' on Heaven's Door"? That's only fair, because a lot of other songs (mostly folk and blues) get evoked in the course of the next few stanzas: "I've been walking that lonesome valley." "Going down the road feeling bad." "Going down to New Orleans." "I've been all around the world boys." "Some trains don't pull no gamblers, no midnight ramblers like they did before." It's like he's living in a garden built of folksong lyrics.

And there's lots more threads connecting these eleven songs. Find your own, it's fun. The most obvious is that every one of these songs is about a love relationship, seemingly the same relationship (with the exception of "Highlands" because the protagonist doesn't get close enough to the antagonist in the long narrative section for her to possibly be the female whose loss or distance is bemoaned in the other tunes, except in the one interesting sense that Dylan again suggests to us on this album, as in *Renaldo & Clara*, that all the women in a man's life can be seen by him as the separate manifestations of one Woman who is present throughout his life). The most powerful threads connecting the songs may be musical ones: the reference to Elvis's Sun sessions in the sound of "Dirt Road Blues" is quite appropriate, as Dylan's mix of blues, r&b, folk, and country on *Time Out of Mind* is very much an exploration of the ground that Elvis and band staked out on their astonishing first single, "That's All Right" backed with "Blue Moon of Kentucky." Then how marvelous to realize that the sound of "Million Miles" is built around some kinda organ played by Auggie Meyers who as a member of Texas' Sir Douglas Quintet was responsible for that great organ sound on "She's About a Mover" that Dylan like me fell in love with the first time he heard it on the radio in 1965. And ... Hey, every song on this album has its own great and unique sound, and all eleven of 'em talk to each other musically, and sweetly and evocatively and hilariously.

*   *   *

I feel inadequate (displaced) (got a low-down feeling). I have to wrap up this essay soon, and I fear it's gonna be too long and too short both at once. Too short because there are so many songs here that I love (eleven), and I want to say *a lot* about the words and sound and vocal & ensemble performance of every one of them. Maybe someday ...

Every one of these songs and performances on *Time Out of Mind* deserves a champion, and I guess it's a knights-and-damsels thing, I want to demonstrate (energetically) to each song how much I care about it. Hey, I'm driven by my hormones – it's a man thing, okay? "I'd go hungry I'd go black and blue, I'd go crawling down the avenue. No, there's nothing that I wouldn't do, to make you feel my love." Guys are supposed to deliver something, and their fulfillment comes from knowing it's been received. The romantic urge. How we're wired.

Um, what I kinda wanna do is rave on for many sentences about specific moments of Bob Dylan's singing on this album, and the way (as on *Blood on the Tracks* and *Blonde on Blonde* and *Highway 61 Revisited* and *John Wesley Harding*) he uses his voice to give overtones and nuance and often a unique character to words and phrases, so they come to mean more than they might if you only encountered them on a page – the singing gets feelings across that enhance and often contradict what the words say (or would have said, without the music and the singing). "Meantime life outside goes on all around you" ("It's Alright, Ma"). "Some things last longer than you think they will" ("Cold Irons Bound").

But since I find myself quoting "Make You Feel My Love," what I have to do now is protect a damsel from a dragon. Greg Kot in the lead record review (paired with the Stones) in the 10/2/97 *Rolling Stone*, says, "Only 'Make You Feel My Love,' a spare ballad undermined by greeting-card lyrics, breaks the album's spell." I don't agree, sir (but you're not alone, I've heard from at least two Dylan fans who find this song lyrically inferior. Of course, I suspect their real problem is that they gave in to the temptation to read the lyrics – available in connection with an already recorded Billy Joel cover version – before hearing the author sing 'em). For me, there is no track on the album that "breaks the spell," except in the positive sense that "Not Dark Yet" suddenly confronts the listener with a close-to-home personal issue that is more unsettling than hearing about someone else's hard-luck love affair. In a similarly favorable way, "Feel My Love" breaks the spell by being the least country-blues-based song here, more related to the side of Bob that likes to sing Gershwin and "We Three" – and, appropriately, by simultaneously stepping away from the oh-so-clever, playfully ironic and sometimes slapstick lyric-writing style of most of the other songs. But the ultimate effect is to strengthen the spell the whole record casts – this musical and verbal break is exactly in place, I find it refreshing when I hear it. I like the sound of his voice here and I relate to what I hear the singer/album-persona saying. Indeed, I think the total "fiction" would be missing something without this one clear statement of what the nature of the album-protagonist's longing is. In various songs he tells us it's about (a response to) her beauty. In some of the songs he also mentions memories of past closeness as part of what's driving him. But in "Make You Feel My Love" we get another side of this Joe Divorcée character who tells us his story all over this song cycle. What does he want from this woman, besides salvation or freedom? Here he gets down on his knees and I think it's quite an important scene in the whole diorama. Ultimately, if one is truly "sick of love," perhaps it would make sense to consider that only one of the causes of my suffering is your beauty and femaleness; another is my maleness. And by the way, I like these lyrics, they are no more or less "greeting card" than "Forever Young"; and sentiments like "I could offer you a warm embrace" and "when evening shatters and the stars appear" mean a lot to me when he sings them with his voice the way he does here on the second song of side two (think vinyl) of *Time Out of Mind*.

My other small disagreement with the *Rolling Stone* review – which I certainly appreciate for giving me a framework for a few comments that otherwise would have to be based on my awkward guesses as to where one of my readers might be hearing something different from what I hear on *Time Out of Mind* – is the way it strongly suggests, in its retelling of the "Highlands" narrative, that the singer is referring to the waitress character when he speaks of a "mangy dog." Well, I suspect the songwriter was aware that a listener could make that connection, more of his playfulness ... but I'm also sure that at this point we're in a post-narrative section of the song, bookended with the pre-narrative section, in which every verse is almost a long chorus, which takes place not in specific sequence to the restaurant scene but rather takes place in the I'm-walking-through-the-world environment of the rest of the album.

There's a real four-legged dog he's avoiding, those are real young men and women he's admiring (maybe walking in Boston Common, if you like to imagine we're still in Boston) and coyly suggesting he'd trade places with in a minute without specifying the gender of the ones he'd trade with. He is talking to himself in a monologue (which, charmingly, could be the text of this album), but not necessarily about the waitress. She's from a different scene. And now he's thinking about buying a coat. I myself first misinterpreted a later part of this verse, thinking someone asked him if he, Bob Dylan, registers to vote, definitely the sort of loaded question a fan with a political ax to grind might have come up with in the '60s or '70s.... Then I realized it's just part of a normal street scene, you're walking around and someone who wants a petition signed talks at you, "Are you registered?" Anyway, somehow the review makes it sound like the singer/character is glorying in his escape from the waitress. Maybe, but not necessarily. Remember, it's a Rorschach test.

This essay is too short because I haven't said anything about how much I love the sound and specific vocal moments (phrasings) of and in "'Til I Fell in Love with You" and "Can't Wait" and "Standing in the Doorway" and every one of the eight other stand-outs. And too long because there's too much here I want to talk about. Which reminds me, I feel like I've hardly even begun to quote favorite lyric/performance moments ("the last thing you said before you hit the street/'Gonna find me a janitor to sweep me off my feet'") (son of "Idiot Wind," "If You See Her ..."), nor have I really had a chance to catalogue moments when the writer/singer consciously and forthrightly refers to other songs he's written and sung: "I can hear the churchbells ringing in the yard/I wonder who they're ringing for." Presumably most listeners quickly hear a remembered voice singing, "for the blind and the dead, for all of us who are left ..." And how about: "I'm breathing hard, standing at the gate"? Right. Still carrying those drums, buddy?

Finally, since not everyone has a copy of Bartlett's *Familiar Quotations* at hand or informative Internet communiqués from Ron Mura in Boston town, I do want to mention here that Robert Burns published his poem "My Heart's in the Highlands" about 200 years ago ("My heart's in the Highlands, my heart is not here,/My heart's in the Highlands a-chasing the deer") and William Saroyan's play with that title (his first) debuted in 1939. Ron points out, as I suppose one must, that the Border Country is far from the

Highlands in actual Scotland, despite what Dylan says in his song, but of course the song is not about actual Scotland. It's more a sequel to John and Paul's "There's a Place."

Of course, I could go on and on. But I'll restrict myself to a final twit of the poor *Rolling Stone* guy, who says "When he recorded *Blood on the Tracks* Dylan was just entering middle age" – okay, I think only in the milieu of youth pop culture magazines is a man "middle-aged" at 33.

And then a footnote to a piece I wrote recently in which I rave about the tape of Dylan's superb April 1, 1997 show. My piece is called "Drivin' Me Insane," and starts with two of my favorite Dylan quotes, from 1963 and '65 ("Oh every thought that's strung a knot in my mind, I might go insane if it couldn't be sprung") ("I wake in the morning, fold my hands and pray for rain; I got a head full of ideas that are drivin' me insane"). Little did I know that he'd already written and recorded this 1997 lyric (from "Highlands"), just about his only overt reference to insanity in his songs since "Isis" ("what drives me to you is what drives me insane"): "Insanity is smashin' up against my soul." So you see, Mr. *Rolling Stone* etc., my point is that he was already feeling that way in 1963/65. Yes, this album is partly about getting older. But it's also a magnificent demonstration that he's still precisely the same tuned-in poet/ singer/visionary he always was. And if record sales and TV ratings don't offer evidence of his continued relevance and immediacy, you know what you can do with that stuff. And finally, finally, let me close with this quote my friend Bob gave me too late to stick on my new book *Love to Burn:* "I'm listening to Neil Young, I gotta turn up the sound. Someone's always yelling, 'turn it down!'"

Bob Dylan has once again given us a record to make the heart soar and make the neighbors shout. Turn it up! So it is, so it will be, and so it has been, time out of mind. Happy 1997.

VI. Golgonooza

May 2001 and "no time"

15.

[This essay/review of Dylan's then-new album was written in November 2001 and was published in *Crawdaddy!* and *On the Tracks* under the title "Stolen Kisses (Sweeter than Wine)."]

In the first *Performing Artist* book, I wrote: "Among other things, *Bringing It All Back Home* had a substantial effect on the language of a generation (if we recognize that language is made of phrases as well as words, and that a phrase that is repeated often in conversation and written communication will influence us not only by its content but by its form and style, the way it puts words together; this is so basic to the thought process that a handful of powerful phrases can actually affect the way people think in a particular culture at a particular time). Dylan like Benjamin Franklin can list among his many achievements the authorship of a remarkable number of successful aphorisms." I went on to cite "Even the president of the United States sometimes must have to stand naked," "Money doesn't talk, it swears," "He who is not busy being born is busy dying," etc. etc.

So suppose you were Bob Dylan and you read that, and

321

thought to yourself, "Wonder if I could do that again?" And supposin' you wanted to, how would you go about trying to write/record/perform a hot batch of fresh new, right-on-time, deathless language in, um, two-thousand-one? For sure, your action-steps would be primarily in the realm of what Carlos Castaneda's teacher Don Juan called "not-doing": you would *not* try to be relevant, not let yourself get caught trying to write a "Bob Dylan song," not pay any attention to thoughts that arise regarding the things you did and didn't do when you were writing and recording "It's Alright, Ma" and "Visions of Johanna," etc. Instead, you might think about language-makers you admire and are inspired by, like Shakespeare, Blake, Charley Patton, Big Joe Turner, Frank Sinatra and others. You would carefully *not* imitate them. Instead, grinning to yourself, you might proudly decide to be both the joker and the thief, and to dialogue between your selves all along that there watchtower till the cows came home, stealing from your heroes as well as from the most mundane, ordinary sources, as you've always done. As every old bluesman worth his salt has always done, musically and verbally. You'd decide to follow your heart and intuition and to put all your will power into *not* following your mind, in order to leave it wide open to whatever might want to jump into it.

And then you would let yourself be delighted by and really sink your teeth into what does jump in: "Well, I'm stranded in the city that never sleeps!" "Hmm," you congratulate yourself, "pretty good epigram for 21st Century Man" – and then you resolutely take care not to let that insight into the phrase have any influence on the content of the rest of the song. "Nah," you mutter, "I ain't gonna chase that. I'm just gonna be honest with me, that's the only way to do it." So you follow your intuitive storyline, and a couple moments later you hear your mouth saying, "Lot of things can get in the way when you're tryin' to do what's right." "Hmm," you think. "Sounds like the First Law or anyway a fundamental principle of Not-Doing." Then you resolutely ignore that thought, and let the language flow, go on with your storyline. "I'm not sorry for nothing I've done." Indeed. The rest of the couplet seems obvious, inescapable, just bubbles forth: "I'm glad I fought, I only wish we'd won." Then you hear yourself saying (and you hear the music along with it at the same time), "The Siamese twins are comin' to town ..." You love it. You sing it to yourself, you assemble your band, get them to start playing it before you even sing it to them.

Language. I've read close to a hundred reviews of *"Love And Theft"* by now, and yet Bob Dylan sums it up best, puts into words how I feel about this new and fabulous verbomusical experience. Says what I wanna say to you on this 7th day of November, 2001: "I know a place where there's still somethin' going on." Yeah! Wow. He does, when so few seem to, and he takes me there. Over and over, whenever I listen to this album. And now I too know such a place, thank you very much. And then how about this (not just the words but the sound of his voice and the music that floats around it) as a description of the *L&T* experience?: "Another one of them endless days ..." Oh yes.

It's such a listenable record. The sound, the melodies, the feel, the variety, the connectedness of it all. Each song, I find myself lingering in the car or wherever it's playing so I can hear it to the end. I get caught by each of 'em again and again in quite a number of pleasing and satisfying ways. And like I say, I like the wholeness, the connectedness, of the album, the way it all hangs together and becomes a single experience, single narrative, in some mysterious and pleasing way that's not easily pointed to or articulated.

I like the echoes. Lots of musical ones, of course, but I'm thinking of the lyrical echoes, the recurring phrases and themes. Whether done consciously or unconsciously, this is a great technique for turning a bunch of seemingly disconnected word-bursts into something that feels meaningful as a whole in, again, very mysterious and satisfying ways. Some examples:

First of all, the perspective of being on a boat. This is overt (the title) in "Floater": "From the boat, I fish for bullheads." "A squall is setting in. Sometimes it's just plain stupid to get into any kind of wind." But as we let all these songs wash over us, we also hear: "I came ashore in the dead of the night" ("Honest with Me") and "My ship's been split to splinters and it's sinking fast" ("Mississippi") and "Throw your panties overboard" ("High Water") and "The fog's so thick you can't spy the land" ("Summer Days") and "My captain he's decorated" ("Lonesome Day Blues") and "They're making a voyage to the sun" ("Tweedle Dee & Tweedle Dum") and "I'll take you 'cross the river, Dear" ("Moonlight"). *Rivers* is a whole other theme and set of echoes: "I crossed that river just to be where you are" ("Mississippi") and "Standin' by God's river my soul's beginning to shake" ("Summer Days") and "They went down the Ohio,

the Cumberland, the Tennessee, all the rest of them rebel rivers"
("Floater").

We hear these echoes much as the album's narrator keeps
listening for footsteps, and tries to make out what the wind is whis-
pering. "I'm preaching the word of God, I'm puttin' out your eyes."
("High Water") "I'm preaching peace and harmony ... yet I know
when the time is right to strike." ("Moonlight") Was that the same
guy talking? Possibly the same guy who does sort of preach near the
end of "Sugar Baby"? – "Look up, look up, seek your Maker, 'fore
Gabriel blows his horn." Often the echoes just seem a reflection of
the way this character or this singer likes to talk: "I never slept with
her even once" ("Lonesome Day Blues.") "I've never seen him
quarrel with my mother even once" ("Floater"). "I'm telling myself
I've found true happiness" ("Bye and Bye"). "I tell myself I could be
happy forever with her" ("Floater"). "I can't tell my heart that
you're no good" ("Honest with Me").

Some echoes seem deliberately thematic: "Why don't you
break my heart one more time, just for good luck?" ("Summer
Days") "To break a trusting heart like mine was just your style"
("Cry a While"). "Your charms have broken many a heart and
mine is surely one" ("Sugar Baby"). Others might be unconscious
or Freudian: "My pa he died and left me ... My brother ... My
sister ..." ("Lonesome Day Blues") "My old man, he's like some
feudal lord ... My grandfather ... My grandmother ..." ("Floater")
"My mother was the daughter of a wealthy farmer ... My father ...
My uncle ..." ("Po' Boy").

And all of them ring together and add to the musicality and
coherent flavor of *"Love And Theft"*, this musically and lyrically dis-
jointed yet marvelously homogenous work of music and language
and performance.

These bits of information (or deliberate misinformation?) about
the making of *"Love And Theft"* have trickled through: it was recorded
in two weeks in May '01 in a studio in midtown Manhattan, with
Dylan's touring band (the lineup that has been with him for the last
two years: Larry Campbell, guitar, violin, banjo, mandolin; Charlie
Sexton, guitar; Tony Garnier, bass; David Kemper, drums) plus
keyboard player Auggie Meyers, produced by Dylan and recorded
and mixed by Chris Shaw. Much of the writing was done at the
sessions. Meyers told *Rolling Stone*: "Dylan would fool around for a
while with a song, then we'd cut it. And he'd say, 'I think I'm gonna

write a couple more verses,' sit down and write five more verses. Each verse had six or eight lines. It's complicated stuff, and he was doing it right there." The songs were mostly recorded live, with minimal overdubs.

At a press conference in Rome in July, Dylan was asked if the lines "I wish my mother was still alive" ("Lonesome Day Blues") and "My mother died" ("Po' Boy") were inspired by the death of his mother last year. "Probably," he said slowly. "I can't understand how it couldn't be like that. Many of these songs were written in some kind of stream-of-consciousness kind of mood, and I don't sit and linger, meditate on every line afterwards. My approach is just to let it happen and then reject the things that don't work."

Also at that press conference, when asked, "How do you go about writing?" he said, "I have so many ways that I can't talk about any one in particular. I take notes. I retrieve them. I pull ideas together. There are lots of ways." And a few moments later: "I don't sit down to write. My lines go into songs and they have a certain structure. They have to conform to an idiom that has an established form. They're not free-form and there's no point trying to throw in some ideological idea. It doesn't interest me at all. It can't be done in a song."

Yet in late September Dylan told Mikal Gilmore, in an interview for *Rolling Stone*, "The whole album deals with power ... the album deals with power, wealth, knowledge and salvation – the way I look at it. If it's a great album – which I hope it is – it's a great album because it deals with great themes. It speaks in a noble language. It speaks of the issues or the ideals of an age in some nation, and hopefully it would also speak across the ages."

If some of these comments seem contradictory, it might help to know that Dylan in July followed up "there's no point trying to throw in some ideological idea" by saying, "I've never intentionally started out with that in mind." So although ideology is "a systematic body of concepts about human life or culture," Dylan isn't telling Gilmore he intended to write songs about power or about the ideals of an age. He's saying that's what this group of songs seems to him to be about now that they've written themselves. He did also tell Gilmore, "A song is just a mood that an artist is trying to convey."

Dylan has told us in past interviews that his best songs have come to him very quickly, and seemingly out of the air. Where does a saxophone or trumpet solo come from during a jazz band

performance? Certainly not from thinking, or some kind of pre-
meditation. It's a kind of art that arises spontaneously in response to
a flow of conversation between co-creators (musicians), and that
draws on all of the life experience and idiosyncrasies and listening
experiences and awarenesses of the horn player or the poet/story-
teller/troubadour. So I (inevitably) see the writing of the *"Love And
Theft"* songs as a performance. A language-master conveying a
mood, a set of moods, in collaboration with other music-makers in a
spirit of passionate interest in expressing what it's like to stand here
in this skin at this historical and personal moment. "Hopefully, it
would speak across the ages," Dylan blurted out to Gilmore. "It'd
be as good tomorrow as it is today and would've been as good
yesterday. That's what I was trying to make happen...."

Performance implies and requires audience. As I am presently
engaged in trying to write a massive work of scholarship (*Bob Dylan –
Mind Out of Time*) which argues that Dylan as an artist sees himself as
a mind, a consciousness, unfettered by human notions of time ... I
am of course encouraged in my madness by this further evidence that
Bob Dylan as a performer aspires to speak to (and exchange sly
in-jokes with) an audience of peers and contemporaries-in-timelessness like Shakespeare, Charley Patton, Jesus, Charlie Sexton, and
possibly your and my great-grandchildren. Nevertheless here we are
in this songwriter's own lifetime and historical era, and what are we
supposed to make of *"Love And Theft"*?

To further complicate matters, Dylan told Edna Gundersen of
USA Today just before *"Love And Theft"* came out, "I've never
recorded an album with more autobiographical songs." Gilmore
followed this up: "In a recent interview you said that you saw this
album as autobiographical." Dylan replied, "Oh, *absolutely*. It would
be autobiographical on every front." This means one thing to a
listening public who've tended to wonder whether "Queen Jane
Approximately" is about Joan Baez ... Will they (we) interpret
Dylan's "autobiographical" comments to mean that he evidently
has been through some epochal flood ("high water everywhere")
we're not aware of? Or that he really is "here to create the new
imperial empire" and intends to "establish my rule through civil
war"? Certainly they won't be far off if they assume that he's
expressing his own convictions when he sings, "There ain't no limit
to the amount of trouble women bring." And if they (we) have often
told themselves they love Bob Dylan's work because he speaks their

own feelings and experiences with such uncanny accuracy, how will they (I) come to terms with the just-quoted statements?

First we might wanna ask ourselves what the word "autobiographical" means to Bob Dylan. The next sentence he said to Gundersen was, "This is the way I really feel about things." And then: "It's not me dragging around a bottle of absinthe and coming up with Baudelairean poems. It's me using everything I know to be true." And his next sentences to Gilmore: "It obviously plays by its own set of rules, but a listener wouldn't really have to be aware of those rules when hearing it. It's not like the songs were written by some kind of Socrates, you know, some kind of buffoon, the man about town pretending to be happy [laughs]." Okay, scratch Socrates and Baudelaire. Translation: this album isn't about who *you* think Bob Dylan is! It's about (he asserts, with a twinkle in his ever-evasive eyes), the *real* Bob Dylan. Many would agree that one of the most obviously wonderful couplets on the album is, "They've got Charles Darwin trapped out there on Highway 5; Judge says to the high sheriff, 'I want 'im dead or alive.'" Your assignment for tonight, class, is to write a paragraph about what this tells us about how Bob Dylan really feels about things. Have fun. And don't be too distracted by the fact that the day after this album came out, the president of the United States used the judge's very words in reference to some new demonic celebrity and evolutionary instrument.

The first thing I was going to say about this album, months ago when I first started contemplating this review-essay, was that it's a Rorschach test, an inkblot that provides a portrait of its observer via whatever he or she sees in it. Then I noticed, because I had to proofread a book in which the article is reprinted, that I said the same thing when I reviewed *World Gone Wrong* in 1993, and further asserted that in this respect *WGW* "fits the classic concept of a new Dylan album." This says something about me, I suppose, but also about who Bob Dylan has been for those of us who've been the immediate audience of his new albums during his and our lifetimes. There was an era, famously, when a whole international generation found out who they were by the patterns their psyches perceived, individually and collectively, in Dylan's new batches of song-performances. That era is gone, but this artist's peculiar power is not. And because this happens to be *this* era, I had it called to my attention via a news item and link on bobdylan.com that I could read (and even print, which I did) 171 short reviews that a cross-section of listeners, not journalists or professional critics, had written about *"Love And Theft"* for the "Customer Reviews" section of the Amazon.com retail book and record website. Yikes! Not just the inkblot but an instant glimpse into the psyche of "us." "I can see what everybody in the world is up against. One day you'll open up your eyes [the Prophet spake] and you'll see where you are. Sugar Baby get on down the road...."

Some people hated the album, of course. Most were very enthusiastic, for many different reasons, not like a consensus but more like an off-the-wall collective portrait (collage) of the issues and ideals of an age in some nation or network of nations. Maybe those reviews should be archived somewhere. There's lots of poetry in them: "Dylan's contribution to the world of art can NOT be understated. *"Love And Theft"* finds him as edgy, obtuse, wise, and downright enthralling as ever. His facility with multilayered phrase-ology and his innate understanding of how to use music to deliver a vision of humanity that is timeless blows me away every time I listen to him. Dylan's music is so real, you can feel it." – Greg Martin, Missoula, Montana.

And I was delighted by those who made connections for me, sharing and furthering the process of discovery. Phil Teece of Wanniassa, Australia, spotted this wonderful trans-album echo: "In his liner notes for *The Songs of Jimmie Rodgers: A Tribute* in 1997, Bob wrote: 'Jimmie Rodgers of course is one of the guiding lights of the 20th century whose way with song has always been an inspiration to those of us who followed the path.... his voice gives hope to the vanquished and humility to the mighty.' NB 'I'm going to teach peace to the conquered/I'm going to tame the proud' – 'Lonesome Day Blues.'" Wonderful, Phil and Bob!

So what do I hear on *"Love And Theft"*? *Lots* of very good singing and very good music-making and a thousand instants of delightful phrasing and um, a house of inkblot mirrors to get joyously (and sometimes terrifyingly) lost in. Some days I'm discovering I love the sound and every line of "Floater" or of "Honest with Me" even more than I thought I did. Other days I'm noticing I still am thor-oughly delighted by all of "Summer Days" even though I have a low tolerance for Dylan uptempo kitchen-sink jump-shuffle numbers like most live versions of "Everything Is Broken" and "Highway 61." But "Summer Days" seems to me to break the mold, musically and lyrically and attitudinally fresh in ways that never stop tickling me.

And, um, the album sequence is as rich and pleasing as we came to expect in the glory days of rock albums in the late '60s and early '70s. Always a pleasure and often a surprise that "Mississippi" comes just when it does and that "High Water" makes such an extraordinary bridge between "Floater" and "Moonlight" and in turn that those two bookend that masterpiece so effectively. And "Po' Boy" sounding so perfect after "Honest with Me"; and the great satisfaction of "Sugar Baby" at the end even though one can then ache at the silent implications of this message stood up against "Where Are You Tonight?" or "Sara" or even "Sad Eyed Lady of the Lowlands" ...

And so forth. And though I apologize for what an infodump this essay has turned out to be, my own sense of the needs of my imagined audience (some of you on expectingrain.com every night but others not even wired, and a few hopefully somewhere across the ages) presses me to pass on to you some of the less-obvious-than-Romeo-and-Juliet-and-Othello "thefts" that I am happy were passed on to me by friends and strangers the world over. There are many, of course, and keep in mind that these songs were written quickly, parts in the recording studio, rather than late at night in some Malibu mansion room with reference books cracked open and pored over ... which is to say, speaking of infodumps, "I need a dump truck mama to unload my head" was certainly autobiographical and hasn't seemed to change as those much-abused brain cells have grown older.

"Bye and Bye": "Well I'm scufflin' and I'm shufflin' and I'm walkin' on briars/I'm not even acquainted with my own desires." William Blake, "The Garden of Love" (1794): "I saw it was filled with graves/And tombstones where flowers should be/And priests in black gowns were walking their rounds/and binding with briars my joys and desires."

Okay, that's an obscure reference rather than a theft. Here's another – not obscure, but it helped me to have it pointed out. "Tweedle Dee & Tweedle Dum": "Livin' in the Land of Nod/Trusting their fate to the hands of God." *Genesis*, 4:16: "And Cain went out from the presence of the Lord, and dwelt in the land of Nod, on the east of Eden."

You've probably already heard that Charley Patton recorded his own "High Water Everywhere," parts one and two, in Grafton, Wisconsin around October 1929; and of course Dylan does

dedicate his song to CP, and even said in the Rome press conference: " *"Love And Theft"* is not an album I've recorded to please
myself. If I really wanted to do that, I would record some Charley
Patton songs." But did you know, and would you believe, that the
haunting penultimate words of "Sugar Baby," "Look up, look up,
seek your Maker, 'fore Gabriel blows his horn," are taken verbatim
from a song sung by Frank Sinatra called "The Lonesome Road"?
And that Sinatra also recorded a song called "I Cried for You (Now
It's Your Turn to Cry Over Me)"?

There's lots more, of course. One subtle one that I noticed
myself is the nod to Bo Diddley as a source of the rather special
sound of "Tweedle Dee & Tweedle Dum" when Dylan sings, "My
pretty baby, she's looking around" in the last verse, a phrase and a
way of talking taken from Bo's first hit, the song "Bo Diddley." I
also recently stumbled on this precursor to "I'm staying with Aunt
Sally [of course, many have noted the *Huckleberry Finn* allusion], but
you know she's not really my aunt" ("Sugar Baby"): "He's not really
my uncle." "They never are." – dialog from the 1990 film *Pretty
Woman*.

One that I wouldn't have known without help from my fellow
L&T annotators is that the "Only one thing I did wrong/Stayed in
Mississippi a day too long" chorus of "Mississippi" is borrowed from
a folk song called "Rosie" recorded in the field and transcribed in a
book by Alan Lomax. The rest of Dylan's song seems to be his own
invention.

And because I absolutely love the couplet from the first verse of
"High Water [For Charley Patton]" (possibly my favorite moment
on the whole album, today anyway) "Big Joe Turner looking east
and west from the dark room of his mind/He made it to Kansas
City, Twelfth Street and Vine," I want to say that I don't know
whether Big Joe Turner ever recorded Wilbert Harrison's 1959 hit
"Kansas City" (which includes the phrase, "Twelfth Street and
Vine"), but that I did find out from *The Faber Companion to
20th-Century Popular Music* that Big Joe was born in KC and was a
bartender there in his youth, a factoid I imagine stuck in Dylan's
mind along with the familiar Harrison lyric and thus led by process
of free association to this magnificent couplet. And I also wanna
quote a sentence from the *Faber Companion* entry that strikes me as
relevant to the album at hand: "Turner did much to create the
jazz-blues singing style in which the voice is used less to narrate than

to contribute a quasi-instrumental melody strand to the orchestral texture."

Moving on from the endless footnoting the texts and musics of this album relentlessly invite, I've just encountered a fine comment on echoes in Dylan's 1978 album *Street-Legal*, by Jonathan Cott in his *Rolling Stone* interview/conversation with BD that year: "As in a dream lines from one song seem to connect with lines from another. For example: 'I couldn't tell her what my private thoughts were/ But she had some way of finding them out' in 'Where Are You Tonight?' and 'The captain waits above the celebration/Sending his thoughts to a beloved maid' in 'Changing of the Guards'." Dylan responds: "I'm the first person who'll put it to you and the last person who'll explain it to you. Those questions can be answered dozens of different ways, and I'm sure they're all legitimate. Everybody sees in the mirror what he sees – no two people see the same thing."

Thus: BD on the Rorschach test effect. A moment later in this conversation he provides another glimpse of what "autobiographical" might or might not mean to him: "I've heard it said that Dylan was never as truthful as when he wrote *Blood on the Tracks*, but that wasn't necessarily truth, it was just perceptive. Or when people say 'Sara' [on *Desire*] was written for 'his wife Sara' – it doesn't necessarily have to be about her just because my wife's name happened to be Sara. Anyway, was it the real Sara or the one in the dream? I still don't know."

No two people seeing the same thing is an exciting and scary aspect of this album, *"Love And Theft"*, made up of quickly written and sometimes improvised songs that may be soliloquies from all sorts of invented characters in other places and times, or may be autobiographical confessions or outbursts, or may be almost random (but brilliant) lines ad-libbed to conform to a musical idiom that has an established form and structure. Depending on who's listening. "Those questions can be answered dozens of different ways."

Just to be honest, or maybe to reassure you that you're not alone if you're not sure that you "get" several of these songs, I want to share with you three very articulate and appealing interpretations of *"Love And Theft"* songs that I'd like to embrace but can't manage to sell myself on. Not that I think these commentators are wrong. There are no correct or incorrect answers when it comes to interpreting inkblots.

First Bob Dylan himself on "Mississippi" (while explaining to David Fricke of *Rolling Stone* that he didn't include the song on *Time Out of Mind* because he was dissatisfied with the recording of it he made with Daniel Lanois at the 1997 sessions): "Polyrhythm has its place, but it doesn't work for knifelike lyrics trying to convey majesty and heroism." And "I tried to explain [to Lanois] that the song had more to do with the Declaration of Independence, the Constitution and the Bill of Rights than witch doctors. ... I thought too highly of the expressive meaning behind the lyrics to bury them in some steamy cauldron of drum theory. On the performance you're hearing [on *"Love And Theft"*], the bass is playing a triplet beat, and that adds up to all the multirhythm you need, even in a slow-tempo song."

Then my friend Dan Levy, in a "mailing list" discussion, on what he sees in the inkblot of "Bye and Bye": "In my opinion, that song is written from the point of view of a religious fanatic waiting for the second coming ... and that seeming throwaway line ['Well, I'm sitting on my watch so I can be on time'] is, in fact, straight from the mindset of one of those insincere ('sugarcoated rhyme') proselytizers who is on his watch, making sure he is on time when the messiah comes round once again....""

And, thirdly, Ben Clayton, talking to Alan Davis in an email correspondence published as an album review in *Isis* magazine: "For an example of the sheer mastery of production and voice in tandem, I'd point you at 'Sugar Baby.' Alan, I just can't get my head round the fact that you don't rate it that highly!! Listen to it closely, with no interruptions around you. Let it sink in and you'll discover a complete universe of human feeling and experience in the song. At least, that's what I get from it. Totally, totally perfect – a song you can *live* in, that stops time while it's playing, that opens all sorts of hidden secret doors ..."

"Mississippi" is a beautiful, powerful song, something of an anchor for the album. I can easily believe that the lyrics and the melody are intended to convey majesty and heroism. Dylan's performance of the song gets these feelings across with a lot of charm and humor and empathy. But try as I may, I can't find in the lyrics anything suggesting the song might have something to do with the Declaration of Independence and the Bill of Rights. And I flatter myself that I'm sensitive to this side of Dylan's work – when *John Wesley Harding* came out, I called my review "God Bless America" as my way of acknowledging the shocking (to a hip young Dylan fan in early '68) message I was hearing in some of the songs. And the first time I heard "Tears of Rage" ("We carried you in our arms on Independence Day/And now you'd throw us all aside and put us on our way") I felt and identified with the speaker's love for the America of Jefferson and colleagues, and his anguish at what it had become. "Why must I always be the thief?" indeed! "Oh what kind of love is this?" A song about love and theft, as you see. But listening to "Mississippi," I hear no clues to point me in any such direction. Only after reading Dylan's comments to Fricke about the song (and since when does Bob Dylan explain his own writings?) does it occur to me that the speaker could be Uncle Sam (cast by playwright Dylan into the role of riverboat gambler, the very character the singer himself seems to be portraying on the cover and sleeves of this album). So I imagine Dylan maybe years back hearing (or reading in Lomax's book) "Rosie," and thinking to himself that "only one thing I did wrong, stayed in Mississippi a day too long" could be the story of America and the tragedy of the Civil War less than a century after the glorious Revolution ... and resolving to write his own version of this folk song. So yes, I guess I can sell myself on the Dylan-talking-in-*Rolling-Stone* interpretation of this inkblot, but why couldn't he have just pointed me this way via a phrase like "Independence Day" or "Tom Paine, himself" somewhere in "Mississippi" itself instead of planting stories in the press?

I blush to say it took me more than a week after reading Dan's post about "Bye and Bye" (in response to other participants complaining about Dylan's corny puns throughout *"Love And Theft"*, including "I'm sitting on my watch....") before it occurred to me that he might be joking. I kept going back to "Bye and Bye" searching in its lyrics for the clues my friend must have found (and I overlooked) to Dylan's creation of a fictional religious fanatic narrator/ point of view. "Baptize you in fire," surely, but why is he so certain the guy's waiting for the Second Coming? A better question might be, why was I so ready to believe this really was my friend's opinion, and so slow to see his tongue in his cheek? Well, I think that throughout *"Love And Theft"* one gets the sense of hearing voices, and of thereby meeting and getting to know a whole batch of screwball characters whose identities can be deduced by the ways they speak and the things they talk about. "Some of these bootleggers, they make pretty good stuff" – must be a backwoods gentleman drinker speaking, probably in the Prohibition era. And also, I've noticed like other Dylan fans that he includes at least one old bluegrass song with a specifically religious message in all of his concerts for the past couple of years … and I know he was once quite fascinated with a book called *The Late Great Planet Earth* and its message that we are indeed living in the End Times. And I once had a friend, a science fiction novelist, Philip K. Dick, who peopled his novels with characters most of whom seemed to be extensions of various sides of his own personality. So I was very ready to believe that this "baptize you in fire" song could be Dylan playfully or fiendishly speaking through the mask of the "insincere proselytizer" side of himself. Similarly, like other friends of mine, I believed Dylan was singing "I'm not even familiar with my *old* desires," until I listened carefully and determined it really was "own"… I guess this was easy to hear and imagine because it seemed such a natural extension of various *Time Out of Mind* songs and themes. Anyway, the moral is: I'm philosophically against interpretation but in practice very ready and even eager to swallow any confidently delivered explanation of who is speaking in any of these new Dylan vignettes. I guess partly I do want them to be vignettes, fictions, and not the purely autobiographical accounts he keeps telling me they are via the media.

As for "Sugar Baby," I like it and find it rich and rewarding, but I'm not as crazy about it as Ben Clayton is, though I want to be – I'd love to "discover a whole universe of human feeling and experience" in the song and let it stop time for me. But so far, though I'm thrilled and delighted by Dylan's delivery of individual lines in "Sugar Baby" (the aforementioned "bootlegger" sentence, for example), something stops me from fully opening my heart to this track's "message." My problem is six words in the chorus (repeated four times): "You ain't got no brains nohow." I hunger to identify with this beguiling love song, but I can't think of a lover, past, present or imaginary, I'd want to say that to, or have that said to me by. The best I can do so far is notice that this phrase is an expression of the speaker's vulnerability, something he tells himself (and her) so he can possibly feel better about his weakness in the face of her charms, her power over him. The same is true, of course, of this character's memorable pronouncement: "There ain't no limit to the amount of trouble women bring." Sounds very genderist, but it's really a portrait of the speaker, another way of saying "I'm sick of love." You could change "women" to "that men" and have a woman (or a gay man) speaking. But I'm reminded unpleasantly of cultures where women are beaten or murdered for wearing clothing that reveals their femaleness. And one must also deal with the echoes of this sentiment throughout *"Love And Theft"*: "Keepin' away from the women, I'm givin' them lots of room" ("High Water"). "Some of these women they just give me the creeps" ("Honest with Me"). In any event, it's clear why Dylan says "the whole album deals with power." To the album's author (not just some odd character speaking in one particular song), it seems, love *is* theft because by its nature it creates an "other" and gives her (or him) the ability to steal one's power. " 'What happened to that poison wine?' 'I gave it to you, you drank it.' " "Juliet said back to Romeo, 'Why don't you just shove off if it bothers you so much?' " (A switch, because in this vignette we get to identify with and root for *her* instead of him.)

So recognizing what a po' boy the speaker in "Sugar Baby" is isn't quite enough to let me hear the song and its chorus as speaking for me. But here's another odd notion that might help a little. "Like a Rolling Stone" is certainly condescending towards the person being addressed, but all of us have had no trouble letting its chorus speak for the entity in ourselves that feels like it's on its own, with no direction home, etc. ... and I've long accepted that the writer of the song was primarily speaking to himself or a part of himself that, um, acts like it went to the finest schools. "Dead man, dead man, when will you arise?" is also a harsh thing to say to someone, and Dylan once mentioned in concert that he wrote that song while looking in a mirror. So, why don't I let myself hear "Sugar Baby" as being addressed to the speaker's (and therefore my) ego? "You went years without me [my true self and values], might as well keep going now ..." Get on down the road, charmer! Hmm. I think I like this spin.

But, you know, happiness can come suddenly, and leave just as quick. Any minute of the day, the bubble could burst and I could be back hearing "Sugar Baby" 's chorus as an expression of contempt for a life partner – which didn't bother me in "Idiot Wind," I think because he also acknowledged that *"we're* idiots, babe" and because it was in a dramatic context, an "autobiographical" story of loss. Context is everything, right? Greil Marcus in his *L&T* review in *The New York Times* reports that Dock Boggs, "a stone-faced singer from the Virginia mountains who first recorded in 1927," had a song called "Sugar Baby" which was "real killer-inside-me stuff; 'Sugar Baby' was what Boggs called his lover, who you weren't sure would survive the song." Creepy. So what was Bob Dylan, whose album "obviously plays by its own set of rules," hearing in his mind as he sang *his* response to (or variation on) Boggs? I don't know. Marcus does provide still another spin, suggesting that, listening to Dylan's performance, a person might suppose "Sugar Baby" is "the name of a horse." Right, further evidence that context is primarily provided by the listener. In this sense, it was *our* inspired and communal listening that made Dylan's spontaneous compositions so brilliant in the first place.

Can we do it again? Well, times have changed. But *"Love And Theft"*, remarkably, truly gives us the opportunity. See what can happen when a man finds a way to get back in touch with the free flow of music and language that is his God-given gift? According to *Time* magazine: "The veteran folk-rocker says his inspiration comes directly from God. 'I've had a God-given sense of destiny,' says Dylan. 'This is what I was put on Earth to do.'" Thus, if we choose to, we can recognize in a line from "Summer Days" the author/performer's autobiographical account of his joyful experience writing and recording this album: "Standin' by God's river, my soul's beginning to shake." As does mine, listening to *"Love And Theft"* at those moments when I happen to get outside of my head and its need to be aware of the rules and know the "intended" meanings of things. But anyway, forgive me for blurting out that in this context I hear the next line, "I'm countin' on you, Love, to give me a break," as addressed to God.

I also hear as autobiographical, in a similar way, "I keep listening for footsteps, but I ain't ever hearing any" ("Floater"). Reference: "I hear the ancient footsteps like the motion of the sea/Sometimes I turn, there's Someone there, other times it's only me" ("Every Grain of Sand").

Regardless of which song is your favorite on any given day (Alan Davis: " 'Mississippi' must be one of his very finest, ever ... Above all, the shifts of emphasis in the voice are breathtakingly sensitive – 'walking though the leaves/falling from the trees' – each syllable given additional meaning and feeling from the way it's sung/breathed"), the joy of *"Love And Theft"* is that, for so many of us, it is so rich in felt truths, brand new ones jumping out of any song almost any time we listen, or so it seems. If you're *not* listening for footsteps, you'll find you just can't stop hearing many many. Not-doing works for the listener as it did for the author and his collaborators. Bob Dylan let go and let God, this time, and my soul's beginning to shake, okay? I just wanna testify.

And because I can't stop quoting the collective consciousness I hear talking about and through this album, here's one more comment that delights me, from the Postscript to John Gibbens's excellent new book *The Nightingale's Code, A Poetic Study of Bob Dylan*: "When we speak of 'I' on this record [*L&T*], I think we'll have to see it as it was described on *Highway 61*: 'There is no eye, there is only a series of mouths.' Dylan has resurrected the persona of Everyman; where once he was a kind of cipher though, a wandering *anyone*, here he's become a streetful, a whole townful of people at once."

Amen. And yes, I do realize that Bob wasn't necessarily telling Lanois that "Mississippi" is *about* the Declaration of Independence and the Bill of Rights ... those might have been the only examples he could think of of the sort of historical majesty and heroism he perceived his song's hero's struggles and character as being expressive of. And, um, if you were a member of the band of musicians that did such superlative work at these sessions, it must have been nice to hear him say, "I got nothing but affection for all those who've sailed with me." Nice for us audience persons to hear also. Which sends me back to the Rome press conference. Dylan's comment "Absolutely. It is not an album I've recorded to please myself ..." was in response to the question "Is *"Love And Theft"* an album intended to conquer a new audience?" Which doesn't mean he no longer believes (per "Restless Farewell," 1963) "It's for myself and my friends my stories are sung." It's just that "a new audience" (including an old audience made new) is his current definition of "my friends," and the reason he doesn't stop recording and performing and energetically following his God-given sense of destiny. Tomorrow night, November 19, 2001, he'll play in New York City, and possibly he'll tell the concertgoers:

> "Well, I got here following the southern star.
> I crossed that river just to be where you are."

16.

After my *"Love And Theft"* review was published, I received a fascinating email letter from John Gibbens, author of *The Nightingale's Code, A Poetic Study of Bob Dylan*. He wrote:

"Your line, 'Dylan … aspires to speak to (and exchange sly in-jokes with) an audience of peers and contemporaries-in-timelessness … etc.' reminded me of a passage from Northrop Frye's magnificent book, *Fearful Symmetry: a study of William Blake*:

> All imaginative and creative acts, being eternal, go to build up a permanent structure, which Blake calls Golgonooza, above time, and, when this structure is finished, nature, its scaffolding, will be knocked away and man will live in it. Golgonooza will then be the city of God, the New Jerusalem which is the total form of all human culture and civilization. Nothing that the heroes, martyrs, prophets and poets of the past have done for it has been wasted; no anonymous and unrecognized contribution to it has been overlooked. In it is conserved all the good man has done, and in it is completed all that he hoped and intended to do. And the artist who uses the same energy and genius that Homer and Isaiah had will find that he not

only lives in the same palace of art as Homer and Isaiah, but lives in it at the same time."

Bingo! Thank you, John. So, "You want to live forever, right, Allen? Huh?" means, you want to live in the same palace of art as Homer and Isaiah. And "stopping time" presumably means, using the same energy and genius that Homer and Isaiah and Blake had. In your chosen art form(s). In order to enter and live in (and help build) the city of God. And presumably, going back to Dylan's 2001 interview with Mikal Gilmore quoted in the previous chapter, stopping time also means speaking across the ages (in a noble language). Dylan told Gilmore he had done that, or hoped he had done that, in *"Love And Theft"*, just as he told Ginsberg that he and his collaborators had stopped time in *Renaldo & Clara*. The important thing, of course, is not that the artist is boasting, but what he chooses to boast of … which tells us what he aspires to. ("My heart's in the Highlands – can't see any other way to go. There's a way to get there, and I'll figure it out somehow. But I'm already there in my mind. And that's good enough for now.")

APPENDIX I

The Roll of Honor

The researching and writing of this book was made possible by the generous financial support of the following individuals (and one foundation), who may be considered its co-authors. Readers who find something of value in this work should know that it could not have been written without the faith and participation of these good persons.

Benefactors:
Andy Hertzfeld
Robert A. Johnson
The Center for the Preservation of
    Modern History

Patrons:
Justin Bairamian
John Baldwin
Patrick B. Bauer
Stephen T. Bishop
Bennett Brier
Robert Brummer
Stephen Burton
Geoff Craig
The Dylan Pool
Maggie Flinn
Walker Forsyth
Ken Glance
Larry S. Greenfield
Robert Kavanagh
Paddy & Fiona Kelleghan
Steve Klemz
Alan G. Laughlin
Jonathan Lethem
Dan Levy
Maurice Moylett
Erik Nelson
New West Records
Brendan More O'Ferrall

Roland Pabst
William C. Parr
Michael Riccardi
Åke Rondin
Richard Rousseau
Jacob T. Sandoval
Gerhard Schinzel
Gary Schulstad
Dr. Wolfgang Schwass
Monika Sommer
Martin Sternstein
Marty Traynor
David van den Berg
James Whitworth
Mark Withrow
John Wraith & Mike Wyvill

Sponsors:
Watt. D. Alexander
Dana Alioto
Dr. Peter Allen
Sven Erick Alm
Douglas Bank
Kenneth Baroy
Carl Baugher
Carsten Baumann
Greg Berberich
Karin Berg
Olof Björner
Michael Brenner

David Bristow
Alessandro Cavazzuti
Sheila Clarke
Philip Cunningham
Judy Dardeck
Chris Davies
Klaus de Buhr
Timothy Dent
Peter Dixon
Mervyn Duddy
Victor Edmonds
John Faldborg
Andrea Falesi
Michelle Finlay
John C. Fischer
Christopher Gabb
Curt Gardner
David Ginsburg
Rebecca Haag
Peter Harrar
Jeremy Heist
Jim Heppell
John Hinchey
John Hume
Gene Interlandi
Peter Jesperson
Jeffrey K. Jones
James C. Klagge
Stephen Knowlton
Stephen J. Lamb
Bart Lazar
Dale Leopold
Jörgen Lindström
Rod MacBeath
Chrissy Marcum
Douglas Marklein
Alfred J. Masciocchi
John & Rita McCarthy
James McElwee
Ben Meltzer
Jami Morgan
Matt Morrison
William Nash
Michael Niebuhr
Rick Nielsen
Bob Palmer
Martyn Pass

Manfred Piltorp
Mel Prussack/The Dylan Shrine
Marty Revels (& the members of
    Small Talk)
Peter Rice
Craig F. Robieson
Steve Rostkoski
Tom & Thea Russell
Sy Safransky/*The Sun*
Lee Sargent
Varady Soma
Andrew Steed
Arnie Stodolsky
Jeff Taylor
Ira Transport
Nick Weinreb
Patrik Winquist
Jerry Withrow
Alice Young

Subscribers:
Frank Ahern
David Allen
Michael Anderson
Terry Baldwin
Michael Belke
Tom Bowles
Øyvind Brunvoll
Dr. Hanns Peter Bushoff
Dale Carter
Steven Castan
Lawrence Chalif
Adrian Childs-Clarke
Randal Churchill
Ken Cowley
Ken R. Crouch
Sebastian Cucullu
Michelle & Gary DeBeck
Thomas Deneke
Arie de Reus
Bob Edwards
Theodore Elliott
Dave Elworthy
Steve Farowich
Thomas Favata
Stephan Fehlau
James Franey

John Gibbens
Monika Glaus
Steve Golston
Kees Goubitz
Dee Granger
Bryan Gray
Tony Gray
Roderick Hines
Darren Hird
Kurt Hoffman
Harri Huhtanen
Bob Hunt
Elaine & Mike Jackson
Richard Kruss
Raymond Landry
Kim Larsen
Dr. John Lattanzio
Dean Lavis
Peter Lee
Robert Levinson
Hedley Lewis
Robert Lichtman
Joseph H. Lilly
Robert Lowery
Beverly Martin
Yoko Masuda
Mick & Laurie McCuistion
Bert Michielsen
Blair Miller
Nick Molland
Andrew Muir

Norazman Mustapha
Richard Oppenheimer
Arthur Osha
Chuck Owen
Steve Park
Gerard Profiti
Zelie Prussack
Paula Radice
Michael Rapp
Beate & Bernd Seuser
Pete Shanks
Robert Shuman
Peter Signell
David Snively
Andrew Sturm
Akiko & Heckel Sugano
Paul Sutcliffe
Mike Sutton
Gabriel Swossil
Jim Tankard
Phil Teece
Keith Venturoni
Peter Vincent
Steve Watson
Jim Weiskircher
Knut-Arne Wensaas
Robert W. Williams
Matthew Wilson
Bill Windsor
Jens Winter

APPENDIX II

Shows I've Seen

As I have no college degree so far (55 years old as I write this), I have to offer some other sort of credential qualifying me to write this series of books. Hence the following list of 148 performances by Bob Dylan that I have attended in the past four decades:

Jordan Hall, Boston, MA, November 2, 1963
Symphony Hall, Boston, October 24, 1964
Academy of Music, Philadelphia, PA, February 24 and 25, 1966
Carnegie Hall, New York City, evening show, January 20, 1968
Madison Square Garden, New York City, evening show, January 31, 1974
Veterans' Memorial Coliseum, New Haven, CT, afternoon show, November 13, 1975
Oakland Coliseum, Oakland, CA, November 13 and 14, 1978
Warfield Theater, San Francisco, CA, November 1, 2, 3, 4, 6, 7, 8, and 15, 1979
Warfield Theater, San Francisco, November 9, 10, 12, 15, 19, and 22, 1980
Sports Arena, San Diego, CA, June 9, 1986
Lawlor Events Center, Reno, NV, June 11, 1986
Cal Expo Amphitheater, Sacramento, CA, June 12, 1986
Greek Theater, Berkeley, CA, June 13 and 14, 1986
Pacific Amphitheater, Costa Mesa, CA, June 16 and 17, 1986
Veterans' Memorial Coliseum, Phoenix, AZ, June 18, 1986
Southern Star Amphitheater, Houston, TX, June 20, 1986
Irwin Center, Austin, TX, June 21, 1986
Reunion Arena, Dallas, TX, June 22, 1986
Market Square Arena, Indianapolis, IN, June 24, 1986
Metrodome, Minneapolis, MN, June 26, 1986
Alpine Valley Amphitheater, East Troy, WI, June 27, 1986
Poplar Creek Music Theater, Chicago, IL, June 29, 1986
Pine Knob Music Theater, Clarkston, MI, June 30 and July 1, 1986
Rubber Bowl, Akron, OH, July 2, 1986
Rich Stadium, Buffalo, NY, July 4, 1986
RFK Stadium, Washington, DC, July 6 and 7, 1986
Great Woods Performing Arts Center, Mansfield, MA, July 8 and 9, 1986
Civic Center Auditorium, Hartford, CT, July 11, 1986
Saratoga Performing Arts Center, Saratoga Springs, NY, July 13, 1986
Madison Square Garden, New York City, July 15, 16 and 17, 1986

The Spectrum, Philadelphia, PA, July 19, 1986
Shoreline Amphitheater, Mountain View, CA, August 5, 1986
Autzen Stadium, Eugene, OR, July 19, 1987
Oakland Stadium, Oakland, CA, July 24, 1987
National Exhibition Centre, Birmingham, England, October 12, 1987
Wembley Arena, London, England, October 14, 1987
Concord Pavilion, Concord, CA, June 7, 1988
Cal Expo Amphitheater, Sacramento, CA, June 9, 1988
Greek Theater, Berkeley, CA, June 10, 1988
Shoreline Amphitheater, Mountain View, CA, June 11, 1988
Pacific Amphitheater, Costa Mesa, CA, July 31, 1988
Greek Theater, Hollywood, CA, August 2, 3 and 4, 1988
Sammis Pavilion, Carlsbad, CA, August 6, 1988
Santa Barbara County Bowl, Santa Barbara, CA, August 7, 1988
Oakland Coliseum, Oakland, CA, December 4, 1988
Greek Theater, Berkeley, CA, September 3, 1989
Santa Barbara County Bowl, Santa Barbara, CA, September 5, 1989
Starlight Bowl, San Diego, CA, September 6, 1989
Pacific Amphitheater, Costa Mesa, CA, September 8, 1989
Greek Theater, Hollywood, CA, September 9 and 10, 1989
Champs de Brionne Music Theater, George, WA, August 18, 1990
Memorial Auditorium, Victoria, B.C., Canada, August 19, 1990
Pacific Coliseum, Vancouver, B.C., Canada, August 20, 1990
Arlene Schnitzer Concert Hall, Portland, OR, August 21, 1990
Kalvoya Festivalen, Kalvoya, Norway, June 28, 1991
Midtfyn Rock Festival, Ringe, Denmark, June 29, 1991
Paramount Northwest Theater, Seattle, WA, April 27 and 28, 1992
Hult Center for the Performing Arts, Eugene, OR, April 30, 1992
Sun County Fairgrounds, Red Bluff, CA, May 1, 1992
Sonoma County Fairgrounds, Santa Rosa, CA, May 2, 1992
Warfield Theater, San Francisco, CA, May 4 and 5, 1992
Berkeley Community Theater, Berkeley, CA, May 7 and 8, 1992
San Jose State University, San Jose, CA, May 9, 1992
Pantages Theater, Hollywood, CA, May 13, 14, 16, 17, 19, 20 and 21, 1992
Oregon Memorial Coliseum, Portland, OR, August 20, 1993
The Waterfront, Seattle, WA, August 21, 1993
Palac Kultury, Congress Hall, Prague, Czech Republic, March 11, 12 and 13, 1995
Stadthalle, Furth, Germany, March 14, 1995
Unterfrankenhalle, Aschaffenburg, Germany, March 15, 1995
Stadthalle, Bielefeld, Germany, March 16, 1995
Martinihal, Groningen, The Netherlands, March 18, 1995
Rodahal, Kerkrade, The Netherlands, March 19, 1995
Musiek Centrum Vredenburg, Utrecht, The Netherlands, March 20, 1995
Zenith Arena, Lille, France, March 22, 1995
Vorst Nationaal, Brussels, Belgium, March 23, 1995
Le Zenith, Paris, France, March 24, 1995

Santa Barbara County Bowl, Santa Barbara, CA, May 20, 1995
O'Neill Center, Western Connecticut State University, Danbury, CT, December 7, 1995
Worcester Memorial Auditorium, Worcester, MA, December 8, 1995
Orpheum Theater, Boston, MA, December 9 and 10, 1995
Beacon Theater, New York City, December 11, 1995
Austin Music Hall, Austin, TX, October 26 and 27, 1996
Capitol Music Hall, Wheeling, WV, April 28, 1997
El Rey Theater, Los Angeles, CA, December 16, 17, 18, 19, and 20, 1997
San Jose Arena, San Jose, CA, May 19, 1998
Pauley Pavilion, University of California at Los Angeles, Los Angeles, CA, May 21 and 22, 1998
Coors Amphitheater, Chula Vista, CA, June 25, 1999
Baltimore Arena, Baltimore, MD, November 8, 1999
The Apollo of Temple, Temple University, Philadelphia, PA, November 9, 1999
Veterans' Memorial Coliseum, New Haven, CT, November 10, 1999
Sun Theatre, Anaheim, CA, afternoon show and evening show, March 10, 2000
Rec Center, Cal Poly University, San Luis Obispo, CA, March 11, 2000
Bakersfield Centennial Garden, Bakersfield, CA, March 12, 2000
Visalia Convention Center, Visalia, CA, March 14, 2000
Chronicle Pavilion, Concord, CA, June 23, 2000
House of Blues, Mandalay Bay Resort & Casino, Las Vegas, NV, June 27, 2000
Verizon Wireless Amphitheater, Irvine, CA, June 29, 2000
Arena, Ventura County Fairgrounds, Ventura, CA, June 30, 2000
Grandstand, Del Mar Fairgrounds, Del Mar, CA, July 1, 2000
Mesa Del Sol Amphitheater, Albuquerque, NM, July 3, 2000
Sundome For The Performing Arts, Sun City West, AZ, August 23, 2001
The Joint, Hard Rock Hotel & Casino, Las Vegas, NV, August 24, 2001
Antelope Valley Fair, Lancaster, CA, August 25, 2001
Wiltern Theater, Los Angeles, CA, October 16, 2002
Open Air Theater, San Diego State University, San Diego, CA, October 19, 2002
Pacific Amphitheater, Orange County Fairgrounds, Costa Mesa, CA, July 27, 2003

APPENDIX III

Discography

I. Albums by Bob Dylan

All of the following are available from Columbia Records (note that *Masterpieces* and *Live 1961–2000* were not released in the U.S. or Europe). Date of first release is given, and the sequence of songs is the order in which they appeared on the original release. For albums first released as vinyl LPs, "A" indicates side one and "B" indicates side two.

1. *Bob Dylan*, released 3/19/62. A: You're No Good/ Talkin' New York/ In My Time of Dyin'/ Man of Constant Sorrow/ Fixin' to Die/ Pretty Peggy-O/ Highway 51. B: Gospel Plow/ Baby, Let Me Follow You Down/ House of the Risin' Sun/ Freight Train Blues/ Song to Woody/ See That My Grave Is Kept Clean.

2. *The Freewheelin' Bob Dylan*, released 5/27/63. A: Blowin' in the Wind/ Girl from the North Country/ Masters of War/Down the Highway/ Bob Dylan's Blues/ A Hard Rain's A-Gonna Fall. B: Don't Think Twice, It's All Right/ Bob Dylan's Dream/ Oxford Town/ Talking World War III Blues/ Corrina, Corrina/ Honey, Just Allow Me One More Chance/ I Shall Be Free.

3. *The Times They Are A-Changin'*, released 1/13/64. A: The Times They Are A-Changin'/ Ballad of Hollis Brown/ With God on Our Side/ One Too Many Mornings/ North Country Blues. B: Only a Pawn in Their Game/ Boots of Spanish Leather/ When the Ship Comes In/ The Lonesome Death of Hattie Carroll/ Restless Farewell.

4. *Another Side of Bob Dylan*, released 8/8/64. A: All I Really Want to Do/ Black Crow Blues/ Spanish Harlem Incident/ Chimes of Freedom/ I Shall Be Free No. 10/ To Ramona. B: Motorpsycho Nightmare/ My Back Pages/ I Don't Believe You/ Ballad in Plain D/ It Ain't Me Babe.

5. *Bringing It All Back Home*, released 3/22/65. A: Subterranean Homesick Blues/ She Belongs to Me/ Maggie's Farm/ Love Minus Zero-No Limit/ Outlaw Blues/ On the Road Again/ Bob Dylan's 115th Dream. B: Mr.

Tambourine Man/ Gates of Eden/ It's Alright, Ma (I'm Only Bleeding)/ It's All Over Now, Baby Blue.

6.   *Highway 61 Revisited,* released 8/30/65. A: Like a Rolling Stone/ Tombstone Blues/ It Takes a Lot to Laugh, It Takes a Train to Cry/ From a Buick 6/ Ballad of a Thin Man. B: Queen Jane Approximately/ Highway 61 Revisited/ Just Like Tom Thumb's Blues/ Desolation Row.

7.   *Blonde on Blonde,* released 5/16/66. 1A: Rainy Day Women #12 & 35/ Pledging My Time/ Visions of Johanna/ One of Us Must Know (Sooner or Later). 1B: I Want You/ Stuck Inside of Mobile with the Memphis Blues Again/ Leopard-Skin Pill-Box Hat/ Just Like a Woman. 2A: Most Likely You Go Your Way (and I'll Go Mine)/ Temporary Like Achilles/ Absolutely Sweet Marie/ 4th Time Around/ Obviously 5 Believers. 2B: Sad Eyed Lady of the Lowlands.

8.   *Bob Dylan's Greatest Hits,* released 3/27/67. A: Rainy Day Women #12 & 35/ Blowin' in the Wind/ The Times They Are A-Changin'/ It Ain't Me Babe/ Like a Rolling Stone. B: Mr. Tambourine Man/ Subterranean Homesick Blues/ I Want You/ Positively 4th Street/ Just Like a Woman.

9.   *John Wesley Harding,* released 12/27/67. A: John Wesley Harding/ As I Went Out One Morning/ I Dreamed I Saw St. Augustine/ All Along the Watchtower/ The Ballad of Frankie Lee and Judas Priest/ Drifter's Escape. B: Dear Landlord/ I Am a Lonesome Hobo/ I Pity the Poor Immigrant/ The Wicked Messenger/ Down Along the Cove/ I'll Be Your Baby Tonight.

10.   *Nashville Skyline,* released 4/9/69. A: Girl from the North Country/ Nashville Skyline Rag/ To Be Alone with You/ I Threw It All Away/ Peggy Day. B: Lay Lady Lay/ One More Night/ Tell Me That It Isn't True/ Country Pie/ Tonight I'll Be Staying Here with You.

11.   *Self Portrait,* released 6/8/70. 1A: All the Tired Horses/ Alberta #1/ I Forgot More Than You'll Ever Know/ Days of 49/ Early Mornin' Rain/ In Search of Little Sadie. 1B: Let It Be Me/ Little Sadie/ Woogie Boogie/ Belle Isle/ Living the Blues/ Like a Rolling Stone. 2A: Copper Kettle (the Pale Moonlight)/ Gotta Travel On/ Blue Moon/ The Boxer/ The Mighty Quinn (Quinn the Eskimo)/ Take Me As I Am (or Let Me Go). 2B: Take a Message to Mary/ It Hurts Me Too/ Minstrel Boy/ She Belongs to Me/ Wigwam/ Alberta #2.

12.   *New Morning,* released 10/21/70. A: If Not for You/ Day of the Locusts/ Time Passes Slowly/ Went to See the Gypsy/ Winterlude/ If Dogs Run Free. B: New Morning/ Sign on the Window/ One More Weekend/ The Man in Me/ Three Angels/ Father of Night.

13.   *Bob Dylan's Greatest Hits, Vol. 2,* released 11/17/71. 1A: Watching the River Flow/ Don't Think Twice, It's All Right/ Lay Lady Lay/ Stuck Inside of Mobile with the Memphis Blues Again. 1B: I'll Be Your Baby Tonight/ All I Really

Want to Do/ My Back Pages/ Maggie's Farm/ Tonight I'll Be Staying Here with You. 2A: She Belongs to Me/ All Along the Watchtower/ The Mighty Quinn (Quinn the Eskimo)/ Just Like Tom Thumb's Blues/ A Hard Rain's A-Gonna Fall. 2B: If Not for You/ It's All Over Now, Baby Blue/ Tomorrow Is a Long Time/ When I Paint My Masterpiece/ I Shall Be Released/ You Ain't Goin' Nowhere/ Down in the Flood.

14. *Pat Garrett & Billy the Kid*, released 7/13/73. A: Main Title Theme (Billy)/ Cantina Theme (Workin' for the Law)/ Billy 1/ Bunkhouse Theme/ River Theme. B: Turkey Chase/ Knockin' on Heaven's Door/ Final Theme/ Billy 4/ Billy 7.

15. *Dylan*, released 11/16/73. A: Lily of the West/ Can't Help Falling in Love/ Sarah Jane/ The Ballad of Ira Hayes. B: Mr. Bojangles/ Mary Ann/ Big Yellow Taxi/ A Fool Such as I/ Spanish Is the Loving Tongue.

16. *Planet Waves*, released 1/17/74. A: On a Night Like This/ Going Going Gone/ Tough Mama/ Hazel/ Something There Is About You/ Forever Young. B: Forever Young/ Dirge/ You Angel You/ Never Say Goodbye/ Wedding Song.

17. *Before the Flood*, released 6/20/74. 1A: Most Likely You Go Your Way (and I'll Go Mine)/ Lay Lady Lay/ Rainy Day Women #12 & 35/ Knockin' on Heaven's Door/ It Ain't Me Babe/ Ballad of a Thin Man. 1B: five songs by the Band. 2A:Don't Think Twice, It's All Right/ Just Like a Woman/ It's Alright, Ma (I'm Only Bleeding)/ three songs by the Band. 2B: All Along the Watchtower/ Highway 61 Revisited/ Like a Rolling Stone/ Blowin' in the Wind. (live album)

18. *Blood on the Tracks*, released 1/17/75. A: Tangled Up in Blue/ Simple Twist of Fate/ You're a Big Girl Now/ Idiot Wind/ You're Gonna Make Me Lonesome When You Go. B: Meet Me in the Morning/ Lily, Rosemary and the Jack of Hearts/ If You See Her, Say Hello/ Shelter from the Storm/ Buckets of Rain.

19. *The Basement Tapes*, released 6/26/75. 1A: Odds and Ends/ *Orange Juice Blues (Blues for Breakfast)/ Million Dollar Bash/ *Yazoo Street Scandal/ Goin' to Acapulco/ *Katie's Been Gone. 1B: Lo and Behold!/ *Bessie Smith/ Clothes Line Saga/ Apple Suckling Tree/ Please, Mrs. Henry/ Tears of Rage. 2A: Too Much of Nothing/ Yea! Heavy and a Bottle of Bread/ *Ain't No More Cane/ Crash on the Levee (Down in the Flood)/ *Ruben Remus/ Tiny Montgomery. 2B: You Ain't Goin' Nowhere/ *Don't Ya Tell Henry/ Nothing Was Delivered/ Open the Door Homer/ *Long Distance Operator/ This Wheel's on Fire. (songs marked * are performed by the Band without Dylan)

20. *Desire*, released 1/16/76. A: Hurricane/ Isis/ Mozambique/ One More Cup of Coffee/ Oh Sister. B: Joey/ Romance in Durango/ Black Diamond Bay/ Sara.

21. *Hard Rain,* released 9/10/76. A: Maggie's Farm/ One Too Many Mornings/ Stuck Inside of Mobile with the Memphis Blues Again/ Oh Sister/ Lay Lady Lay. B: Shelter from the Storm/ You're a Big Girl Now/ I Threw It All Away/ Idiot Wind. (live album)

22. *Masterpieces,* released 2/25/78 in Japan, Australia, and New Zealand only. 1A: Knockin' on Heaven's Door/ Mr. Tambourine Man/ Just Like a Woman/ I Shall Be Released/ Tears of Rage/ All Along the Watchtower/ One More Cup of Coffee. 1B: Like a Rolling Stone (from *Self Portrait*)/ The Mighty Quinn (Quinn the Eskimo) (from *Self Portrait*)/ Tomorrow Is a Long Time/ Lay Lady Lay (from *Hard Rain*)/ Idiot Wind (from *Hard Rain*). 2A: Mixed Up Confusion/ Positively 4th Street/ Can You Please Crawl Out Your Window?/ *Just Like Tom Thumb's Blues/ *Spanish Is the Loving Tongue/ *George Jackson (big band version)/ *Rita May. 2B: Blowin' in the Wind/ A Hard Rain's A-Gonna Fall/ The Times They Are A-Changin'/ Masters of War/ Hurricane. 3A: Maggie's Farm (from *Hard Rain*)/ Subterranean Homesick Blues/ Ballad of a Thin Man/ Mozambique/ This Wheel's on Fire/ I Want You/ Rainy Day Women #12 & 35. 3B: Don't Think Twice, It's All Right/ Song to Woody/ It Ain't Me Babe/ Love Minus Zero–No Limit/ I'll Be Your Baby Tonight/ If Not for You/ If You See Her, Say Hello/ Sara. (performances marked * are not available on any American album)

23. *Street-Legal,* released 6/15/78. A: Changing of the Guards/ New Pony/ No Time to Think/ Baby Stop Crying. B: Is Your Love in Vain?/ Senor (Tales of Yankee Power)/ True Love Tends to Forget/ We Better Talk This Over/ Where Are You Tonight? (Journey through Dark Heat).

24. *Bob Dylan at Budokan,* released in the U.S. 4/23/79. 1A: Mr. Tambourine Man/ Shelter from the Storm/ Love Minus Zero–No Limit/ Ballad of a Thin Man/ Don't Think Twice, It's All Right. 1B: Maggie's Farm/ One More Cup of Coffee (Valley Below)/ Like a Rolling Stone/ I Shall Be Released/ Is Your Love in Vain?/ Going Going Gone. 2A: Blowin' in the Wind/ Just Like a Woman/ Oh Sister/ Simple Twist of Fate/ All Along the Watchtower/ I Want You. 2B: All I Really Want to Do/ Knockin' on Heaven's Door/ It's Alright, Ma (I'm Only Bleeding)/ Forever Young/ The Times They Are A-Changin'. (live album)

25. *Slow Train Coming,* released 8/18/79. A: Gotta Serve Somebody/ Precious Angel/ I Believe in You/ Slow Train. B: Gonna Change My Way of Thinking/ Do Right to Me, Baby (Do Unto Others)/ When You Gonna Wake Up/ Man Gave Names to All the Animals/ When He Returns.

26. *Saved,* released 6/20/80. A: A Satisfied Mind/ Saved/ Covenant Woman/ What Can I Do for You?/ Solid Rock. B: Pressing On/ In the Garden/ Saving Grace/ Are You Ready?

27. *Shot Of Love,* released 8/12/81. A: Shot of Love/ Heart of Mine/ Property of Jesus/ Lenny Bruce/ Watered-Down Love. B: Dead Man, Dead Man/ In the

Summertime/ Trouble/ Every Grain of Sand. (Later pressings include The Groom's Still Waiting at the Altar at the start of side two.)

28. *Infidels*, released 11/1/83. A: Jokerman/ Sweetheart Like You/ Neighborhood Bully/ License to Kill. B: Man of Peace/ Union Sundown/ I and I/ Don't Fall Apart on Me Tonight.

29. *Real Live*, released 11/29/84. A: Highway 61 Revisited/ Maggie's Farm/ I and I/ License to Kill/ It Ain't Me Babe. B: Tangled Up in Blue/ Masters of War/ Ballad of a Thin Man/ Girl from the North Country/ Tombstone Blues. (live album)

30. *Empire Burlesque*, released 5/27/85. A: Tight Connection to My Heart (Has Anybody Seen My Love?)/ Seeing the Real You at Last/ I'll Remember You/ Clean-Cut Kid/ Never Gonna Be the Same Again. B: Trust Yourself/ Emotionally Yours/ When the Night Comes Falling from the Sky/ Something's Burning, Baby/ Dark Eyes.

31. *Biograph*, released 11/4/85. 1A: Lay Lady Lay/ Baby, Let Me Follow You Down/ If Not for You/ I'll Be Your Baby Tonight/ *I'll Keep It with Mine. 1B: The Times They Are A-Changin'/ Blowin' in the Wind/ Masters of War/ The Lonesome Death of Hattie Carroll/ *Percy's Song. 2A: *Mixed-Up Confusion/ Tombstone Blues/ *The Groom's Still Waiting at the Altar/ Most Likely You Go Your Way (and I'll Go Mine) (from *Before the Flood*)/ Like a Rolling Stone/ *Jet Pilot. 2B: *Lay Down Your Weary Tune/ Subterranean Homesick Blues/ *I Don't Believe You (She Acts Like We Never Have Met)/ *Visions of Johanna/ Every Grain of Sand. 3A: *Quinn the Eskimo/ Mr. Tambourine Man/ Dear Landlord/ It Ain't Me Babe/ You Angel You/ *Million Dollar Bash. 3B: To Ramona/ *You're a Big Girl Now/ *Abandoned Love/ Tangled Up in Blue/ It's All Over Now, Baby Blue. 4A: *Can You Please Crawl out Your Window?/ Positively 4th Street/ *Isis/ *Caribbean Wind/ *Up to Me. 4B: *Baby, I'm in the Mood for You/ *I Wanna Be Your Lover/ I Want You/ Heart of Mine/ On a Night Like This/ Just Like a Woman. 5A: *Romance in Durango/ Senor (Tales of Yankee Power)/ Gotta Serve Somebody/ I Believe in You/ Time Passes Slowly. 5B: I Shall Be Released/ Knockin' on Heaven's Door/ All Along the Watchtower/ Solid Rock/ *Forever Young. (performances marked * are not available on any other American album)

32. *Knocked Out Loaded*, released 7/14/86. A: You Wanna Ramble/ They Killed Him/ Driftin' Too Far from Shore/ Precious Memories/ Maybe Someday. B: Brownsville Girl/ Got My Mind Made Up/ Under Your Spell.

33. *Down in the Groove*, released 5/31/88. A: Let's Stick Together/ When Did You Leave Heaven?/ Sally Sue Brown/ Death Is Not the End/ Had a Dream About You, Baby. B: Ugliest Girl in the World/ Silvio/ Ninety Miles an Hour (Down a Dead End Street)/ Shenandoah/ Rank Strangers to Me.

34. *Dylan & the Dead*, released 2/6/89. A: Slow Train/ I Want You/ Gotta Serve Somebody/ Queen Jane Approximately. B: Joey/ All Along the Watchtower/ Knockin' on Heaven's Door. (live album)

35 *Oh Mercy*, released 9/19/89. A: Political World/ Where Teardrops Fall/ Everything Is Broken/ Ring Them Bells/ Man in the Long Black Coat. B: Most of the Time/ What Good Am I?/ Disease of Conceit/ What Was It You Wanted/ Shooting Star.

36. *Under the Red Sky*, released 9/11/90. A: Wiggle Wiggle/ Under the Red Sky/ Unbelievable/ Born in Time/ T.V. Talkin' Song. B: 10,000 Men/ 2X2/ God Knows/ Handy Dandy/ Cat's in the Well.

37. *The Bootleg Series, Volumes 1–3 [Rare and Unreleased], 1961–1991*, released 3/26/91. Disc one: Hard Times in New York Town/ He Was a Friend of Mine/ Man on the Street/ No More Auction Block/ House Carpenter/ Talkin' Bear Mountain Picnic Massacre Blues/ Let Me Die in My Footsteps/ Rambling, Gambling Willie/ Talkin' Hava Negeilah Blues/ Quit Your Low Down Ways/ Worried Blues/ Kingsport Town/ Walkin' Down the Line/ Walls of Red Wing/ Paths of Victory/ Talkin' John Birch Paranoid Blues/ Who Killed Davey Moore?/ Only a Hobo/ Moonshiner/ When the Ship Comes In/ The Times They Are A-Changin'/ Last Thoughts on Woody Guthrie. Disc two: Seven Curses/ Eternal Circle/ Suze (the Cough Song)/ Mama, You Been on My Mind/ Farewell, Angelina/ Subterranean Homesick Blues/ If You Gotta Go, Go Now/ Sitting on a Barbed Wire Fence/ Like a Rolling Stone/ It Takes a Lot to Laugh, It Takes a Train to Cry/ I'll Keep It with Mine/ She's Your Lover Now/ I Shall Be Released/ Santa-Fe/ If Not for You/ Wallflower/ Nobody 'cept You/ Tangled Up in Blue/ Call Letter Blues/ Idiot Wind. Disc three: If You See Her, Say Hello/ Golden Loom/ Catfish/ Seven Days/ Ye Shall Be Changed/ Every Grain of Sand/ You Changed my Life/ Need a Woman/ Angelina/ Someone's Got a Hold of My Heart/ Tell Me/ Lord Protect My Child/ Foot of Pride/ Blind Willie McTell/ When the Night Comes Falling from the Sky/ Series of Dreams.

38. *Good As I Been to You*, released 11/3/92. Frankie & Albert/ Jim Jones/ Blackjack Davey/ Canadee-i-o/ Sittin' on Top of the World/ Little Maggie/ Hard Times/ Step It Up and Go/ Tomorrow Night/ Arthur McBride/ You're Gonna Quit Me/ Diamond Joe/ Froggie Went a Courtin'.

39. *World Gone Wrong*, released 10/26/93. World Gone Wrong/ Love Henry/ Ragged & Dirty/ Blood in My Eyes/ Broke Down Engine/ Delia/ Stack a Lee/ Two Soldiers/ Jack-a-Roe/ Lone Pilgrim.

40. *Bob Dylan's Greatest Hits, Vol. 3*, released 11/15/94. Tangled Up in Blue/ Changing of the Guards/ Groom's Still Waiting at the Altar/ Hurricane/ Forever Young/ Jokerman/ Dignity/ Silvio/ Ring Them Bells/ Gotta Serve

Somebody/ Series of Dreams/ Brownsville Girl/ Under the Red Sky/ Knockin'
on Heaven's Door.

41. *MTV Unplugged*, released 4/25/95. Tombstone Blues/ Shooting Star/ All
Along the Watchtower/ The Times They Are A-Changin'/ John Brown/ Rainy
Day Women #12 & 35/ Desolation Row/ Love Minus Zero–No Limit/
Dignity/ Knockin' on Heaven's Door/ Like a Rolling Stone/ With God on Our
Side.

42. *Time Out of Mind*, released 9/30/97. Love Sick/ Dirt Road Blues/ Standing
in the Doorway/ Million Miles/ Tryin' to Get to Heaven/ 'Til I Fell in Love with
You/ Not Dark Yet/ Cold Irons Bound/ Make You Feel My Love/ Can't Wait/
Highlands.

43. *Live 1966*, released 10/13/98. She Belongs to Me/ Fourth Time Around/
Visions of Johanna/ It's All Over Now, Baby Blue/ Desolation Row/ Just Like a
Woman/ Mr. Tambourine Man/ Tell Me, Mama/ I Don't Believe You/ Baby,
Let Me Follow You Down/ Just Like Tom Thumb's Blues/ Leopard-Skin
Pill-Box Hat/ One Too Many Mornings/ Ballad of a Thin Man/ Like a Rolling
Stone.

44. *The Essential Bob Dylan*, released 10/31/2000. Disc one: Blowin' in the
Wind/ Don't Think Twice, It's All Right/ The Times They Are A-Changin'/ It
Ain't Me Babe/ Maggie's Farm/ It's All Over Now, Baby Blue/ Mr. Tambour-
ine Man/ Subterranean Homesick Blues/ Like a Rolling Stone/ Positively 4th
Street/ Just Like a Woman/ Rainy Day Women #12 & 35/ All Along the
Watchtower/ Quinn the Eskimo (The Mighty Quinn)/ I'll Be Your Baby
Tonight. Disc two: Lay Lady Lay/ If Not for You/ I Shall Be Released/ You
Ain't Goin' Nowhere/ Knockin' on Heaven's Door/ Forever Young/ Tangled
Up in Blue/ Shelter from the Storm/ Hurricane/ Gotta Serve Somebody/
Jokerman/ Silvio/ Everything Is Broken/ Not Dark Yet/ Things Have Changed.

45. *Bob Dylan Live 1961–2000*, released 2/28/2001 in Japan only. Somebody
Touched Me/ Wade in the Water/ Handsome Molly/ To Ramona/ I Don't
Believe You/ Grand Coulee Dam/ Knockin' on Heaven's Door/ It Ain't Me
Babe/ Shelter from the Storm/ Dead Man, Dead Man/ Slow Train/ Dignity/
Cold Irons Bound/ Born in Time/ Country Pie/ Things Have Changed.

46. *"Love And Theft"*, released 9/11/2001. Tweedle Dee & Tweedle Dum/ Mis-
sissippi/ Summer Days/ Bye and Bye/ Lonesome Day Blues/ Floater (Too
Much to Ask)/ High Water (for Charley Patton)/ Moonlight/ Honest with Me/
Po' Boy/ Cry a While/ Sugar Baby.

47. *Live 1975*, released 11/26/2002. Disc one: Tonight I'll Be Staying Here with
You/ It Ain't Me Babe/ A Hard Rain's A-Gonna Fall/ The Lonesome Death of
Hattie Carroll/ Romance in Durango/ Isis/ Mr. Tambourine Man/ Simple
Twist of Fate/ Blowin' in the Wind/ Mama, You Been on My Mind/ I Shall Be

Released. Disc two: It's All Over Now, Baby Blue/ Love Minus Zero–No Limit/ Tangled Up in Blue/ The Water Is Wide/ It Takes a Lot to Laugh, It Takes a Train to Cry/ Oh, Sister/ Hurricane/ One More Cup of Coffee (Valley Below)/ Sara/ Just Like a Woman/ Knockin' on Heaven's Door.

48. *Live 1964*, released 3/23/2004. Disc one: The Times They Are A-Changin'/ Spanish Harlem Incident/ Talkin' John Birch Paranoid Blues/ To Ramona/ Who Killed Davey Moore?/ Gates of Eden/ If You Gotta Go, Go Now/ It's Alright Ma, (I'm Only Bleeding)/ I Don't Believe You/ Mr. Tambourine Man/ A Hard Rain's A-Gonna Fall. Disc two: Talkin' World War III Blues/ Don't Think Twice, It's All Right/ The Lonesome Death of Hattie Carroll/ Mama, You Been on My Mind/ Silver Dagger/ With God on Our Side/ It Ain't Me Babe/ All I Really Want to Do.

II. Other Officially Released Recordings by Bob Dylan

These are legally released Bob Dylan performances that are not available on any of the albums listed in the first part of this discography, but that have been officially released elsewhere.

Midnight Special (Dylan on harmonica), on Harry Belafonte: *Midnight Special,* RCA, 3/62.

I'll Fly Away/ Swing and Turn Jubilee/ Come Back, Baby (all Dylan on harmonica), on Carolyn Hester: *Carolyn Hester,* Columbia, summer 1962.

Corrina Corrina (B-side of the 7″ single Mixed Up Confusion, released 12/62).

Rocks and Gravel/ Talking John Birch Paranoid Blues, on *The Freewheelin' Bob Dylan* (early promotional edition), Columbia, 4/63.

John Brown/ Only a Hobo/ Talkin' Devil (under the pseudonym Blind Boy Grunt), on *Broadside Ballads, Volume I,* Broadside/Folkways, 9/63.

Only a Pawn in Their Game (live from the March on Washington, 8/63), on *We Shall Overcome,* Folkways, winter 1964.

Blowin' in the Wind/ We Shall Overcome (ensemble performances from Newport Folk Festival, 7/63), on *Evening Concerts at Newport, Volume I,* Vanguard, May 1964.

Playboys and Playgirls (sung with Pete Seeger)/ With God on Our Side (sung with Joan Baez) (from Newport 7/63), on *Newport Broadside,* Vanguard, May 1964.

Sitting on Top of the World/ Wichita (Dylan on harmonica and background vocals, backing Big Joe Williams, late 1961), on Victoria Spivey: *Three Kings and a Queen,* Spivey, 10/64.

George Jackson (the acoustic version was the B-side of a 7″ single released 11/71 with the big band version of this song as the A-side).

A Hard Rain's A-Gonna Fall/ It Takes a Lot to Laugh, It Takes a Train to Cry/ Blowin' in the Wind/ Mr. Tambourine Man/ Just Like a Woman, on *The Concert for Bangladesh,* Apple, 12/71.

Grand Coulee Dan/ Dear Mrs. Roosevelt/ I Ain't Got No Home (in This World

Anymore) (from Carnegie Hall, 1/68), on *A Tribute to Woody Guthrie, Part One*, Columbia, 1/72.

Train A-Travelin'/ I'd Hate to Be You on That Dreadful Day/ The Death of Emmett Till/ Ballad of Donald White (as Blind Boy Grunt) (recorded 1962), on *Broadside Reunion*, Folkways, 1972. (Ballad of Donald White and John Brown also available on *The Best of Broadside* CD, Folkways, 8/2000.)

Big Joe, Dylan and Victoria/ It's Dangerous (Dylan on harmonica, backing Big Joe Williams and Victoria Spivey, late 1961), on *Victoria Spivey: Three Kings and a Queen, Volume 2*, Spivey, 7/72.

People Get Ready/ Never Let Me Go/ Isis (live from fall 1975), on *4 Songs from Renaldo & Clara*, Columbia (promotional disc), 1/78.

Baby Let Me Follow You Down (two versions)/ I Don't Believe You/ Forever Young/ I Shall Be Released (live from 11/76), on The Band: *The Last Waltz*, Warner, 4/78.

Trouble in Mind (B-side of the 7″ single Gotta Serve Somebody, released 9/79).

Let It Be Me (B-side of the 7″ single Heart of Mine, released 9/81 in Europe only).

interview with occasional guitar accompaniment, on *Dylan London Interview* 1981, Columbia (promotional disc), 9/81.

Angel Flying Too Close to the Ground (B-side of the 7″ single Union Sundown, released 10/83 in Europe only).

We Are the World (shared vocal; Dylan's role is small), released as single and on USA for Africa: *We Are the World*, Columbia, 3/85.

Sun City (shared vocal; Dylan's role is small), released as single and on Artists United Against Apartheid: *Sun City*, Manhattan, 12/85.

Band of the Hand (movie theme song) (backed by Tom Petty and the Heartbreakers and the Queens of Rhythm) on soundtrack album of the same title, and 7″ single, MCA, 5/86.

Most of the Time, released on a Columbia Records promotional CD and as a promotional video, 4/90.

The Usual/ Had a Dream About You, Baby/ Night after Night, on Fiona, Bob Dylan, Rupert Everett: *Hearts of Fire*, Columbia (soundtrack album), 10/87.

Important Words, on advance promotional cassette of *Down in the Groove*, 5/88.

Got Love If You Want It, on Argentinian release of *Down in the Groove*, 6/88.

Pretty Boy Floyd, on *Folkways: A Vision Shared*, Columbia, 8/88.

Dirty World/ Congratulations/ Tweeter and the Monkey Man (lead vocals; other tracks on the album also feature Dylan on shared vocals and guitar and keyboards), on *Traveling Wilburys, Volume One*, Warner, 10/88.

People Get Ready, on *Flashback*, WTG (soundtrack album), 1/90.

Nobody's Child (shared vocal with the Traveling Wilburys), on *Nobody's Child: Romanian Angel Appeal*, Warner, 7/90.

She's My Baby/ If You Belonged to Me/ 7 Deadly Sins/ Where Were You Last Night? (lead vocals; other tracks on album also feature Dylan on shared vocals and guitar), on *Traveling Wilburys: Vol. 3*, Warner, 10/90.

This Old Man, on *For Our Children*, Disney, 5/91.

Heartland (song written by Dylan and Nelson) (shared vocal), on Willie Nelson: *Across the Borderline*, Columbia, 3/93.

It's Alright, Ma/ My Back Pages/ Knockin' on Heaven's Door/ Girl from the North Country, on *Bob Dylan: The 30th Anniversary Concert Celebration*, Columbia, 8/93.

Troubled and I Don't Know Why/ Mama, You Been on My Mind/ Blowin' in the Wind (duets with Joan Baez from 1963, 1964 and 1976), on *Joan Baez: Rare, Live & Classic*, 8/93.

You Belong to Me, on soundtrack album for *Natural Born Killers*, recorded 8/92, released by Uni 8/94

Ballad of Hollis Brown, on *Mike Seeger – Third Annual Farewell Reunion*, Rounder, 11/94.

Highway 61 Revisited, on *Woodstock 94*, A&M, 11/94.

Baby Please Don't Go/ Blowin' in the Wind/ Dink's Song/ I Ain't Got No Home/ Medicine Sunday/ Rocks and Gravel (Solid Road)/ The Story of East Orange, New Jersey/ Wade in the Water/ My Blue-Eyed Jane/ House of the Rising Sun/ I Shall Be Free No. 10/ Like a Rolling Stone/ When He Returns/ One Too Many Mornings/ Queen Jane Approximately, on *Highway 61 Interactive* (CD-ROM), Columbia/Graphix Zone, 2/95.

Boogie Woogie Country Girl, on *Till The Night Is Gone: A Tribute to Doc Pomus*, Rhino 3/95.

A Hard Rain's A-Gonna Fall (performed live with a symphony orchestra), on *Dignity* CD single, Columbia, released in Europe, 4/95.

Ring of Fire, on soundtrack album for *Feeling Minnesota*, Atlantic, 8/96.

All Along the Watchtower, on *The Concert for the Rock and Roll Hall of Fame*, Columbia, 9/96.

Shelter from the Storm (rare alternate take), on *Jerry Maguire* soundtrack album, Epic 12/96.

My Blue Eyed Jane, on *The Songs of Jimmie Rodgers – A Tribute*, Egyptian, 8/97.

Boots of Spanish Leather/ Ballad of a Thin Man/ Tombstone Blues, on *Live '96* (promotional disc), 11/97 and on *Not Dark Yet* CD single, Columbia, released in Europe 2/98.

The Lonesome River (duet with Ralph Stanley), on Ralph Stanley: *Clinch Mountain Country*, Rebel 5/98.

Love Sick/ Cold Irons Bound/ Cocaine Blues/ Born in Time/ Can't Wait, Roving Gambler/ Blind Willie McTell (live tracks from 1997 and '98), on *Love Sick* CD singles, Columbia, released in Europe and Japan, 6/98.

Million Miles, on *Million Miles: Live Recordings 1997–1999* CD single, Columbia, 6/99.

To Ramona/ Love Minus Zero–No Limit/ The Lonesome Death of Hattie Carroll/ It's All Over Now, Baby Blue/ It Ain't Me Babe (previously unreleased complete live performances from 1965), on *Don't Look Back* DVD, Docurama, 1/2000.

Highlands/ Blowin' in the Wind/ Make You Feel My Love (live tracks from 2000 and 1998), on *Things Have Changed* CD single, Sony (Japan), 5/2000.

Friend of the Devil, on *Stolen Roses*, Grateful Dead Records, 7/2000.

Return To Me (Dean Martin song), on the TV soundtrack album, *Sopranos. Peppers & Eggs*, 5/2001.

Crash On The Levee/ When I Paint My Masterpiece/ Don't Ya Tell Henry/ Like a Rolling Stone (previously unreleased performances with the Band from a New Year's Eve concert, 1971), on the Band, *Rock Of Ages* (CD reissue), Capitol, 5/2001.

I Was Young When I Left Home/ The Times They Are A-Changin' on "special limited edition" CD packaged with *"Love And Theft"* when it was first released, Columbia, 9/2001.

I Can't Get You Off of My Mind, on *Timeless* (Hank Williams tribute album), Lost Highway, 9/2001.

Roll on, John (previously unreleased 1962 performance), on *There Is No Eye: Music for Photographs*, Smithsonian Folkways Recordings, 10/2001.

Red Cadillac and a Black Moustache, on *Good Rockin' Tonight – The Legacy of Sun Records*, WEA/London/Sire, 10/2001.

Gonna Change My Way of Thinking (duet with Mavis Staples), on *Gotta Serve Somebody, The Gospel Songs of Bob Dylan*, Columbia, 4/2003.

Down in the Flood/ Diamond Joe/ Dixie/ Cold Irons Bound, on soundtrack album for *Masked and Anonymous*, Columbia, 8/2003.

Some of the otherwise unavailable Dylan performances above, notably ones included on Japanese and European CD singles, first became available as downloads from the Sony-Records-sponsored official website bobdylan.com. More such material continues to be available from the site, but it may not be apparent to a visitor where to find it. A query posted on the discussion board at bobdylan.com or to a newsgroup like rec.music.dylan might be a way to get information about what can currently be heard via the site and where and how to find it.

APPENDIX IV

Filmography

I. Films by Bob Dylan

Eat the Document. Filmed 5/66 by D. A. Pennebaker, edited 1967 by Bob Dylan, Howard Alk, and Robbie Robertson. First shown publicly 2/8/71. Not currently available. Circa one hour.

Renaldo & Clara. Directed by Bob Dylan. Filmed fall 1975, edited 1977 by Dylan with Howard Alk. First shown publicly 1/25/78. Not currently available in any form except bootleg or privately circulating copies. Original is close to four hours with an intermission. A second, two-hour edited version was released in fall 1978.

Masked and Anonymous. Directed by Larry Charles. Written by Bob Dylan and Larry Charles under pseudonyms. Starring Bob Dylan as "Jack Fate." Theatrical release in the U.S. summer 2003. Video/DVD release expected in 2004.

II. Films about Bob Dylan

Don't Look Back. Directed by D. A. Pennebaker. Filmed 4–5/65. First shown publicly 5/17/67. Circa 90 minutes. Available on videocassette and now in a somewhat expanded form on DVD.

Hard Rain. Live concert footage shot 5/23/76 in Fort Collins, Colorado, by TVTV (Top Value Television); edited by TVTV. Broadcast on NBC 9/14/76. Circa 55 minutes. Not currently available.

Hard to Handle. Live concert footage filmed by Gillian Armstrong in Sydney, Australia, 2/24 and 2/25/86. Edited by Armstrong. Broadcast by HBO, 6/20/86. Circa one hour. Available on videocassette.

Getting to Dylan. A one-hour segment of the BBC programme *Omnibus*. Directed by Christopher Sykes. Broadcast 9/18/87. Not currently available.

Bob Dylan: The 30th Anniversary Concert Celebration. Broadcast and filmed 10/18/92. A three and a half hour tribute to Dylan organized by Columbia Records, with many different artists performing his songs backed by Booker T. & the MGs and G. E. Smith. Dylan performs five songs. Released in 8/93 as an audio CD, videocassette and laser disc.

The Supper Club (unreleased, except for excerpts on the *Highway 61 Interactive* CD-ROM). Dylan and his touring band played four shows, using acoustic instruments only, on October 16 and 17, 1993 before a live audience in a small New York City club. Dylan had these performances filmed at his expense for possible use as a television program, but ultimately chose against releasing the excellent results.

MTV Unplugged. Recorded 11/94, broadcast 12/94, released as a videocassette and laser disc (and audio CD and LP) 5/95.

Bob Dylan Anthology (tentative title). Documentary directed and assembled by Martin Scorsese, to be released in 2005.

1966 World Tour: The Home Movies. DVD, released 2004.

III. Films in which Bob Dylan appears as an actor

The Madhouse on Castle Street. Dylan acted and sang in this British television drama, made and shown by the BBC, 1/63.

Pat Garrett & Billy the Kid. Directed by Sam Peckinpah. Released 5/73. Circa 106 minutes. Available on videocassette (director's original version has now been released).

Hearts of Fire. Directed by Richard Marquand. Released 10/87, UK only. Circa 90 minutes. Dylan stars as singer Billy Parker. Available on videocassette.

Catchfire (aka *Backtrack*). Directed by Dennis Hopper. First released (Australia) 1989. Dylan has a small, cameo role.

Masked and Anonymous. See above.

IV. Films that include performances by Bob Dylan

Festival. Directed by Murray Lerner. Released 1967. Footage from Newport Folk Festival, 7/64 and 7/65, including All I Really Want to Do/ Maggie's Farm/ Mr. Tambourine Man. Available in film format.

The Concert for Bangladesh. Edited by George Harrison, with help from Dylan. Released 3/72. Includes If Not for You (partial)/ A Hard Rain's A-Gonna Fall/ It Takes a Lot to Laugh/ Blowin' in the Wind/ Just Like a Woman. Available on videocassette and DVD.

The Last Waltz. Directed by Martin Scorsese. Released 4/78. Includes Forever Young/ Baby, Let Me Follow You Down/ I Shall Be Released. Available on videocassette and DVD.

At present, some short (i.e. 30 seconds) film clips of Dylan performing can be found at bobdylan.com, usually by following the "albums" link and then looking for a "WindowsMedia" link after the name of a song in the list of songs you see when you click on an album's title. At present, 22 such clips, mostly from *Renaldo & Clara*, can be found associated with the *Live 95* album listing on this website.

V. Noteworthy television appearances

The Madhouse on Castle Street. 1/63. (see above)

The Times They Are A-Changin', half-hour segment of the Canadian Broadcasting Company program *Quest*, recorded 2/1/64 and broadcast by CBC 3/10/64. Includes Restless Farewell and five other songs. Archived in video form. Prior to this, Dylan made three known television appearances in the U.S. in 1963, including one song on Johnny Carson's *Tonight* show.

The Steve Allen Show, live, 2/25/64. The Lonesome Death of Hattie Carroll and conversation with host. Archived in video form.

Les Crane Show, live, WABC, New York, 2/17/65. Dylan sings two songs accompanied by Bruce Langhorne and is witty and cutting in conversation. Archived in audio only.

BBC programmes recorded in BBC studios, 6/1/65, and broadcast in two parts in 6/65. 12 songs, approximately 70 minutes. Archived in audio only, apparently.

San Francisco Press Conference, KQED Studios, 12/3/65, broadcast by KQED later that day. Circa one hour. Archived in video form.

The Johnny Cash Show. Three songs, taped 5/1/69, broadcast on ABC 6/7/69. All items from here forward are archived in video form.

The World of John Hammond, part of the National Educational Television *Soundstage* series. Includes three songs by Dylan. Recorded 9/10/75. First broadcast 12/13/75.

Hard Rain. Broadcast 9/10/76. (see above)

Saturday Night Live. Three songs. NBC, 10/20/79.

Grammy Award Show. CBS, 2/27/80. One song: Gotta Serve Somebody.

Late Night with David Letterman. NBC, 3/22/84. Three songs, including Don't Start Me to Talkin'.

Live Aid Concert. Three songs. 7/14/85. Broadcast live by satellite around the world.

Farm Aid Concert. 9/22/85. Four songs were broadcast live by the Nashville Network.

20–20, ABC, 10/10/85. Interview.

Hard to Handle. HBO, 6/20/86. (see above)

Farm Aid 2 Broadcast. 7/4/86. Three songs from Dylan's concert in Buffalo, New York were broadcast live by VH-1 TV; much of the concert was shot and transmitted live by satellite in preparation for the broadcast.

Getting to Dylan. BBC, 9/18/87. (see above)

Grammy Awards Ceremony, 2/20/91. Masters of War with his touring band, introduction by Jack Nicholson, short speech in acceptance of his Lifetime Achievement Award.

One Irish Rover – Van Morrison in Performance, Arena, BBC-TV, 3/16/91. Dylan and Morrison sing three songs together filmed in Greece, June 1989.

Bob Dylan: The 30th Anniversary Concert Celebration, 10/18/92. (see above)

Bill Clinton Inauguration Concert, 1/17/93. Broadcast by TV stations around the world. Dylan performs Chimes of Freedom backed by an orchestra led by Quincy Jones.

A Country Music Celebration, CBS TV, 2/6/93. Dylan and Willie Nelson perform Heartland.

Willie Nelson: The Big Six-0. American television, 5/93. Dylan sings Pancho and Lefty with Nelson and performs Hard Times with his own touring band, and is interviewed. Later released on videocassette.

The Great Music Experience Countdown, 5/22/94. Broadcast on TV (and radio) stations around the world. Dylan performs Hard Rain, I Shall Be Released, and Ring Them Bells backed by the Tokyo New Philharmonic Orchestra.

Woodstock '94, 8/14/94. Dylan and his band's 12-song set at this festival is broadcast live on radio and TV around the world.

MTV Unplugged, 12/14/94. (see above)

Sinatra: 80 Years My Way. Broadcast 12/12/95 by various TV networks around the world. During this tribute concert, Dylan and his band perform Restless Farewell at Sinatra's request.

Masters of Music Concert for the Prince's Trust, performed in Hyde Park, London, 6/29/96; three songs of Dylan's 8-song set were broadcast on European TV in the next two months, and 5 songs were broadcast by HBO in the U.S.A. in 8/96.

World Eucharistic Congress, 9/27/97. Broadcast by Italian state television. Dylan and his band perform three songs at this event in Bologna, and Dylan is seen shaking hands with the Pope and talking with him.

Kennedy Center Honors Lifetime Achievement Awards Ceremony, 12/7/97. Dylan and other artists, including actress Lauren Bacall, are presented with this award by President Clinton at an event broadcast by U.S. television.

Grammy Awards Ceremony, 2/25/98. Love Sick with his band. Broadcast by CBS TV.

Johnny Cash Tribute Show. Broadcast 4/18/99 on U.S. TV. Includes a film of Dylan and his band performing Train of Love (at a tour rehearsal in early April).

Dharma & Greg – Play Lady Play episode, ABC TV, 10/12/99. Dylan acted in this episode of the American TV series.

Oscar Awards Ceremony, 3/25/01. Dylan won an Oscar for and performed Things Have Changed by satellite from a studio in Australia, where he and his band were on tour.

VI. Promotional Videos

Between 1983 and 1997 Dylan participated to some degree in the making of promotional videotapes to accompany the following songs. All of these are studio recordings attached to footage shot later, so there are no actual new performances on these tapes, with one exception: Dylan performs live in the studio on the video of "Most of the Time."

Jokerman
Sweetheart Like You
Tight Connection to My Heart
Emotionally Yours
When the Night Comes Falling from the Sky
Tangled Up in Blue (from *Renaldo & Clara*)
Handle with Care (Traveling Wilburys)
End of the Line (Traveling Wilburys)
Political World
Most of the Time
She's My Baby (Traveling Wilburys)
Unbelievable
Wilbury Twist (Traveling Wilburys)
Series of Dreams (the best Dylan video by far)
Blood in My Eyes
Love Sick
Not Dark Yet
Things Have Changed

APPENDIX V

Bibliography

I. Books by Bob Dylan

Tarantula. New York: Macmillan, 1971
Writings and Drawings. New York: Alfred A. Knopf, 1973
Lyrics, 1962–1985. New York: Alfred A. Knopf, 1985 (Expansion of *Writings and Drawings*; a further expanded edition is planned in 2004 or soon after)
The Songs of Bob Dylan from 1966 through 1975. New York: Random House, 1978
Drawn Blank. New York: Random House, 1994 (sketches in pencil and charcoal "done over a two- or three-year period from about 1989 to about 1991 or '92 in various locations mainly to relax and refocus a restless mind")
Chronicles, Vol. I (forthcoming). New York: Simon & Schuster, 2005 (tentative)

II. Key references used in preparing this text

Björner, Olof. *Olof's Files: A Bob Dylan Performance Guide* (11 volumes, 1958–2000), Devon, England: Hardinge Simpole, 2002. (Previously available only on Internet websites.) Lists all known recorded performances, including audience tapes of concerts, studio outtakes, etc., with full song lists for each performance and lots of additional information, including "Bob Talk" – i.e., "We played that last song for everybody here who doesn't know anybody" (after "Rank Strangers to Me" at a 1999 show).

Krogsgaard, Michael. *Positively Bob Dylan*, Ann Arbor: Popular Culture, Ink, 1991. Like the Björner series, this book lists all known recorded performances, including audience tapes of concerts, studio outtakes, etc., with full song lists for each performance. Very well indexed. This edition is an update of Krogsgaard's earlier books, *Twenty Years of Recording* and *Master of the Tracks*. For information about ordering in the U.S., call Popular Culture, Ink at 800-678-8828.

Dr. Filth (pseudonym). *The Fiddler Now Upspoke, Volumes 1–5*, privately published in England. Collections of Bob Dylan interviews and press conferences, from 1961 to 1997.

Gates, David. "Dylan Revisited" (interview), in *Newsweek*, October 6, 1997.

Bauldie, John, ed. *Wanted Man: In Search of Bob Dylan*, London: Black Spring Press, 1990. Interviews and essays from *The Telegraph*, including Allen Ginsberg's interview with Bob Dylan about *Renaldo & Clara*, interviews with Richard

Marquand and Iain Smith about *Hearts of Fire*, Traveling Wilburys interviews, quotes from Tom Petty & the Heartbreakers about touring with Dylan, and "Daniel Lanois and *Oh Mercy*" by John Bauldie.

Heylin, Clinton. *Bob Dylan, A Life in Stolen Moments, Day by Day: 1941–1995*, self-published, U.K., 1996. A detailed, highly reliable chronology of Dylan's personal and professional life.

Muir, Andrew. *Razor's Edge: Bob Dylan & the Never Ending Tour*, London: Helter Skelter, 2001. An insightful study from a fan's perspective of Dylan's touring between 1988 and 1999.

Sounes, Howard. *Down the Highway: the Life of Bob Dylan*, New York: Grove Press, 2001.

Heylin, Clinton. *Bob Dylan: Behind the Shades, Take Two*, London: Viking, 2000. Still the best biography so far, particularly for its accuracy and its coverage of Dylan's last few decades.

Cartwright, Bert. *The Bible in the Lyrics of Bob Dylan*, revised edition, self-published in Fort Worth, Texas, 1992.

Dylan, Bob. "Jimi" – two-page fax sent to Alan Douglas in 1988 for use in a traveling exhibit about Jimi Hendrix. Unpublished (copies privately circulated).

The Telegraph, issues #1 (1981) – #56 (1997). Edited by John Bauldie. A phenomenal amount of Dylan information, insight, and entertainment is contained in these pages. Publication ceased in 1997 due to the editor's untimely death. *The Bridge* (see below) is a worthy successor in a similar format.

The Wicked Messenger, issues #1 (1980) – #1849 (2003). Dylan newsletter, written by Ian Woodward. Consistent, obsessive, indispensable. Now available only as a feature in *Isis* (see below).

III. Other sources used in preparing this text

Isis, bimonthly UK Dylan magazine, 109 issues through 7/03, lots of news and information, oriented towards collectors. Edited by Derek Barker. For subscription information, contact Isis, PO Box 1182, Bedworth, Warwickshire CV12 0ZA, U.K., or www.bobdylanisis.com

On the Tracks, American Dylan magazine, 24 issues through 2002. Edited by Mick and Laurie McCuistion. Available from Rolling Tomes (phone and address below). www.b-dylan.com

The Bridge, UK Dylan magazine, a successor to *The Telegraph,* 16 issues through summer 2003. Edited by Mike Wyvill and John Wraith. PO Box 198, Gateshead Tyne and Wear, NE10 8WE, England. www.two-riders.co.uk

Judas, another excellent UK Dylan magazine, 7 issues through 10/03. Edited by Andrew Muir. 8 Laxton Grange, Bluntisham, Cambridgeshire, PE28 3XU, UK. www.judasmagazine.com

Augustine, Saint. *The Confessions of Saint Augustine.*

Beck, Emily Morison, editor, *Bartlett's Familiar Quotations*, fourteenth edition, Boston: Little Brown, 1968.

Buttrick, George Arthur, et al. *The Interpreter's Dictionary of the Bible*, Nashville, 1962.

Casey, Barbara, "Acting and Mindfulness: an interview with Jeffrey King" in *The Mindfulness Bell*, winter 2001–2002.

Cott, Jonathan. "The *Rolling Stone* Interview with Bob Dylan," in *Rolling Stone*, 1/25/78 and 11/16/78.

Crowe, Cameron. *Biograph* booklet and liner notes, included with album, 1985.

Danielson, Virginia. *The Voice of Egypt*, Chicago: The University of Chicago Press, 1997.

Dawidoff, Nicholas. *In the Country of Country*, New York: Pantheon, 1997.

Dundas, Glen. *Tangled Up in Tapes, 4th Edition, A Recording History of Bob Dylan*, Thunder Bay, Canada: SMA Services, 1999. Another fine guide to all of Dylan's performances, organized in a different fashion than Krogsgaard's or Björner's.

Ellington, Duke. *Music Is My Mistress*, Garden City: Doubleday, 1973.

Frye, Northrop. *Fearful Symmetry: A Study of William Blake*. Princeton, NJ: Princeton University Press, 1947.

Gibbens, John. *The Nightingale's Code, A Poetic Study of Bob Dylan*, London: Touched Press, 2001.

Gilot, Françoise. *Matisse and Picasso*, New York: Doubleday, 1990.

Gottlieb, Robert. *Reading Jazz*, New York: Vintage, 1999. Quotes from Duke Ellington and Bill Evans found in this *Performing Artist* volume are on pp. 37 and 426 of Gottlieb's fine anthology.

Graf, Christof. *Bob Dylan, Man on the Road: The Never Ending Tour 1986–1999*, Echternach (Luxembourg), 1999.

Gray, Michael. *Song & Dance Man III*, London: Continuum, 2000.

Hardy, Phil and Laing, Dave. *The Faber Companion to 20th-Century Popular Music*, London: Faber and Faber, 1990.

Heylin, Clinton. *Bob Dylan: The Recording Sessions 1960–1994*, New York: St. Martin's, 1995.

Hilburn, Robert. "Dylan: 'I learned that Jesus is real and I wanted that'," *Los Angeles Times*, November 23, 1980.

Humphries, Patrick and Bauldie, John. *Oh No! Not Another Bob Dylan Book*, Essex: Square One, 1991.

Jackson, Blair. *Garcia: an American Life*, New York: Penguin, 1999.

Kramer, Daniel. *Bob Dylan*, New York: Citadel Press, 1967.

Lindley, John. *7 Days*, self-published, Cheshire, England: 1987.

May, Herbert G. and Metzger, Bruce M., editors, *The New Oxford Annotated Bible*. New York: Oxford University Press, 1973.

Michel, Steve. *The Bob Dylan Concordance*, Grand Junction, CO: Rolling Tomes, 1992.

Scobie, Stephen. *Alias Bob Dylan*, Alberta: Red Deer, 1991.

Wilhelm, Richard and Baynes, Cary, translators. *The I Ching or, Book of Changes*, New York: Bollingen, 1950.

Williams, Richard. *Dylan: A Man Called Alias*, London: Bloomsbury, 1992.

* For assistance in locating and obtaining particular books, you may wish to contact one of the long-established mail order companies specializing in books about Bob Dylan:

My Back Pages, P.O. Box 30, Lancaster LA1 2GH, England, or
www.bobdylanisis.com

Rolling Tomes, P.O. Box 1943, Grand Junction, CO 81502 USA, or
(303) 245–4315, or
www.b-dylan.com

CREDITS

Copyright Citations, and Acknowledgments

Copyright Citations

Acknowledgments

First I'd like to thank my wife, Cindy Lee Berryhill, and my young son, Alexander
Berryhill-Williams, for their love and support.

Plentiful thanks are also due to the persons listed on the Roll of Honor, whose
financial support made it possible for this book to be written.

I am also grateful to those who helped supply research materials, including
Carsten Baumann, Arnie Stodolsky, Heinrich Gerkepott, Stephan Fehlau, and
the fine fellow who called my attention to the "Visions of Madonna" Tramps performance, whose name I've misplaced, alas.

My thanks also to Jeff Rosen and all at Special Rider Music, and to my editor,
Chris Charlesworth, and to you out there who are reading and listening ... and to
David Hartwell, who first introduced me to Bob Dylan's music 40 years ago and
who has remained a good and supportive friend ever since.

INDEX